DRUG WARS AND COVERT NETHERWORLDS

DRUG WARS AND COVERT NETHERWORLDS

The Transformation of Mexico's Narco Cartels

James H. Creechan

THE UNIVERSITY OF
ARIZONA PRESS

TUCSON

The University of Arizona Press
www.uapress.arizona.edu

We respectfully acknowledge the University of Arizona is on the land and territories of Indigenous peoples. Today, Arizona is home to twenty-two federally recognized tribes, with Tucson being home to the O'odham and the Yaqui. Committed to diversity and inclusion, the University strives to build sustainable relationships with sovereign Native Nations and Indigenous communities through education offerings, partnerships, and community service.

ISBN-13: 978-0-8165-4328-1 (hardcover)
ISBN-13: 978-0-8165-4091-4 (paperback)

Cover design by Derek Thornton / Notch Design
Typeset by Sara Thaxton in 10/14 Warnock Pro with Nota (display)

Publication of this book is made possible in part by the proceeds of a permanent endowment created with the assistance of a Challenge Grant from the National Endowment for the Humanities, a federal agency.

Library of Congress Cataloging-in-Publication Data
Names: Creechan, James H., 1945–author.
Title: Drug wars and covert netherworlds : the transformations of Mexico's narco cartels / James H. Creechan.
Description: Tucson : University of Arizona Press, 2021. | Includes bibliographical references and index.
Identifiers: LCCN 2021021566 | ISBN 9780816543281 (hardcover) | ISBN 9780816540914 (paperback)
Subjects: LCSH: Drug traffic—Mexico—History. | Gangs—Mexico—History. | Drug abuse and crime—Mexico—History.
Classification: LCC HV5840.M4 C74 2021 | DDC 364.1/33650972—dc23
LC record available at https://lccn.loc.gov/2021021566

Printed in the United States of America
♾ This paper meets the requirements of ANSI/NISO Z39.48-1992 (Permanence of Paper).

For Mary Lou, as always

CONTENTS

ABBREVIATIONS

AFI   Agencia Federal de Investigación (Federal Ministerial Police)

AMLO   Andrés Manuel López Obrador

BNDD   Bureau of Narcotics and Dangerous Drugs

CDMX   Ciudad de México (Mexico City)

CEFERESO   Centro de Readaptación Social (Center for Social Readaptation)

CIA   Central Intelligence Agency

CISEN   Centro de Investigación y Seguridad Nacional (Center for Investigation and National Security)

CJNG   Cártel de Jalisco Nueva Generación (Jalisco New Generation Cartel)

CNS   Consejo Nacional de Seguridad (National Security Council)

CRS   Congressional Research Service

DEA   Drug Enforcement Administration

DF   Distrito Federal (Federal District)

DFS   Dirección Federal de Seguridad (Federal Security Directorate)

DOJ   Department of Justice

EPIC   El Paso Intelligence Center

FBI   Federal Bureau of Investigation

FBN   Federal Bureau of Narcotics

GAFE   Grupo Aeromóvil de Fuerzas Especiales (Special Forces Airmobile Group)

IACHR	Inter-American Commission on Human Rights
ICE	Immigration and Customs Enforcement
INEGI	Instituto Nacional de Estadística y Geografía (National Institute of Statistics and Geography)
INS	Immigration and Naturalization Services
Morena	Movimiento Regeneración Nacional (National Regeneration Movement)
NAFTA	North American Free Trade Agreement
PAN	Partido Acción Nacional (National Action Party)
PGR	Procuraduría General de la República (Attorney General of the Republic)
PJF	Policía Judicial Federal (Federal Judicial Police)
PRD	Partido de la Revolución Democrática
PRI	Partido Institucional Revolucionario (Institutional Revolutionary Party)
SEDENA	Secretaría de la Defensa Nacional (Secretariat of National Defense)
SEGOB	Secretaría de Gobernación (Secretariat of the Interior)
SEMAR	Secretaría de Marina (Naval Secretariat)
SESNSP	Secretariado Ejecutivo del Sistema Nacional de Seguridad Pública (Secretary General of National Public Security)

DRUG WARS AND COVERT NETHERWORLDS

Introduction

Cradle of Narco Traffickers

I knew little about Culiacán, Sinaloa, before 1998. I realized it was about seven hundred miles south of Tucson, where I had gone to the University of Arizona, and that it was the capital city of a Mexican state primarily known for growing tomatoes. I had also heard more than a few tales about its notoriety as a regional crime capital reportedly populated by gangsters wearing huaraches and having an unparalleled talent for smuggling marijuana and heroin from the adjacent Sierra Madre mountains. And like anyone who attended the university in Tucson or lived near the frontier border, I knew that the coveted sinsemilla strain of marijuana came from there.

In 1997 I was invited to travel to Culiacán and realized I needed to learn more about the city and the state. During the final weeks of a yearlong sabbatical at El Colegio de México in Mexico City, Guillermo Ibarra and Ana Luz Ruelas from the Universidad Autónoma de Sinaloa (UAS, Autonomous University of Sinaloa) invited me to be a visiting professor in a graduate program they had recently established and hoped that I might travel to Sinaloa in the late summer of 1998 to teach one of the initial seminars for the first cohort.

That triggered a quest to learn more about Culiacán and Sinaloa State. Before I returned to my full-time academic position at the University of Alberta in Canada, I bought two books by Luis Astorga (*Mitología del "narcotraficante" en México* and *El siglo de las drogas*) and a short novel by Leonides Alfaro (*Tierra blanca*) at the legendary Mexico City Gandhi

Bookstore. By chance, I picked up a Latin American edition of *GQ* magazine that included the Charles Bowden article "Amado Carrillo Fuentes: The Killer Across the River," in which he described a shadowy Sinaloan family overseeing large-scale drug operations in Ciudad Juárez, Chihuahua. Those three books and that single magazine article provided my first serious introduction to Culiacán and the Sinaloa drug subculture and thus played a significant role in shaping my understanding of the shadowy world that I describe in this book.[1]

Culiacán is the epicenter and the petri dish for subcultural and tribal traditions that spawned all modern drug cartels, and the history of drug production and distribution in northwest Mexico—specifically heroin and marijuana—is an entangled saga of individuals and families going back more than one hundred years. In particular, Astorga and Alfaro describe the birth of a powerful narco-culture and more importantly make it clear that narco memories had inserted themselves deep into the very *carne y hueso*—heart and soul—of Culiacán and Sinaloa and northwest Mexico.

The barrio of Tierra Blanca described in Alfaro's fictional novel is an actual community in Culiacán that spawned what is now the most powerful criminal organization in Mexico and the Americas—the Sinaloa Cartel. Alfaro's protagonist became a powerful narco trafficker in spite of deep moral ambiguity and ascended to become both an influential jefe and a respected community figure. The fictional hero is a composite of several actual men and women in the Tierra Blanca subculture that had gradually seeped outward to dominate regional politics, the economy, and all areas of social and cultural life—and ultimately affect most of modern Mexico.

By the 1950s, the subculture and traditions portrayed in Alfaro's novel had become so deeply engrained that the city of Culiacán and the state of Sinaloa were inseparably linked to drug smuggling and violence. Astorga describes Culiacán and barrio Tierra Blanca in his chapter "Culiacán: Chicago con Gángsters de Huarache":

> Sinaloa is described as "a very rich state, very agricultural and, it pains me to say this, a place where the gunman and his lady, la goma, are a couple that walk boldly in the street." To be Sinaloense is almost synonymous with being a gomero, even though that is not necessarily a disgraceful thing: for example, a notable baseball writer recently wrote that "los gomeros" lost their third series in a row against the Hermosillo baseball team. They say that

Tierra Blanca Colonia "is the center for operations of coyotes and gomeros," that it is a "nest of opium growers" where they reign over "vice and wildness" and "where weapons are everywhere," that it is the "refuge of more than just opium producers" and is a "paradise of vice." (1996, 87)[2]

The two Astorga books and the short Alfaro novel are rich descriptions of a narco subculture and underworld that spread far beyond humble campesino origins to infiltrate, influence, and dominate a broad sphere of politics, economics, and culture. Old traditions, customs, and cultural expressions from Tierra Blanca gradually became normalized and routinized, and eventually had an impact far beyond the boundaries of the city and of Sinaloa State. Shortly after providing that description of daily life in Tierra Blanca, Astorga goes on to note that its denizens had nevertheless become influential figures in Culiacán.

It is widely known that the traffickers with the widest reach have covered up their questionable activities with others that have a more legal respectability: they are "well-known community members" who to all appearances are "honest and hardworking merchants," "professionals," "labor leaders and even authorities at the highest level." (1996, 87)

Those narco roots and links to respectable society are deep, and there are still many families and powerful individuals in Sinaloa whose origins go back to that era of gangsters in huaraches. When I first visited Culiacán in 1998, few outside Sinaloa knew anything of that history or those links, and even fewer had written of them in academic circles. Astorga and Alfaro are native Sinaloans—Astorga grew up on those streets of Tierra Blanca—and they are among a very few who are innately qualified to describe the shadowy connections and linkages binding drugs, culture, politics, family, and community life in Sinaloa. Those of us not from Sinaloa can only imagine the tales shared when families gather to speak of their grandparents, parents, aunts and uncles, and cousins, while writers like Astorga and Alfaro know them from experience.

Unlike them, Bowden was one outsider who did understand the extensive reach and the secretive world of Sinaloan drug subculture long before others, and he especially realized that there were more than a few powerful and influential respectable families from Sinaloa playing key roles in a vast criminal network without drawing attention from the outside world. In the *GQ* article describing Carrillo Fuentes, he metaphorically described a man secure inside his home on a hill surveying the world beyond, while those outside did not see what was taking place behind those walls. His article should now be read as a prescient warning that the world should have paid much more attention to those powerful forces percolating in the shadows. But when he wrote his article in the mid-1990s, few heeded his warning.

This book argues that the popular history of narco Mexico has too often been narrowly framed within a perspective that reflects the ideology of the U.S. War on Drugs and that it overemphasizes the criminal agency of individuals prominent within the drug world. Consequently, much of the common understanding of the narco world is actually based on mythology and misunderstanding, and the public narrative has consistently overlooked links to respectable individuals and legitimate society. The authors I have mentioned here offer a more complex narrative and viscerally understood the broader connections of a narco society that are not reflected in the popularized narratives of narco Mexico. I cannot claim to understand that world to the degree they do, but I did come to learn much more about Sinaloa and its powerful subterranean traditions from years of contact with students and colleagues in the Faculty of International Studies and Public Policy at UAS-Culiacán; from friends I made in Sinaloa; from casual discussions with many individuals in coffee shops, at newsstands, and at sports events; and by discovering the work of excellent Spanish-language journalists and authors who wrote about drugs, cartels, and narco-culture.[3]

The details and the narrative of this book are the product of two things—an academic investigation and a personal journey into a world that was gradually revealed by those I met along the way. It was not my intention to undertake an investigation of narco-culture or Mexican cartels—neither during my sabbatical leave at El Colegio de México nor the appointment to UAS as a visiting professor. But many weeks and months spent in Culiacán over fourteen years and many visits to Mexico City made it increasingly obvious that much of what I had believed about narco-culture and Mexican cartels had been narrowly framed within a silo that constrained its reality and deep connections to normal society. And the more I learned—from new friends, casual encounters, personal experiences, and many journalists—the more it became obvious that popular and official narratives about drugs and Mexican cartels only touched the surface of narco Mexico.

To be fair, distorted conceptions of crime and deviance are not limited to the English-speaking world. Banditry, smuggling, and illegal drugs were a central feature of Mexico's mysterious netherworld long before the concept of drug cartels emerged to overwhelm and dominate all public discourse of crime. Mexico had historically explained criminality and drug addiction by viewing it through a rigid lens of race, gender, and class that defined criminality as the perverted behavior of outlaws, degenerates, the mentally deranged, or social defects. Privileged classes have always remained beyond reproach and immune to suspicion that they might also act in uncivilized ways—especially so when misbehavior involves drugs. Despite many progressive movements demanding reform from within, Mexico's penal codes have remained immutable to revision and have been slow to incorporate modern conceptions of law and justice, and Mexico's penal institutions are stubbornly bound to an ancient inquisitorial ideal that it is necessary to control dangerous classes and maintain rigid boundaries between elites and threatening underclasses (see Buffington 2000).

The Limit of Official Views

The popular understanding of narco Mexico has been disproportionately influenced by a U.S. Drug Enforcement Administration (DEA) narrative of a War on Drugs and has also been informed by the statistics and data in official U.S. government reports.[4] Much of what is found in those reports has been constrained to fit a rigid "official" vision that illicit drug use must be suppressed through punitive reaction since those involved in the drug trade are disproportionately from a dangerous and threatening underclass. Undeniably, DEA files describe the actions of individuals situated lower in the pecking order of a broader, extensive narco-traffic enterprise, and arguably, those *official* records serve to reinforce the popular assumption that the drug enterprise is indeed dominated by modern versions of outlaws, degenerates, mentally deranged, or social defects. But the following chapters demonstrate that is not the case in Mexico, and that an elite and respectable ruling and business class has long played a central contributing role in what may be described as a covert netherworld.

Because crime statistics and court recordings emphasize individual action and agency, an understanding of broader criminal connections is not easily constructed from official data sources. In light of that, much of this book relies on secondary sources that are not traditionally used in the formal study of criminology and which are not widely known in the English-speaking world—primarily, the large body of work of authors, academics, investigators, and journalists writing in Spanish and publishing in magazines, newspapers, and publishing houses throughout Mexico and Latin America. It was those non-English sources that became particularly important and valuable for my personal understanding of cartels, and they provided much of the specific information and contextual material I depend on to present the history of narco Mexico and to describe the transformations within cartels and narco Mexico over three decades.

The DEA and Intelligence Reports

DEA agents arrived in Mexico early in the U.S. War on Drugs, and they undertook surveillance almost exclusively dedicated to identifying moles and snitches within the cartels and gangs—individuals known variously as *informadores, soplones,* and *sapos* in Spanish. Dozens of agents, who cultivated and pressured informants to provide intel about the covert world of production and distribution in Mexico, were especially focused on tracking drug movement into the United States.[5] Over the course of many years, DEA agents were committed to a deliberate and systematic process that usually began by targeting lower-echelon targets with exposed vulnerabilities. Then, each entrapped informant was manipulated to identify someone further up the chain, and that next higher-level informant was subsequently pressured to identify those even closer to the top. Agents were skilled in using a threat-and-reward tactic, and routinely offered incentives and protected-witness status that included immunity, reduced sentences, and even relocation and new identities—even if the targeted informant had committed serious crimes such as murder. One recent book by a controversial former agent, Hector Bellerrez, describes an insider's view of how the DEA routinely recruited and nurtured informants using that strategy, and one earlier Spanish-language book by Andrés López López included many specific details about the carrot-and-stick approach employed by agents in the field (Berrellez 2021; López López 2008).

Informants and protected witnesses did give agents valuable information about the subterranean world of opium and marijuana production in remote regions of Mexico, and most importantly provided critical evidence leading to criminal conviction in an estimated 70 percent of the cartel-related trials in the USA (de Córdoba and Pérez 2020). Electronic surveillance and monitoring were introduced much later in the long history of the U.S. War on Drugs and only began to make significant contributions after 2012, when the DEA and other American agencies came to use it to verify intel otherwise coerced or purchased from shadowy sources and protected witnesses.[6] Regional centers such as the El Paso Intelligence Center (EPIC) and the DEA Special Operations Division in Virginia became increasingly important as data centers and coordinating units during the high-profile trials of major drug lords such as Joaquín Archivaldo "El Chapo" Guzmán Loera, Jesús Reynaldo "El Rey" Zambada García and Vicente "Vicentillo" Zambada Niebla (see DEA n.d.).

Relatively little information from archival DEA records has been used to present the history of cartels in this book. Access was highly restricted until recently and remains significantly bureaucratic and expensive to arrange, and furthermore it was obvious that many records of interest had been sealed and designated as privileged information through court orders.[7] Instead, I have relied almost exclusively on the work and research of academic and journalistic observers who gathered information about cartels through the difficult and sometimes dangerous work of investigative journalism.

Official DEA narratives have nevertheless dominated and framed our cultural and popular representations of cartels and capos—especially as they become reflected in populist tales and sagas portraying heroic special agents battling ruthless, brutal drug lords: Don Winslow's fact-based cartel trilogy (2005, 2015, 2019a) and the Netflix series *Narco: Mexico* are only two examples of how narco Mexico is largely portrayed through a DEA lens. It is worth noting that DEA directors have only emulated what other justice agencies previously did to establish their bureaucratic legitimacy and secure Congressional funding; high-profile takedowns of criminals by heroic G-Men were regularly staged by J. Edgar Hoover in a sophisticated claims-making process that promoted the Federal Bureau of Investigation (FBI) as a bastion against evil and as the agency within the Department of Justice (DOJ) that should be supported at all costs.

The Restrictive Lens of the U.S. War on Drugs

President Richard Nixon proclaimed a War on Drugs in 1971, and five decades onward, it remains the longest war the United States has ever undertaken under a specious and false pretense. The following year, the Nixon DOJ created the DEA and made it the lead agency in a global crusade to impose a criminalized narrative of drug use. Even after many tweaks and modifications during the five-decade course of this crusade, the DEA has maintained an unwavering commitment to a militarized and punitive vision that emphasizes eradication at the source of production, interdiction at point of delivery, and the arrest and extradition of kingpins.

Initially, the war focused on Andes cocaine production and Colombian cartels, but Mexican marijuana and heroin were also targeted for eradication.[8] For thirty years, the U.S. Congress and the Office of Management and Budget allocated resources to governments that voluntarily conformed to the American vision through a certification program and primarily rewarded those countries that destroyed crops at the source. In those early years, funding also went to the Mexican military to underwrite the cost of eradication of opium and marijuana crops (Beittel 2009, 2011, 2015; Cook 2007; Library of Congress 1988). The emphasis of the U.S. drug war shifted from eradication to emphasizing the hunt for drug lords in the 1990s with the enactment of the Foreign Narcotics Kingpin Designation Act (the Kingpin Act) (1999): it encouraged the surveillance and arrest of high-level drug lords and the seizure and freezing of financial assets.[9] The U.S. vision of the drug war was modified again in 2007 and funding allocated to several different U.S. agencies during the George W. Bush presidency under the broad bilateral initiative known as Plan Mérida (Ribando Seelke 2009, 2021; Ribando Seelke and Finklea 2014). Plan Mérida delivered U.S. dollars to Mexican initiatives that focused on justice reform and social programs but also introduced new measures and incentives for information sharing and bilateral cooperation that would lead to the arrest of drug *capos* and *jefes*.

Drug Narratives and Presidential Sexenios

For forty-five years, the discourse about narco traffickers, cartels, and drugs dominated Mexico's internal security landscape and policy. Insecurity and violence dragged on across seven presidential terms, beginning with José López Portillo's *sexenio* (1976–82) and most recently through Enrique Peña Nieto's (2012–18)—and they have also marred the first half of Andrés Manuel López Obrador's presidency. This book describes the five decades between 1976 and 2020 and presents an overview of how drug cartels began and how they transformed across those presidential terms, known as sexenios. It also describes how the drug organizations became the essential component of what I describe as a covert netherworld—a conceptualization proposed by historian Alfred J. McCoy (2018).

Initially, Mexico half-heartedly committed troops and police to wage a version of a proxy war that selectively targeted regional drug barons and destroyed the fields of a few scapegoat producers of marijuana and opium. When Ronald Reagan rejuvenated the Nixonian crusade against drugs for his own political reasons in 1982, President Miguel de la Madrid Hurtado (1982–88) was governing Mexico with a weak mandate, and he conveniently chose to overlook increasingly aggressive incursions of the DEA and the CIA onto Mexican soil. In 1985 a U.S. constitutional crisis was triggered by events in the Middle East, and the threat of border closures related to trade issues dominated the political relationship between Mexico and the United States. Two memorable and historical incidents came to the forefront during that year of crisis: first, DEA agent Enrique "Kiki" Camarena was tortured and murdered in February by Guadalajara Cartel drug lords (Shannon 1988); and second, a few short months later the Iran-Contra affair implicated both the CIA and Mexican drug lords in the illegal transportation of arms to Contras opposed to a leftist Nicaraguan government (Bartley and Bartley 2015). What were seemingly unconnected events were in fact intricately bound together by the growing power and influence of Mexican criminal organizations: Mexican cartel bosses in Guadalajara had contracted with American dark operatives to ship arms intended for Iranian rebels through Mexico and had then used those same planes to transport cocaine back to the United States. In fact, those planes were operated by the very cartel leaders who had also kidnapped agent Camarena.[10]

The Camarena kidnapping, torture, and murder dramatically changed the trajectory and organization of Mexican drug cartels when the DEA demanded an immediate punitive response from the Mexican government. Subsequently, three high-level drug lords were imprisoned at the insistence of the Americans, based on information that was provided to the Mexican federal government by American sources. The unprosecuted cartel bosses, subordinates, and lieutenants then entered into what was a new Pax Mafiosa and created an umbrella cooperative agreement that the DEA tagged as the Federation. Drug operations had not been destroyed by the removal and jailing of three of its top bosses but instead thrived in a subterranean underworld for the next six years, during which its new bosses worked efficiently in the shadows with the knowledge and cooperation of many well-respected members of society, business, and government.

That convenient accommodation among narco traffickers solidified during the first few years of the Carlos Salinas de Gortari sexenio, and the Pax Narca allowed his administration to remain relatively unaffected by security distractions. Simultaneously, it gave the remaining drug lords breathing room to restructure and expand and create ties in a covert netherworld. Arguably, the DEA had not remained focused on gathering additional detailed intelligence on the remnants and stragglers from the Guadalajara Cartel collapse during that interlude at the beginning of the Salinas years: U.S. attention and resources had almost entirely shifted to cocaine eradication in the Andes. The public pursuit of Pablo Escobar Gaviria in Colombia and the avowed destruction of Andean and Caribbean routes of cocaine into U.S. markets had become the main focus for the agency.

Journalism and Cartels

Transformation and expansion of Mexico's cartels after 2000 have been extensively described by many Spanish-language authors and journalists in both national and regional publications. Much of their work remains untranslated and therefore is unknown to unilingual English audiences. Their reports, investigative studies, and books are the principal documents of record that I use in the following chapters to describe internal wars *within* cartels, several wars *between* cartels, and the official state war *against* cartels triggered by President Felipe de Jesús Calderón Hinojosa (2006–12). Each of those three war fronts continued with varying degrees of intensity right through the Peña Nieto sexenio. During the first three years of the López Obrador sexenio, the aftermath of those wars continued to play out and even moved in new deadly directions as two cartels, the Sinaloa Cartel and the Cártel de Jalisco Nueva Generación, challenged each other for dominance.

For more than twenty years, the dangerous crime beats covered by many Mexican authors and journalists reported on what anthropologist Howard Campbell (2009) has astutely described as low-grade battle zones; many brave journalists and writers who have covered those events have been the principal inspiration and the key source of information for most of this book. The chapters that follow would never have been possible without relying on the information and the insight first printed in Mexican newspapers and in online news portals by dozens of *periodistas*.

The structure of this book and its description of cartel history are also guided by timeline descriptions I first read about in Mexican newspapers, magazines, and digital sites. In particular, chapters 4 and 5 have been inspired and informed by interactive pages and graphic timelines reproduced in national magazines and newspapers of record such as *Proceso Seminario*, *La Jornada*, *Reforma/El Norte*, and *El Universal* as well as others found on several Internet portals. The following chapters also incorporate many details and observations first described in influential regional papers and magazines such as *Ríodoce* and *Noroeste* in Sinaloa and *Zeta Seminario* in Tijuana. In particular, the news portals of *Ríodoce*, *Sin Embargo*, and *Animal Político* served as reliable sources and go-to sites to uncover basic information and to fact check and identify trustworthy reports.

The El Chapo Trial and Public Interest

The trial of El Chapo Guzmán in the first two months of 2019 gave the DEA a rare dramaturgical opportunity to showcase and brag about its accomplishments in that five-decade U.S.-led War on Drugs. In the first few years of the twenty-first century, the DEA had gradually slipped down the pecking order within the Homeland Security umbrella and the DOJ as security priorities exclusively focused on terrorism following the September 11 attacks, and then shifted in response to the immigration and border security xenophobia inspired and fed by Donald J. Trump. The security emphasis on the border resulted in the rapid expansion of Customs and Border Patrol, which became the largest federal police agency with more than thirty-seven thousand agents in the field compared to the four thousand assigned to the DEA (Graff 2020).

The DEA had a chance to return to the spotlight and remind the world—and its political overseers—about its role with the arrest, extradition, and public trial of Guzmán. A curious public was riveted by the expected revelations about Mexico's narco enterprise during the intensely watched trial of a man the DEA had proclaimed to be the most important Mexican narco trafficker ever captured and put on trial. To guarantee a conviction, the charges against Guzmán were strategically limited to a narrow range of events that occurred over a couple of years leading up to 2012. Members of the public camped out in the middle of winter hoping to gain access to the courtroom, while untold others eagerly consumed daily reports about the drug lord known as El Chapo and the details of sensational crimes he had committed or ordered to be committed while he was head of the now widely known Sinaloa Cartel. The trial of Guzmán Loera represented a crowning achievement in the U.S. War on Drugs and an opportunity for the DEA to swagger in public adulation, but the events discussed in that trial represent only a small part of a larger history of narco traffic and cartels described in the pages that follow.

In many ways, the core of this book unfolds as the history of four distinct but interconnected wars—the global *War on Drugs* called for by the United States, internal civil *Wars Within Cartels* and *Wars Between Cartels*, and a Mexican state futile intervention that grew into its own never-ending *War Against Cartels*. Those distinct war fronts have melded together and are too often compounded into one in cultural representations; they have been further muddled by a great deal of misinformation being spread amid the intensified xenophobia about the border characterizing the misinformed Trump era. The different wars playing out in Mexico are inextricably linked together and have regularly exploded beyond the boundaries of low-grade battle zones to bring chaos and spread bloodshed throughout Mexico.

But each of those four wars are nevertheless unique events with their own distinct trajectories. The U.S. War on Drugs is now five decades old and shows few signs of ending in spite of increasingly liberalized views about the legalization of drugs across North America. The wars within cartels and the wars between cartels have surged and faded, and continue in 2021 as the Sinaloa Cartel and the Cártel de Jalisco Nueva Generación compete to control and dominate dozens of smaller gangs and organizations that have emerged since 2004; the Mexican military and its newly established Guardia Nacional (National Guard) are still waging a war in the streets even though Mexico's president proclaimed that war had finished in 2018.

Admittedly, the internal civil wars between cartels subsided from the extreme levels of violence seen in the years bookmarking 2010, but by no means have they ended: vicious factions are still battling violently to control plazas and achieve domination in several states and regions of Mexico in 2021, and areas such as Guanajuato State, Michoacán, and the State of Mexico remain contested battlefields. The Mexican military's war against cartels was already twelve years old when Mexico's newly elected president, Andrés Manuel López Obrador (AMLO), boldly declared it had ended; but violence continued unabated and Mexican troops remained in the streets in the guise of the newly created Guardia Nacional, which contradicted his presidential declaration of an end to war, *abrazos no balazos* (hugs, not bullets), and his electoral promises to return troops to barracks (Fredrick 2018).[11]

The following eight chapters describe the world of narco Mexico based on three decades of personal observation, and a personal archive of news reports, articles, studies, and Spanish-language books collected over that time.[12] The most important information has been extracted from the thousands of news reports and columns published by Mexican journalists and academics who have consistently placed their lives at risk in a dangerous environment plagued by threats, violence, and corruption from the narco traffickers and from the state. Most of those men and women *periodistas* are unknown to English speakers, and much of their material describes a subterranean Mexico unknown to outsiders. The body of work of those journalists provides a look into a world that has been distorted beyond all recognition by xenophobic and dishonest cultural representations horrifically reinforced by politicians like Donald Trump and his enablers. It goes beyond saying that no one should believe that a reasonable view of Mexican narco traffic and cartels can come from anyone who has foolishly reduced it to a claim that it is caused by bad hombres. And the sources that I have used do not look at the world in such a simple way.

This book describes the world of cartels and narco traffic in eight substantive chapters. I believe that two types of readers are attracted to the subject matter and themes described in this book: on the one hand, there is a surprisingly large network of experts and professionals who monitor Mexico or whose professional advancement increasingly demands they pay close attention, while on the other hand, there are many readers who simply hope to learn about something that has piqued their interest because it has increasingly become the subject of many cultural representations in literature and popular culture. I have tried to keep both audiences in mind and have told the story of narco Mexico so that it is useful to both.

The next two chapters expand on the themes that I briefly touched upon in this introduction, and then chapter 3 moves on to describe the Mexico of 2020 as it collectively held its breath and hoped for a miracle as it awaited a promised era of transformational change. Their president, López Obrador, had promised that he would establish what he called a Fourth Transformation. Lamentably, his vision of *la 4T* faced daunting obstacles and threats—including continuing violence, a collapsing economy, and the devastating impact of the global pandemic that had not been managed well within Mexico or elsewhere—but AMLO's electoral victory sent strong signals that 2018 represented a watershed moment ending a long dark cycle during which a covert netherworld had dominated and been nourished by a widespread corruption that had seeped into every nook and cranny of Mexican life. Chapter 4 describes the history of drugs and banditry in Mexico and explores how a relatively unsophisticated subterranean culture situated in northwest Mexico gradually and perhaps unintentionally gave birth to the sophisticated criminal organizations and remarkable characters who created thriving enterprises within a secretive and powerful underworld described in more detail in chapter 5. Chapter 6 looks specifically at the significance of El Chapo—the man who has been elevated in popular culture as the archetypical embodiment of a Mexican drug lord—especially in the aftermath of a showcase trial in a Brooklyn, New York, courtroom. Facts do not always support the widely held and popularized view of his importance, and the reality of his status and power within the criminal underworld is much more complex than the DOJ and DEA assertions would have the world believe. Chapter 7 outlines more recent events leading to the rise and fall of Mexican criminal organizations within Mexico's covert netherworld, and identifies key events, prominent personalities, and individuals who were skilled entrepreneurs operating outside the bounds of civil society. The eighth and final chapter returns to the present—2021—and reflects on Mexico's future. Modern Mexico's struggles to end corruption and dismantle the covert netherworld remain ongoing challenges, and the trends and events of Mexico's past are still deep and powerful forces that continue to resist change and make the hope of transformation difficult.

Narco Traffickers, Cartels, and Academia

American academia has been sadly neglectful in viewing organized crime as a substantive area of research; in the grand scheme of things, there has been little formal investigation into narco traffic and cartels in Mexico. It does not overstate reality to point out that European criminologists and sociologists have made more important contributions to research on transnational and organized crime, and the most important seminal investigations and textbooks have originated outside the United States and North America. On the other hand, those European researchers rarely made Mexico the focus of scholarly work. They and others were late to recognize that organized crime and transnational mafias existed as a powerful force in Mexico. For instance, Jean-François Gayraud's influential book *El G9 de las mafias en el mundo* (2007) made no reference to Mexican crime organizations in his list of the most important global mafias, even though by then the Sinaloa Cartel had an international presence. But the European focus elsewhere and the non-attention to Mexico do not explain why so few academic studies of Mexican crime organizations have happened in the United States.

The American Society of Criminology (ASC) is the largest and indisputably the most prestigious professional association for crime scholars; its annual meeting showcases contemporary research, emerging issues, and exploratory ideas about the causes and consequences of crime.[13] A content analysis of conference proceedings between 2007 and 2017 based on various combinations of search terms—*cartel, Mexico, narco, narco traffic, organized crime, drug lord,* and *drug smuggling*—easily demonstrates that Mexico and crime in Mexico were barely an afterthought for academic criminologists. An exponential spike upward in Mexico's homicide rates began between 2005 and 2007, and there was a continual unabated ten-year period when the various cartel wars raged across Mexico. But while that bloodshed and chaos was unfolding in Mexico, there were at least 6,200 academic sessions at the ASC annual meeting exploring crime in the world that made little reference to Mexico.[14] In that ten-year cycle (2007–17) when Mexico recorded 242,082 known homicides, academic criminologists had apparently not even noticed that something extraordinarily violent was unfolding, and the concepts narco trafficker, narco, and cartel appeared almost nowhere in academic discourse.[15]

This raises an obvious question about where to find *reliable* information about narco traffic and narco traffickers outside the DEA archives, and also suggests a related secondary question about how the information about current events and crime actually filters into the public domain. First, it should be obvious that studying organized crime represents an inherent personal risk to anyone who delves too deeply into it, and it is virtually impossible for outsiders to engage in direct observation or directly gather primary data from within the hidden world of organized crime, mafias, and cartels. The people who do have detailed knowledge will not talk unless coerced, induced by legal threat, or tempted by promises of immunity. It is extremely rare for anyone from the inside to publish memoirs or voluntarily write insider accounts of life inside a mafia. In the case of Mexico, there has been no source equivalent to *The Valachi Papers* (Maas 1986), even though an older publication by José Alfredo Andrade Bojorges (1999) claimed to be a Mexican mafia tell-all before it was widely discredited by both insiders and by knowlegable investigators.[16] The December 2019 publication of *El traidor: El diario secreto del hijo del Mayo* (Hernández 2020) promised to be the first legitimate insider account of Mexican crime syndicates—and its appearance triggered a vigorous reexamination of much of what was previously written and believed about cartels—especially in details about the history and operations of the powerful Sinaloa Cartel.

There are few primary data sources available to sociologists, criminologists, security experts, and political scientists—especially since much in the DEA archives remains effectively closed to outsiders. Mexican scholar Luis Alejandro Astorga Almanza is one of the few academics who has delved deeply into older historical archives and primary sources; he effectively used that information to produce his two classic books that remain canonical overviews of the trajectory of narco Mexico (Astorga 1996, 2003).[17] But recently, no professional scholar has been granted extensive access to primary sources of information such as the sealed testimony from protected witnesses or details gathered using electronic surveillance. The DEA and the DOJ selectively released additional information following the sentencing of Guzmán, but those documents relate to only a very small slice of the overall history of narco traffic and cartel Mexico. But encouragingly, the material that has been released supports information and facts that were already in the public domain, and the selective release of secretive data has almost always validated details that were previously reported by Mexican journalists who had uncovered the story. The fact that little has been so far contradicted by the release of DEA and DOJ data gives hope to the premise that the history known up to this point in time by journalists is largely accurate.

Until the DEA archives and EPIC databases are fully accessible, the main source of information about Mexico's narco traffickers and cartels will necessarily be that broad category of data that academics refer to as secondary sources. Many authors and journalists in Mexico have covered organized crime and written about it for decades, and their work and observations provide the backbone material for much of this book and for that of other researchers. But at the same time, some of that journalistic material propagates false claims or repeats anecdotes and sheer nonsense that should be dismissed as nonsense or myth. In addition, many lies about narco traffic have been deliberately circulated in the public domain by journalists working for both the government and on behalf of narco traffickers. The legitimation and identification of trustworthy accounts and the debunking of nonsensical reports ultimately depend on a detailed and critical reading of the material that is available in the public domain. Given what I have just written, it should be obvious that I am asking the reader to accept my personal interpretation and selection of relevant material, and to trust that I have done my best to use only reliable and trustworthy sources.

This book is based on material and authors that I came to trust through my personal contacts and professional academic training and from five decades of observing, teaching, and working in Mexico and the borderlands of southern Arizona. Much of my knowledge and understanding has been especially informed by long conversations and emails with many friends and scholars, such as the late George Grayson at William and Mary College. Several sections of this book heavily rely on notes and personal exchanges I had with him; I have specifically made an effort to credit those parts that were formed in discussion with him.

My doctoral studies between 1971 and 1975 at the University of Arizona involved routine travel to several communities sitting on both sides of the Arizona–Sonora border south of Tucson.[18] My research brought me to towns and communities such as Ajo, Nogales, Naco, Agua Prieta, Bisbee, Wilcox, and Douglas for extended observational visits and data collection— and sometimes just to be a tourist, eat wonderful food, and experience the Sonoran Desert. This research employed a wide range of sociological techniques, which included analysis of court records, random sample interviews of citizen respondents, and the administration of self-report surveys to high school students across that border region in a specific stretch of the Arizona–Sonora border where the Mexican civil war had been fought just south of the American line and now sits exactly where the Sinaloa Cartel and El Chapo later constructed border tunnels.

Nixon's declaration of a War on Drugs actually had a personal impact when it temporarily held up research funding on my PhD dissertation until a secondary review by the Republican administration determined that it still fit into the new priorities established by the DOJ in the aftermath of the declaration of the War on Drugs. My particular research represented only one part of an umbrella research project funded by the National Science Foundation to specifically explore marijuana and drug use, and also to examine community and police reaction to crime and drug consumption in that region. The broader narrative and concern focused on Mexican organized crime and narco traffic was unknown at the time I was involved in gathering data (in the early 1970s) and did not enter into the equation; nor would any description of drug organizations and transnational crime appear anywhere in the public discourse during the initial years of the War on Drugs.

Later, I did undertake research following those same themes while I taught sociology, criminology, and research methods courses at the University of Alberta over the next three decades. During those years, I regularly returned for extended periods to Tucson, Arizona, where I continued to track border issues and pursue my own research in crime and delinquent behavior—but even in those subsequent years, I rarely encountered references to or saw a great concern about organized crime along the border, with the exception of occasional news items about Joe Bonano and his family life in Tucson at a house located around the corner from where we lived during graduate school.

The passage of the North American Free Trade Agreement (NAFTA) opened opportunities to pursue additional research in Mexico, and the University of Alberta supported a sabbatical year over 1996–97 during which I planned to initiate a comparative project examining public perceptions of crime and delinquency in Mexico and Arizona. I spent the first two months of my sabbatical at the University of Arizona in Tucson and followed up immediately by spending a full year as a visiting scholar at El Colegio de México in the southern part of Mexico City. It was during those years that the terms *cartel* and *narco* first began to seep into the public discourse and appear in popular narratives about drugs and the U.S. War on Drugs. The most dramatic event during that year living in Mexico City was the execution of the "Lord of the Skies" in a hospital not far from where I lived, but it was actually several months later that some of the details became known and general discussions of organized crime dominated news reports. However, my attention to organized crime shifted to a level of heightened awareness following a number of high-profile shoot-outs and the public arrests of high-profile criminals in the Pedregal area near my apartment and the El Colegio de México campus located in the Ajusco area. After that, references to cartels and organized crime in Mexico began to regularly appear in the public discourse and were regularly reported in important newspapers such as the centrist *Reforma* and leftist *La Jornada.*

Near the end of my sabbatical leave, I received an invitation to become a visiting scholar and adjunct faculty member in a North American Studies graduate program newly created in Culiacán, Mexico, at the Autonomous University of Sinaloa. One year later, in 1998, and almost completely oblivious to the reality that Sinaloa State was the *cuna del narcotráfico*—the so-called cradle of narco traffic—I began what turned out to be a fourteen-year association with the UAS as professor and lecturer in a graduate-level program that eventually produced dozens of university professors and researchers who are still working in Mexico. That by-chance opportunity brought many adventures and left me with many friends in Sinaloa who have coincidently remained my eyes and ears in Mexico and with whom I still communicate on a regular basis.

I am *güero* and anglo *foráneo*—a white, English-speaking foreigner—but my years in Sinaloa and travels to Mexico have provided a modicum of cultural capital and the assuredness to write about a covert netherworld of Mexican cartels that I had come to know over time. But even more importantly, those years in Sinaloa allowed me to identify reliable and trustworthy observers of the subterranean world of narco Mexico. The sources cited in this book have been identified and culled from those personal experiences in Sinaloa and from those ongoing friendships with many Mexican professors and graduate students who have become longtime correspondents.

More than once, I happened to be Sinaloa or in Mexico when a major tipping point in narco history unfolded. The most notable was a 2004 trip to Culiacán when I narrowly avoided the ambush where Rodolfo Carrillo Fuentes was gunned down at the Cinépolis Plaza in Culiacán and triggered a bloody war within cartels between the El Chapo faction and the Carrillo Fuentes family from nearby Guamulchilito. Another frightening experience happened in 2008 when I was locked down in my hotel room after Arturo Beltrán Leyva had brutally arranged the execution of five state police two blocks away in the initial salvo signaling his break from the Sinaloa Cartel and specifically from El Chapo.

My ongoing contact with more than seventy-five graduate students and dozens of faculty and staff from the Autonomous University of Sinaloa and the Faculty of International Studies and Public Policy has left me with a personal pool of friends, observers, and informants who I regularly lean on to give me details about events in Culiacán and Mexico and from whom I receive advice about trustworthy journalistic sources. Those personal and professional experiences have hopefully made me a trustworthy narrator of narco Mexico in the pages and chapters that follow.

CHAPTER 1

Cartels and Covert Netherworlds

Jefe de Jefes
A mí me gustan los corridos
Porque son los hechos reales de nuestro pueblo
Sí, a mí también me gustan porque
En ellos canta la pura verdad

—Los Tigres del Norte, "Jefe de Jefes," 1997

On the eve of revolution, John Kenneth Turner (1912) wrote that life for the majority of Mexicans was barbaric.[1] The authoritarian president Porfirio Díaz oversaw a government that produced immense wealth for its elite by consigning *los de abajo* to lifetimes of crushing poverty and slavery.[2] Turner's angry words were aimed at the Progress and Order ethos of Díaz and his bureaucracy made up of liberal *científicos*, but he also had no kind words for U.S. president Howard Taft and American foreign policy.[3] By the time a first edition of *Barbarous Mexico* circulated, Taft had deployed thirty thousand American troops to the border region to remind Mexican dissidents that the USA firmly supported Díaz's authoritarian regime and its economic goals (Turner 1912, 1999). The unquestionable threat of U.S. invasion did not deter populist uprising, and civil war and revolution erupted to leave several million dead and hundreds of thousands permanently displaced.[4]

Marginalized Mexicans paid the price for that revolution; millions of impoverished people were displaced and served as the cannon fodder in revolutionary battles that raged on for fourteen years. Carnage waxed and waned as competing factions strategically battled for control, but by the mid-1920s, most confrontations had ended and killing shifted from producing the carcasses of war to a pattern where the dead were now victims of brute power, venality, or anger. Years of war had normalized violence, and too many Mexicans had come to believe that murder was an acceptable option for resolving personal and economic disputes—especially given the prevalent impunity in the absence of effective policing and justice institutions. During the first years of peace, homicide rates continued to sit at unacceptably brutal levels even as the slaughter shifted from the product of war to acts of force, the product of criminal action, or simply the consequences of human anger or desire for revenge.

But the rate of killing eventually did slow. There were non-dramatic changes at first, but the long-term historical trends clearly indicate that Mexican homicide rates began a trajectory downward to reach a rate of about 9 per 100,000 murders in 1969, before jumping briefly to 22 per 100,000 in 1974, and then declining once again to about 9 per 100,000 by 2004 (Global Change Data Lab n.d.; Policzer 2019, 83–92).[5]

A momentous shift beginning in 2004 precipitously ended the trend of a seven-decade cycle wherein the better angels of nature had dominated. By 2006 mindboggling levels of violence had reappeared to leave rivers of blood flowing everywhere for the next sixteen years. At least 400,000 Mexicans have now been murdered in the first two decades of the twenty-first century—exactly at a time when Mexico has aspired to become a fully functioning partner in the global world and had been firmly committed to pursuing neoliberal economic policies that promised to bring peace along with prosperity.[6] Sadly, the vast majority of those who were murdered as well as those who did the killing came from marginalized classes, while those at the top of the economic ladder rarely paid the price with their life.

The bloody carnage shows no sign of slowing as these words are written in the spring of 2021. Mexico recorded an additional 135,587 homicidios dolosos from 2017 through 2020, wherein each subsequent year established a new shameful high for the most murders ever recorded in one year. The year 2020 ended that cycle of record increases—but only barely: the 35,554 homicidios dolosos recorded in 2020 fell a mere 104 homicides short of equaling the dubious record of 35,588 in 2019 (SESNSP 2021).

Routine savagery and shattered social bonds have now contaminated four presidential terms and tainted the first three years of a fifth with no end in sight. Sadly, official tallies of violence underestimate the true carnage and impact on society—especially for marginalized Mexicans: another sixty thousand have disappeared and remain untraceable in 2020, and there are entire rural communities that sit empty and have been abandoned to the elements

(SESNSP 2019; Sheridan 2020b). The nature of that excessive brutal violence has remained remarkably consistent across the most recent five sexenios: seven of ten murders were committed with firearms, the firearms used are almost always military grade, six of every ten killings can be attributed to organized criminality, and with increasing regularity the victims show signs of brutal mutilation (Angel 2020).

One hundred years ago, a classic vision of a liberal state that had created gaping economic and social inequality was brought down by unrest, calls for democratization, demands for transparency, and anger about the corruption favoring a privileged elite. Ultimately, civil society fractured and an ensuing revolutionary war left at least 1,500,000 dead and 200,000 missing by 1917 (McCaa 2003). More recently, Mexican cartels have prospered within a neoliberal economy that had promised much but had done far too little to reduce social inequality, deliver prosperity, or end Mexico's endemic corruption. Neoliberalism's failures and Mexico's institutional inefficiency are directly responsible for fostering the conditions that allowed organized crime groups to thrive, and both are indirectly responsible for engendering the current levels of violence.[7]

The Paradox of Cartel Power in a Time of Prosperity?

No statistical measure of homicide truly captures the total impact of bloody, violent vortices of murder and mayhem—but precise counts should not be necessary to arrive at a conclusion that the Mexican state has failed in its moral obligation to provide security for its people.

As mentioned earlier, violence in Mexico had consistently fallen over many decades, including during the 1980s. Those declining levels were recorded even though Mexican politicians and the bureaucratic state of that era were unquestionably corrupt, and even though Mexico's juridical and social institutions had by then become tangled thickets of inefficiency and incompetence leaving many *vacíos de poder* (Buscaglia 2013).[8] In what can be described as a puzzling phenomenon, violence actually had *declined* for fifteen consecutive years, even though criminal groups were fusing into powerful entities that would eventually dominate the American continents and establish an extensive transnational presence.

Paradoxically, a perverse version of government oversight, a Pax Narca, had managed to constrain violence for many years—not necessarily because the jefes of crime groups sought peace but because agents of the state demanded it.

Secretive pacts between state agents and emergent narco traffickers had created a stable equilibrium wherein everyone profited—and where excessive violence was held in check by subterranean codes and a shared understanding that harmonious partnerships were beneficial to everyone. Mayhem and chaos attracted too much attention from the outside world—especially from all-seeing eyes monitoring on behalf of the United States—and disruption and mayhem were best kept suppressed.

The criminal-state stasis that had successfully limited violence in Mexico was eventually stretched to a breaking point with the arrival of a new millennium. Sociopolitical conditions changed and there were once again widespread popular expectations for democratization and transparent governance, a rapid geopolitical expansion of global markets, and the persistent and nagging drumbeat from the United States to conform to its vision of a global War on Drugs. Social and economic arrangements that had previously fostered stable pacts among capos, corrupt officials, and justice agencies were increasingly undermined by disruptive pressures and fissures that appeared in all of Mexico's cities and states—but especially those along the northern border with the USA. The breaking point came in 2004 when several plaza disputes and internal challenges for leadership could no longer be held in check by state dictate; matters were exacerbated even more with the unexpected appearance of a novel narco insurgency and radically different criminal force known as Los Zetas. The equilibrium between narco traffickers and the state imploded, and Mexico erupted in a wave of violence that dragged on without signs of slowing for the next fifteen years.

Covert Netherworlds, Narco Wars, and Broken Pax Mafiosas

The following chapters describe the alliances of corrupt government officials and agencies, narco organizations, and criminal justice institutions responsible for the extreme violence afflicting modern Mexico. One common narrative insists that powerful drug lords and a violent criminal underworld are responsible, but that is a one-dimensional explanation that overlooks the wide extent of corruption, the roles played by many in a powerful elite, and the tragic weaknesses of Mexico's social institutions.

In reality, drug lords are but one component in a complex criminal network that has entangled entire communities, legitimate businesses, respectable institutions, elected officials, high-level bureaucrats, military generals, and thousands of police and justice agencies in a perverse social contract. Organized crime has often been described as a distinct *parallel* institution that competes directly for power with the state (e.g., Fernández Menéndez 2001), but a more accurate interpretation is that the Mexican state and criminal networks are intrinsically linked: criminals and agents of the legitimate state work cooperatively in symbiotic interdependence and are motivated to cooperate by a shared economic interest. The principal coordinators and intermediaries of that perverse interface are located in Mexico's police agencies, the military, and in many other parts of Mexico's dysfunctional justice institutions; the integrative glue binding them together is an enormous underground economy lubricated with vast sums of dark money.

The criminal-state alliance is conceptualized in these pages as a covert netherworld where the members of a criminal organization and government officials and respectable individuals work together in mutual cooperation. This viewpoint has been consistently dismissed in official circles, but it is widely accepted as reality by most Mexicans who have learned about it from folklore and popular culture over decades—especially from *narcocorridos*.[9] In many ways the description of cartels and narco traffic in this book reflects the common knowledge on the street rather than what has been fully described in books or academic research. The popular appeal of songs about corruption and official involvement in narco trafficking has frequently angered state governors and national politicians to the point where they sometimes moved to ban narcocorrido groups and deny radio airtime (see Wald n.d.). The *norteño* group Los Tigres del Norte is just one musical group that experienced the wrath of officialdom, but they have remained immensely popular for almost four decades and are seen as truth tellers by most: their iconic double CD, *Jefe de Jefes*, is arguably one of the most complete and comprehensive descriptions of that complex world populated by drug lords, politicians, military generals, police officials, and ordinary people entangled in a shadowy alliance (Bello et al. 1997; Ramirez 2019).[10]

In the following chapters, the five-decade-long U.S. War on Drugs is not the main focus, even though it is frequently referenced and was undeniably important in influencing the way the criminal underworld evolved and transformed in Mexico. The narrative of narco Mexico as reflected in the official U.S. viewpoint focuses almost exclusively on the kingpins and capos, and provides little information about "the invisible interstice between the formal and informal sectors where these illicit activities seem to survive and thrive" (McCoy 2003, 1). Rather, the substantive focus in this book is broader and describes the connections between narco traffickers, their allies, and their facilitators as Alfred McCoy has suggested.

> A covert netherworld takes form when three critical components—*social milieu, covert operations,* and *illicit commerce*—converge in a particular and potent array. At its core, this netherworld is an invisible interstice inhabited by criminal and clandestine actors who are practitioners of what famed intelligence operative Lucien Conein once called "the clandestine arts"—that is, the skill of conducting complex operations beyond the bounds of civil society. (2018, 2, emphasis added)

The Mexican underworld and criminal organizations were first described and entered into public consciousness during the early years of the U.S. War on Drugs when they were specifically targeted by the newly established DEA. Initially the view of drug cartels was painted with a very broad and nonspecific brush, especially in the way it minimalized interactions with state agents and politicians. The broader world of Mexican crime and drug-trafficking networks—the social milieu, the covert operations, and the illicit commerce mentioned by McCoy—has never been comprehensively described before in one book or publication. There *are* many excellent books and government reports that describe many aspects of the narco history that will be expanded in the following chapters: for example, books by British journalists Ioan Grillo (2012) and Malcolm Beith (2010) and the late political scientist George Grayson (2008b, 2010, 2014) remain highly recommended reference points for anyone seeking to know more about narco history. And a Spanish-language book by Guillermo Valdés Castellanos (2013) provides an overview of Mexican cartels from a high-level government insider, and it should be viewed as an essential historical reference for all scholars of cartels in modern Mexico.

The narratives describing cartels and the criminal underworld of Mexico in fiction and popular entertainment have been heavily influenced by the official DEA accounts of cartels, and they almost always portray narco traffickers, cartels, and Mexican criminal organizations as malevolent and unpredictable protagonists operating in defiance of the state. The popularity of *Breaking Bad* and *Better Call Saul*; several streaming series, such as Netflix's *Narcos* and *Narcos: Mexico*; and best-selling novels like Don Winslow's *The Border* (2019) have amplified and shaped the public conception of Mexico's complex and invisible world of clandestine actors operating beyond the boundaries of civil society and state control. But those cultural representations are fictionalized, and they do borrow as much from imagination and a tunnel vision as from reality and fact.

Cartels and Narco Insurgency

The subterranean underworld that had evolved under the watchful eye of the Partido Institucional Revolucionario (PRI, Institutional Revolutionary Party) governments of 1998–2000 managed to keep violence in check, and had successfully suppressed the identity of most of the key players. But that period of stability was disrupted not long after Vicente Fox Quesada of the Partido Acción Nacional (PAN, National Action Party) won the presidency in 2000.[11] For a few short years, not much appeared different, but after 2004 violence began to surge to levels unseen since the revolutionary era. This book argues that the emergence of the paramilitary criminal group known as Los Zetas was one of the major factors unleashing a disruptive power and spreading violence across the nation. There had always been arguments and disputes that threatened the stability within the underworld, and later chapters will describe the more important ones that affected narco Mexico. But before Los Zetas appeared, disputing factions had always managed to renegotiate Pax Mafiosas and restore alliances before violence escalated out of control.[12]

Competition between cartels grew more brutal and violent by the third year of the Fox presidency, but it was in the fourth year of his sexenio that homicides and forced disappearances began to surge upward. In the beginning, Los Zetas seemed to be little more than a couple of dozen army deserters recruited as foot soldiers and sicarios for the Gulf Cartel plazas in five states (Coahuila, Nuevo León, Tamaulipas, San Luis Potosí, and Veracruz), but it soon became evident that its members were much more than body-guards. They were the enforcers and advance invasionary force for Gulf Cartel expansion into new plazas, and in stark contrast to the cartels based in northwest and central Mexico, they relied on force, raw power, and intimidation to enforce compliance in communities they invaded. Los Zetas had been indoctrinated to follow a code of extreme military discipline, and each of the original recruits was expert in using military tactics to sow terror and create fear, and they had little patience for negotiating reciprocal arrangements or forging cooperation in the communities they invaded and controlled.

The startling and rapid success of Los Zetas forced a dramatic reaction in established criminal organizations that had historically expanded and grown by using consensus, cooperation, and shared economic interests to cement bonds with other groups and even the wider community. Los Zetas had emerged as a type of criminal insurgency reliant on terror tactics, and the older criminal organizations in Mexico were challenged by the new and dangerous threat; they reacted quickly to create their own squadrons of heavily armed foot soldiers. This is not to say that the older organizations hadn't used violence over the years, but they had never done so to the extent it became normalized after 2004.[13]

Shortly after those developments in Mexico, a new narrative of narco insurgency appeared in U.S. analyses of narco Mexico. In 2008 the U.S. Pentagon and the Military Joint Forces Command testified before Congress that Mexico was in danger of becoming a failed state after Los Zetas and the Gulf Cartel had expanded their territorial reach across northeast Mexico. The introduction of the term *narco insurgency* represented a significant shift for sociopolitical explanations of organized crime in Mexico: cartels were not only being conceptualized as criminal groups but had been elevated into full-blown enemies of the state and competitors with it for legitimacy in the community. President Felipe Calderón vehemently rejected the idea that his nation should be classified alongside pariah nations such as Pakistan, which the Joint Forces had also identified as a failed state, but nevertheless Calderón, Mexican intelligence agencies, and even the international press increasingly began to refer to narco insurgency and the war against cartels (Grayson 2010; Lacey 2009). The term *insurgency* soon became the rationalizing justification to legitimate President Calderón's view that the only way to eliminate Mexico's narco-trafficking threat was to wage war against cartels and to task the responsibility for waging it to Mexico's armed forces.

In spite of its popular use after 2008, the narrative of narco insurgency as it was applied to Los Zetas does not explain the perseverant power and success of the older cartels, which had organically depended on links to power and economic institutions. Guadalupe Correa-Cabrera (2017) has provided the most comprehensive English-language description of Los Zetas, but neither did she categorize Los Zetas as a narco insurgency: rather, she describes them as a criminal corporation and a capitalist enterprise dedicated to pursuing economic gain. Her comprehensive overview portrays a criminal enterprise that did usurp and weaken the legitimate authority of the state, including the power to sanction and punish those who didn't follow rules or obey orders, but it never intended to replace the state. However, two recent Spanish-language books by Juan Alberto Cedillo (2018) and Ricardo Raphael (2019) have resurrected the narrative language of war and insurgency to argue that Los Zetas should be thought of as a narco-insurgent movement. In fact, Cedillo claims it was a narco insurgency that severely disrupted governance in Mexico and delegitimated the state to the point it was incapable of controlling other narco cartels or even maintaining order in many parts of northeast Mexico.[14]

■ ■ ■

In 2021 many facts about narco Mexico remain unknown, especially to those who have depended only on English-language accounts. Much that is written in English about cartels is surprisingly incomplete and shallow, or has been distorted by myth and infused with rumor rather than presenting factual evidence and documented detail. And as mentioned previously, most media depictions of narco traffickers and narco Mexico have muddied the understanding of the true nature of cartels through an overreliance on fictionalized accounts about the rise of Mexican cartels and the power of Mexican capos—especially so in how cartel figures have been portrayed in the Netflix series *Narcos: Mexico.*

In contrast to the fictional versions of narco reality, there are many dedicated journalists and investigators who have published detailed and accurate descriptions of cartels and organized crime in Mexico, and their reports have been consistently and increasingly validated with each release of unsealed documents and archives from the American judicial processes. The exact details of brutal slaughters, the pacts between narco traffickers and government officials, longtime symbiotic connections between narco traffickers and legitimate businesses, the actual tallies of massacres, and the underlying factors triggering internecine cartel attacks have been trickling into the public domain with each new release of court and archival documents.

For instance, hundreds of pages of previously sealed documents were released after El Chapo Guzmán was found guilty in a Brooklyn court on February 12, 2019, of leading a criminal enterprise (DOJ 2019). During that showcase trial, U.S. prosecutors introduced an impressive treasure trove of information based on telephone surveillance and Internet hacks, informants, protected witnesses, and indicted individuals who had proffered evidence under oath in exchange for reduced criminal sentences, cash, and guaranteed protection. Many of the documents introduced in the trial or released afterward had been known to exist but they had also been sealed and therefore inaccessible to reporters and researchers.[15] There are still hundreds of thousands of pages based on wiretaps and records of electronic surveillance that have never been made public. A highly recommended account of the capture and trial of Guzmán is Alan Feuer's *El Jefe: The Stalking of Chapo Guzmán* (2020), which describes in explicit detail how much of that information was collected; it also describes the complications involved in using it for the historical record.

Many archival records are accessible to those with the patience and funds to search the public portal Public Access to Court Electronic Records (Federal Judiciary n.d.), and Mexican journalist Juan Alberto Cedillo recognizes what that source of information meant for his investigations and potentially means for his colleagues: "In just a few years, this portal had become the fundamental archival source for writing the history of Mexico, thanks to the large number of confessions that have been gathered in trials and collected there" (2018, Kindle Location 103–4).[16]

The eventual release of American juridical transcripts and unsealed documents will either revise the history of narco Mexico or expand on the narrative documented by Mexican journalists before 2018. Three books have already used that material to add to our knowledge of cartels and more importantly to expose specific links to public officials and Mexican security agencies that worked directly with Mexican cartel bosses (Cedillo 2018; Hernández 2020; Raphael 2019). As these words are written, a trial for money laundering and other narco-trafficking charges against Genaro García Luna, Mexico's former secretary of public security, is scheduled for a New York court and will certainly involve the release of additional wiretaps and cables that implicate other high-level government officials (Cruz 2020; Estevez 2020a; Hernández Norzargaray 2020; Sumners 2020). DOJ documents released in the aftermath of El Chapo's trial also led to the extradition from Spain of Emilio Lozoya, the former head of Petróleos Mexicanos (Pemex, Mexican Petroleum) during the Peña Nieto presidency (Sheridan 2020a). But until all those cables and wiretaps are finally made public, and until trials are completed for men like García Luna and Lozoya, the full extent of the interstices between respected figures and narco traffickers will continue to sit in the realm of rumor rather than in the concrete world of demonstrable fact.

The Sinaloa Cartel and Covert Netherworlds

Anabel Hernández's book *El traidor: El diario secreto del hijo del Mayo* (2020) also used U.S. DOJ documents to expose the innermost details of the Sinaloa Cartel. Her book primarily relies on material reprinted directly from the personal diary of Vicente "Vicentillo" Zambada Niebla and long interviews with a Zambada family lawyer named Fernando Gaxiola, but their first-person accounts are corroborated by her descriptions of other documents that he shared with her, and the Chicago court transcripts of the trials of Vicente, his uncle Jesús Reynaldo "El Rey" Zambada García, and the Flores brothers, who were the key Sinaloa Cartel operatives in Illinois and later the key prosecution witnesses against both Zambadas. Additionally, she provides detailed accounts of her personal investigation into the legitimate businesses that laundered millions of dollars for the Sinaloa Cartel and more specifically on behalf of Vicente's father, Ismael "El Mayo" Zambada García.

Relying heavily on the accounts related by Fernando Glaxiola and by Vicentillo, Hernández maintains that El Mayo *founded* the Sinaloa Cartel in the late 1970s, and has remained entrenched as de facto boss for more than four decades. Both Glaxiola and Zambada Niebla told her that the Sinaloa Cartel had materialized out of a drug-smuggling business operated by El Mayo's brother-in-law Antonio Cruz Vásquez in Las Vegas, Nevada, until his arrest in 1978. The elder Zambada Gárcia, who had been introduced to the narco-trafficking trade by the Cuban national Cruz, subsequently shifted operations to Los Angeles about the same time that the Guadalajara Cartel was emerging in Jalisco State. Unlike many Sinaloan narco traffickers described in this book, El Mayo had never lived in the high sierra and instead was a native of El Alamo on the southern outskirts of Culiacán: rather than fleeing to Guadalajara like many others, he relocated instead to Los Angeles, California, following Operation Condor. He remained in that Southern Califorina megalopolis for about five years before returning to Sinaloa around 1982, but most of his drug operations remained centered north of the border in Southern California (Hernández 2020, 37–42).

Most importantly, Hernánez reveals the extensive links connecting key operatives of the modern Sinaloa Cartel to individuals in government, business, and respectable circles. Over decades, it had developed deep ties to national corporations such as the Mexican state monopoly Pemex, corrupt politicians at state and federal levels, Mexican military leaders, police officials, and several prominent entrepreneurs who had managed to remain anonymous until their names were revealed during the trials of El Rey Zambada, El Chapo Guzmán, and Vicentillo Zambada. She points an accusatory finger at many high-ranking public officials—most notably the aforementioned Genaro García Luna, who is under arrest in the United States and awaiting trial for narco trafficking (Cruz 2020; Estevez 2020a; Hernández Norzargaray 2020; Sumners 2020).

El traidor provided specific details about the Sinaloa Cartel operations never published before and also represented the first extensive biography of its founder, El Mayo. Hernández's revelations validate my argument that the Sinaloa Cartel is best conceptualized as a covert netherworld rather than seen as a criminal enterprise operating in functional opposition to the state or as a counterinsurgent power attempting to replace it. For more than four decades, the Sinaloa Cartel has successfully interwoven the three critical components of a covert netherworld specifically mentioned by McCoy—a social milieu, covert operations, and illicit commerce—and established stable symbiotic relationships with key actors within the state apparatus, with entrepreneurs, and with a powerful economic and social class. The Sinaloa Cartel is arguably unique in pursuing a relationship that sociologists have described as mutual reciprocity: its power and permanence had thrived in official invisibility, and most of its organizational structure and inner workings have remained largely unknown until now amid the revelations from these high-profile criminal cases. In effect, the Sinaloa Cartel has been hiding in plain sight for several decades—and continues to do so even in 2021.

Even so, the Sinaloa Cartel has admittedly transformed and adapted over time, and that trajectory will be described in the following chapter, which reviews the adaptive and aggressive changes that happened over five presidential terms. Internal disputes within the Sinaloa Federation led to eruptions of violence in the past, but even after severe disruptions, it continued to be a powerful force because its subterranean horizontal and vertical links to social-economic-political institutions always remained intact and were largely unaffected by turmoil—even during this especially tumultuous period at the first two decades of this century.

Indisputable evidence of the Sinaloa Cartel's resiliency was most recently demonstrated in a 2020 incident that is now infamously known as Jueves Negro (Black Thursday) or El Culiacanazo. The Mexican army was humiliated and forced into an embarrassing stand-down following the failed arrest of Ovidio Guzmán López—one of El Chapo's sons. An army unit had surrounded Guzmán's Culiacán residence and had actually arrested Ovidio, but cartel bosses and *lugartenientes* (subcommanders) rapidly deployed heavily armed foot soldiers to surround his house while simultaneously seizing control of most of Culiacán's major arteries, intersections, and municipal exit points. Cartel operatives manning .50 caliber machine guns streamed operations directly to social media from pickup trucks as Sinaloa foot soldiers and hit men surrounded all the military and police checkpoints across the city. Furthermore, a prison break coordinated by the cartel bosses released dozens of criminals onto Culiacán's streets to create additional mayhem. The speed of the cartel counterattack following an attempted arrest and the sophisticated operation involving coordinated teams were an undeniable demonstration of power. The Sinaloa Cartel's reaction to the attempted arrest left no one questioning who actually controlled Culiacán and Sinaloa State.

The audacious display of cartel power was unleashed even as Alfredo Durazo Montaño, then federal cabinet director of security and citizen protection, was hosting a high-level meeting with security officials to discuss and plan regional security measures in Culiacán and Sinaloa State.[17] An army captain had arrested Ovidio Guzmán at gunpoint but wisely made the decision to retreat after Ovidio spoke to his half-brother Iván Archivaldo Guzmán on a cell phone that the arresting officer himself passed over for him to use.[18] The humiliating retreat was captured on several cell phones and streamed instantaneously to social media. Unshaken by the day's events,

Ovidio celebrated with friends at a popular *antro* (nightclub) later that evening—an event also streamed live for public consumption. Months later,
President López Obrador admitted that it was he who personally gave the
order for the army to stand down and retreat (García 2020).

El Culiacanzo represents overwhelming proof that the Sinaloa Cartel is
intact and remains powerful even though El Chapo was by that time serving a life sentence in an American federal prison for narco trafficking. The
interested reader can find much more information about this incident in
several reports by Romain Le Cour Grandmaison, such as "The Narco Spectacle Can End" (n.d.). One year following the confinement of El Chapo in
a high-security supermax prison, nothing appeared to have changed nor
diminished the power of the Sinaloa Cartel in Culiacán and Sinaloa State
(Gándara 2020).

Insurgency: The Gulf Cartel and Los Zetas

In the years before the Vicente Fox presidency, one powerful national criminal mafia—a federation with deep roots in Sinaloa State that had unquestionably been the dominant player in the covert netherworld—had established a presence in thirteen states. In those years, U.S. agents used various
names to describe that dominant organization and variously referred to it
as the Guadalajara Cartel and sometimes the Juárez Cartel before eventually settling on the Federation. Distinct factions and groups operated within
that unitary criminal enterprise, but almost all were connected by family or
historical roots to Sinaloa State.

However, within the first few years of Vicente Fox's sexenio, at least four distinct and competing criminal organizations emerged to establish a national or
broad regional presence (Tijuana, Juárez, Sinaloa, and Gulf). The Tijuana and
Ciudad Juárez syndicates emerged after fractious disputes led them to withdraw, renegotiate plazas, or arguably be expelled from a broader Sinaloa Federation. Specifically, the Arellano Félix family asserted its dominance in Tijuana
and Baja California, while the Carrillo Fuentes brothers led by Amado Carrillo
cemented their firm grip on the Juárez corridor—an era that one Spanish-
language author describes as the coming of the barbarians (Tercero 2011).

In the northeast, a distinct organization known as the Gulf criminal organization emerged as a powerful criminal drug syndicate when its leader,

Juan García Abrego, added cocaine distribution to a diversified heroin and commodity-smuggling organization that had been created decades earlier by his uncle Juan Nepomuceno Guerra. The emergent Gulf Cartel seized a golden opportunity after the DEA had effectively shut down most of the Caribbean routes used by Colombian cartels to move drugs into Miami and south Florida. García Abrego himself was arrested and extradited during the initial years of expansion of that *fayuquero* operation into cocaine smuggling, and almost immediately the nascent Gulf criminal organization was writhing with mistrust, brutal blood sport, and chaotic competition among aspiring leaders.

By the time the Fox sexenio reached its midpoint, the Gulf syndicate had descended into routine spectacles of viciousness and brutal backstabbing largely attributable to the cocaine-fueled paranoia of men aspiring to replace García Abrego. Eventually, a relatively stable model of organizational governance based on brute power and intimidation emerged when Osiel Cárdenas Guillén and his brother Antonio recruited army deserters to serve as their personal guards and act as organization enforcers. Twenty highly trained deserters from a special Mexican army unit known as the Grupo Aeromóvil de Fuerzas Especiales (GAFE, Special Forces Airmobile Group) were engaged by the Gulf Cartel and formed a paramilitary wing called Los Zetas.[19] Recently released U.S. court documents add credence to the long-standing rumor that the original GAFE deserters were also employed as federal police at the same time that they were working for the Gulf Cartel—and those documents further indicate that they had been directly assigned to the Cárdenas Guillén brothers by high-ranking military and judicial officials entrusted with high-level authority by the federal government. This meant that the original twenty Zetas were simultaneously on the payroll of the Mexican army, the Mexican federal police (Federales), and the Gulf Cartel (Cedillo 2018; Raphael 2019). Each of the original Zetas formed his personal *estaca*, a military force of twenty enforcers, and by 2010, when they finally broke from the Gulf Cartel under the leadership of Heriberto "Z-3" Lazcano Lazcano, there were at least four hundred heavily armed criminals operating under the banner of Los Zetas. Soon, the twenty rogue paramilitaries turned on former allies within the Gulf; waged turf wars with competing cartels, including those who were former allies; and tragically unleashed a river of blood that overwhelmed a wide swath of Mexico.

In marked contrast to the Sinaloa Federation, the Gulf Cartel's emergence followed a radically different trajectory, and the following chapters provide

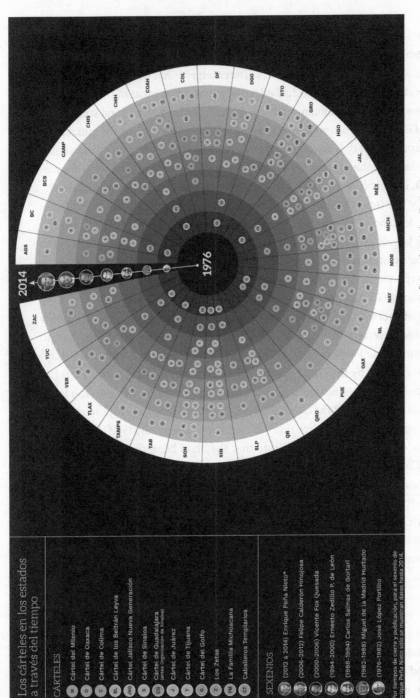

FIGURE 1 Presence and expansion of cartels in Mexican states across seven sexenios. "Un país rehén: Todos los estados ocupados por el crimen organizado," https://narcodata.animalpolitico.com/pais-invadido/. Used with permission of *Animal Político*.

more evidence of how these two criminal organizations were different. The Sinaloa Cartel will be described as a covert netherworld wherein norms of mutual reciprocity bound criminal and legitimate worlds together in a common enterprise, whereas such norms were less important for the Gulf Cartel, especially after Los Zetas were recruited to spread mayhem and fear: in fact, entrepreneurial activities and expansion of the Gulf Cartel depended much more on fear, power, dominance, and brutalization.

■ ■ ■

Without question, the violence of the past two decades is the consequence of cartel expansion and drug wars, but it is increasingly evident that generalized greed and corruption as well as the failure of state institutions contributed to its meteoric rise and the horrific tallies seen in official statistics. Why did violence escalate during the first two decades of this century? After all, Mexican cartels did not suddenly materialize out of nowhere at the beginning of the twenty-first century, and corruption and institutional inefficiency had an even longer presence in Mexico's sociopolitical reality. Furthermore, in spite of long-standing and known connections between cartel bosses and corrupt authorities, most regions of Mexico had experienced extended periods of time when violence was nowhere near as barbarous and had in fact been consistently declining. Mexican drug cartels existed long before the violence surged. The next chapter provides an overview of their emergence and their gradual, deepening entanglement with corrupt politicians, army generals, and police. Those pages also provide a broad introduction to the various cartel wars that shattered an equilibrium that had been established, and those wars will be elaborated in even more detail in chapters 4 and 5.

All of the following chapters expand on the history and events that are referenced in figure 1. This specific image is a grayscale version of an interactive page that is accesible through an archival link maintained by the Mexican news portal *Animal Político*. Figure 1 summarizes the formation and expansion of cartels across the Mexican presidential sexenios impacted by the U.S. War on Drugs in a static form, and the original interactive version (https://www.animalpolitico.com/root/diez-de-guerra/index.html) is a dynamic roadmap that graphically captures the transformation, expansion, and spread of Mexican cartels across those seven presidential sexenios.

CHAPTER 2

A Five-Decade Trajectory

Did we know we were lying about the drugs? Of course we did.
—John Ehrlichman in an interview with Dan Baum, 2016

Drug cartels did not exist when Richard Nixon unilaterally declared his War on Drugs. In 1971 there were no criminal organizations identified with such a label in Mexico—literally or in fact. The term *cartel* would not become the official tag applied to drug organizations until twenty years later, and during those early years of the War on Drugs, no Mexican or Latin American crime group had achieved a transnational reach or developed an organizational structure anywhere akin to other mafias of the world.[1] Rather, subcultural patterns of criminality had established deep roots in three distinct regions spread across seven different Mexican states (Sinaloa, Durango, Sonora, Chihuahua, Baja California, Tamaulipas, and Oaxaca). The most extensive and interconnected network of criminality was located in the Sierra Madre Occidental, where many individuals and groups were dedicated to marijuana and heroin production; another was based in Tamaulipas State on the Gulf Coast and was dedicated to heroin smuggling and the routine smuggling of goods known as fayuquero; and a third was a personal fiefdom of a regional boss or cacique in the mountains of Oaxaca producing vast crops of marijuana.

Nevertheless, five years into Nixon's global war against drugs, the nascent DEA financed a Mexican military operation in the area known as the Golden Triangle, where Sinaloa, Durango, and Chihuahua converge high in the remote sierra. The adversaries of the United States in that initial skirmish were marijuana and amapola producers rather than transnational drug organizations. The administrative designation of a cartel as the enemy in the U.S. War on Drugs did not exist, and that label was not used to identify the targets of those initial operations. No formalized crime group was identified, nor was the DEA focused on hunting down notorious drug capos on its most-wanted list. Operation Condor was a raze and burn operation meant to disrupt the production of the drugs that Nixon had argued were harming the morals of youth in the USA. A transformational shift to identifying cartels the enemy in the War on Drugs would come about much later as the result of tenacious claims making within the DEA and within the Nixon White House.[2] But in the beginning, growers large and small were targeted in that first attack of the War on Drugs in Mexico.[3]

Over the next five decades, the DEA would eventually designate thirteen distinct Mexican groups as cartels and identify their leaders as jefes with the same status as mafia dons.[4] Demonstrably, many of those originally designated crime groups never actually achieved an organizational structure, permanence, criminal diversity, or transnational reach to merit a broad classification that elevated them to mafia-like organizations. Notwithstanding the loose definitional parameters inherent in the term *cartel*, the DEA persisted in categorizing many groups as its organizational enemy in that ongoing War on Drugs. Three of the groups that the DEA had initially designated as powerful cartels were no longer operating on a large scale by the end of 2006: the Milenio, Oaxaca, and Colima organizations and their operatives had by then been absorbed into gangs and affiliates within a larger federation dominated by a Sinaloa faction.[5]

When Mexican president Enrique Peña Nieto left office in late 2018, the DEA was still tracking nine distinct cartels it had identified and between sixty and eighty criminal entities affiliated with those larger groups (see chapter 7). Those nine cartels had expanded to operate in twenty-three of Mexico's thirty-two states, and at least two among them competed for dominance in a dozen states—often with violent consequences. Five of the cartels operating in 2015 traced their roots directly back to subcultural traditions and to specific groups that emerged first in Mexico's Golden Triangle: at different times over a protracted thirty-five-year period, the Sinaloa, Beltrán Leyva, Juárez, Tijuana, and Cártel de Jalisco Nueva Generación (CJNG, Jalisco New Generation Cartel) cartels had worked together in unified federations (twice), formed alliances to wage war against upstart cartels, and had even fought with former allies in bitter civil wars. Two cartels, the Gulf and Los Zetas, had evolved together in a complicated and bloody pattern of alternating cooperation and mistrust, and both were operating and remained dangerous in 2014 even though each had diminished in reach and power and were considerably weaker than the Sinaloa faction. Two other regional organizations, La Familia Michoacana and Los Caballeros Templarios (the Knights Templar), continued to operate on a smaller scale; they remained unsuppressed by Mexican authorities and in competition with each other in Michoacán State, where they fought to control lucrative agricultural commodities (e.g., avocado plantations) and for the right to demand payment for use of drug routes connecting the Pacific Coast to central and northeast Mexico. In 2021 there are only two large cartels that remain standing and in direct competition with each other for control of Mexico's major plazas—the Sinaloa Cartel and the CJNG—while there are at least eighteen smaller organizations that are working with and/or under the domination of the large cartels (Raziel and Montalvo 2020).

Sexenios and Cartel Wars

Mexican temporal cycles are routinely parsed into six-year presidential terms known as sexenios. This chapter uses this convention to present an overview of the transitions and expansions of Mexican criminal organizations across seven presidential terms. The following pages describe the cartel presence across five decades, beginning and ending with a Mexican military operation that targeted the mountainous Sierra range where the states of Sinaloa, Durango, and Chihuahua converge. The roots of banditry, marijuana and opium, and drug smuggling are even older and will be described elsewhere (chapter 4), but the history of cartels in this book will begin in 1976 with a military invasion known as Operation Condor. From that point, it moves on to trace the trajectory of Mexican cartels until Mexican marines invaded the very same area in a massive manhunt for El Chapo Guzmán in 2018. The history does not end there, and some of the changes and ongoing developments during the first three years of the Andrés Manuel López Obrador presidency will be reviewed in the final chapter.

Mexican crime organizations grew more sophisticated and powerful over this specific period bookmarked by those two different military operations in the Golden Triangle. Simultaneously, a powerful covert nether-world expanded its reach to touch all areas of political, economic, social, and cultural life. In the immediate aftermath of the first military invasion described here—Operation Condor—a first generation of drug lords established a criminal organization that in due course fragmented into three parts, headed by a second generation of jefes, before re-forming a second federation that itself would eventually be plagued by internal disputes and eventually collapse by 2008.

The radiography of those changes is broken down into five distinct periods delimited by specific presidential sexenios: (1) the José López Portillo and Miguel de la Madrid Hurtado sexenios, during which three distinct factions first emerged; (2) the Carlos Salinas de Gortari and Ernesto Zedillo Ponce de León sexenios, when the factions merged into a unitary federation with a broad transnational reach; (3) the Vicente Fox Quesada sexenio and the fragmentation of the second federation that was triggered by the collapse of a PRI hegemony and the decentralization of the federal state; (4) the sexenio of Felipe de Jesús Calderón Hinojosa, dominated by brutal, bloody, and violent internal wars of cartels and an ill-advised direct state war against cartels; and finally, (5) the Enrique Peña Nieto sexenio, which fostered the deliberate fragmentation of cartels.

Later chapters situate the drug lords and criminal organizations within an even broader historical and sociopolitical context and will revisit several themes described in the following pages, but the first broad overview of Mexican cartel trajectories begins with 1976 and the López Portillo sexenio.

Period 1: The López Portillo–de la Madrid Era

By 1976 three regional and loosely affiliated groups were the primary source for all Mexican drug production—primarily and almost exclusively dedicated to the propagation and smuggling of marijuana and heroin. The Sinaloa cluster was embedded deep in the Golden Triangle; a bootleg and smuggling operation was based in Tamaulipas State opposite Brownsville, Texas, on the Mexican Gulf; and a large marijuana operation was situated in Oaxaca State. No group was organized to a degree that the term *mafia* could be applied, and all three fit into a conceptualization that criminologists would label deviant subcultural traditions.

The Sinaloa cluster arguably had the most sophisticated, entrenched, and diverse organizational structure among that first generation of criminal networks. It was the oldest and had linked diverse individuals in a horizontal and cooperative alliance wherein authority was negotiated and mediated through a subterranean code rooted in banditry and outlaw traditions. For six decades, the remoteness and microclimate of the Golden Triangle offered perfect conditions for growing marijuana and amapola poppy, and isolation and neglect from the central government provided safe haven for many occupying the fringes of lawful society. One man who rose to prominence was Pedro Avilés Pérez; he would eventually emerge as the key facilitator, intermediary, logistics manager, and dependable smuggler for the region's largest landowners. It was those landowners who would eventually come together to create the Sinaloa Cartel.

In contrast to the Sinaloa faction and its organic horizontal leadership, the other two criminal traditions were decidedly more hierarchical and led by regional strongmen in a cacique tradition.[6] The Gulf group was dedicated to alcohol smuggling and had a monopolistic control over fayuquero (bootlegging). Although Mexican brown heroin was moved alongside alcohol, the Gulf leader, Juan Nepomuceno Guerra, concentrated on illegal transport of a wide range of commodities throughout the 1970s. South of the capital, Mexico City, Pedro Díaz Parada was a powerful cacique who owned hundreds of acres in Oaxaca dedicated to marijuana plantations, had a reputation for violence, and maintained extensive political connections obtained through bribery (Relea 2007).

These three clusters thrived within a subcultural tradition of criminality for years, but it is misleading to describe them as organized crime groups even though they were remarkably efficient, profitable, and headed by individuals with deep regional roots and a deeply engrained local base of support. That generation of criminals had achieved a stability within social-political-cultural traditions where powerful local bosses (*caciquismo*) made the rules in the absence of legitimate state control. Longevity and success were largely attributable to personal power and subcultural traditions rather than the hierarchical structure characteristic of classical mafias.

The three groups were headed by powerful regional figures who were overlords in those communities by virtue of their wealth but also because of family and religious connections such as *compadrazgo*. They legitimated their influence and status by constructing schools, building churches, and underwriting infrastructural projects like paving streets and supplying electricity in the absence of government infrastructure.

In Sinaloa there were many such men, but the most prominent during the mid-1970s were Ernesto Fonseca Carrillo and Miguel Ángel Félix Gallardo. In Tamaulipas, the legendary cacique Nepomuceno was unchallenged in his authority and influence (Peralta González 2001). Marijuana plantations enriched Díaz Parada and were the source of his power in Oaxaca State, but even more than the others he relied on violence as often as he demonstrated munificence.

Operation Condor and the War on Drugs

In November 1975, during the waning days of Luis Echeverría Álvarez's presidency and the transition to the López Portillo sexenio, Mexico unleashed a military operation known as Operation Condor (Vinson 2009, 40) with the purported intent of disrupting marijuana and opium production in remote municipalities and ranchos of the Golden Triangle. Badiguarato Municipality was ground zero; military helicopters transported troops there to destroy marijuana and poppy crops and to roust local landowners and campesinos. The operation triggered a mass exodus wherein dozens and dozens relocated to Culiacán's historically notorious barrio Tierra Blanca, while larger landowners moved their families to Guadalajara in Jalisco State, or to Tijuana and Mexicali in Baja California, and others, such as Ismael Zambada García, headed as far afield as Los Angeles, California, and Reno, Nevada.

A dominant narrative asserts that Operation Condor had unintended consequences, resulting in the consolidation of power among regional bosses and the emergence of a unified criminal organization more powerful than previously existed. It argues that the forced displacement devastated smaller producers, while larger landowners simply shifted opium and marijuana operations to terrain they owned elsewhere—specifically to rural Guerrero, Durango, Chihuahua, and parts of Michoacán State. Those who relocated to Guadalajara, Jalisco, soon reactivated and returned to using their traditional smuggling routes and reestablished contact with operatives such as Jaime Herrera Nevares in Ciudad Juárez. As Anabel Hernández reported in 2020, men like Zambada established endpoint destinations for marijuana and opium in Nevada and California.

Significantly, the Guadalajara contingent also developed alternate smuggling routes operated by family members and compañero Sinaloans who had relocated to Tijuana, Mexicali, and other border cities following that 1976 invasion. In particular, Mexicali held new opportunities at reduced risk, and those who had moved to Guadalajara began to move drugs into the United States through existing tunnels built by Chinese gangsters many years previously. The tunnels' original purpose was to move Chinese migrants across the border during the era of Baja California's corrupt governor Esteban Cantú.

Sinaloans Miguel Ángel Félix Gallardo, Ernesto Fonseca Carillo, and Rafael Caro Quintero were among those who relocated to Guadalajara to eventually establish contact with Colombian intermediaries looking to move Andean cocaine as ancillary routes to an existing Caribbean pipeline. The initial partnerships between Mexican marijuana-opium smugglers and Colombian cartels have routinely been described as a serendipitous and unintended result of Operation Condor, but there is support for a claim that it was never accidental and rather that the move to Guadalajara was part of a long-term plan by Sinaloans and corrupt Mexican officials who had been working with Colombian brokers long before 1976. Major operatives such as Cuban national Alberto Sicilia Falcón were already moving drugs from Mexico to the USA before Operation Condor; Sicilia did it with the full knowledge and cooperation of high-level government officials—and arguably through CIA agents who had infiltrated Mexico in the aftermath of the Cuban Revolution (Mills 1988).

The Guadalajara Cartel Emerges

The formative years of the emergent Guadalajara Cartel are not well documented—and most details perhaps will never be known—but those inclined to believe that Sinaloan transplants to Guadalajara were country bumpkins who had stumbled into fantastic wealth will continue to accept a narrative of serendipity and unintended consequences. However, those who argue that Félix Gallardo and others were in fact visionary entrepreneurs intent on expansion will support the competing premise that Operation Condor was a brilliant maneuver prearranged with the full cooperation of Mexican authorities hoping to establish an urban and metropolitan base for a new criminal organization and a new promising product—cocaine.

Much is indisputable. Operation Condor did not eradicate marijuana and heroin but instead triggered a rapid expansion of the cocaine market and the emergence of a powerful criminal organization that came to be known as the Guadalajara Cartel. The Sinaloans in charge were already efficient producers and shippers of heroin and marijuana, and they became astoundingly rich in a short period of time after adding Andean cocaine to their traditional inventory. Furthermore, the new income financed a massive expansion of marijuana and opium poppy production across Mexico. It also underwrote the expenses of paying off even more government officials as well as financing their expansion into legitimate businesses such as major hotel chains. As mentioned previously, long before Operation Condor, Sicilia was already working with federal government officials and several Sinaloans to move marijuana and cocaine along older and traditional smuggling routes through Tijuana and Ciudad Juárez, but the overall volume shipped by the Sinaloans expanded exponentially following their relocation to Guadalajara and after new connections to Santiago Ocampo of Colombia's Cali Cartel were formalized.[7] Sicilia was arrested in 1975, but his Sinaloan partners had already switched to work with a Honduran intermediary named Juan Matta Ballesteros, who had even more extensive Colombian connections—especially to the increasingly powerful Medellín Cartel of Pablo Escobar Gaviria.

Operation Condor was initially heralded as evidence that the Mexican government was cooperating in the U.S. War on Drugs triggered by President Nixon, but there is growing and compelling evidence that it was actually an elaborate ruse to give the impression of compliance. The Mexican military had been gifted Bell and Howell helicopters and additional modern military ordnance for carrying out the operation, and several Mexican politicians and government officials at the highest levels of political and economic power were inexplicably enriched during that Guadalajara Cartel expansion (Craig 1980).

Contact with federal officials and bureaucrats was mediated by Miguel Ángel Félix Gallardo, a former police officer and trusted bodyguard for Sinaloa governor Leopoldo Sánchez Celis.[8] Specifically, the Mexican intelligence agency, the Dirección Federal de Seguridad (DFS, Federal Security Directorate), and its director, Miguel Nazar Haro, worked hand in hand with the Sinaloans through Félix Gallardo.[9]

The Guadalajara Cartel's connections to high-ranking Mexican politicians, intelligence agencies, and police in a shadowy organization should have left it immune from any chance of prosecution within Mexico. But the Guadalajara bosses—and arguably others, including CIA agents—made a fatal miscalculation in kidnapping, torturing, and killing a U.S. DEA agent, Enrique "Kiki"

Camarena. That mistake happened when the Sinaloans decided to retaliate in response to Camarena's single-minded investigation that had uncovered mega-marijuana production fields in San Luis Potosí and Chihuahua States. Testimony and legal documentation support allegations that Camarena's murder actually represented much more than simple payback for loss of those mega-plantations, and instead was driven by the realization that Camarena's investigations could expose broad, illegal, and insidious links between cartel capos, high-level Mexican government officials, and CIA agents operating illegally as agents in the Iran-Contra affair: archival evidence supports rumor and speculation that Camarena's murder successfully derailed the exposure of CIA agents and operatives who had been directly involved in the Iran-Contra arms scandal that unfolded during the Ronald Reagan presidency and almost brought him down (Bartley and Bartley 2015).

Supportive evidence of the CIA involvement is buried deep in dark archives and may never be revealed, but an undeniable reality is that pressure to identify and arrest Camarena's killers was spearheaded by another U.S. agency. DEA directors put pressure on the U.S. government and led Washington to impose measures that left President de la Madrid with no reasonable option but to arrest the Guadalajara Cartel bosses for Camarena's murder (Shannon 1988).

Dozens involved in DEA agent Camarena's murder and the bungled cover-up disappeared unsurprisingly, but the three main Guadalajara jefes were ultimately arrested, and each was sentenced to life imprisonment following a massive manhunt code-named Operation Leyenda. In all, more than three dozen people were indicted and linked to the torture and murder of Camarena, but only two individuals ended up serving time in a U.S. prison: Rubén Zuno Arce, who was son-in-law of former Mexican president Luis Echeverría, and Mexican pediatrician Humberto Álvarez Machaín were the only ones found guilty following their extradition and trial in a U.S. courtroom.[10] No American and no Mexican judicial figures were ever indicted or prosecuted—in spite of many rumors and widespread speculation about the degree of high-level involvement and interference.

Removing that first generation of cartel jefes triggered an era of regeneration and tremendous opportunities for a second generation of entrepreneurial capos to advance and dominate the drug trade for the next fifteen years. The imprisonment of the three major Guadalajara Cartel capos did not cripple the production and shipping of drugs: in fact, several enterprising leaders emerged to oversee expansion, diversification, and efficiency of drug and money operations. Specifically, they renegotiated agreements and reestablished and solidified important partnerships with corrupt Mexican government officials—especially those in the newly created Centro de Investigación y Seguridad Nacional (CISEN, Center for Investigation and National Security) and the Policía Federal Preventiva (Federal Preventive Police), which resulted from the merger of four other departments in the aftermath of Operation Leyenda. Furthermore, that second generation of capos formed an alliance now referred to as the First Federation; that arrangement proved remarkably efficient for business and was successful in resolving and constraining internal disputes for many years afterward.

When it became inevitable that the elders of the Guadalajara Cartel would be imprisoned, Félix Gallardo reportedly convened a summit of regional deputies to oversee the dissolution of the Guadalajara Cartel and reallocation of responsibilities. Most accounts have reported that the meeting took place at a luxurious resort outside Acapulco, but more recent evidence places the actual meeting in Mexico City.[11] No matter the location, Félix Gallardo reputedly oversaw a "dissolution of the Guadalajara Cartel" and proposed a new framework that acknowledged the semi-independence of three distinct plazas. Some accounts claim that it was Juan José "El Azul" Esparragoza Moreno, not Félix Gallardo, who organized that meeting and that the original agenda was actually hijacked by subordinates and lieutenants who felt emboldened to take control.[12] But everyone agrees and uniformly acknowledges that three distinct subgroups emerged from that summit in the aftermath of the arrests of the first-generation capos. The three factions controlled 85 to 90 percent of the drug trade in and through Mexico, and an outsider, Nepomuceno, and his nephew García Abrego oversaw the remainder, which moved through northeast Mexico.

Three Cartels

The high-level summit in the late 1980s divided the Mexican drug trade along territorial lines and formalized the existence of three organizational affiliates led by loyalists, allies, and established partners who all had Sinaloan and northwest Mexican roots. Two of those affiliates were handed to large and cohesive families with many siblings; those family connections and ties left them largely immune to external challenges.[13]

The Juárez Cartel

Chihuahua and Ciudad Juárez were assigned to the Carrillo Fuentes family. Their home was in Guamulchilito, near Navolato, Sinaloa—just north of Culiacán—but they had already established a dominant presence in Juárez in the aftermath of Operation Condor. Family members had long been involved in the drug trade in Sinaloa and Navolato and had emerged as a dominant power thanks to Amado Carrillo Fuentes, who had been mentored by his uncle Ernesto "Don Neto" Fonseca Carrillo. Carrillo Fuentes apprenticed under Don Neto in Guadalajara before creating a sophisticated smuggling organization in Chihuahua State by usurping routes originally developed by an older-generation smuggler, Pablo "El Zorro" Acosta Villareal. Carrillo Fuentes worked hand in glove with one of the most notoriously corrupt Mexican Agencia Federal de Investigación (AFI, Federal Ministerial Police) agents, Guillermo González Calderoni, to assassinate Acosta Villareal and to seize dominant control over police and city officials in Ciudad Juárez. Over time, that branch of the organization would be commonly referred to as the Juárez Cartel, and occasionally the Carrillo Fuentes Organization (CFO). Within a decade, it would emerge as the most dominant faction among the three divisions emerging in the aftermath of the dissolution of the Guadalajara Cartel.

The Tijuana Cartel

Tijuana and Baja California were entrusted to the thirteen siblings of the Arellano Félix family, which had also migrated from Sinaloa and seized control of major smuggling routes into California: over time, it came to be known as the Tijuana Cartel and just as frequently referred to by the name Arellano Félix Organization (AFO).

The Sinaloa Cartel

Héctor Luis "El Güero" Palma Salazar was designated to oversee the traditional home base of narco Mexico—Sinaloa and the Golden Triangle.[14] By the 1980s, the narco business had become far too complex to designate it to a single powerful overseer, and other longtime foot soldiers, such as Juan José Esparragoza, Joaquín Guzmán, the Beltrán Leyva brothers, and others, were named lieutenants with specific responsibilities. The Sinaloa faction had already established many businesses and laundered money through dozens of enterprises that stretched from Sinaloa, Jalisco, Sonora, Durango, and

Chihuahua to the Distrito Federal (DF, Federal District). The Sinaloa faction was heavily invested in marijuana and opium poppy production and owned its own plantations, contracted with independent landowners, and regularly employed thousands of workers to produce and process its product. The Sinaloans also controlled and protected smuggling routes north into Tijuana, Mexicali, Juárez, and other border points; those routes were relatively easy to monitor and control because of the scarcity of highways along the Pacific Coast. Increasingly, it began moving Andes cocaine through Mexico to the USA along those same routes after connections to Andean suppliers had developed.

It is worth noting that Ismael Zambada García is often described as or assumed to be one of the lesser personalities and junior associates within an array of powerful lieutenants in that second generation of Sinaloa Cartel leaders. Interestingly, the most common narratives from this era of narco Mexico rarely mention his name, and when they do, they imply that El Mayo was a minor player in those early years. But more recent accounts, specifically that of Anabel Hernández, argue that he had a much more important place in narco history than previously understood. Fernando Gaxiola's description of the importance of his client is quoted by Hernández in *El traidor*:

> The true boss of El Chapo is Ismael Zambada. The real driving force of everything is El Mayo. He and El Chapo know each other and have common friends, but at the beginning they did not work together. El Mayo has always been independent, and he is a man to be feared—a man to be respected. When El Mayo kills, he will do so, but in those days the rules for narco traffickers were different. They were unwilling to target the general population. (2020, 42)[15]

Stability

The initial tripartite division of the Guadalajara Cartel remained relatively stable for almost a full decade. The Juaréz and Tijuana plazas were stabilized and constrained by the dynamics of family cohesion and loyalty. The Sinaloa faction faced unique challenges, since its designated boss and lieutenants were linked through the putatively weaker bonds of common experience, birthplace, and ritualistic compadrazgo. The potential for infighting, dispute, resentment, and jockeying for power always lay superficially below the surface, but the Sinaloa group proved to be surprisingly stable in spite of many strong and volatile personalities working together.

When the Salinas government came to power, all three factions would coalesce once again and reenter into a confederated partnership under the leadership of Carrillo Fuentes; at that point, the Juárez faction appeared to take a dominant role and act as first among equals.

Period 2: Salinas, Zedillo, and the Narco Federation

The presidential term of Carlos Salinas de Gortari began in controversy and amid compelling evidence that he had stolen the presidency through vote manipulation.[16] He pushed through NAFTA and promised a modern era of neoliberal political reform that included opening up the border through free-trade zones (Preston and Dillon 2004). That period of free trade and reduced tariffs was accompanied by the rapid expansion of highway and railway crossings at the border, especially along the corridor that moved goods from Mexico City through the State of Nuevo León and into Texas. Border cities like Ciudad Juárez and Tijuana in the west and Matamoros and Nuevo Laredo in the east attracted new businesses and factories known as maquiladoras, and Mexicans migrated to the frontier by the tens of thousands seeking employment. Border traffic increased exponentially; new customs ports were created and agents hired to meet the demands of increased trade.

The drug business boomed alongside that burgeoning free-trade economy in Mexico, and it was primarily dedicated to delivering product to an external market—the USA. The demand for marijuana and cocaine was on an insatiable trajectory upward within the United States, and NAFTA had opened up new options for the Mexican crime organizations to deliver the product. The sheer volume of automobile, transport, and railway traffic meant shipments could easily move across the border alongside legitimate products—especially when the contraband was transported inside large container shipments or disguised as a legitimate export product. Furthermore, hundreds of human mules were available to transport small amounts of cocaine by simply crossing alongside the thousands of others who moved daily to jobs on either side of the border.

Carrillo Fuentes established an iron-clad grip on all drug traffic passing through Ciudad Juárez and neighboring border ports where new factories operated in tariff-free zones. But his operation grew especially powerful after he purchased his own air fleet. Initially, Carrillo Fuentes agreed to transport Colombian cartel cocaine for a fee—but gradually, he and his Sinaloan partners bought cocaine directly in the Andes and used his air fleet to transport it to several collection points across southern Mexico. It was first warehoused in many different points in the Yucatán, Oaxaca, and Nayarit before eventually moving through northern border crossings alongside legitimate commercial traffic.[17] The safe-house collection points in Mexico required partnerships with local groups, and consequently new gangs and partner groups such as the Valencia family first emerged as players and partners playing significant roles in the trafficking of drugs. By the mid-1990s, Carrillo Fuentes was arguably the most influential narco trafficker in the Americas, and it was he who had reputedly unified most of the drug organizations in Mexico around his leadership—primarily because he controlled the endpoint destination for delivering drugs directly to the American market. His ability to deliver product made him an essential partner for everyone in the drug trade—with the possible exception of the Gulf Cartel, which had built upon its older fayuquero routes.

A high-profile assassination and spectacular shoot-out in 1993 came close to shattering the Pax Mafiosa that had been patched together in the aftermath of the Camarena murder, but the Salinas government quickly intervened before fractious drug wars could derail the ongoing trade negotiations with the United States and Canada. Cardinal Juan Jesús Posadas Ocampo was gunned down when two disgruntled factions of the Federation triggered a wild shoot-out at the Guadalajara International airport. Salinas quickly moved to reestablish order among the cartel factions during a crucial stage of NAFTA negotiations: most notably, Salinas's response resulted in the arrest and imprisonment of El Chapo, and the government followed up by launching a successful public relations campaign to sell a specious narrative that this short man from rural Sinaloa was actually the supreme boss of all of Mexico's underworld.

The Salinas administration's quick response successfully deflected attention away from drugs and cartels, and much of the discussion about mafias and drug lords faded into the background to remain virtually unmentioned for the next four years. Salinas's reaction to salvage NAFTA arguably guaranteed that the six-decade hegemonic rule of the PRI would extend into at least one more sexenio, and consequently Ernesto Zedillo Ponce de León became the president in December 2004 under the banner of the PRI—even without the full support of the Salinas family.

The drug organizations in Mexico continued to operate in the shadows, but everything came to a screeching halt in 1997 when the Jefe de Jefes (Boss of Bosses), Amado "El Señor de los Cielos" Carrillo Fuentes, died in a Mexico City hospital while undergoing surgery. On July 4, 1997, almost at the midpoint of the Zedillo sexenio, the prominent drug lord from Sinaloa unexpectedly died during liposuction and plastic surgery. Truth be told, Carrillo Fuentes was actually executed by unknown usurpers to leadership, and the narrative of narco Mexico and dangerous drug cartels returned to the forefront of news reports and brought renewed attention from the DEA. To complicate matters, the Gulf Cartel by then had emerged as a legitimate challenger to the power of the Federation under the leadership of García Abrego and later Cárdenas Guillén based on a model rooted in threat and intimidation.

The DEA was quick to reclaim a prominent role in the aftermath of Carrillo Fuentes's murder. The capo's bloated body had been mutilated beyond recognition in his ill-advised attempt to undergo simultaneous liposuction and facial plastic surgery and reportedly even after he had snorted massive amounts of cocaine for twenty-four hours straight. The DEA provided the DNA samples and other supporting evidence confirming his identification; this information allowed the release of his mutilated corpse to his grieving mother in Guamuchilito, Sinaloa. She and family members arranged a dramaturgical funeral that was attended by dozens of politicians, prominent citizens, and businessmen before a final interment in a spectacular mausoleum constructed in Los Jardines de Humaya in Culiacán—now widely known as the cemetery of narco traffickers.

The DEA released additional details about the executed drug lord infamously referred to as "The Lord of the Skies" and about his powerful crime organization that the DEA had identified as the Juárez Cartel. But in the aftermath of his mysterious assassination, nobody knew with certainty who had actually ordered his death or whether it represented the beginning of major reorganization.[18] Internal battles and wrangling took place deep within the covert netherworld and festered there for the next three years. The events within Mexican cartels during last three years of the twentieth century have never been fully revealed and are arguably the most mysterious period in the long history of narco Mexico.

The specific details may never be fully known, but it was also clear that cartels continued to expand their reach into more states across Mexico. At the end of Zedillo's sexenio, the DEA was now tracking seven cartels operating in Mexico. The three smallest and most recent were the Milenio, Oaxaca, and Colima Cartels. The three larger factions that had sluiced off from the Guadalajara Cartel—Sinaloa, Tijuana, and Juárez—were viewed as equivalently dangerous by the Americans. But all six of those identified organizations were considered to be cooperating within a second narco federation that had reached agreements about the allocation of routes and had determined appropriate right-of-passage payments where warranted. The Gulf Cartel was increasingly drawing attention of the DEA as it expanded its cocaine routes and increasingly resorted to violence in the northeast border region. But what was most alarming at the end of the 1990s was the realization that cartels were now operating in twenty-six states—doubling their presence in the few short years after NAFTA came into effect. Thirteen of those states now had two cartels competing or sharing routes. Seven states had three cartels competing or sharing routes, and one state (Jalisco) had four. Only Oaxaca had not seen a major change or invasion from elsewhere.

It is now paradoxical that obvious and major expansion into twice as many states was not accompanied by a noticeable or significant increase in violence in Mexico. In fact, the overall homicide rate showed another steep decline about the midpoint of the Salinas sexenio and had dropped from a rate of 19.7 murders per 100,000 to 11 per 100,000 in the last year of the Zedillo presidency. The expansion of cartels was inexplicably and unaccountably accompanied by what appeared to be a generalized Pax Mafiosa or Pax Narca.

Period 3: Fox Sexenio, Second Federation Internal Wars, and Gulf Cartel Emergence

The electoral victory of PAN candidate Vicente Fox Quesada in 2000 created circumstances that ultimately made it impossible for one single overarching criminal federation to ever establish full control and dominate the drug trade. Ultimately the changes he introduced led to the collapse of a Pax Mafiosa bequeathed to him. Perhaps counterintuitively, those changes did not immediately disrupt equilibrium and the internal peace that had governed the covert netherworld, and there was not an immediate impact on generalized violence. In fact, President Fox oversaw the only four-year era in Mexican history where the national homicide rate was consistently lower than 10 per 100,000.[19]

Immediately after Fox ended the seventy-one-year rule of the PRI, he advanced structural and policy changes that would set the stage for two internal Wars Between Cartels that have now played out across the first two decades of this century. The most important action was Fox's immediate decentralization of governance and the allocation of more power to Mexico's thirty-one governors and municipalities.[20] That action immediately weakened federal jurisdiction and its influence over security, trade, and commerce; large and small regional crime organizations quickly seized the opportunity to circumvent oversight from Mexico City and instead forged direct links with state and municipal governments—especially in the northeast and northwest corners of Mexico, where the NAFTA trade routes were now firmly entrenched. The covert netherworld had suddenly become more complex and had expanded to open up new interstices of connection and corruption.

Wars Within Cartels

Vicente Fox, perhaps unwittingly, triggered additional Wars Between Cartels through his second executive action. He followed through on his election promise to overturn the long tradition of denying U.S. requests for the extradition of criminals charged with U.S. crimes. When it became clear that President Fox would keep his promise, and when he faced imminent removal to the United States, El Chapo Guzmán engineered what would be his first escape from a maximum-security prison and soon disappeared into the shadows and protective cover of the underworld before he could be handed over to the Americans.[21] Chaos and disruption inevitably erupted within the second narco federation, which was El Chapo's home, and a series of Wars Within Cartels became inevitable once he had returned.

El Chapo managed to reassert his influence through the direct intervention of his longtime allies within the powerful Sinaloa faction. He assembled a gang of *sicarios* and launched two large-scale strikes against other factions of the Federation. Those two operations triggered internal Wars Within Cartels that turned border cities like Ciudad Juárez and Tijuana into full-scale battle zones. The attacks were deliberately launched to marginalize the Juárez and Tijuana cartels and to reestablish dominant control of the Federation, now indisputably led by the triumvirate of Ismael Zambada García, Juan José Esparragoza Moreno, and Joaquín Guzmán Loera. There were clear economic advantages motivating the attacks launched by El Mayo, El Azul, and El Chapo, but those two internal cartel wars were also fueled by festering historical grudges, the desire for payback, and a lingering hatred of the Carrillo Fuentes and Arellano Félix families.

The first skirmish and direct challenge came on November 11, 2004, when Guzmán sent a team of sicarios to assassinate Rodolfo Carrillo Fuentes, the youngest brother of the family controlling the Juárez faction. "El Niño del Oro" (The Golden Boy) and his wife were gunned down outside the Cinépolis Plaza in Culiacán, Sinaloa, along with an innocent parking attendant. For many, such as *Ríodoce* editor Ismael Bojorquez (2015), that execution was the initial salvo in an internal war that would play out over the next fifteen years.

The Juárez faction was not the only Federation ally attacked and betrayed by the Sinaloa triumvirate. Arellano Félix operations were directly targeted with armed attacks by Sinaloa sicarios, but the Tijuana faction was simultaneously under siege by DEA agents who seized drug shipments and arrested operatives and even family members. The logistics and details allowing those confiscations and arrests were fed directly to U.S. agents by the Arellano Félix family's putative allies and partners Ismael Zambada and Joaquín Guzmán (Hernández 2020).

Wars Between Cartels

Thirty years after beginning the War on Drugs and establishing the DEA, the United States returned its focus to Mexico in the aftermath of what has been described as a perfect storm of events (Hope 2013; Payan 2014) that disrupted Andean cocaine pipeline routes in the Caribbean.[22] Mexico had emerged as the alternate and the preferred trampoline for delivering cocaine and synthetic drugs into the USA. By 2004 Mexican criminal cartels were in competition to control the lucrative routes that had opened up, and an arms race soon developed when some cartels established paramilitary wings to protect their money-making routes and entry ports into the United States. The Gulf Cartel triggered this arms race when it recruited the twenty military deserters who became known as Los Zetas, but the Sinaloa faction almost immediately reacted by forming its own paramilitary unit known as Los Pelones—formed from recruits who had served time in both Mexican and American prisons.

Bloody internal Wars Between Cartels erupted on several fronts along the border shared with the United States: five different groups waged war with each other for control of those lucrative trade routes that had opened up after NAFTA was implemented in 1994. Some began as internal skirmishes and eventually escalated into a prolonged low-grade war, and initially most of the casualties were the foot soldiers and combatants working directly for the cartels. But that pattern would change dramatically over the next fifteen years as those Wars Between Cartels expanded and became even more complicated after the Mexican military was deployed by the next administration.

Period 4: Calderón and Four Overlapping Wars

When Felipe de Jesús Calderón Hinojosa assumed office, nine cartels were operating across Mexico in twenty-eight different states. In the fourth year of the Fox sexenio, Los Zetas and the Gulf Cartel had split and were in direct conflict. Six different states had emerged as extreme red-alert zones where four or more cartels competed for dominance: Durango, Guerrero, Jalisco, Sonora, and Sinaloa each had four distinct cartels looking to control routes, and Michoacán had five different cartels hoping to dominate in that state. All nine recognized cartels engaged in a campaign to recruit new bodies for expansion and did so in different ways—by creating franchises, by forming alliances with extant regional gangs, or by simply usurping existing regional gangs and their territory through brute force.

The Sinaloa Cartel formed alliances with many smaller gangs and ocassionally created new groups by recruiting and training ex-prisoners. The Gulf Cartel and Los Zetas were more inclined to simply invade and usurp control through fear and force (Raphael 2019). The presence of so many smaller gangs complicated the radiography of narco Mexico even more and made it extremely difficult to keep track of the players and combatants. At least sixty gangs were working as affiliates or proxies for the nine larger cartels that remained operational during the Calderón sexenio.

In 2007 the Mexican military was directly deployed by President Calderón to confront the now heavily weaponized criminal cartels, which had formed alliances with at least five-dozen smaller gangs. Calderón's initial objective was to eliminate drug organizations in his home state, Michoacán, where La Familia Michoacana and Los Caballeros Templarios had emerged as two competing entities. But Calderón Hinojosa soon expanded his initiative and launched what became known within Mexico as the War Against Cartels. This meant that four distinct wars were ongoing simultaneously in Mexico— the thirty-five-year-old War on Drugs directed by the DEA in pursuit of an American political agenda; a Mexican government War Against Cartels led by the military and pursuing the personal agenda of the president and his security cabinet; a third, ever-shifting War Between Cartels that most often saw sicarios of Sinaloa allies fighting against the Gulf Cartel for contested turf; and an even more complicated civil War Within Cartels resulting from divisions and disputes within the criminal underworld. It was those four wars that generated an almost unfathomable increase in violence described earlier.

That fourth internal civil war of cartels splintered the larger cartels into extremely dangerous and violent offshoots, such as the emergent Beltrán-Leyva Cartel and the independent Los Zetas operation. Those two specific spin-offs were arguably the most ruthlessly violent and simultaneously the most hunted targets in the Mexican military's War Against Cartels. Their emergence and the army response left the nation soaked in blood and filled countless graveyards and random fields with bodies of victims.[23] At least 280,000 were murdered and more than 35,000 went missing between January 2007 and December 2018 (INEGI 2019; SESNSP 2019).[24]

Period 5: Peña Nieto, Fragmentation, and a New Consolidation

Enrique Peña Nieto hoped to take a different approach when he appointed a Colombian national, General Óscar Naranjo Trujillo, to serve as his chief security adviser. Naranjo's strategy was specifically aimed at fragmenting larger organizations and breaking them into so-called smaller and putatively manageable *cartelitos*. The logic was that no single criminal organization should be allowed to compete directly with the federal government as an alternate power; during the Naranjo period, the federal government fostered a climate of benign tolerance toward smaller organizations it believed less likely to create international scandals or draw attention to corruption at the national level. That strategy had been proclaimed successful in Colombia, where it had helped promote the impression that the drug problem was under control. In fact, it represented a shell game, which simply demanded that drug lords and organizations shift gears and operate without generating excessive disruptions and not engage in excessive violence.

By the end of 2015 and the beginning of 2016, there were at least eight major drug organizations identified as operating in Mexico: the Sinaloa, Cártel de Jalisco Nueva Generación, Beltrán-Leyva, Juárez, Gulf, Los Zetas, La Familia, and Knights Templar of Michoacán organizations. One notable absence from the list at that time was the Tijuana criminal organization, which was no longer being mentioned prominently in DEA drug threat reports at that time.[25] Furthermore, by then there were at least forty-eight and as many as sixty-eight smaller groups that were working with or for the largest cartels as a result of Naranjo's fragmentation initiative.

Those organizations did not have equivalent power, reach, and scope: in fact, the differences are so great that most observers now agree that only two or three organizations are worthy of being designated cartels. Unquestionably, the two most powerful crime groups operating in 2015 were the Sinaloa Cartel and the remnants of the Gulf Cartel / Los Zetas, although the Cártel de Jalisco Nueva Generación (CJNG) had by then become decidedly independent and wealthy because of synthetic drug production, its new international partnerships, and its delivery routes that did not compete directly with Sinaloa or the Gulf. It had served a frightening notice of its existence by brazenly attacking Mexican military forces and engaging them in armed firefights (Guerrero Gutiérrez 2015b). Among all these groups, only the Sinaloa Cartel and the CJNG would remain to compete with each other as comprehensive cartels by mid-2021 (see chapter 8).

El Chapo became the obvious target for the Peña Nieto government, given his international profile, his continuing visibility, and his legendary reputation for instigating violence. Accordingly, Mexican security forces and CISEN prioritized the hunt for Joaquín Guzmán, and Operation Gargoyle kicked into high gear shortly after Peña Nieto's inauguration (those events and the impact on the Peña Nieto presidency will be described in much more detail in chapter 6).

Drug Wars, Transformations, and Netherworlds

La historia no estudia el pasado, lo construye. Toda historia nacional es una mitología, y las mitologías sirven para estructurar la mente de un pueblo.

—Juan Miguel Zunzunegui, *El mito de las tres transformaciones*, 2019

In December 2018, Andrés Manuel López Obrador and the Movimiento Regeneración Nacional (Morena, National Regeneration Movement) were handed the reins of a country battered, beaten, and bloodied by violence and ongoing drug wars. Mexico's demoralized people had elected a populist politician who they hoped would finally end the chaos and the routine cycles of violence, and eliminate the corruption that had seeped into all levels of government and daily life.

This is where my in-depth overview of cartels and narco traffic will begin—at a critical juncture when more than thirty million Mexicans voted for a man who promised transformation and whom they prayed would mend the social fabric of a nation left in tatters. Venality and brutality had become deeply entrenched in Mexican institutions and had continually been nurtured by traditions of corruption that had thrived for more than five decades in the shadows and in the open. By 2018, drug wars had dragged on for sixteen years and left rivers of blood and corpses in their wake—and heavily armed troops patrolling the streets.

The ongoing drug wars were the manifestation of other deeply engrained structural problems. Corruption had seeped into all institutions and stained all aspects of governance, business, and even everyday norms of existence. The endemic problems fed by corruption had become routinized almost to the point of routine and invisibility—but there were recurring cycles when corruption and dysfunction made themselves obvious and shifted into a higher degree of frenzied activity. Those reoccurring times have been named on the street and in cultural tradition as the hour of the grasshopper, the Year of Hidalgo, and *la narcopolítica*.

Politicians, bureaucrats, and entrepreneurs routinely treated the sixth and final year of presidential terms as the propitious moment to collect debts, realize outstanding favors, and pursue new opportunities for self-enrichment. Corruption among public officials was so evident that the last year of every sexenio was colloquially known as the Year of Hidalgo.[1] That final year before a handover to a new administration signaled the beginning of a vicious cycle where politicians and bureaucrats competed to drain the coffers of Mexico's corrupt national oil company (Pemex), the Secretaría de Desarrollo Social (Ministry of Social Development of Mexico), or any other agency that dispersed public funds. The final year of sexenios were also the auspicious time for entrepreneurs and privileged business elites to put together sweetheart deals and begin megaconstruction projects that would continue deep into the next presidential term.

With frightening regularity since 1984, the final year of Mexico's presidential terms had also become the season of la narcopolítica—the frenzied months when the underworld of drug lords conspired with corrupt politicians to ensure that Mexico's covert netherworld would continue to thrive in the next sexenio.

The dance card in those reoccurring Years of Hidalgo parties was not restricted to only bureaucrats and politicians. A distinctive feature of the Mexican Constitution—and arguably a fundamental tenet of Mexico's revolutionary ideal—is that reelection and reappointment were not allowed.[2] That revolutionary commitment to no reelection had unintentionally generated a social milieu where individuals were motivated to put themselves first and made institutions dysfunctional; it had created an environment where covert negotiation and illicit commerce converged in a particular and potent array to disrupt continuity.

Mexico's Revolution began under a banner of *sufragio efectivo, no reelección*, and the principle was encoded when edicts against reelection were permanently enshrined in law, tradition, and practice by the Constitution of 1917. Subsequently, Mexico's president, governors, mayors, congressmen, senators, university presidents, and most government bureaucrats have been restricted by federal organic law and a customary understanding that it is not possible to return to the same electoral or administrative position across consecutive terms. Unintentionally, the final months of electoral terms became a recurring season colloquially called *la hora de chapulines* (the time of grasshoppers). When it arrives, hundreds if not thousands of politicians, senior bureaucrats, and functionaries begin a personal and frenzied quest to hop into an alternate well-paid and secure post in the next electoral term.

Politicians established a special way to protect themselves and circumvent the negative impact of lost income and diminished status when sexenios ended. They incorporated a structural safety valve that reserved political appointments for the party militants and set aside one-third of all congressional and senate seats for appointed candidates; the party militants, elite, and faithful are thus assigned to Congress and the Senate based on a formula tied to the percentage of a party's popular vote. The system offers no guarantees except for those highly placed within the party hierarchy and perhaps the most militant members, but any unfortunate soul not placed on the list for a guaranteed congressional or senate post still had a promising alternative—they could be appointed to direct agencies and institutions of government, and if ever there were not enough placements, they could count on their friends in power to create new ones. This century-old constitutional adherence to no reappointment has consistently disrupted and destabilized institutions that are arguably better served by continuity and the guiding hand of competent and qualified appointments.

The unintended consequences of sufragio efectivo, no reelección were especially disruptive in justice institutions and police forces of Mexico. Daniel Sabet (2012) describes the chaotic impact on Mexican police departments in his case study investigation that examined five different police departments in years of transition: in one city, a municipal police chief returned to walking the streets as a beat officer following the electoral defeat of his party; and in another city, there was a wasteful three-year cyclical repainting of police and security vehicles to restore the colors of the winning party after PAN and PRI traded electoral victories.

That revolutionary ideal of no reappointment had been putatively institutionalized in constitutional law to introduce transparency and prevent corruption but instead had routinely and cyclically destabilized institutions that managed state revenues or were mandated to ensure safety.

Situational and rational-choice criminologists explain that criminality thrives whenever motivated offenders, criminal opportunity, and the lack of an effective deterrent converge—and the cyclic routines institutionalized in the Year of Hidalgo regularly bring all three factors together in a recurring tradition where bribery and corruption are tolerated and made necessary for individual economic survival. The great paradoxical tragedy of the Constitution of 1917 was that in seeking to institutionalize transparency and openness, it inadvertently built in a motivational push for corruption and established the conditions where narco politics would eventually come to dominate.

The covert netherworld interlinking politicians, bureaucrats, and cartel bosses feeds upon flaws and fissures that leave institutions vulnerable to corruption. Arguably, those weaknesses become especially evident during Years of Hidalgo and the time of grasshoppers when state agencies are directed by individuals concerned about their own future. Capos and cartel bosses have systematically intervened during these periods to ensure that their business is neither exposed nor disrupted. Drug lords, flush with bundles of cash, work diligently during such recurring cycles to ensure that their choice will be appointed as the temporary replacement for grasshopper officials who leave early and make it even harder to guarantee that the postelectoral appointment goes to someone they control. To state the obvious link to politics, the postelectoral appointments are made by the party that wins the election, and thus the Year of Hidalgo has also transformed into a season of la narcopolítica where dark money is at play.

The Vicente Fox Quesada sexenio (2000–2006) triggered the start of a new feverish era of narco politics and intense bargaining in all the interstices of Mexico's subterranean world. The prospect of PAN's electoral victory meant that, for the first time in seventy-one years, incoming politicians and bureaucrats would not be appointed from the predictable and known list of candidates recorded in PRI dossiers. Furthermore, President Fox also planned to devolve significant authoritative and spending power to Mexico's thirty-one governors.[3] The criminal underworld could no longer selectively concentrate on negotiating and overseeing appointments in only the national capital; in fact, its denizens eagerly welcomed an opportunity to control states and cities that would have increased authority and oversight in the future. In effect, the devolution of power to states represented an opportunity for cartels to exert direct control at the local level with less interference from federal overseers. Unsurprisingly, many governors welcomed the change— and the consequences and expanded reach on Mexico's covert netherworld would soon become evident. When Andrés Manuel López Obrador took the oath of office after those modifications had been in place for three sexenios, eighteen former governors were either serving prison terms for corruption, under indictment for malfeasance and bribery, or fugitives from the law.

Popular narratives emphasize a *plata o plomo* (silver or lead) trope where politicians or others become narco traffickers when they are presented with a win-or-lose option—that is, they are offered a bribe or threatened should they refuse it. But such views assume that relatively few individuals find themselves in that position, and also overlook the extent to which narco traffickers are tolerated and even respected in specific communities because they give back to the community and provide services that the government has failed to deliver. And that silver or lead narrative also overlooks the extent to which ordinary men and women are willingly corruptible when they believe things are unfair and the system is rigged. It's just as likely that narco corruption is primarily a synchronous two-way arrangement where the mutual benefit is perfectly understood by two parties, and where the terms of agreement are negotiated beyond the boundaries of respectable society.[4] The narco-political deals common in the covert netherworld do not always involve violence or physical intimidation, while admittedly there is always an unspoken understanding that the consequence of breaking the arrangement will have deadly consequences. Many politicians, bureaucrats, and businessmen willingly join with narco traffickers to practice such "clandestine arts" and to "conduct complex operations beyond the bounds of civil society" (McCoy 2018, 2).

Corruption is deeply engrained in many of Mexico's institutions and becomes routinely visible during la hora de chapulines and Years of Hidalgo when the pools of motivated offenders increase. The bundles of cash that flowed to politicians and operatives of the state during the era of first-generation drug lords were managed directly by bagmen within the federal police. The late George Grayson (2010) colorfully described the routinized process as a traveling suitcase, where an intermediary literally transported bundles of money that had been partitioned into thirds for distribution to drug lords, administrators, and gatekeepers and to elite political overseers who looked the other way—or who actually supervised the distribution to their subordinates. The routine became a deeply engrained expectation that drug lords and politicians understood and expected for six long decades. Arguably, the Year of Hidalgo became even more widespread and institutionalized when the pool of available chapulines and the number of cartels expanded exponentially following President Fox's decentralization of federal power and devolution of responsibility to states in 2000. After the collapse of the old PRI hegemony, the Year of Hidalgo reached a fever pitch and was most certainly in full-blown ascendancy by the end of the Fox sexenio;

la narcopolítica was operating at a heightened state during the last year of Fox's sexenio and perhaps even more intensely at the end of Calderón's presidency.

One undetermined point of history is whether, and how, those engrained traditions of corruption and narco politics unfurled during the final years of the Enrique Peña Nieto presidency. Early in 2017, it was obvious that the PRI government was certain to be defeated by a populist movement (Morena) that had waged an aggressive campaign against corruption and Mexico's privileged oligarchy. The public support for a change in government was unmistakable, and President Peña Nieto and his PRI compatriots were dead men walking as early as 2016. Did the drug lords and bureaucrats who had adjusted to the Years of Hidalgo during the two PAN sexenios have an alternate path—a plan B—to circumvent the certain rejection of the old ways promised by presidential candidate López Obrador and Morena? Or were the pull, power, and tradition of *narcocultura*, narcopolítica, la hora de chapulines, and the Year of Hidalgo too deeply engrained to be disassembled in one election? In 2021 it's unknown how that old game of la narcopolítica actually played out in 2017, but the long trajectory of narco Mexico and the remarkable adaptability of those in the covert netherworld suggest that the old ways and expectations did not end and found a way to adapt.

Cynical fatalism about politics and corruption is deeply engrained in Mexico; the average person believes that politicians and political leaders are habitually and deeply addicted to corruption, and that la narcopolítica routinely determines electoral outcome. Even though those sentiments are widely held and spoken, confirmatory evidence of such dark clandestine arrangements were rare until the El Chapo Guzmán trial introduced two high-profile protected witnesses to testify against him in 2019. Specific financial figures about bribes were revealed during his trial, and the magnitude of the numbers was staggering.[5] Testimony from Sinaloa drug lord El Rey Zambada and from Guzmán's righthand man Alex Cifuentes revealed that hundreds of millions of dollars had been routinely set aside to bribe politicians and officials—and that those bribes reached the highest level of politics and governance. The magnitude of dollars set aside for bribery affixed an actual financial number on the degree of corruption and validated what had long been rumored but never proven. As novelist Don Winslow characterized the bribery testimony from the El Chapo trial:

The "revelations" that these witnesses have brought forward aren't revelatory—they merely confirm what we've always known. I've been writing about the Mexican drug world for two decades, and I've heard credible accounts of these bribes and payoffs continually from day one. I'm not unique in this regard—one highly respected journalist after another has reported these stories, some at the cost of their lives. (2019b)

El Chapo's sensational trial in Brooklyn unmasked secrets of the Sinaloa Cartel and offered compelling evidence that much previously consigned to the realm of rumor was demonstrably true. The posttrial release of additional documents verifies that the DEA had many significant case files implicating organized crime syndicates, politicians, entrepreneurs, and justice officials in systematic and routine corruption. As already suggested, those files will certainly become central pieces of evidence in future prosecutions of specific drug kingpins and prominent political figures, such as former secretary of public security Genaro García Luna, who was arrested in 2019. Nevertheless, the consensus and personal experience of the average Mexican are that even these or future revelations will have little immediate impact on the recurring cycles of corruption. The tradition and cultural norms of the Year of Hidalgo and la narcopolítica are deeply engrained, and the pool of job-hopping chapulines seems endless—and the motivational push and opportunities for personal enrichment continue.

The remaining sections of this chapter describe a historical context wherein Mexicans came to place their hope in Andrés Manuel López Obrador in 2018 with the expectation he would finally end corruption and destroy the tradition of narco politics. But a 2020 incident involving former secretary of national defense Salvador Cienfuegos Zepeda suggests that voters may have overestimated President AMLO's commitment or his ability to get things done, and that their confidence in his promise to bring change represented little more than a momentary suspension of disbelief and everyone's failure to recognize the entrenched power of la narcopolítica.

General Cienfuegos was arrested at Los Angeles International Airport in October 2020 as he arrived with his family for a Disneyland vacation. American DOJ marshals apprehended him to enforce an arrest order relating to a sealed indictment issued in 2019 by the same American grand jury that reviewed evidence against El Chapo. Agents had effectively extradited Cienfuegos because of his own decision to travel to the United States, and they immediately flew him to New York to await trial on those sealed charges (Ahmed 2020). The evidence presented to the grand jury was based on a years-long investigation that had been code-named Operation Padrino; U.S. agents had gathered a treasure trove of evidence from cell-phone intercepts, money trails, and cooperative witness testimony. For DOJ prosecutors, that evidence definitively supported accusations that, while secretary of national defense during Peña Nieto's sexenio, Cienfuegos had conspired with a cartel leader in Nayarit State to smuggle cocaine, methamphetamine, and marijuana into the USA between 2012 and 2018.[6] The general was specifically accused of working with and protecting Franciso Patrón Sánchez to guarantee that the Mexican army did not intercept shipments and furthermore of being the *padrino* of the H-2 Cartel, several military subordinates, police officials, state and federal functionaries, and several state governors.[7]

The evidence presented to the grand jury had been tightly sealed, and most importantly had never been shared in advance with the Mexican government prior to arresting the general. In fact, it had been deliberately hidden from them in spite of existing agreements in the Mérida Initiative to share intelligence with Mexican officials.

The Mexican government protested vehemently when it learned of the de facto extradition and impending trial of General Cienfuegos. Foreign secretary Marcelo Ebrard Casaubón immediately relayed an official response on behalf of the Mexican government threatening to expel or restrict the activities of all fifty-four U.S. agents working on counterdrug activities in Mexico unless the charges against him were immediately dropped and the general returned to Mexico ex post haste. In fact, the Mexican government did exactly what Ebrard threatened to do even when the charges were eventually dropped and Cienfuegos had been returned to Toluca, Mexico (Esquivel 2021; Kitroeff, Feuer, and Lopez 2021; Pradilla and Ángel 2020; Tourliere 2021).

It was widely expected that the Mexican government would rely on some technical or evidentiary mistake to avoid prosecuting the general in a Mexican court—for instance, by arguing that the charges did not contravene any specific Mexican statute, or that contacts with narco traffickers were required because of his position as secretary of national defense, or perhaps even that he had been set up by false accusations planted by rival cartels hoping to diminish the power of the H-2 Cartel. Shockingly, none of those options were used. Instead, they fully exonerated General Cienfuegos and declared he was not guilty in January 2021 (Castillo García 2021; de Córdoba and Harrup 2021; Esquivel 2021; Tourliere 2021).

Furthermore, President López Obrador used much of his early morning press conference (*la mañanera*) of January 15, 2021, to denounce the DOJ's actions and specifically accuse the DEA of manufacturing evidence. Ebrard was only slightly more circumspect; he specifically stated that the decision was made because of uncompelling and ambiguous evidence provided to Mexico by the acting DEA head. Later the same day, the Mexican government uploaded more than 750 pages of transcripts of intercepted Blackberry SMS messages sent to it by DEA acting director Timothy Shea.[8]

Mexico did not release actual tapes of intercepted audio recordings or any other evidence that the DEA might have gathered from cooperative witnesses, and it did not indicate whether it had received any supporting evidence from the DOJ that offered further evidence of General Cienfuegos's direct involvement in trafficking and money-laundering cartels. J. Jesús Esquivel (2021) reported factually that the evidence uploaded to the Mexican government site represented only a small part of that which had been collected by the DEA and that only some of the information from Operation Padrino had been unsealed in the aftermath of the El Chapo trial.

All the facts of the Cienfuegos incident are not available; they remain inaccessible in secret files and sealed documents that the DEA and other American agencies have maintained since at least 1985.[9] For lack of revealed evidence, it is premature to claim that General Cienfuegos was in fact el padrino in Mexico's covert netherworld. But even if he was falsely accused, the DEA documents and the released SMS messages undoubtedly confirm the widespread level of corruption and reveal the inner workings of the Mexican underworld. In 2021, two years after the inauguration of López Obrador, it appears that little has changed and la narcopolítica remains as entrenched and as powerful as it was during the previous five sexenios. The year 2018 may have seemed a moment of hope, but the promised transformation has not happened as these words are written in mid-2021.

A Critical Moment and New Trajectory?

The Peña Nieto administration abandoned all pretense of governance following the crushing electoral rejection of July 2018. Presumably, the traditional expectations and routines of the Year of Hidalgo had also been disrupted, and that led to frantic scrambling in the covert netherworld to operationalize a plan B to ensure its survival.

Rather than follow the example of previous transition periods where incoming administrations observed and learned while outgoing governments continued to act, president-elect López Obrador immediately began to govern by fiat and routinely issued press releases from his Mexico City home during the five-month transition period between July and the December inauguration. Two governments were in place, but the public had clearly shifted loyalty to the government-in-waiting and effectively ignored the PRI government that technically remained in charge. The outgoing government and its appointees were hopelessly enfeebled during those last few months of the 2018 Year of Hidalgo (Overa 2020), and the incoming government had served advance notice that it would not be participatating in the clandestine dance of corruption that traditionally accompanied transition.

The incoming president and his transition team held daily press conferences wherein they routinely issued broad statements and laid out their plans for governance. Several statements about eliminating corruption were frequent and fiercely critical of the old order, but at the same time the few pronouncements that spoke to security and violence were arguably short on substance and often self-contradictory: for instance, AMLO's overall Plan for Security was heavily infused with broad symbolic statements about the need for moral regeneration and a promise of a Fourth Transformation (President Elect Transition Team 2018).[10]

In those final five months of 2018, one long era of narco politics had reached an apparent end point and an alternate trajectory for the nation and for security about to be implemented. One century after the bloody revolution, Mexico was apparently on the verge of revisiting the difficult challenge of transformational reform and restoration of civil society—even as barbaric violence continued unchecked across the nation and Mexican troops patrolled the streets. AMLO's promise to end endemic corruption was encouraging but in reality had little chance of bringing about real change if it were not also accompanied by plans for concrete action and institutional reform. Engrained tradition and routine norms are inherently resistant to change—and la narcocultura and narco corruption were deeply imbedded in the social-political-cultural life of the nation.

Sadly, in the modern Mexico of horror, promises and rhetoric are not enough to bring a quick end to the long nightmare of violence nor break cycles of corruption or eliminate the ingrained influence of narcocultura.[11] Sinaloan journalist Ismael Bojorquez (2019a) zeroed in on the limits of the presidential oratory in one terse observation: "Homicides are increasing: the narcos don't know about the fourth transformation."[12]

President López Obrador won victory when Mexicans overwhelmingly grew weary of corruption and self-enrichment by PRI and PAN politicians and people finally took a leap of faith and entrusted governance to the populist and putatively left-leaning National Regeneration Movement (Morena). During the long pre-election and transition period, the Morena team had focused on corruption, entitlement, and the self-enrichment of a ruling oligarchy that had long manipulated the strings of power, but it also said surprisingly little about how a populist government might specifically deal with security issues.[13] That which was said was vague, often contradictory, and did not proffer anything resembling a road map for bringing an end to the drug wars or the corrupting influence of the powerful narco-political culture. Instead, López Obrador offered an optimistic narrative about a Fourth Transformation and a continuity with Mexico's idealized past along with a promise to introduce a moral constitution that would restore and repair shattered social bonds (el tejido social) (Ackerman 2019; Xantomila 2018).

Reimagining social values and appealing to past ideals can be a powerful political tool when a country's social fabric is in tatters and its norms have been corrupted—but it is also prone to the reductionist error of oversimplifying complex history when looking for solutions to new problems. The line between hopeful rhetoric and manipulative propaganda is nebulous, and there are many apprehensive voices fearful that AMLO's populist appeal was illusory and would soon transmogrify into an authoritarianism of the left. In the immediate postelection period, López Obrador's Fourth Transformation came under intense scrutiny, and several articulate accusations of historical oversimplification were circulating widely (Zunzunegui 2019). Several critics argued that his plan represented a mindless propaganda designed to legitimize a populist government in the absence of substantive, realistic, or concrete proposals for change and reform (Sicilia 2018).

President López Obrador's commitment to a moral constitution borrows directly from the 1940s works of Mexican liberal philosopher Alfonso

Reyes. His short treatise *Cartilla Moral, 1944* (1952) was referenced frequently during the election campaign, and in fact was eventually updated and reprinted for wide distribution shortly after AMLO assumed office in December (Sicilia 2018; Xantomila 2018). Reyes's vision of transformation was inspired by ideas initially proposed by the classical French sociologist Émile Durkheim, who had written extensively about morality, order, and progress at the beginning of the twentieth century.[14] Durkheim believed that stable societies successfully bind members to a common purpose through two distinct and parallel processes that he envisioned as *regulation* and *integration*. Regulation referred to a comprehensive set of rules, norms, and laws that were part of rational governance and engrained in stable institutions that produced continuity and security. Integration was a parallel force that is less tangible and saturated in the shared core values that are symbolically and viscerally reinforced through language, music, rhetoric, celebration, sport, worship of national icons, and ritual ceremonies. Reyes and his twenty-first-century advocate López Obrador both placed more importance on the integrative dimension described in Durkheimian theory, and both have given less attention to the regulatory dimension that Durkheim saw as more essential for stability. Integration can be promoted with symbols and rhetoric, but total institutional reform would also have to occur in order for integration to contribute significantly to order and progress. But rather than offering specific and concrete proposals to address security, AMLO and his inspirational guide apparently believe that change will occur if people can be convinced to change their values or aspire to follow the terms of a new morality. The task of institutional reform is much more complex than making a simple appeal to moral values, and even now, three years into his sexenio, there are few indications that it is happening.

Mexican institutions have long been handicapped by that commitment to the sufragio efectivo, no reelección code. Constant rotating appointments among senior administrators made it difficult if not impossible for any state institution to provide a continuity of vision and the regulatory stability Durkheim argued was essential to modernity. But in most ways, AMLO is not unique, and to an inordinate degree, Mexican governments have always compensated for institutional deficiencies in regulatory governance by appealing to the integrative power of patriotic symbols and rituals to reinforce social bonds. Mexicans are a fiercely proud people and deeply attached to the flag;

the green, white, and red colors attached to clothing; their national soccer team, *el tri*; and many other symbols of nationhood—even as many of their institutions have failed to live up to their promise to serve them well. But on the day that AMLO assumed power, he could no longer count on the integrative power of older symbolic forces that had drawn the country together in a common cause—since even the most historically influential symbols of mexicanismo had been tainted by scandal and weakened by corruption and the impact of never-ending narco wars.

There are specific examples where the integrative power of symbolically important institutions had been badly undermined by years of public insecurity and rampant corruption that had instead turned them into additional representations of incompetence and corruption. The first is Pemex, whose nationalization by President Lázaro Cárdenas del Río in the late 1930s had inspired a profound sense of mexicanismo. But by 2018, massive corruption and incompetence of Pemex managers had left it a tattered remnant of inspiration. Second, respect for Mexico's military had plummeted to historic lows: there had always been a historic, deep-rooted, and sacrosanct respect for the Mexican army and its revolutionary generals, and many military figures had served as a patriotic touchstone over the years—but by 2018, incompetence in suppressing cartel violence and blatant abuses of power had undermined its remaining symbolic power.[15]

López Obrador assumed office at a time when the integrative symbolism of both Pemex and the military were badly tarnished by incompetence, corruption, scandal, and general disrespect. The three sexenios immediately prior to his had expended most of the cultural capital that had historically accrued to both. Those two iconic unifying symbols of Mexico had been badly harmed by the blatant corruption within Pemex and by the incompetence in battles and civil rights abuse at the hands of military forces deployed in a futile War Against Cartels.

Grand Narratives

President López Obrador arrived with little in his playbook beyond a vague promise to bring about a Fourth Transformation. He did not come into office with a fully conceived plan for bringing change and he had not presented specific details for rebuilding Mexico's institutions—especially to those responsible for security and justice. There is a historical predilection for all Mexican leaders to propose grand narratives and introduce change using a top-down framework, and in his actions AMLO is not unique.

Octavio Paz (1970, 1979) made reference to that traditional pattern when he wrote that European and American institutions were built upon Enlightenment principles of egalitarianism, rationality, and countervailing powers, whereas Mexico continued with the counter-reformative tradition where ideas and ideals were built upon pyramidical values. Many have noted how that long-established hierarchical tradition of governance has left Mexican institutions weak and underdeveloped and incapable of implementing the high ideals that are regularly expressed by leaders: Enrique Krauze (1997) published several accounts of the hierarchical and pyramidical tradition and exercise of power that has dominated Mexico's imperial presidencies since World War II, and Daron Acemoglu and James Robinson (2012) presented powerful and damning empirical evidence that Mexican institutions are weak to a degree that they actually impede development and modernization—especially the agencies charged with overseeing the well-being, security, and education of its citizens.

Mexicans are justifiably proud of their history, and especially self-congratulatory about the words and ideals contained in three magnificent constitutional documents that emerged in the aftermath of three historic disruptions: the Constitutions of 1825, 1857, and 1917 are engraved into collective memory and rightfully celebrated as watershed moments when the nation emerged from chaos to frame an ideal future. Each is an aspirational document inspired by impressive visions of democracy and equality, but not one of those ambitious frameworks ever led to the creation of a comprehensive network of interconnected institutions capable of carrying out the ideals they championed.

The 2018 electoral victory of López Obrador and Morena cannot be interpreted as anything other than a watershed moment in Mexican history because of the size of its mandate, but it remains to be seen whether it actually represents a new transformation and the end to a long era of narco politics and the eradication of la narcocultura. Unless the Morena government successfully establishes security, all the goodwill and optimism that led up to the victory of AMLO will prove transitory and violence will continue.

Since the 1960s, Mexican governments have been committed to a neo-liberal model that puportedly would make Mexico competitive in global markets and finally admit it to membership in the modern world. López Obrador has argued that it has been those neoliberal ideals that actually fomented the routine acceptance of corruption and created the context in which covert netherworlds of criminality have thrived. Through his words and actions, AMLO has specifically targeted neoliberalism as the enemy, and he has blamed it for all the woes that have befallen Mexico. But he was imprecise about what would take its place.

Andrés Manuel López Obrador profoundly believed in the power of symbolism and the integrative goal it might achieve. But at the same time, his political vision was conspicuously imprecise about how he would bring an end to the twelve years of staggering bloodshed and violence that left more than 310,000 dead and more than 60,000 missing during the sexenios of his neoliberal predecessors. His rhetorical call for a Fourth Transformation and his optimism about the educative potential of a new moral constitution did not specify how those would end Mexico's deep entanglement in the five-decade U.S. War on Drugs, nor had he outlined a specific multidimensional strategy that would eradicate organized crime and reduce the violence from ongoing wars within cartels and wars between cartels.

His three immediate predecessors and neoliberal governments had failed to provide an effective security policy that protected its citizens. Violence, and more problematically massacres attributable to cartels as well as to police and the army, had become increasingly routine occurrences over their eighteen years of governance. The impact on the social bond was demoralizing as citizen confidence in the state and its key institutions plummeted to abysmal levels: homicides had reached unimaginable highs, and tens of thousands had disappeared; the army, police, courts, and paramilitary forces seemed to be operating without any pretense of a commitment to human rights; the police and military were directly responsible for horrific incidents such as the repression of protest at San Salvador Atenco (2006), the cold-blooded massacre of twenty-two young people at Tlatlaya (2014), and the murder of six people and the disappearance of forty-three Raúl Isidro Burgos Normal School students at Iguala (2014) whose whereabouts remained unknown and let those who are responsible remain free (EFE 2016). The first two decades of the new millennium had not seen any improvement in Mexican security institutions and instead the symbolic trust that Mexicans had previously placed in two institutions that were historically the source of inspirational pride—the military and Pemex—had shredded.

Despite many failures of the state that were obvious by the late 1990s, it took long years of hard and vicious campaigning before the populist vision of AMLO and Morena finally claimed victory in 2018. A majority of Mexicans had grown so weary of violence and thoroughly revulsed by the endemic corruption that they finally turned their backs on neoliberal parties and placed their trust in a party that was viewed as leftist and opposed to neoliberalism.

The campaign platform that finally produced Morena's electoral win featured a commitment to end corruption and a nebulous promise to bring about a Fourth Transformation (*la 4T*) and introduce a new moral constitution (Rodríguez García 2018; Sicilia 2018; Xantomila 2018). But López Obrador was handed a nation plagued by massive economic problems and served by weak and corrupt institutions, and his vague, idealistic, and hopeful campaign promises would be severely tested by reality. He was also faced with the immediate and daunting challenge of bringing an end to the three lingering wars—the war between cartels, internal wars within cartels, and a futile twelve-year-old war against cartels that was still being waged by the army and navy.

Three Sexenios and Three Wars

Criminal organizations have thrived in the new millennium, and brutal violence exponentially rose to staggering levels while they have prospered (see figure 2). At the beginning of Vicente Fox's presidency, three criminal cartels operated regionally across thirteen Mexican states, but by the end of 2018, nine were operating in twenty-eight of the thirty-one Mexican states and the Federal District. Only four Mexican states were unified plazas controlled by a single cartel, and the other twenty-four had at least two cartels operating and often competing within its boundaries (D. Ramos 2015).

Localized turf wars escalated into wider regional battles soon after Vicente Fox (2000–2006) decentralized the federal state and devolved power to state and municipal governments. In the fourth year of Fox's term, an internal war broke out within the Sinaloa Cartel when Joaquín Guzmán assassinated the youngest brother of the Carrillo Fuentes family in an attack carried out at the Cinépolis Plaza in Culiacán. That incident was arguably the beginning point of a decade-long struggle for dominance within and between cartels: a series of skirmishes and attacks and low-grade war erupted across Mexico—

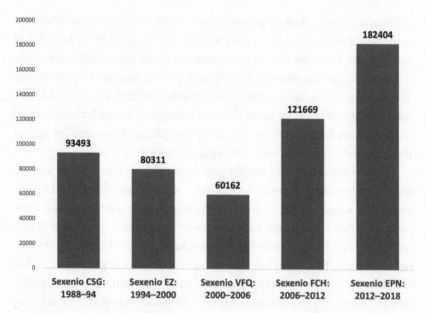

FIGURE 2 Homicide totals by sexenio, 1989–2018. Data from Instituto Nacional de Estadística y Geografía (INEGI).

but especially across the northern states sharing a border with the USA. And then in 2006, the new president, Felipe Calderón, recklessly committed the nation to undertake a war against cartels that would continue through the Peña Nieto presidency and into the AMLO sexenio.

The six-year term of Felipe de Jesús Calderón Hinojosa (2006–12) was dominated by cartel wars that will forever be remembered as the defining events of his presidency. Throughout his sexenio, Mexico's generals and admirals waged war against cartels—and specifically focused on hunting cartel bosses and capos. He remained stubbornly committed to that approach, even though military and security experts alike warned that his *kingpin strategy* to hunt down capos using the military was a questionable strategy. Elsewhere in the world, terrorist organizations had been wiped out by targeting their leaders, but those groups were ideologically driven, diffusely organized, and led by charismatic personalities: unlike them, Mexico's cartels were complex organizations with community ties, high-level official support, and innumerable numbers of lower-level narcos and sicarios ready and willing to step up and take over the leadership whenever a jefe was arrested or killed. Felipe Calderón and his generals misunderstood the reality of organized crime in

Mexico, and overlooked the perverse trade-off that many of its members had made—to live ten years like a *güey* instead of forty years like a *büey*.[16] And furthermore, Calderón did not seem to care or understand that the American decision to target kingpins was actually an economic sanction used by the U.S. Treasury, and it was not a justification for waging military attacks. Calderón's unrelenting commitment to his vision of a kingpin strategy had unintended consequences for Mexico: the larger cartels splintered into smaller groups that were led by unpredictable and arguably more desperate leaders.[17]

The new capos of those smaller groups proved to be even more violent, less intimidated by threats of confrontation with military forces, and far less inclined to negotiate Pax Mafiosas with authorities or even with rival competitors. Offshoots of larger cartels—known as *cartelitos*—emerged during his sexenio and engaged in violent internecine challenges for control of product and routes. To cite but one example, a violent younger generation within the older Milenio Cartel—a longtime ally and subservient faction within the Sinaloa Cartel—fought among themselves for leadership after Ignacio Coronel Villareal was killed in a skirmish with the Mexican army in 2010. Coronel Villareal had been sanctioned as a kingpin by the U.S. Treasury in 2005, and consequently was a prime target of the Mexican army in Calderón's war. But the younger generation that stepped up to replace him proved more dangerous, unpredictable, and violent (Malkin 2010). The Milenio Cartel had established a foothold in Jalisco and dominated Mexico's synthetic drug trade using smuggling routes largely independent of Sinaloa Cartel oversight: by the time of "Nacho" Coronel's death, the profits from the synthetic drug trade had skyrocketed with increasing consumer demand. His killing left a power vacuum and enormous riches up for grabs, and several contenders were ready to step up: initially two factions known as Los Cuinis and Los Menchos emerged as rivals, but they managed to remain unified in the face of continuing attacks from the military and also from Los Zetas. They set aside differences and reemerged as the Cártel de Jalisco Nueva Generación to attack Mexican troops in aggressive confrontations and battles—including one where a Mexican army helicopter was shockingly shot out of the sky with military-level ordnance (de Mauleón 2017a).

■ ■ ■

The first skirmish in what eventually became known as Mexico's War Against Cartels can be traced to December 11, 2006, when Calderón surprisingly and unexpectedly mobilized seven thousand troops to attack drug organizations in his native state.[18] Joint Operation Michoacán State was a surprising action undertaken a mere ten days into his sexenio.[19] Emboldened by the initial impact, Calderón quickly authorized further joint operations against identified kingpins and cartels in Baja California, Guerrero, and the Golden Triangle (Sinaloa, Durango, and Chihuahua) over the first two months of 2007 (Guerrero Gutiérrez 2017). By mid-May, Calderón's War Against Cartels had broadened to include political rivals, and an operation known as the Michoacanazo brought indictments against ten mayors and twenty state functionaries for narco trafficking and money laundering.[20]

The military interventions nudged Calderón's personal popularity upward from pre-inauguration levels barely hovering around 50 percent, and afterward nothing that happened over the next five years would dissuade Calderón from his personal conviction that war and military intervention had become absolutely necessary to bring an end to the power and influence of cartels. At the end of Calderón's presidency and 2,180 days of continuous war with no evidence of success, Ismael Bojorquez (2017) summarized the president's willful blindness and commitment to war as akin to that of some ploughshare beast fitted with blinders to block out anything except the path it was on.[21]

Any optimism that emerged after the initial joint military operations and political crackdown in early 2007 proved illusionary when drug lords organized to launch brutal counteroffensives. Casualty rates soared, and Mexico's generals and admirals realized that their ill-trained *pelones* (foot soldiers) and marines had become engaged with formidable adversaries.[22] At least three different cartels had amassed powerful arsenals after the 2004 expiration of a U.S. assault weapons ban made powerful weapons readily obtainable, and those drug lords also established training camps for foot soldiers to entrusted and brutally sanguine lieutenants.[23] By mid-2007, Calderón's government was entangled in proverbial briarwood and Mexico's ill-equipped military was fighting a war in which it had quickly become the defender rather than aggressor. Héctor Aguilar Camín's metaphor perfectly describes what happened: "The wild beast of organized crime was quick to sense the jab to its loin and it never stopped lashing back" (qtd. in Editorial Nexos 2017).[24]

To make matters worse, traditional respect for the Mexican military in Mexico was soon undermined when generals authorized dubious strategies and maneuvers that resulted in citizens and human rights groups filing formal complaints with both state and federal human rights organizations

(Krauze 2016; Open Society Foundations 2016; Scherer García 2011; Suárez-Enríquez and Meyer 2017; Ward 2009).

Momentum in the war had dissipated within the first few months of the very first year of his term, but Calderón would never waver from his conviction that it was necessary to pursue drug bosses. Mexico remained entrenched in a war that left a legacy of savagery and bloodshed in its wake: by the end of his sexenio (2006–12), an estimated 135,000 had been murdered, more than 30,000 were missing or disappeared, and countless thousands of innocent victims had been displaced by violence, fear, and intimidation. Calderón's impulsive declaration of a War Against Cartels had engendered years of blood and lead for ordinary citizens while the cartels expanded and thrived. Rather than being crushed, the mafias and their leaders flourished, and their influence expanded into new illegal enterprises and markets. When Calderón assumed office, six cartels were operating in Mexico, but by 2010 the number had grown to nine powerful groups overseeing at least fifty-nine smaller affiliates.[25]

Calderón's obsession with waging a *War Against Cartels* shredded Mexico's social cohesion (tejido social) and ripped apart the social fabric with each passing year. His futile war also brought a screeching halt to democratic reform that had begun in an era of hope in the mid-1990s: instead of eliminating violence and ending drug smuggling, Calderón's unsuccessful war left Mexico yearning for some semblance of efficiency and primed the nation for the return of authoritarian rule when his term ended. Calderón not only failed in his quixotic quest to eliminate cartels by concentrating on bringing down kingpins, but he also fostered the conditions that demeaned democratic reform as inefficient and left a majority of Mexicans willing to return to the old authoritarian ways of the PRI.

President Calderón had boldly predicted that Mexico's generals would eliminate kingpins, defeat the cartels, and restore confidence in government. Instead, his personal reputation was diminished by the bloody disaster he had blindly unleashed. Violence and suffering reached sickening levels—ones that he woefully justified with a claim that at least he had tried and that there was no other option. "What would you have had me do? That I had greeted them? That I had invited them to spend time with me? That I had taken them for a coffee?" (Astorga Almanza 2015, Kindle Location 1592).[26]

Felipe Calderón squandered any chance that the Partido Acción Nacional had to govern beyond the first two sexenios of the new millennium.

That ignominious outcome is truly astonishing given the optimism that was unleashed when PAN had finally ended the PRI's seven-decade reign in 2000: after the Fox victory, most reasonable observers believed it would require at least one generation before the old ruling party could hope to recover from that crushing defeat. Fox had won the presidency when voters had finally wearied of PRI's authoritarian ways and of the corruption and enrichment of its oligarchic class—a long era that Mario Vargas Llosa had characterized as a *perfect dictatorship* (*El País* 1990). But millennial prophecies of an extended or permanent demise were wildly incorrect: Fox's chaotic management did not lead to a reformative redistribution of power sharing across Mexico's major institutions, and then Calderón's disastrous war once again opened a yearning among many for PRI's resurrection from obscurity and from its stronghold in Mexico State.

Taking advantage of the widespread anger directed at Calderón's disastrous War Against Cartels and his party's mismanagement of the economy, the elite and wealthy members of the neoliberal oligarchy (Grupo Atlocomulco) effectively organized support for Mexico State ex-governor Enrique Peña Nieto. The PRI resorted to a Machiavellian strategy to ensure its return to power: it took full advantage of the media power Televisa to frame a narrative of competence for Peña Nieto while it denigrated his opponents. The PRI also targeted and bribed vulnerable voters with gifts of major household appliances and shopping cards, and ran a campaign built around the theme of *Saving Mexico*. Undoubtedly, the PRI manipulated the vote by resurrecting historical tactics of cheating to ensure its candidates won. The dark money of the covert netherworld and cartels assuredly financed much of that campaign and its strategies.

The PRI returned to power in 2012 faced with the challenge of governing under conditions that Lorenzo Meyer (2017) classified as "the very definition of political system that, even now, is an unstable and failed hybrid; a bad mix of old authoritarianism with a dash of democratic elements and wrapped in rampant corruption." The PRI returned to govern a nation emotionally drained by violence and even more deeply distrustful of its political class. But the people were willing to overlook their doubts because of the hope that it would return stability and security. New patterns of governance had emerged during the Fox and Calderón sexenios, and incoming president Pena Nieto could not re-establish the imperial presidency typified by the PRI's seven-decade reign of the twentieth century. There could be no return to centralized and hierarchical governance, nor any immediate re-establishment of a top-down containment model of crime control where PRI functionaries served as the direct brokers in a power syndicate with entrepreneurial gangs.[27] Constitutional amendments had since delegated autonomy to states, and Mexico's criminal mafias had by then forged accommodations at the subnational level beginning in 2001 (Ribando Seelke 2021).

In retrospect, it is not surprising that Peña Nieto was no more successful than Calderón in reining in the cartels or curbing the bloody violence plaguing Mexico. He had also assumed office without offering a well-defined or clear strategy for containing cartels, nor had he even bothered to make specific promises about organized crime during his electoral campaign. Instead, he spoke in broad generalities about implementing a *Pact for Mexico* that would transform all its institutions. He placed most of the security functions directly in the control of the Secretaría de Gobernación (SEGOB, Secretariat of the Interior), which continued to pursue kingpins, and he left troops on the streets to battle cartels.[28]

But one noticeable difference soon became apparent—the new PRI government made it more difficult to obtain information, find relevant statistics, or use objective measures related to violence and disappearances (CFR .org Editors 2017). The curtain had been closed on transparency. For a short period at the beginning of the Peña Nieto sexenio, there was statistical evidence released that suggested violence was subsiding. Journalists writing for newspapers and regional magazines quickly undermined official claims of a drop and reported contradictory evidence showing that violence was still on a long trajectory upward as cartels continued their internecine battles for turf in ongoing wars *between* cartels. Disputing the official reports, journalists offered proof that no justice agency at the federal or state level was having success in ending the bloodshed, halting forced disappearances, or intervening to prevent massive internal displacement from remote communities.

Many had hoped that a PRI government would restore efficiency and stability, but the Peña Nieto administration became embroiled in three crises that demonstrated it had no greater competence than PAN in controlling drug organizations. The first crisis exposed the brutality of Mexican federal troops. A journalist from *Esquire* magazine exposed the brutal and unjustified execution of twenty-two young people at Tlatlaya in Mexico State (Ferri Tórtola 2014; see also Ahmed and Schmitt 2016; Meyer 2016). A second crisis emerged from the woeful mismanagement of internecine wars in

Michoacán State: the government had encouraged the re-establishment of armed citizen militias to contain La Familia Michoacana and Los Caballeros Templarios, but their encouragement and support unintentionally worsened matters when those populist militias became the source of violence. A third crisis damaged government credibility even more, and left its credibility shattered and totally diminished. On the night of September 25 and the early morning September 26, 2014, six people were murdered by municipal police in Iguala, Guerrero, and forty-three Raúl Isidro Burgos Normal School students from Ayoztinapa disappeared. The investigation spurred on by fact-filled reports from journalists revealed the extent of nefarious ties between drug cartels, politicians, local and state police, and the army: in the aftermath, preposterous official investigations by the federal attorney general exposed the utter shamelessness of state institutions and its disingenuous commitment to justice and transparency (Devereaux 2017; Goldman 2015; Guillermoprieto 2015; Rosagel and Rodríguez 2016; Villa et al. 2015).

As his term limped to an end, it became increasingly evident that Peña Nieto had proven no more successful than his predecessor—and by some measures, he had done worse: the homicide numbers reached a historic high of 31,174 in 2017 and 33,341 in 2018, there were more violent crime groups operating than ever seen before (Baltazar 2017), there were turf battles in states that were previously cartel-free zones and no longer immune to violence (e.g., Edomex, Puebla, Ciudad de México [CDMX, Mexico City]), and eighteen former governors were under indictment or arrested for links to cartels and corruptio (Overa 2020).[29]

Transformations and Mythmaking

The futility of using military force to fight a war against cartels was a fiasco easily foretold (see Aguilar V. and Castañeda 2010; Buscaglia 2010; Payan, Staudt, and Kruszewski 2013). But it had already dragged on for twelve years when López Obrador finally declared that he wanted no part of that war and proclaimed, "Ya se acabó la guerra" (The war has finished) (qtd. in López Ponce 2019):

> Right at the end of his January 30 press conference, a journalist asked President Andrés Manuel López Obrador "has the War Against Cartels ended?"

"There is no war" responded the head of state. "Officially there is now no war. We want peace." (Nájar 2019)

Were those idle words casually tossed out in the spur of the moment? Or was Mexico at a critical point where a government was truly committed to ending all drug wars? Only time will tell, but what is certain is that a new narrative and new discourse had replaced the old, and 2019 marked the end of a period dominated by the language of war against cartels. Much of that narrative was based on a newer and vaguer promise of transformation.

Andrés Manuel López Obrador is the first Mexican president elected as head of a populist and leftist party, and the first claiming to disavow the principles of the dominant global neoliberal economic philosophy. He is also the first modern Mexican president to reject the symbolic and attendant frills of an imperial presidency: he disbanded the military unit formed to protect and act at the service of the president—the Estado Mayor Presidencial—and he travels unencumbered in public without guards; he refused to occupy the presidential mansion, Los Pinos, and opened it to the public and turned it into a museum; he mothballed the recently purchased luxurious presidential plane and instead travels around the country on commercial flights; he cut his own salary and that of the cabinet, staff, and appointed heads of agencies. He holds daily press briefings and question-and-answer periods—la mañanera—and was the first to proclaim that he would rely on public referenda for feedback on financial proposals and major projects. Finally, he is the first president in many years to show no concern for international politics, even in the aftermath of the racist and xenophobic rantings of an authoritarian U.S. president who made Mexico the enemy on the borders.

The first three years of his presidency have indicated that he would continue in the Mexican tradition of relying on myth and symbolism to counteract all problems—even insecurity. In June 2020, the Cártel de Jalisco Nueva Generación staged a bold and blatant assassination attack on Omar García Harfuch, the secretary of security for Mexico City (González Díaz 2020). Five days later, on the occasion of the first mañanera held after that attack, AMLO reaffirmed his conviction that the cartels would be defeated because the state has the *moral force* that will defeat and suppress all illegal activity (Martínez and Muñoz 2020). That will surely not be enough to destroy the entrenched narcopolítica, or narco-culture, and bring an end to the neverending wars.

Disruption and transformation are recurrent tropes in the Mexican origin narrative, and like most other constructions of national identity, the actual disruption and resultant transformations blend fact and myth together to create fable.

The grand Mexican narrative is based on the events that followed several great disruptions and transformations. Undoubtedly, the most catastrophic was in 1519 and the arrival of Hernán Cortés and European invaders. A vast Mejica Empire established as early as March 1325 collapsed with unexpected rapidity when vassal states such as the Tlaxcalans and Cholulans defected to support a small band of bearded newcomers. But even those older myths that have served as the basis of Mexican identity have recently been undermined with the publication of revealing histories based on events and interpretations written by the descendants of the catastrophe (Townsend 2020).

In those mythological narratives, many ethnohistorians attributed the abruptness of the collapse to the Aztec belief in recurrent temporal cycles and celestial omens signifying new beginnings (Malmström 2010). Mesoamerican calendars delineated time into repeating fifty-two-year solar cycles with designated dark days set aside for ceremonies that would reveal either an end of days or a new beginning. One enduring postcolonial myth maintains that the arrival of bearded Castilians coincided with those dark days of the solar calendar and a misreading of signs by the Tlatoani Motecuhzoma Xocoyotzin and priest oracles. The widely accepted fable would have the world believe that a great Mejica empire, founded where an "Eagle on a Cactus consumed a Snake," arrived at its end of days during a fourth solar cycle when Tlatoani Moctezuma mistakenly believed Cortés was the incarnation of the returning Toltec god (Restall 2003). Three previous solar cycles had renewed with the successful kindling of a new sun following the rituals of extreme bloodletting and sacrifice—anthropological narratives and the archaeological uncovering mounds of skulls are testament to the magnitude of a blood-soaked dramaturgy where prisoners of proxy wars had hearts ripped out atop the Templo Mayor.

The darkness caused by the failure to ignite the ceremonial fifth solar sun represented an end of days for Moctezuma and the Mejica. But even as it mythically collapsed, the actual sun rose in the east to illuminate all the days and months and years of a five-century era that brought more disruptions and cycles of change to Mexico—a revolution to gain independence from Spain, a liberal movement to shed colonial institutions, a chaotic revolution at the beginning of the twentieth century—and now in 2019, a Fourth Transformation proposed by another man from Tabasco.

In Mexico, such broad cycles and eras are important markers of time, and despite the incursion of modernism, there has been an enduring and deep affinity for history and the signaling of momentous events. Admittedly, few Mexicans remain attentive to rhythms and cycles marked in Mesoamerican calendars, and fewer still are guided by cosmological projections drawn from dual cylinders co-linking linear time and ritual cycles. Modernity requires that linear measurement of time guides rational action, and consigns the cyclic rhythms and accompanying rituals to memory and replaces them with ceremonies marking the change of governments and election of new leaders.

The pageantry of AMLO's inauguration day signified the beginning of what he promised would begin a new sociopolitical trajectory terminating five decades of neoliberal hegemony in Mexico. For the first time, a leftist president was given the chance to govern by voters grown weary of eighteen years of corruption and fifteen years of escalating violence. No one expected that López Obrador could end Mexico's long nightmare of corruption and violence and Wars Between Cartels by simply assuming office, but all eyes eagerly watched for specific signs of the new era when he assumed office.

For the incoming president, the rituals of investiture were the apex of a personal eighteen-year odyssey and began on day one of his self-styled moral crusade to bring about that Fourth Transformation. For a generation of long-suffering leftists, AMLO's electoral victory was the high point of a prolonged quest to bring democratic reform—quashed fifty years earlier by the Tlatelolco and Corpus Christi massacres and waged from the shadows during President Echeverría Álvarez's *guerra sucia*. For millennials, December 1, 2018, brought sweet vindication for electoral disappointments of Cuauhtémoc Cárdenas Solórzano in 2000, of AMLO in 2006 when Enrique Krauze demonized him as a "tropical messiah" (Krauze 2006; López Obrador 2007), and for a third time in the 2012 election that López Obrador obstinately insisted he had legitimately won.

But then, on the first official day of the new presidency, the memory of those three defeats was blurred by the spectacle of inauguration, the dramaturgical pageantry, and AMLO's oratorical promise of that Fourth Transformation. López Obrador participated in the traditional postrevolutionary ceremonial rituals that invested him in the office of an imperial presidency (Angulo and Esposito 2018), but immediately after swearing the traditional oath of office and newly garlanded with the ceremonial green, white, and red sash, he unleashed a withering critique of his immediate predecessor, Peña Nieto, and the neoliberal imperative that had dominated the five previous sexenios:

> And this is what I insist that you recognize. The hallmark of neoliberal-
> ism is corruption. This sounds harsh, but privatization in Mexico has been
> synonymous with corruption. Disgracefully this evil always existed in our
> country, but the neoliberal period had no precedent for the degree to which
> it operated hand in hand with corruption. Political power and the economic
> power have fed and nurtured each other and were implanted as the modus
> operandi for the theft of the people's goods and the riches of the nation.
> (Lopez Obrador 2018)[30]

Then he unexpectedly and symbolically acknowledged the Other Mexico—that "isolated, Indian and agrarian country excluded from modern development" (qtd. in Fuentes 1973). Unaccompanied by guards, he walked across the great Plaza of the Constitution toward the ruins of the Templo Mayor to receive a blessing from indigenous leaders and accept the *bastón de mando* signifying his role as *tlatoani*—their traditional leader (Sanchez and McDonnell 2018).

Those two ceremonies on the eastern side of Mexico's grand Zócalo literally and symbolically signified that a new trajectory had begun and that an economic continuity that had endured over nine sexenios might be coming to an end.[31] Given the bloodshed that was the hallmark symbol of the preceding twelve years, the new president had many well-wishers—but it is far too early to predict a positive outcome for his avowed Fourth Transformation or whether it can even begin to end the violence. In reality, the odds are stacked against it.

Political organizations dedicated to neoliberal economics had governed for nine sexenios and had coursed unchallenged by any meaningful opposition for fifty-four years. During forty-seven of those years, six PRI and two PAN presidents pursued market and economic expansion into the United States and had accepted the encumbrance of its demands to serve as a proxy partner in its War on Drugs. AMLO vehemently rejected that dominant neoliberal economy that his predecessors had worshipped, but he spoke only vaguely about that proxy drug war and the violence it had engendered.

Instead, he simply repeated his often-stated assertion that violence would disappear when the root problem—corruption—was eliminated.

> In other words, as I have repeatedly said over the course of many years, nothing has damaged Mexico more than the dishonesty of governments and the small minority that has profited from insider connections and influence. . . . That is the principal cause of economic and social inequality, and also for the insecurity and the violence that we suffer. (López Obrador 2018)[32]

Other than committing to the creation of a new National Guard, he said nothing in his inaugural speech about Mexico's continued participation in the War on Drugs, nor did he present a specific plan for reining in the powerful cartels that thrived during the neoliberal era and had bloodied the country in the internecine battles known as wars between cartels. In the long five-month period of the pre-inaugural transition, he had speculated about the legalization of some drugs (marijuana) and perhaps even negotiating amnesty with drug gangs, but he made no reference to those proposals in his first speech as president. Instead, López Obrador made it clear that neoliberalism and corruption were his targets and that cartels and wars with cartels would be considered later. But the covert netherworld was still in place and presumably ready to oppose any of these measures.

Following the catastrophic economic collapse during Miguel de la Madrid Hurtado's sexenio (1982–88), Mexico had consistently repudiated every leftist presidential aspirant who challenged the neoliberal economic orthodoxy that had been embraced as an absolute necessity for modernization. The forces and parties of neoliberalism won all elections that mattered and usually by any means necessary.

An inexplicable twilight computer crash zeroed out early electoral counts, and the rebooted count tabulated results indicating that Carlos Salinas de Gortari had come from behind to win that election of June 1988. The dubious malfunction ushered in a sexenio wherein the neoliberal economy became firmly entrenched with the signing of NAFTA and a massive dumping of national utilities at bargain-basement prices: two-thirds of the public corporations that were privatized during the Salinas sexenio generated lottery windfalls for twenty-three families and set aside a place for them at tables reserved for superbillionaires. The dominance of neoliberal economies at the expense of public institutions was reinforced when those newly admitted into the ranks of the moneyed class became willing participants in a recursive monetary loop that promoted the glories of a neoliberal narrative and guaranteed that their own wealth would grow (Overa 2019a). During the final year of the Salinas sexenio, twenty-five of Mexico's richest men were gathered together in a room by Carlos "El Profesor" Hank González and compelled to turn over $1 million of their windfall to ensure that the PRI and Ernesto Zedillo Ponce de León would defeat Cuauhtémoc Cárdenas and keep the presidency in PRI hands in 1994 (Oppenheimer 1996). At the millennium's end, rampant corruption, elitism, and the impunity in the aftermath of brutal massacres had enraged many Mexicans and reignited an activism akin to that which drove Mexican students to the streets back in 1968. The older generation had believed protest was the route to change but instead discovered that it had simply ushered in a dark era of repression and allowed a covert netherworld to operate in the shadows: the millennial generation believed that change came at the ballot box and withdrew allegiance from the PRI dynasty to support the opposition PAN, only to belatedly realize that PAN enforced the same hegemony of neoliberalism and the protection of privilege.

Millennial discontent bubbled below the surface and was kept alive by veterans of Mexico's dirty war in their activity as artists, intellectuals, and journalists. They were joyful and celebratory on the day that AMLO became president and openly promised transformation and an end to the old ways. But few of them remembered Octavio Paz's cautionary observation about the final outcome of all previous great transformative disruptions in Mexican history: Mexico's great poet laureate had observed that the only winners in the aftermath of previous disruptions were those already occupying the top of structurally and deeply divided societies, while "one half is denied any real social, cultural or political participation" (qtd. in Fuentes 1973).[33] In his bittersweet reflection of the crushed 1968 protests (*Posdata*), Paz critically mourned how the continuity of power for those at the top was the inevitable outcome following the great transformations of Mexico's past—the Conquest, the Wars of Independence from Spain, the liberal wars against colonization, and even the bloody Revolution (Paz 1970, 1978).

Paz recognized that Mexico is a pyramidical society where the concentration of power remains permanently fixed even when the entirety has been disrupted by transition and transformation. The pain of the disruption never touches the elite but is exclusively felt by *the Other*—and the cost is always paid with their blood. His peer Carlos Fuentes summarized the inevitable outcome of Mexico's great disruptions in his magnificent review of Paz's *Posdata.*

> Octavio Paz was struck by the continuity of a power structure, masked by different ideologies, serving equally well the needs of Indian theocracy, Spanish colonialism, and modern *desarrollismo*, development for development's sake. He presents us with the drama of a people, suffering and silent, but given to periodic explosions that have formed the conscience of Mexico: the revolution to gain political independence from Spain, the liberal movement to achieve independence from colonial institutions, and the vast, bloody, chaotic revolution of this century, inflamed by the cultural passion for self-knowledge, the democratic passion for self-government, and by an economic passion for success as a modern nation. (Fuentes 1973)

By the late 1990s, the established and recently admitted beneficiaries entrenched at the top of Mexico's pyramid remained true believers in the benefits of a neoliberal narrative, and they were aware that an outwardly crushing electoral defeat for the PRI in 2000 would not have the dramatic consequences that the other Mexico envisioned. And too many of them were active participants and members of a covert netherworld that had been taking form since the mid-1970s. Vicente Fox had seemingly wrestled the presidency from the seventy-one-year cycle of domination by the PRI, but the elite still sitting at the peak of the pyramid recognized it to be a minor structural modification in the neoliberal continuity of power. PAN remained guided, perhaps even more than PRI, by those same neoliberal principles of governance during its twelve years at the top of the pyramid, while those on the bottom awaited authentic social, cultural, and political participation.

Neoliberal Governance and Cartels

Neoliberal hegemony dominated Mexican politics between 1982 and 2018, and during those years organized crime worked closely with the elite in a covert netherworld so that both would profit at the expense of everyone else. Drug cartels and drug capos thrived during the initial rush to embed and enshrine neoliberal policies in law and trade agreements. The cartels emerged as truly powerful forces with resources that matched or even surpassed the wealth of Mexico's oligarchy when the U.S.-Mexico border was finally opened to trade.

Criminal cartels and crime organizations grew especially powerful after they expanded their presence to almost all Mexican states and cities during the years 2004 to 2012: not surprisingly, the violence spiked during those years of internecine battles for turf and open war between competing cartels within many states. As usually happened, it would be the poor and the underclass who paid with blood. While Mexican politicians were busy promoting globalism and the benefits of neoliberalism, mysterious and figures from the underworld emerged as powerful figures in the world of transnational crime. They did so with the implicit acceptance of government and the elite.

There are competing and unresolvable narratives about the exact manner in which those underworld figures are directly linked to the legitimate world of neoliberalism: one view is that they were nurtured and supervised by key players in that world (Grayson 2010, 2014), but an alternate narrative claims that cartels brutalized their way to dominance as parallel powers because of the weakness of state security agencies (Fernández Menéndez 2001), and finally there are many narratives asserting that organized crime was empowered only because of the ruthless and brilliant criminal personalities applying the principles of entrepreneurial capitalism (Emmot 2010). No matter what accounts for the emergent power of cartels in the last two decades of the twentieth century, the undeniable reality is that the emergence of a narco state and la narcopolítica dovetail perfectly with an intensified commitment to neoliberal models of globalization.

A note of caution must be provided here. While it is definitely true that Mexican cartels emerged as powerful entities and thrived simultaneously alongside neoliberal presidencies, this should not be interpreted as proof that neoliberalism has been the prime causal factor leading to the emergence of cartels. Obviously, there are many neoliberal states that do not have drug organizations, and there are narco states not swayed by a neoliberal model of economies (e.g., Afghanistan). The rise of cartels in Mexico has been perfectly described by Phil Williams and others as the confluence and emergence "from a perfect storm of conditions," and a neoliberal economy has been only one of several factors leading to the rise of cartels (Creechan 2012; Sullivan, Cook, and Durand 2008; Williams 1999).[34] This book will return to these themes when it describes the origins and development of cartels in later chapters.

But for the moment, we should recognize that we have arrived at a critical point in Mexican history and in the cartel wars. The integrative power and symbolism explicit in the words and rhetoric of AMLO and his promise of a Fourth Transformation cannot be enough to end the power of criminal organizations, nor quickly or permanently bring an end to violence and social disruption.

Any real change awaits the implementation of a multidimensional plan of action and the true strengthening of Mexico's security institutions and social support networks. Mexican institutions addressing poverty, education, and social welfare must be simultaneously reconstructed and strengthened. Words may matter, but they are no match for guns and will not be powerful enough to destroy the appeal of narco politics and end la narcocultura.

CHAPTER 4

The Roots of Narco Mexico

Badges? We ain't got no badges. We don't need no badges. I don't have to show you any stinking badges.

—Alfonso Bedoya, Gold Hat, bandit in *The Treasure of the Sierra Madre*, 1967

In *The Treasure of the Sierra Madre*, five misfits search for a gold mine that will rescue them from a life of misery, only to descend into venality in their quest. Trapped in marginality and living lives of wretchedness, they eventually do discover an El Dorado in a remote Mexican sierra populated by impoverished villages—but in a cruel twist of fate, none survive to live out their dream of heaven on earth. Tantalizingly close to realizing his dream, the final survivor is killed by the bandit Gold Hat, who himself is fleeing Mexican Federales: author B. Traven (1967) spins a Hobbesian tale of a quest for treasure and salvation in a turbulent kingdom of darkness where life is nasty, brutish, and short, and where the chances of success are stacked against everyone.[1]

In the end, the last adventurer is killed, and his gold dust is scattered to the winds by Gold Hat, who believes it is only fool's gold. The antihero, Fred Dobbs, had earlier crossed paths with his executioner when the hapless bandit demanded he surrender his rifle—"If you are the police, then where are your *badges*?" Dobbs challenged.[2] In John Huston's movie adaptation, Mexican actor Alfonso Bedoya sneers back at Humphrey Bogart and grunts the well-known retort—"Badges? We ain't got no badges. We don't need no badges. I don't have to show you any stinking badges"—before slinking away in retreat.

Traven's novel was set in the 1920s during a time when Los Federales actually did carry badges that were effectively licenses to kill, and they hunted down bandits in Mexico's Sierra Madre Occidental justified by a deadly *ley fuga* (extrajudicial assassination). Huston's adaptation of Traven's noire tale was filmed shortly after World War II in remote areas of Mexico where the Mexican government had tenuous control and where any federal presence was feared more than welcomed.[3]

By the 1970s—five decades after the era described in Traven's fictional morality tale of distrust and lawlessness—those same mountainous regions were still spotted with impoverished communities where the rule of law had made little gain, and where all but a few scratched out a precarious existence. That part of Mexico's sierra was now known as the Golden Triangle and was still attracting dreamers in pursuit of their holy grail, but rather than gold, those latest adventurers came in search of a golden dream that was fed by plants—marijuana and amapola. A half century after Dobbs and his marginalized misfits began their quest for gold, the Sierra Madre Occidental was still a sanctuary for bandits and outlaws. There were also modern manifestations of Los Federales with badges—but, unlike the fictional tale, those lawmen were now partners with those misfits and desperados. The men with badges worked closely with that new generation of renegades in the quest for a modern El Dorado. The riches they found were shared by virtue of a silver platter colloquially known as *la charola*, and the potential payoff far exceeded any that might have been achieved with real gold dust.

■ ■ ■

By the late 1970s and early 1980s, badge-carrying members of Mexico's DFS were working directly with bandits and outlaws to routinize the production and distribution of marijuana and opium, backed by the power of their "charolas"—the silver platter of immunity authorized by Mexico's federal state (Aguayo 2001). In Sinaloa, one member of the DFS, Miguel Ángel Félix Gallardo, worked hand in glove with regional caciques and campesinos such as Pedro Avilés Pérez, Ernesto Fonseca Carrillo, and Rafael Caro Quintero to form a partnership that enriched them and their families. Elsewhere, police commanders such as Guillermo González Calderoni of the Policía Judicial Federal (PJF, Federal Judicial Police) used the power of his silver badge to smooth the way for powerful drug lords like Amado Carrillo Fuentes to extend the reach of those Sinaloa bandits to border cities such as Ciudad Juárez in Chihuahua State: González Calderoni eliminated a few recalcitrant stumbling blocks, including Pablo Acosta Villareal, who proved to be an unpredictable link and unwilling believer in the tradition of the traveling suitcase, and by killing him he cleared the way for other Sinaloans to consolidate a burgeoning narco enterprise.[4]

George Grayson describes the power of the badge—la charola—in his book *Mexico: Narco-Violence and a Failed State?* (2010). President Miguel Alemán Valdés had created the DFS in late 1946 as the federal agency responsible for gathering intelligence, but it soon expanded its original mandate and in fact became a criminal enterprise legitimated by the state and working for the state. Grayson writes:

> The DFS epitomized the worst in police forces. It recruited poorly educated individuals, mostly men aged 30 to 45; its roster included both civilians and military personnel; it demanded that operatives show loyalty to their individual sponsors, thus privileging personal commitments over institutional loyalties; it paid relatively low salaries and turned a blind eye when members supplemented their incomes by trafficking in drugs, extorting money, or selling protection to hapless businessmen and prostitutes. It also suffered high turnover as its agents, once having learned the ropes of criminality, gravitated to more lucrative endeavors—most often in the underworld. Moreover, the agency was a loose cannon whose activities often overlapped with those of the Federal Judicial Police, state and local forces, and the military— that is, it engaged in reckless intelligence gathering, crime promotion, the illegal investigation of lawful behavior, and political espionage. . . .
>
> The organization's identification card—known as the *charola* or collection plate—provided a license to abuse civil liberties, intimidate suspects, make false arrests, procure prostitutes, protect cronies, and extort money. In addition to paid employees, the director invited several hundred members of the armed services, civilians, and agents of other police units to serve as honorary DFS affiliates. They, too, could use their badges for legitimate or illegitimate purposes. (2010, 134)

That state-sanctioned corruption and misuse of the badge by agents working directly with drug capos operated with impunity until President Miguel de la Madrid Hurtado was finally forced to disband the DFS in 1986 when it directed the assassination of prominent Mexican journalist Manuel Buendía Tellezgirón. That well-known and influential journalist had discovered the links between DFS commanders, drug lords, and CIA operatives working together in the Iran-Contra Affair; he was murdered to prevent exposing

DFS involvement in the drug trade and more widely in illegal actions contravening U.S. Congressional directives (Bartley and Bartley 2015).

The Iran-Contra Affair has been widely described by investigative journalists and documented in Congressional hearings as a complicated and twisted geopolitical plot involving the illegal shipments of arms, the blatant diversion of Congressional funds, and the turning of a blind eye when the Guadalajara Cartel shipped crack cocaine unimpeded into the U.S. market. High-level operatives in Ronald Reagan's presidential team ignored Congressional directives and surreptitiously supplied powerful arms and training to rebels (the Contras) plotting to overthrow a leftist Sandinista government of Nicaragua. Congress had banned direct aid to those Contras, but operatives such as Oliver North hatched a plan that would divert arms approved for Iran and then used Mexico-based CIA personnel as his field operatives to carry it out: Mexico became staging ground for the Iran-Contra operation, and American CIA operatives worked closely with the Mexican DFS and with the emergent Guadalajara Cartel to establish a training camp for rebels and to provide them with military-grade weapons for an invasion. Sinaloan drug lord Miguel Ángel Caro Quintero provided personal land he owned in Veracruz State to serve as the Contra training camp; he also arranged for Guadalajara Cartel airplanes to deliver the diverted arms directly to the Contras in training in exchange for U.S. officials to look the other way when those same planes shipped cocaine north into Arkansas. Russell H. Bartley and Sylvia Erickson Bartley document how the discovery of this plot led to the killing of investigative reporter Manuel Buendía in 1984 when he was about to expose those covert and illegal arrangements. The Bartleys further argue that DEA agent Enrique Camarena was tortured and murdered shortly afterward when the American CIA and the Mexican DFS both realized that Camarena had learned about the shadowy complicity and was planning to expose the details (cf. Bartley and Bartley 2015; C. Bowden and Molloy 2014; Schou 2015; U.S. Congress 1988).

The disbanding of the DFS in 1986 did little to roll back the advance of narco trafficking or destroy connections between federal officials and increasingly powerful narco traffickers: drug trafficking had flourished and was firmly entrenched because agents of the state exploited institutional weaknesses and significant flaws in Mexico's dysfunctional judicial system, and they continued to operate with impunity from new positions in the new agencies that were created. Originally, the center of state-sanctioned drug trafficking was embedded within the DFS, but it shifted to other parts of the Procuraduría General de la República (PGR, Attorney General of the Republic) when the DFS was officially disbanded in 1986. By the mid 1980s, a drug economy and a culture of corruption had become firmly reestablished in institutional gaps that Edgardo Buscaglia (2013) describes as *los vacíos de poder*. State agents routinely flashed their badges to signal their untouchable status while their directors and supervisors distributed those shields to known criminals, and literally and symbolically passed the special silver platter to collect their share of the profits—usually one-third, according to the now customary rule of the traveling suitcase.

By the 1970s and 1980s, Traven's version of banditry and criminality had faded into distant memory, but la charola had become a powerful virtual tool used by new generations of state-sponsored bandits to institutionalize the drug trade, forge entrepreneurial criminal franchises, and distribute the money that bound everyone together in a covert netherworld. The elimination of the DFS in 1986 did not eliminate the symbolic and real power that came from flashing a DFS charola, and official state oversight of the drug business would continue operating for another two decades and ensure the success of the burgeoning drug trade. In fact, the stubborn permanence of narco trafficking in Mexico cannot be explained without acknowledging the role of corruption and the direct involvement of the state in providing protection and allowing the drug trade to operate in a covert netherworld that grew stronger and stronger with each Mexican presidential term.

Culture, Geography, and Gaps in Governance

Narco trafficking is routinely described by narratives that emphasize individual criminals, outrageous bandits, and mythologized outlaws rather than situating it within the powerful context that allows many people to thrive with impunity. Far too much attention is devoted to the criminal trajectories of individuals like El Chapo Guzmán Loera and other prominent kingpins, and far too little written about the socioeconomic and political corruption that sustains and empowers them to operate successfully and with impunity in a subterranean world. Bandits and outlaws flourish because they are tolerated by authorities and because the state fails in its obligation to control them, but the emergence of powerful narco gangs in Mexico is attributable to much more than a tolerant acceptance of banditry or the incompetent prosecution of organized criminals. The Mexican state has been directly and indirectly complicit in creating those powerful drug-trafficking organizations, and any strategy that focuses exclusive attention on criminal kingpins must be interpreted as a cynical attempt to create a myth that drug capos and jefes are responsible for everything that has gone wrong. That misguided attention deflects the public view away from the compelling evidence that collusion, corruption, and flaws in governance are actually responsible for creating those criminal groups and for allowing them to prosper.

Narco trafficking originated in a remote area of Mexico's northwest where generations of subsistence farmers harvested marijuana and opium poppies in relative obscurity until the winds of change brought them into contact with transnational crime and trafficking operations. The epicenter was in the Sierra Madre Occidental, where the borders of Sinaloa, Durango, and Chihuahua formed a Golden Triangle, and it was there that geopolitical forces and a perfect storm of circumstances would converge. Subsistence-level *marijuaneros* (marijuana farmers) and *gomeros* (amapola farmers) were eventually introduced to a broader world of commerce and trade that subsequently evolved into sophisticated institutionalized configurations far beyond the routines of subsistence production. The isolation of the northwest sierra provided the nurturing environment where sophisticated narco traffickers seized on the opportunity to exploit illicit trade routes that had emerged over a century. The remoteness of the area can be easily seen by the absence of major highways across the central plateau—especially in the northwest. Map 1 is reproduced from Richard Rhoda and Tony Burton's book *Geo-Mexico: The Geography and Dynamics of Modern Mexico* (2010), but the interested reader can also see the remoteness by opening Google Earth and searching for Badiguarato, Sinaloa, or other cities and towns mentioned in this chapter.

A rudimentary drug commerce had emerged within the bounds of the Golden Triangle amid recurring cycles of rebellion and disorder that predated Mexico's revolutionary war; those routines slowly evolved into an entrenched cultural tradition during the chaos that the revolution had unleashed. During the Porfiriato, rebels, bandits, and outlaws roamed freely across outlying territories and districts of northern Mexico, and some had even metastasized into dangerous gangs and formidable organizations doing the bidding of agitators, *hacendados*, regional caciques, and local mayors and governors.[5] A few even emerged to become the defenders of the downtrodden, abused, and

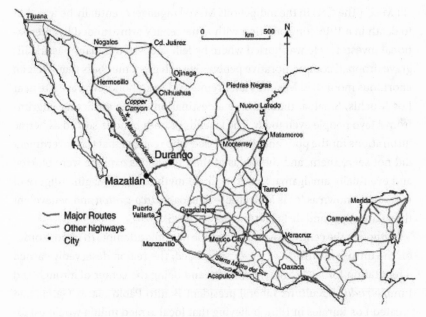

MAP 1 Major highways and roads in Mexico. From Richard Rhoda and Tony Burton, *Geo-Mexico: The Geography and Dynamics of Modern Mexico* (Ladysmith, B.C.: Sombrero Books, 2010), https://geo-mexico.com/wp-content/uploads/2013/10/Fig-17-3-Highways-color.ai_.jpg. Used with permission.

mistreated—the victims of state brutality and indifference—and exploited for their labor in foreign factories.

Two rebellious gangs were headed by the legendary figures Heraclio Bernal and Felipe Bachomo. Bernal, known as "El Rayo de Sinaloa" (The Sinaloan Thunderbolt), led rebellious miners aggrieved by Porifirio Díaz's land expropriations that favored international investors in the years before the revolution: in 1888 bounty hunters and three military units from Díaz's National Guard trapped and executed Bernal near the municipality of Cosalá on the Sinaloa-Durango border, and they ruthlessly hung his body from a tree and posted an edict forbidding burial.[6] Disruption did not end with his execution, and disorderly mobs and bandits continued to roam the sierra even as the revolution roiled across the central plains of Mexico. Outlaws and folk heroes such as Felipe Bachomo conducted raids on American-owned sugar factories, South Pacific Railway supply lines, and the American distilleries on the Sinaloa-Sonora border. Bachomo was popularly known as

"El Misi" (The Cat) in the indigenous Mayo language; eventually he was shot to death in a 1916 confrontation with a mercenary army funded by international investors. He was buried where he fell, and Mayo Indians passing his grave dropped commemorative pebbles in such great numbers that it left an enormous mound. El Misi was later reinterred to an honored grave site near Los Mochis, Sinaloa, that became a destination shrine attracting pilgrims from Mayo people even today. The legends of both bandits served as heroic inspirations for the poor and dispossessed who realized that the government did not serve them, and the fables of their rebellious exploits were blurred and eventually amalgamated into a single mythical and imagined figure of resistance known as Jesús Malverde—Sinaloa's *narco-santón* and benevolent thief (Creechan and de la Herrán Garcia 2005).

Although the central government made periodic attempts to impose order on the unruly northwest, it never succeeded; the region deservedly earned a reputation for lawlessness, rebellion, and being the center of a rough and tumble *rudo* subculture. Liberal president Benito Pablo Juaréz García had created Los Rurales in 1861, believing that local armed militia would establish order, and later the dictator Porfirio Díaz created his own version and authorized it to use any means necessary to rein in bandits, criminals, rebels, and malcontents. Los Rurales deservedly acquired a black reputation for brutality when its members routinely applied la ley fuga.

During the 1920s and 1930s, wide swaths of the Golden Triangle were controlled by local bosses and henchmen who were de facto agents of authority and control. By default, and through disinterest from federal authorities, power had accrued to numerous regional land barons and caciques, and that authority would never be fully recouped by later versions of the central or even local state. When revolutionary battles ended, instead of eradicating the bandits and armed groups who remained in the northwest, the federal and many state authorities opted to negotiate dubious accommodations with any armed group that was a perceived threat to state legitimacy.[7] In effect, that strategy was a version of *don't ask, don't tell* accommodation with marijuana and opium farmers who had by then developed a rudimentary and illegal commerce that was regularly shipping golden harvests northward and across the border into an American market (Astorga Almanza 2003).

It is routinely believed that Mexico's drug trade emerged from the Golden Triangle and frequently said that Sinaloa and Culiacán were the cradle of narco traffic, but this should not be interpreted to mean that full-blown criminal mafias emerged from this region to dominate all organized crime in Mexico. Rather, those ideas describe the subterranean tradition of narco trafficking that evolved organically, gradually, and by chance within a rugged, lawless, and remote area of the Sierra Madre Occidental where the state was unable or unwilling to impose a legitimate social order. In the absence of stable governance and alternate economic opportunities, marijuana and amapola production became the focal point of the economy and community life and what Mexicans refer to as the tejido social (social bond). The isolation of the region left few options for inhabitants short of leaving or participating in that nascent drug economy—and generations of campesinos had long been sowing marijuana and opium poppies. Everyone was involved in one way or another within a routinized division of labor centered on a single economy—including children who were regularly excused from school to work the harvests (Valdez Cárdenas 2011), and to regional politicians who looked the other way and recognized how things really worked.

The full embodiment of an organized drug enterprise would not occur until decades later. The history of the gradual emergence and transformation of Mexico's drug organizations will be described later in this chapter and in chapter 6, but the following section explores how Mexican narco trafficking emerged from such humble beginnings in an impoverished area to eventually emerge as a major player on the global stage. The transformation of the early Mexican drug trade into criminal organizations and cartels spanned several decades and only became possible because of accommodations reached with corrupt government officials and agencies to create a covert netherworld—originally at a local level, and eventually at the national and transnational stage.

The Stages of Narco Trafficking

Functionally and organizationally, it is a very complicated process to move drugs from production to market while simultaneously managing the economic transactions involved. The movement of drugs on a large scale requires the foresight of advance planning and a large labor force—all of which must operate in shadows and in secrecy because the state has declared those activities illegal. The model described here represents a generalized and ideal representation of the components and processes trajectory of the drug trade.

Figure 3 shows an ideal representation of a drug enterprise and conceives of it as consisting of nine distinct institutional activities.[8] The first four stages of this model describe the narco-trafficking traditions that had evolved and were fixed in place in Mexico's Golden Triangle prior to 1975. Marijuana and amapola poppies had been grown in that region for at least one hundred years—and both commodities had been selectively modified into marketable versions for distribution to markets outside the region. The isolation and the fertile environment in the sierra range allowed the production of a potent marijuana and significant quantities of opium resin that could be transformed into brown heroin: both were produced in significant numbers in a region where there was low risk of detection or threat of crop eradication. For decades, scattered fields, small and large, were set aside for marijuana and poppy production in that remote terrain to the east of the Sea of Cortés. The production of the two main commercial products— marijuana and heroin—fostered drug traditions that would permanently remain at the root of the narco-trafficking enterprise in Mexico, but other illegal substances would later be introduced and generate a diversification and requirement for specialized skills and a much more complicated division of labor. Andean cocaine became the new commodity moving through

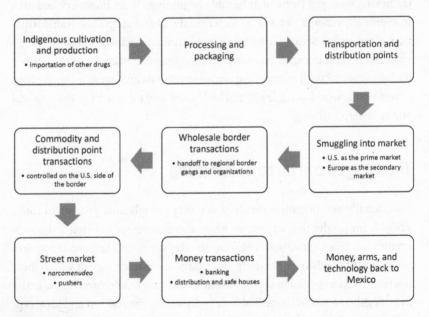

FIGURE 3 The drug trade process: production to market. Graphic created by author.

Mexican intermediaries at significant levels beginning in the mid-1970s, and synthetic drugs would later be added to the mix by Milenio Cartel leaders Armando Valencia Cornelio and Óscar Orlando Nava Valencia to the south in Michoacán shortly after cocaine appeared.

The Golden Triangle was home turf to what has become recognized as the first generation of large-volume drug smugglers like Pedro "El León de la Sierra" Avilés Pérez. He was an expert at moving marijuana and heroin through mountain paths that snaked through the Sierra Madre Occidental to border distribution points: Avilés was a skilled expeditor and routinized the delivery of drugs to end-point destinations in Chihuahua and Durango where they were turned over—sold—to border gangs and local drug dealers such as Ignacia "La Nacha" González on the Mexican side of the Rio Bravo (Linares 2010; Lupsha 1991). By the 1960s, Avilés and several partners had developed a few interspersed routes moving northward through Sonora and westward to Baja California, where resident gangs moved it into Arizona and California markets. The marijuana and opium producers of the sierra also developed partnerships with ambitious, large-scale smugglers like Pablo "El Zorro" Acosta Villareal, who was famously creative and entrepreneurial in moving tons of marijuana directly into the U.S. market from a home base in Ojinaga, Chihuahua, using a fleet of pickup trucks with modified gas tanks (cf. Poppa 1990, 1998).

By the end of the 1970s and the beginning of the 1980s, Mexico's Golden Triangle had established a cultural tradition and developed a network for cultivating drugs—specifically marijuana and heroin. Parallel networks of supportive criminality had emerged based on individual skill and expertise in delivering contraband to borderlands for direct transfer to regional gangs and criminals who sold directly to consumers. Those interactions grew more routinized, structured, and formalized through the 1970s, and they had organically emerged from long-established and customary routines and tradition: overall, that first business model of the drug trade could never be characterized as a hierarchically structured institutional enterprise, nor viewed as what would later be called a *holding company* backed by a shadowy group of investors.[9] It was more akin to a trade and barter arrangement, although the scale of money far exceeded that common to most informal economies or traditional trading arrangements. Furthermore, the movement of drugs and the success of the model were cemented by a mutual understanding and rooted in shared agreements sealed by handshakes and by family connections: money exchanged hands at every point of the process until commodities reached the frontier, where little or no control remained in the hands of Mexican nationals when the product moved across the line into the U.S. market.

Before cocaine was introduced into the equation, the first four stages of this idealized nine-step model of a drug business had emerged from a century-long tradition of producing and moving marijuana in the Golden Triangle, and it operated as an efficient and effective delivery model because it was rooted in common needs, historical tradition, understanding, and friendship. By 1975 the introduction of cocaine had yet to happen on a large scale, and the formalization into a fully developed drug enterprise had not occurred, but a new generation of narco traffickers such as Miguel Ángel Félix Gallardo, Ernesto Fonseca Carrillo, and Rafael Caro Quintero would soon push beyond those initial stages. The drug enterprise expanded from a simple informal model of production and delivery from within a regional base after cocaine was introduced into the traditional business: the efficient transport of drugs originating in the Andes required adaptation and the creation of more sophisticated delivery models to import it in bulk into Mexico, warehouse and package it for distribution, and develop trustworthy and safe distribution networks connecting more and more points in the south and central Mexico in far more extensive and organized ways than had been already established.

A formal way of describing those changes is to say that the functional prerequisites of an institutionalized organization were not in place by the mid-1970s, but traditional routines and practices had developed to the point that they could be used as the core for an extensive formalization and expansion of the drug trade. The Golden Triangle had been home to a routinized tradition of drug production and had established an organized distribution network that had been successful for at least three decades. There were even rudimentary security forces in place, but those relied on local thugs and ruffians to safeguard the production and the shipping routes, and they were relatively unsophisticated, poorly trained, and inadequately armed compared to the full-scale security teams that would eventually be formed to oversee the production and distribution of product, minimize loss during transportation, serve as the strong-arm agents of expansionist activities, mete out punishment, and counteract threats and challenges from competitors or elements of the state. Until Félix Gallardo, Fonseca Carrillo, Caro Quintero, and others formalized links to legitimate institutions and agencies, all relationships with authorities and competitors remained capricious and unpredictable and were routinely influenced by regional politics and quarrels.[10] It took many years before Mexican narco traffickers entered into sophisticated contractual arrangements with government and with businessmen, accountants, and lawyers to manage the funds for laundering and to oversee the expansion and diversification into new businesses. When it finally happened and a covert netherworld was stabilized, the Mexican cartels were ready to expand internationally and competed with the most efficient and powerful mafias of the world.

Arguably, the most important element in the formalization of organized drug trafficking in Mexico was the routinization of drug connections with corrupt officials—especially power brokers based in the DFS. In the beginning, those links were asymmetrical, and the direct initiative and management spread downward from state officials to the local level: institutionalized corruption within the DFS, and later within the PGR and CISEN, were recognized and denounced by journalists and investigators who specifically described normative expectations for purchasing plazas according to pro-rated fees based on potential profitability (Grayson 2008a, 2010). Once the links of corruption were formalized and the covert relations became routinized, the DFS patronage and direction linked organized crime leaders to dedicated protectors (*madrinas*) and highly placed collaborators within the state apparatus. Those contacts in the covert netherworld provided the capos and the business the necessary immunity and protection that promoted drug trafficking in the shadows.

Organizational links with legitimate authority have long been known to exist but were always described in quiet whispers and spoken of in rumors until the powerful hegemony of the PRI finally unraveled over the last few years of the twentieth century.[11] Luis Astorga has described that erosion of the enduring political arrangements and the transformation in governance that eventually exposed those essential political ties to the drug trade. Investigations and reports such as his have gradually made those perverse connections within the covert netherworld visible. With the collapse of the PRI hegemony in 2000, there came a freedom for observers to describe how Mexico's drug organizations had achieved their power through the corrupt officials who imposed an institutional efficiency and helped establish the criminal organizations as irrepressible and virtually unstoppable forces (Astorga 2002a; Astorga and Shirk 2010). Two decades afterward, the public trials in the United States of drug bosses like Joaquín Guzmán Loera, Jesús Reynaldo Zambada García, and Vicente Zambada Niebla would provide confirmatory documented evidence that those ties had been initially forged into formal patterns in the late 1980s and early 1990s.

The Cradle of Narco Traffic

Sinaloa is known for its agricultural diversity but is arguably more infamous for its sinister history. It is la cuna del narcotráfico (the cradle of drug traffic)—the birthplace, the home turf, and even today the sentimental homeland for many leaders of the most powerful drug organizations operating in Mexico.

Sinaloa is an agricultural oasis bounded on the west by the Sea of Cortés, and it shares borders in the north with Sonora and Chihuahua and to the east with Durango in the remote Sierra Madre Occidental. It has eleven rivers, several dams, and an abundance of mountain runoffs that feed a sophisticated irrigation system stretching across its entire littoral plain. Sinaloa's agricultural economy is based on the exportation of produce within Mexico and internationally to the United States and Canada: tomatoes are Sinaloa's iconic export, but an impressive diversification policy led to the successful production of other commodities, such as white corn for biofuel production, eggplant, broccoli, and even lychee.[12] Sinaloa's largest cities—Mazatlán, Culiacán, and Los Mochis—sit on constricted and flat coastlands laying west of the Sierra Madre Occidental: the narrowest stretches between the foothills and ocean are the stretches just north of Culiacán, where mountain runoffs feed a network of mangroves that drain into many concealed coves.

The topography of the state is such that there are relatively few suitable places to build major highways, and the inland roads leading eastward are quickly blocked by ranges of hills, countless valleys, and rivers that drain to the Sea of Cortés.[13] Highways leading eastward into the sierra quickly taper into dirt roads and dead ends, and until the 2013 opening of the Durango-Mazatlán Super Highway, the simplest land route to Durango required travel south before turning east to Cuernavaca for the highways leading north—a trip of six to eight hours under ideal conditions (Rhoda and Burton 2010).

In the mid-1990s, NAFTA injected a major boost into Sinaloa's economy when commercial traffic from central and southern Mexico was forced to use Highway 15 as the only viable Pacific and Western shipping route west of Mexico's great central plateau. Culiacán became the most important international logistical access point for all commercial traffic serving the United

States through a terminus border port at Ambos Nogales on the Sonora-Arizona border. From there, the U.S. interstate highway system was accessed for all products and produce shipping north to Tucson and Phoenix, Arizona. In no short order, it was that single shipping route through Sinaloa that fed all interstate routes connecting Los Angeles to New Orleans via U.S. Interstate 10, or north toward the Pacific Northwest via U.S. Interstate 5.

Sinaloa had been the epicenter for opium and marijuana production for 150 years or longer. In the 1950s, its people were pejoratively demeaned as gomeros—a slur referring to the seasonal harvesters required for the amapola and resinous poppy gum production just northeast of Culiacán. The municipality of Culiacán also earned a reputation for violence even while it simultaneously emerged as a moneyed and civilized urban center that hosted a respected university and cultural enterprises such as its full-scale symphony orchestra. Drug signifiers came to be the master status assigned to everyone who came from Sinaloa and most of its cities—whether or not they had any connection to the drug trade. In the 1960s, newspapers and journalists described Culiacán as a *little Chicago* because of violence, and because hoodlums and drug runners had established themselves in rough and tumble neighborhoods like Tierra Blanca. Because many of those men and women had migrated from the sierra and dressed in a unique rural style, the streets and bars of Culiacán were regularly described as swarming with gangsters in huaraches. By the 1960s and 1970s, the region and specifically the city had attained an international notoriety—to the point that Sinaloa and Culiacan were specifically targeted by a major initiative in the War on Drugs unleashed by President Nixon. In 1975 a military intervention code-named Operation Condor deployed Mexican army troops and DEA and FBI operatives to the sierra region and environs of Badiguarato to eradicate crops and evict the major marijuana and opium producers from the Golden Triangle.[14]

Marijuana and opium production had become keystone commodities in that burgeoning drug economy, and several *Sinaloense* clans and families had cemented their place at the heart of that business.[15] Drug production was relatively easy because of the near-perfect microclimate and the isolated topography within that Golden Triangle where Sinaloa, Durango, and Chihuahua converged. To the east, only unpaved and unmarked roads meandered through mountain passes to neighboring states. Everywhere, numerous patches of small fertile fields lay interspersed and hidden by dense forestation that provided camouflage for the fields and for the processing centers. To the west and south sat the emerging financial and money-laundering center, the state capital, Culiacán; cash that had accumulated from a half century of marijuana and heroin production had been heavily invested in the state capital and provided the city with an infrastructure and public institutions that were rarely found in provincial cities. But in the banks and financial institutions, there was little evidence such wealth existed. Much of the wealth circulated in a cash-only economy—and even the largest purchases of luxury trucks and autos, homes, and businesses were conducted with bundles of cash—often, U.S. dollars. Further westward, long stretches of uninhabited beaches and clusters of mangrove swamps provided opportunistic sites for launching fast boats and for loading and unloading deep-sea fishing vessels common to the Sea of Cortés.

Geography alone does not explain the emergence and enduring impact of Sinaloa in the modern drug trade: the region had attracted many natural and creative entrepreneurs who exploited the opportunities that came their way. Many took advantage and seized the opportunity to become very rich even as that demanded living on the edge of the law. Their individual success must also be attributed to the close-knit connections and unspoken and shared understandings with neighbors and authorities that provided them the freedom to flourish and yet remain invisible outside Sinaloa. As others have noted, drug organizations are especially successful when their subterranean structure is close-knit, interconnected, and invisible—and that was certainly the fertile and prevailing environment in Sinaloa.

Smuggling Routes

Smuggling routes had been established over a century of experience and perfected by Sinaloans such as Pedro Avilés Pérez, who was also known as El León de la Sierra for his success in moving products efficiently and secretly across narrow and hidden paths. Three main routes led outward from the drug-producing regions of the Golden Triangle. One route snaked along mountain paths and winding valleys northward until finally emerging on the east side of the Sierra Madre in Chihuahua above Chihuahua City, Ojinaga, and Ciudad Juárez. The municipality of Angostura at the northern edge of Culiacán became the central transfer point for two important trafficking routes—one that moved by land, and another using water routes.[16] Angostura is geographically situated at a strategic stretch of the Pacific Coast where the Sierra Madre descends steeply toward the Sea of Cortés, and the municipality sits astride the only major highway (Federal Highway 15) that moves north to south along Mexico's Pacific coastal plain. This route became the important juncture for the transfer of drugs from the sierra in bulk to vehicles for transport north; it also became the route for dollars and arms that traveled south through Sonora State and back into Sinaloa.

Additionally, Angostura was the staging point for the water routes across the Sea of Cortés to the Baja Peninsula and north to the Arizona border. A myriad of coastal bays and inlets in mangrove swamps created countless hidden bays and covert landings for fast boats (*pangas*), deep-sea fishing vessels, and even fiberglass submarines. Many years later, the bays and inlets west of Angostura became the nexus for shipping drugs north toward Puerto Peñasco in Sonora, for offloading synthetic drug precursors from the Orient, and for stockpiling of weapons such as the AK-47's and AR-15's coming from China. Those bays and inlets became strategically crucial many years later when U.S. Homeland Security measures and the construction of border walls tightened inland border points stretching from Baja California, Sonora, New Mexico, and Texas and made the water routes the best option to ship commodities to the remote areas west of Nogales and Naco, Sonora.

Sinaloa also gave birth to a narco society and a *narcocultura* where unwritten norms and codes defined all relationships, and it was also where several feuds and disputes among Sinaloan clans originated to still play out in modern bursts of vengeance that make the Hatfield-McCoy feuds seem tame in comparison. The narco-culture that emerged in Sinaloa gradually spread outward in a narcocultura diaspora, but until that happened, the visible signs and tradition of narco trafficking remained largely invisible to the outside world for decades. Sinaloa's centrality in the North American drug trade operated in the shadows and went largely unnoticed, except when missteps and feuds brought unwanted attention and enmeshed its members in bloody turf battles that could not be ignored.

An Overview of Drug History in Mexico

The remaining pages of this chapter describe a broad and selective history of the drug trade and trace key events and moments in its long trajectory. That history is divided into three eras—*early origins* up until about 1960, *formative years* between 1969 and 1999, and a *modern era* from 2000 until the end of 2018. Many of the incidents described here are increasingly disentangled and gaps are being filled in as new archival material is released from government files and as more and more journalists and scholars have devoted more time and attention to uncovering details.

Although this chapter and the following one make references to specific individual criminals, the emphasis is on the emergence of criminal organizations and their symbiotic relationship with legitimate power to create the covert netherworld of narco traffic and organized crime. This chapter also focuses on events that are relatively well known and that drew widespread attention from the international press. It does not claim to be comprehensive, and it cites many important events only in passing in order to provide a context.[17]

The first two periods of narco-history described here are relatively uncontroversial because there is a rich literature to draw upon: visible leaders were relatively few in number, and their connections to state officials and agencies had been unmasked long ago. But even so, there remains controversy, and some incidents from that golden era of narco trafficking remain enshrouded by mythology and confused by fable. Those first two periods will be described in this chapter, and the third period is given its own separate chapter (5). That most recent history is the most difficult to concisely summarize because there were several major shifts in narco trafficking and disruptions with cartels after the millennium: those changes resulted in a proliferation of criminal organizations and an exponential increase in the number of criminal traffickers.

Period 1: Origins of Narco Trafficking in Mexico

As has been long noted, Sinaloa State is widely acknowledged as la cuna, or the birthplace, of narco trafficking in Mexico. Much of the history of the drug trade remains obscured in myth, but no one disputes that narco-traffic roots lay somewhere in the Sierra Madre mountains above Sinaloa's Pacific coastal plains. Sinaloa remains legendary for producing sinsemilla marijuana and brown heroin from amapola, and its natives have earned a deserved, if exaggerated, reputation for efficiency in delivering drugs to American consumers through mountainous trails and over water routes accessible from its coastal plain. The existence and seclusion of those drug corridors, as well as a long

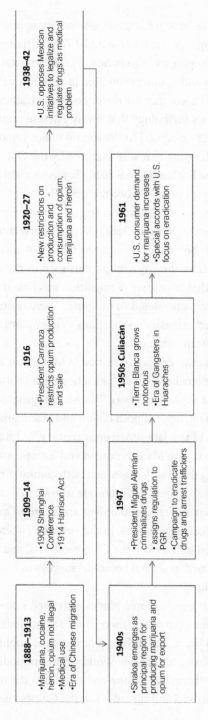

1888–1913
- Marijuana, cocaine, heroin, opium not illegal
- Medical use
- Era of Chinese migration

1909–14
- 1909 Shanghai Conference
- 1914 Harrison Act

1916
- President Carranza restricts opium production and sale

1920–27
- New restrictions on production and consumption of opium, marijuana and heroin

1938–42
- U.S. opposes Mexican initiatives to legalize and regulate drugs as medical problem

1940s
- Sinaloa emerges as principal region for producing marijuana and opium for export

1947
- President Miguel Alemán criminalizes drugs
- assigns regulation to PGR
- Campaign to eradicate drugs and arrest traffickers

1950s Culiacán
- Tierra Blanca grows notorious
- Era of Gangsters in Huaraches

1961
- U.S. consumer demand for marijuana increases
- Special accords with U.S. focus on eradication

FIGURE 4 The shift from deregulation to criminalization, 1888–1961. Graphic created by author.

tradition of smuggling, brought Sinaloenses even more power when cocaine was added to the drug repertoire in the mid-1970s. Although the drug trade would grow more complex and diversified, its fundamental roots are traced directly to marijuana and opium production in remote areas above the capital city, Culiacán. It is there that the history of narco trafficking begins.

There is a tenacious mythology that it was Chinese migrants who introduced opium poppies (amapola) to the mountainous regions of northwest Mexico during the diaspora that was triggered by the Opium Wars and the Boxer Rebellion in the Far East (Lovell 2014). Evidence contradicts this popularized version of history in at least two respects. First, the Chinese migration to the Pacific Northwest of Mexico was triggered more by economic hardship than by the direct flight from Opium Wars or persecution for excessive opium habits in their homeland. In fact, the Opium Wars occurred four or five decades earlier than the large migrations seen at the end of the nineteenth century, and that later wave of migration was linked to uprisings and conditions only marginally related to drug use. There is little evidence that Chinese migrants had extensive connections to the opium trade when they arrived on the American continent.

But more importantly, opium had existed in Mexico for at least 350 years before the origin was attributed to the late nineteenth-century influx of Chinese migrants. Most probably, it was Spanish conquistadores and Portuguese explorers who introduced both opium and marijuana long before the Chinese migrations of the late nineteenth century.[18] Opiates and hashish were ubiquitous across the Mediterranean and Europe and coastal North Africa regions during the Middle Ages, and both commodities were familiar to those Spanish and Portuguese adventurers who arrived in the New World seeking fortune. Many references to opium are found in archives that preserve their personal correspondence, in the *virreinal* (viceregal or colonial-era) reports produced long before the Chinese arrival, and were even more systematically described in several botanical surveys of flora and fauna carried out in New Spain.

Even though both psychotropic plants were well known and used for medicinal and religious purposes, there is no acknowledged authoritative study that describes the actual diffusion of amapola poppies or marijuana plants throughout Mexico or the New World: both commodities were known to exist and flourish there, but no one had examined the trajectory of how they had originally arrived and spread—and the Chinese newcomers would be the ones blamed for introducing them in the absence of any archive that contradicted folklore.

Cannabis may have been inadvertently seeded during several initiatives to propagate hemp for economic gain. Cannabis is a complex genus and a diverse species, but all the botanical distinctions and variants were unknown until long after viceregal administrations had left New Spain: it would be much later that botanists categorized and recognized two distinctive sub-species of cannabis—one primarily a fibrous product with mild psychotropic characteristics, and an alternate version with more marked psychotropic attributes. At one point, virreinal administrators in New Spain mandated the propagation of a cannabis species to create a local economy based on textile and rope production, and in encouraging that enterprise, they may have coincidently and unintentionally seeded the psychotropic version. In 1545 a Spaniard named Pedro Quadrado was the first European to deliber-ately propagate cannabis seed in Mexico after he was granted an *encomienda* that would grow *cáñamo* (the Castilian name for the hemp version of can-nabis) for the commercial production of textiles. Quadrado was unsuccess-ful, but New Spain's administrators encouraged several others to establish hemp plantations elsewhere with the hope that the crop would take root. A fiber hemp industry would belatedly flourish two centuries afterward in the Yucatán, long after those seventeenth-century plantations had faded into obscurity and failure—with the possible exception that it made an unin-tended contribution to seed diversification in Mexico's biosphere. It's prob-able that cannabis seeds distributed during those failed hemp initiatives included sufficient quantities of psychotropic seeds to germinate and even-tually emerge as an indigenous plant in the Americas. Alternatively, any one of Mexico's diverse microclimates may have triggered a natural evolutionary process wherein fiber-producing hemp species transmuted over generations into species with more intense psychotropic qualities.

By the 1770s, cannabis had already been cataloged in several indigenous communities to the point that observers had also noticed its common use in medical-religious practices to foment visions. A psychotropic species of marijuana was also recorded across a wide swath of Mexico, from Oaxaca in the south to Sonora in the northwest. Some early chroniclers even raised warnings about how cannabis was being used, but their admonitions never led to restrictions on marijuana or opiate use. By the 1840s, marijuana had been routinely identified in the scientific surveys of flora and fauna known as *farmacopeas*, and it had become ubiquitous to the extent that it was regulated to a degree by local agencies known as *protomedicatos*—the precursors of regional health boards.[19] Those regional regulatory bodies were overseen by physicians and doctors who were charged with monitoring the use of all medicinal remedies.[20] Early regulations required nothing more than the documentation of use, and they stopped short of introducing rules that would enforce limits on production or restrict access; marijuana and other opiates remained widely accessible from local pharmacies throughout Mexico as long as local pharmacists followed rules of record keeping established by regional medical tribunals and agencies.

Even though marijuana and opium were widely considered to be indigenous crops by the 1850s, a nascent stigmatization of both was already underway—especially in the case of marijuana. Sensationalistic Mexican newspapers—known as the yellow press—published anecdotal reports linking marijuana to extreme violence and insanity (see Campos 2014). During the last two decades of the nineteenth century, Mexico's elite classes were universally targeting any substance that putatively poisoned the race and arguably impeded Mexico's advance toward modernity. Marijuana was targeted as the most harmful and the most dangerous among them, and its widespread popularity was universally denounced as a harmful vice preferred by marginalized men such as prisoners, *indios*, and soldiers.[21]

Before 1880, the western United States had routinely attracted more Chinese migrants than did Mexico. But when the United States passed the Chinese Exclusion Act in 1882, Mexico emerged as the optional fallback destination—both for those expelled from the USA and for the latest arrivals from China. Indeed, migration to Mexico's northwest was actively encouraged by President Porfirio Díaz as part of a broad strategy to establish a labor pool that could be exploited by international investors looking to build factories and construct railways in Mexico's underdeveloped northwest. That investment in Mexico was promoted as representing an ideal jumping point for access to the southwestern United States, which at that point in time had few connections to the Eastern Seaboard. Other than Chinese refugees and migrants, very few took advantage of Díaz's invitation to populate the arid and hot but fertile lands lying along Mexico's northwest coastal plain.

In the final few years before the Mexican Revolution, the Chinese population swelled in the Mexican states of Baja California, Sonora, Sinaloa, and Chihuahua, and major concentrations of migrants had settled in several cities, such as Tijuana and Mexicali in Baja California, Hermosillo in Sonora, Ciudad Juárez in Chihuahua, and as far inland as Torreón and Mexico City. Those migrants fell into two broad categories—a relatively wealthy merchant class and an impoverished labor class. The laboring class also differed from their merchant brethren in at least two important respects: first, it was disproportionately composed of single detached men, and in significant numbers it was they who frequented opium dens; second, the more stable merchant class was actually efficacious in establishing businesses that would thrive until approximately 1930, when an embryonic anti-Chinese backlash led to the expulsion of thousands of Chinese foreigners back to Baja California and to border cities such as Mexicali. Prior to that nativist backlash, many among a Chinese merchant class had successfully integrated into communities of Mexico's northwest and made important contributions to commerce and education (Schiavone Camacho 2012), even as the Chinese laboring class remained precariously vulnerable to the vagaries of economic fluctuation and lived amid a diminished social tolerance. The history of Chinese migrant labor is more complicated than that of the merchant class, and it is they who became the focal point for blame and the primary market for a nascent drug trade.

The archival record is clear—it was not the Chinese who introduced opium and marijuana plants to Mexico. Nevertheless, Chinese migrants were targeted as the consumers who would become the indispensable market for the drug trade. Unfortunately, that laboring class would pay the cost in more ways than one. Marginalized migrant laborers were viciously targeted by an anti-Chinese sentiment that not only resented them for allegedly stealing jobs but also came to stigmatize them for having "endangered public health and drugged and poisoned people with toxic, alien substances" (Schiavone Camacho 2012, 49).[22]

The Chinese presence became important for the establishment of the drug trade in at least three broad ways during a period of intense anti-Chinese sentiment that assailed Mexico's Pacific Northwest at the beginning of the twentieth century.

First, the presence of a significant number of opium users among migrant laborers represented a market opportunity for the growers. Although reliable profiles of drug addicts from that era do not exist, many anecdotal newspaper accounts singled out those Chinese laborers as primary opiate consumers. Undoubtedly, they were also viewed as consumers by enterprising ranchers and politicians who were eager to cultivate amapola to meet that growing market demand. But they may not have been the only group targeted by growers, and there is documentation backed up by folklore that a few producers were actually farsighted entrepreneurs who hoped to establish a legitimate exportation of drugs to the United States—primarily morphine and heroin—to compete with the more far-flung Turkish sources of opium.

According to several newspaper reports, new poppy fields were initially propagated in Baja California due to the high concentration of Chinese workers on the western side of the Sea of Cortés, but production gradually shifted to regions sitting above the municipality of Angostura in Sinaloa, where the microclimate proved to be more favorable and conducive to amapola propagation. Furthermore, Sinaloa's mountainous regions provided important invisibility during a period of unpredictability when it was difficult to ascertain how governments would respond. Local politicians in those remote areas were less likely to hinder production, and in fact, anecdotal evidence suggests that it was local politicians who proved keenest to participate in the establishment of the fields and who were most anxious to establish a foothold in a potentially lucrative trade.

A second way that the Chinese presence affected the drug trade was that the concentration of migrants in the Chinatowns of border cities like Mexicali, Tijuana, and Ciudad Juárez nurtured disorganized social environments where Chinese migrants would become both victim and victimizer, and where everything happened under the attentive watch of corrupt politicians. By 1915 migrants expelled from Sonora and Sinaloa during anti-Chinese threats sought refuge in the same cities where America's banished refugees had converged a few years earlier—and old and new arrivals became easy targets for established Chinese gangs and many corrupt politicians eager to exploit their marginality and vulnerability.[23] To cite one well-documented historical example, the governor of Baja California, Esteban Cantú, demanded a head tax in return for the right to settle in Mexicali. Cantú's tax did not guarantee migrant safety since he had previously decided and apportioned which gangs could operate opium dens and distribute narcotics (Werne 1980), and he personally collected a significant share of profit from wide-ranging illegal activities such as commodity smuggling, human trafficking, and extortion (Werne 1980). Those burgeoning Chinese gangs became powerful forces due to the fact that they had institutionalized a symbiotic collaboration with corrupt politicians for mutual benefit. The synergetic link between criminals and politicians would establish a precedent and serve as a model followed by other Mexican criminal organizations that would emerge during the twentieth century. Coincidentally, those Chinese gangsters were the first to build tunnels to move contraband in and out of the Mexicali area—long before El Chapo Guzmán would gain notoriety as a skilled lord of the tunnels.[24]

A third reason that Chinese migrants are important in the history of narco trafficking is that they represent the first of many convenient scapegoats to become targeted by antidrug entrepreneurs and official policies while simultaneously turning a blind eye to the government corruption that fostered the necessary conditions that made drug sales profitable for an elite few. The migrants were symbolically demonized as folk devils, almost effortlessly because of a prevailing eugenicist rhetoric that made them low-hanging fruit for politicians who could simultaneously use them to deflect attention away from their own misdeeds (Cohen 1972; Cohen and Young 1981). The highlighting of the immigrants' putative vices and a rabidly xenophobic emphasis on their outsider status were convenient and distractive decoys used by corrupt Mexican politicians as well as the incipient drug dealers who were left free to operate in the shadows and beyond reproach of any impropriety linked to marijuana and opium sales.

Narcotic use was not an exclusive habit confined to the Chinese; Mexico's Pacific Northwest was populated by all manner of misfits—but smoking opium was consistently identified and stigmatized in newspaper reports as a Chinese vice.[25] All the while, it remained legal to purchase both marijuana and opium in pharmacies as long as the sale was recorded.

Until Mexico's participation in the Shanghai conference in 1909, marijuana and opium were both viewed through a lens of benign tolerance by all levels of government even though newspapers had been inciting fear about marijuana and other drugs with sensationalist stories that had little basis in fact. Marijuana was the principal target, and Isaac Campos (2014) documents how the mainstream and yellow press fed the public perception by exaggerating two important misconceptions: one conflated marijuana with other distinctly different psychotropic substances, and another promulgated the myth that marijuana inevitably resulted in madness (see also Cambell 2009).

Prodded by his team of científicos, Porfirio Díaz had authorized Mexican delegates to participate in the international 1909 Shanghai opium conference. His successor, Francisco Madero González, also sent a delegate to Hague for the International Opium Convention, which had promulgated the first international drug treaty in 1912, but the Mexican Revolution had pushed aside all matters of internal drug regulation into the background while politicians dealt with the more pressing matters of governance and stabilization. Furthermore, a fundamental disagreement about the scope and power of a federalist state delayed the introduction of national legislation until President Venustiano Carranza De La Garza was finally successful in empowering a relatively strong centralist government in 1916, after he had managed to convene delegates in Santiago de Querétaro to revise the Mexican Constitution of 1857 to institutionalize that mandate.

The first national legislation on drug control emerged from that Querétaro conference after Brigadier General José Maria Rodriguez, the president's personal physician, requested that more powers be delegated to a national Department of Public Sanitation in order to raise the living standards of the "Mexican race." He argued that such a council could effectively campaign against alcoholism "and the sale of substances that poison individuals and degenerate the race" (Campos 2014, 198). His measure passed with overwhelming support and delegated tremendous power to the Sanitary Council for all matters regulating alcohol, marijuana, cocaine, and opiates. The law required support and input from Mexico's national Apothecary Commission, and that was eventually provided in January 1920.

Campos cites a speech by the Sanitary Council president, Fernando Breña Alvírez, that led to a successful vote in favor of his proposal; his speech is quoted at length here since it contains the specific parameters of drug regulation that would govern Mexico for the next two decades.

> It is indispensable that the dispositions dictated to correct this sickness of the race (degeneration), stemming principally from alcoholism and the poisoning by medicinal substances like opium, morphine, ether, cocaine, and marihuana etc., be dictated with such energy that they may offset in an effective and efficacious manner, the abuse from the commerce in these substances that are so poisonous to health, that today have occasioned disasters of such a nature, that they have multiplied mortality to levels amongst the highest in the world. (2014, 199–200)

This measure mandated that drug wholesalers obtain permission to import opiates or cocaine, and it further proscribed that the drugs would be available only from doctors and licensed medical distributors (Campos 2014, 199).

Campos also reports that Mexico's científicos had participated in international conferences calling for the regulation of drugs, but there would be no formal legislative action within Mexico until President Plutarco Elías Calles assumed office. He had been Sonora governor, and was a vocal *antichinista*; it was under his direction that Mexico finally ratified the International Opium Convention, which had been formally agreed to in principle back in 1912. A significant majority of convention precepts had already been incorporated within the 1920 public sanitation guidelines—and in some ways, Mexico had moved even further toward restrictive regulation than other countries when it introduced marijuana prohibitions that predated those international conventions by five years.

It has been commonly argued that, in 1938, Harry Anslinger and the Federal Bureau of Narcotics (FBN) railed against Mexico's policy that made addiction a health issue, and that he had intimidated Mexico into transferring the governance of marijuana and opiates to the criminal code. This assessment that Mexico had caved in face of the ham-fisted American pressure is simplistic and is one of many myths and misconceptions that abound in popular narratives about narco traffic and drugs in Mexico. In fact, Mexico had already moved toward punitive policies, and it had already undertaken initiatives to control trafficking even before Anslinger felt compelled to intervene. This is not to argue that Anslinger and the FBN had no impact, since other evidence indicates that this specific and many subsequent interventions were not helpful. Contrary to his intent, his interventions arguably contributed to an expansion of a drug industry in Mexico.

Trafficking had not faded into the background in Mexico following the revolutionary war readjustments, and in fact it had been the specific focus of a 1937 justice officials' meeting that had been convened by the director of Mexico's Departamento de Salubridad (Department of Health)—medical doctor and army general José Siurob Ramírez. At the meeting, he described Mexico as "un centro de concentración y distribución de estupefacientes" (Astorga Almanza 2005, 39), and in a persuasive speech he described how illegal drug use had been empowered by the full participation of police, the weakness of penal laws, the involvement of governors, the power of underworld gangs of Ciudad Juárez, and serious addiction levels among Mexico's soldiers (39–41). There were many others in Mexico who shared the outlook of Siurob. Luis Astorga Almanza documents how underworld and trafficking gangs had been routinely identified in Salvador Martínez Mancera's investigative news reports in *El Universo Gráfico* for many years prior to the 1937 gathering of experts. Martínez Mancera and other journalists had also published reports describing addiction levels, police campaigns against trafficking gangs (primarily Chinese), the extent of political and police corruption, and the impunity of criminal activities in border cities like Ciudad Juárez.

The historical record is clear. Mexico had introduced many initiatives aimed at controlling both trafficking and addiction prior to any American involvement or persuasive advocacy. For instance, the Federal Penal Code of 1931 introduced fines and jail terms between six months and seven years for trafficking and for drug abuse (*toxicomanía*). In October 1931, a new federal law targeting drug abuse, but not trafficking, assigned responsibility for addiction to the federal Department of Health. El Reglamiento Federal de Toxicomanía mandated the building of hospitals and allocated funds to health authorities for addiction treatment.[26]

In 1935 the Department of Health required pharmacies to report all sales of addictive drugs (*drogas enervantes*). Prior surveys (1920, 1929) had successfully tabulated the legal sale of cocaine, coca leaves, *adormidera* (poppies), laudanum, and any mixtures containing opium, but the 1935 exercise was met with a pushback from doctors, pharmaceutical companies, and mothers of addicts (*madres de familia*) who protested that such inventories were ineffective to control the real problem—widespread illegal trafficking. That backlash led to the formation of a national auxiliary commission to the Department of Health that was mandated to study drug consumption and recommend solutions. The commission quickly made specific recommendations to change the emphasis of the 1931 law and identified specific target areas for action: (1) assign sole responsibility for persecution, apprehension, and incarceration of traffickers to the PGR; (2) undertake a careful invigilation of the border, ports, and customs offices; (3) destroy plantations in several states (Puebla, San Luis Potosí, Oaxaca, Guerrero, Querétaro); (4) improve salaries for narcotraffic police; (5) increase penalties for trafficking; and (6) establish a dedicated hospital to treat addiction (Astorga Almanza 2005, 44–45).[27] These suggestions made eighty-five years ago would not be inconsistent with the recommendations that are regularly proposed today by academics, policy analysts, and enforcement officials based in the USA.

By early 1940, a punitive framework for the 1931 legislation dominated all policy initiatives, and the health-medical frameworks would soon fade away in neglect. Only a few addiction centers were actually created by the 1931 legislation, and none had been established after 1940; more importantly, the funding to existing centers shrank yearly—a death knell by a thousand cuts to the viewpoint that drug abuse is a medical question.[28] But in contradiction to the auxiliary committee belief that trafficking would disappear with increased surveillance, it actually expanded. Astorga Almanza argues that this happened because the 1940 recommendations drove up the price of drugs and increased the profit margins of illegal drugs.[29]

A *mano dura* or hard-line emphasis on control had emerged independently of U.S. pressure and was not forced upon Mexico externally. But paradoxically the United States would make things worse when it moved to ban the export of legal opiates to Mexico when Anslinger and others were obdurately convinced that Mexico had not done enough to root out trafficking. His ill-advised action had the unintended consequence of consolidating power of Mexican gomeros, and it triggered an increase in the production of adormidera poppies in several areas of Mexico—including the Golden Triangle—and even spurred the extension further south to regions of Michoacán, Guerrero, and Oaxaca.

Mexico had moved to criminalize and root out traffickers because of a domestically driven concern about addiction levels and, contrary to popular mythology, had not criminalized treatment only because of those loud threats coming from north of the border (Astorga Almanza 2005, 46). Nevertheless, Anslinger and the FBN recommended that there should be an embargo on medicinal drugs in 1940 after Mexico temporarily delayed the implementation of 1940 recommendations because the war in Europe had disrupted supply routes shipping legal drugs from European laboratories, which had created a shortage within Mexico. The U.S. embargo on shipping drugs to Mexico exacerbated the problem even more, and shortages grew more acute—and it played directly into the hands of illegal drug producers who were able to replace the gap in the market.

The FBN embargo on the export of legal drugs to Mexico generated unanticipated consequences that are widely believed to have occurred but which have never been demonstrably linked to smoking gun official documents or archival sources. There are many tales about those events that are fueled by enduring folklore and rumor often told in the environs of Culiacán and Sinaloa, and they have been repeated for years afterward as dubious "historical truths" in the aftermath of the FBN action. Those legends include one persistent tale that mafia boss Lucky Luciano had personally encouraged the planting of Sinaloa poppy fields to provide the U.S. military with an alternate source for the blockaded Turkish heroin.[30] But underlying those rumors is a reality that is undeniably true—the mountainous region around Badiguarato, Sinaloa, experienced major increases in amapola and heroin production during that period. Other remote areas in Durango, Michoacán, and Guerrero also experienced a boom in poppy production as a result of the American embargo, and several regions also experienced large-scale increases in marijuana production. Badiguarato attracted attention because of the scale of opium production happening there.[31]

This drug production did not go unnoticed in the United States and, in particular, caught the attention of Anslinger, who demanded that the Mexican government move to eradicate poppy fields around Badiguarato. A governor of Sinaloa would do precisely what Anslinger demanded, and it cost him his life.

Coronel Rodolfo T. Loaiza was Sinaloa governor between 1941 until his assassination in 1944 by a hit man named Rodolfo "El Gitano" Valdés Osuna. The assassin had clear links to the governor's political enemies and to land-owners who cultivated poppies. The governor had served as a federal senator and was a prominent member of that National Commission for Public Health, which had amended health codes that emphasized the eradication and control of trafficking. Upon assuming office in Sinaloa, Loaiza ordered anew the eradication of poppies and specifically targeted fields sitting near Badiguarato. In 1944 Loaiza was gunned down in Mazatlán's Hotel Belmar by El Gitano, who had been contracted either by a political enemy or by one of the many outraged poppy growers. Although the intellectual author of the crime has never been identified, there is no doubt the assassination was the result of Loaiza's decision to pursue poppy and opium eradication.[32]

A byzantine political fallout in the aftermath of Loaiza's assassination would only be stabilized when incoming president Miguel Alemán (1947–52) removed all responsibility for drug control from Mexico's Department of Health and transferred it directly to the PGR. The Procuraduría General de la República was legitimized as the only institution with a mandate to monitor trafficking, while eradication was left to the Mexican army. In contrast to the decentralized and regionally diverse Department of Health, the PGR was decisively hierarchical and controlled directly from headquarters in Mexico City—and indirectly by presidential advisors in the headquarters of Los Pinos. With one order, President Alemán had destroyed all remnants of a health care policy targeting treatment and prevention and had created a strong centralized agency that would monitor and control all aspects of drug production and distribution. The transfer to the PGR initiated a new stage where the Mexican state—or at least specific agents of the Mexican state—were handed the power to directly influence the production and distribution of drugs. Alemán's solution was the catalytic move that allowed the drug business to prosper and eventually evolve into a covert netherworld operating in shadows.

The specific form of the arrangements between the PGR and the traffickers would formalize slowly over the next twenty-five years, but the groundwork had now been established and new rules of narco trafficking began to govern the business and the drug trade. The norms and rules that eventually materialized would not lead to the elimination of drugs but would instead guarantee a mutual accommodation for both the agencies of the atate and the narco traffickers—and it would enrich both.

By the mid-1950s, the State of Sinaloa and its capital city, Culiacán, had emerged as the center of drug trafficking in Mexico. This was the result of many factors that converged in close order, but geography was arguably an important contributor. The city was close enough to the sierra and its fertile microclimates favorable to poppy and marijuana production, and yet it was far enough away from Mexico City to allow criminal groups the freedom to operate with relative impunity and in obscurity. Most importantly, Culiacán lay within easy striking distance of a lucrative drug market emerging in the United States, and its gomeros had a proven track record of delivering drugs efficiently and with minimal risk of detection.

In the 1950s and early 1960s, drugs from Sinaloa moved along three different conduits to Tijuana, Mexicali, Nogales, and several points in Chihuahua. One route traversed mountain paths and narrow valleys northward toward Ojinaga and Ciudad Juárez in Chihuahua. A second route used the only major north-south highway (Federal Highway 15) along the narrow coastal plain to connect with Nogales and the Arizona border. That route allowed easy transport and bulk delivery of drugs to the north and passed through several municipalities that would become important drug plazas in their own right—Guasave and Los Mochis in Sinaloa were the two most important. The third option was the water routes that began from myriad coastal bays and inlets situated to Culiacán's northwest to move across the Sea of Cortés toward Mexicali and Tijuana.

To outsiders, being a Sinaloense was synonymous with being a gomero—
the most widely used term in the 1950s for poppy growers or opium producers. Amapola and marijuana were both cultivated in the remote regions of
Sinaloa's Sierra Madre—poppies and marijuana in the north, and marijuana
in the south—but trafficking also required an economic and business hub,
and the municipality of Culiacán provided that environment. There were
bankers and businessmen eager to work with the gomeros, and there was no
shortage of municipal and state politicians willing to look the other way as
long as they received their share of profit.

Specifically, Culiacán's barrio Tierra Blanca was notorious because of the
number of *narcotraficantes* who had settled there during the 1950s.[33] Initially, most were men rooted in country ways, and many had been socialized
into a rough and tumble *bronco* (roughly, a cowboy culture, a redneck culture) ethos. Although those gomeros forged links with bankers, businessmen, and politicians, they largely stuck to their own and lived in specific
barrios and colonias. As Luis Astorga Almanza describes Tierra Blanca, the
infamous community of narcotraficantes:

> It's said that colonia Tierra Blanca "is the center of operations for coyotes
> and gomeros," that it's "the cradle (cuna) of gomeros" where "vice and wan-
> tonness" reign—and that "weapons are everywhere". They also say it's much
> more than "a refuge for a gomero"—it is a "paradise of vice." We can specif-
> ically mention the Zúñiga, Urías and Andrea Inns, and the bars Mi Delirio
> and Montecarlo, as places where besides the gomeros "there are farmers
> from the hills, killers, horse-thieves, cattle-rustlers, and all kinds of no-good
> types who have come from Badiguarato and Durango to waste the money
> they earned in ill-gotten ways." They also say that Tierra Blanca is where
> murders are committed in "the same manner as Chicago gangsters," and that
> Culiacán itself has become "a new Chicago with gangsters wearing huara-
> ches." (2005, 87)

And when the U.S. appetite for drugs began to surge in the 1960s, it was
Sinaloa that provided both marijuana and heroin to feed it. Sinsemilla marijuana was perceived to be high quality and relatively inexpensive, and Mexican brown heroin became the fall-back option for addicts whose supply of
white heroin had seriously diminished after the French Connection operation. But it would also take the action of the Mexican army working with

American drug agents to provide the spark that set off the drug explosion in Mexico.

Period 2: Traditions and Cartel Consolidation

During the 1960s, the growing use of marijuana in the American market led the United States to revisit the long-standing antidrug strategy that followed since the early years of Harry Anslinger and the Federal Bureau of Narcotics (Hari 2015). During the 1950s, the U.S. efforts had concentrated on heroin and opiate abuse, but by the 1960s, the United States had added marijuana and other recreational drugs to the watch list. Washington had specifically fingered Mexico as the primary supplier of marijuana to the American market and had actively pursued specific agreements and accords with Mexican officials to eradicate marijuana crops—particularly those situated in the Golden Triangle and producing the powerful version known as sinsemilla. By then, that region of Mexico had also achieved an international notoriety and became the focal point for many complaints raised by the Federal Bureau of Narcotics and the Bureau of Drug Abuse Control (BDAC).

Mexico's military and federal police periodically seized marijuana shipments and burned a few fields, but those interventions represented little more than symbolic gestures intended to appease Washington and the FBN and BDAC. There were also suspicions that the tonnage of destruction was regularly exaggerated, and that some of the seized product had been returned to the drug producers after a ceremonial public display and media coverage of destruction (O'Day 2001; O'Day and López 2001). Overall, Mexican interdictions had little impact on the flow of drugs northward; Lyndon B. Johnson's administration repeatedly applied pressure on Mexico at the diplomatic level but took few concrete steps to force compliance with the accords and treaties by cutting off aid.

Upon his election, President Nixon authorized Operation Intercept in the third week of September 1969. It was timed to coincide with the prime harvest season of marijuana, and it resulted in a near shutdown of border traffic between Mexico and the United States for three weeks. In spite of the rhetoric that was used to justify the action, there were no significant seizures of marijuana that greatly impacted the drug market, and the most consequential outcome was the deterioration of bilateral relations with Mexico. Nevertheless, the Nixon administration was convinced that it had achieved its goal

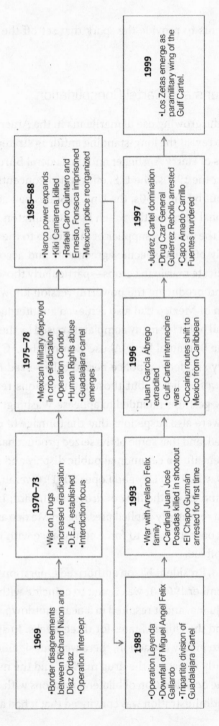

FIGURE 5 The War on Drugs and cartel consolidation, 1969–1999. Graphic created by author.

1969
- Border disagreements between Richard Nixon and Diaz Ordaz
- Operation Intercept

1970–73
- War on Drugs
- Increased eradication
- D.E.A. established
- Interdiction focus

1975–78
- Mexican Military deployed in crop eradication
- Operation Condor
- Human Rights abuse
- Guadalajara cartel emerges

1985–88
- Narco power expands
- Kiki Camarena killed
- Rafael Caro Quintero and Ernesto, Fonseca imprisoned
- Mexican police reorganized

1999
- Los Zetas emerge as paramilitary wing of the Gulf Cartel.

1989
- Operation Leyenda
- Downfall of Miguel Angel Felix Gallardo
- Tripartite division of Guadalajara Cartel

1993
- War with Arellano Felix family
- Cardinal Juan José Posadas killed in shootout
- El Chapo Guzmán arrested for first time

1996
- Juan García Ábrego extradited
- Gulf Cartel internecine wars
- Cocaine routes shift to Mexico from Caribbean

1997
- Juárez Cartel domination
- Drug Czar General Gutiérrez Rebollo arrested
- Capo Amado Carrillo Fuentes murdered

of encouraging the Mexican government to reduce drug production, and that it had also achieved a symbolic political victory (Baum 2016).[34] In some respects, the Nixonian argument was statistically correct since the number of seizures and crop eradications recorded in Mexico did climb steadily during the 1970s. During the 1960s, only 2,400 hectares and 500 tons of marijuana had been decommissioned, but between 1970 and 1976, that had increased to more than 13,300 hectares destroyed and 3,800 tons seized. There are no accurate figures of the total number of hectares actually in production, and therefore there is no way of arriving at an accurate estimate of the proportion of crops that had been destroyed.[35]

U.S. War on Drugs and Unintended Consequences

Richard Nixon escalated the level of rhetoric and declared a War on Drugs in June 1971, and in doing so created new policing institutions with a specific policy mandate to oversee and regulate all aspects of drug and narcotics control.[36] That major reorganization dramatically increased the number of agents monitoring drug use, and it funneled enormous amounts of money to justice and border agencies, while on the legislative side President Nixon also transferred marijuana to the Schedule 1 classification that came with harsher penalties (it was later overturned in a federal court).

In an executive action, he created a new agency that was named the Drug Enforcement Administration to operate under the umbrella of the Department of Justice in 1973, and in so doing he had mandated that one single agency would now be responsible for drug control.[37] The newly formed DEA began operations by assigning agents to DOJ bureaus in Mexico City and Monterrey in Nuevo León (both of which had been operating since 1961), to Hermosillo in Sonora (established in 1971), and to a new foreign office in Mazatlán, Sinaloa, that was opened in 1973. The DOJ, the DEA's parent agency, also established the El Paso Intelligence Center (EPIC) in 1974 and gave it the mandate to coordinate all drug-related intelligence; DEA agents were posted there with a broad directive to cooperate with border and immigration agencies and to dovetail and piggyback on their work. In later years, the border and immigration agencies would benefit from that auxiliary assignment and grow to the point that their numbers represented more than 33 percent of all federal law enforcement officials (Graff 2020; Miller 2014).

Meanwhile, domestic consumption of marijuana in the USA continued to rise, and moreover Mexican brown heroin was increasingly common in many American cities in the aftermath of disruptions caused by the famous French Connection seizures.[38] Sinaloa State, the major producer of both marijuana and brown heroin, became the primary focus of DEA surveillance, and Washington increased the pressure on the Mexican government to reduce the production of both drugs within that state. In 1975 Mexican president Luis Echeverría Álvarez authorized a military intervention in response to U.S. demands, and in 1977 he authorized Operation Condor, which deployed ten thousand Mexican army personnel under the command of General José Hernández Toledo.[39] The operation was also monitored by at least one PGR representative, Carlos Aguilar Garza, and several unnamed DEA agents.

Despite the application of defoliants and an untold number of blatant human right violations, General Hernández's operation would have no long-term success. Instead, hundreds of ordinary farmers fled to other areas, as did the most important drug traffickers of the region, who would eventually grow even richer and come to play important roles on an international scale and in the covert netherworld of Mexico that emerged. As Astorga describes the results of Operation Condor:

> Tons of drugs were destroyed, production was reduced, prices rose, but drugs continued to flow into the American market, although in lesser quantity of Mexican origin. Many villages in the sierra were deserted. Hundreds of people were arrested, tortured and sent to jail, but not a single big boss. The most important group leaders moved to Guadalajara, Jalisco, and continued their business on a bigger scale thanks to cocaine which they had already been smuggling on a large scale since 1975, according to the DEA. The military and political success claimed by the authorities was just a mirage. In the long term, the social cost of the military operation was more important for a large number of people, whose negative attitude towards federal police and the military was reinforced, than the spectacular destruction of illegal plants which made Mexican and American anti-narcotics officials so happy and optimistic. According to both governments, their collaboration—through DEA agents and their counterparts, for example—had never been as good and efficient. This did not last very long. (1999)

Instead of reducing narco traffic, Operation Condor had generated disastrous unintended consequences for the U.S.-inspired War on Drugs—the consolidation of regional rivals and the bolstering of a cocaine market. Both changes would have a long-term impact and shape the organization of drug-trafficking Mexico for the next forty years. In effect, Operation Condor gave birth to the first national drug cartel within Mexico—the Guadalajara Cartel—and introduced cocaine as a staple into the Mexican drug enterprise. Between 1977 and 1985, the skills that had been honed at a regional level would be applied on national and international levels with incredible success; in retrospect, it was a remarkably smooth expansion and transition. The forced relocation of drug barons would bring them immense wealth after they arrived in Guadalajara and allow them to influence events on a scale never seen before. Miguel Ángel Félix Gallardo recognized the opportunities, and he would become the first real Jefe de Jefes among Mexico's narco traffickers.[40]

In hindsight, it's clear that Operation Condor had no chance of destroying a communal network that had been cemented by informal bonds, nor did it stand the chance of dismantling the interpersonal arrangements that were the powerful bonds linking members of that seminal drug fraternity. Soldiers and generals were outsiders and were undermined by the very local authorities whom they had incorrectly assumed to be working with them. In fact, Operation Condor forged even deeper bonds between Félix Gallardo, Caro Quintero, and Fonseca Carillo and introduced external constraints that bound them closer and reduced internal disagreements about turf or product—"the enemy of my enemy is my friend," goes the saying. The drug jefes also realized that local production and distribution routes had been untouched even though Operation Condor had forced them to personally relocate. In reality, the enforced move represented new opportunities to access international markets, and those opportunities guaranteed that all three men would soon join an elite circle among the richest people in Mexico.[41]

The first Mexican drug organization with national and international dimensions has most frequently been called the Guadalajara Cartel, primarily because Don Neto Fonseca Carrillo and Rafael Caro Quintero had relocated to that city and reorganized their criminal syndicate and underworld in the aftermath of Operation Condor with the help of Miguel Ángel Félix Gallardo. When he was located in Sinaloa, Caro Quintero had long smuggled marijuana to the United States in partnership with another infamous Sinaloan named Pedro Avilés Pérez. A Badiguarato native, Fonseca Carrillo owned extensive properties dedicated to producing marijuana and amapola;

he had also been shipping cocaine to the USA on a smaller scale since the late 1970s.[42] Both of those men were the principal figures in a fledgling drug cartel along with Félix Gallardo, who operated out of Culiacán itself and was a prominent figure in political and social circles.

Félix Gallardo is indisputably the most important figure during that formational period of Mexican narco-trafficking organizations because he was essentially the cogwheel of a network that linked Sinaloan narcotraficantes; corrupt government, army, and police officials; and Colombian cocaine producers and forged them together to create a covert netherworld. A native of Culiacán, Félix Gallardo was a badge-carrying member of Mexico's DFS and a bodyguard to Sinaloa governor Leopoldo Sánchez Celis. He also had direct links to the Cali Cartel in Colombia through his Honduran contact Ramón Matta Ballesteros.[43] Unlike his partners, Félix Gallardo was not driven away from Sinaloa by Operation Condor; he remained in Culiacán, where he passed as a successful entrepreneur and was a frequent participant at important social and political events in the capital. Another partner in the Sinaloa Cartel who strengthened his power at the time of the move to Guadalajara was Juan José Esparragoza Moreno, known as El Azul: he was a man who mysteriously managed to remain silently operating in the background—and ultimately would turn out to be the longest-lasting survivor from that original group that formed the Guadalajara Cartel.

In light of the assertion by Anabel Hernández (2020, 42) that Ismael Zambada García had founded the Sinaloa Cartel, it may seem strange that El Mayo has not been mentioned more frequently in historical accounts describing the formation of the first major cartel in Guadalajara. But there are reasons his name rarely appears, and is only briefly mentioned in the following pages. This section of the book focuses on the emergence of the Guadalajara Cartel, and the organization known as the Sinaloa Cartel did not have a national presence until much later. Furthermore, Zambada was not an especially close associate of Fonseca Carillo or Caro Quintero: he was from El Alamo, Sinaloa, which lies south of Culiacán and not in the Golden Triangle, where the others had roots. El Mayo's Cuban-born brother-in-law Antonio Cruz Vásquez had introduced him to the drug trade, and his trajectory was different than those of Fonseca Carrillo or Carto Quintero. And it is important to emphasize, in the aftermath of Operation Condor, that El Mayo had not gone to Guadalajara but instead relocated to Las Vegas, Nevada, and soon after to Los Angeles, California (Hernández 2020, 40–42). The history in the following pages describes the foundational years of the Guadalajara Cartel, which was the dominant national crime syndicate in the 1980s.

A narcocorrido by Los Tucanes de Tijuana refers to the three little animals of the drug trade—*el gallo, la chiva*, and *el perico* (the rooster, the goat, and the papagayo [toucan])—slang for marijuana, heroin, and cocaine. All three had become firmly rooted in the subterranean culture by the late 1970s, and all three had become keystone commodities moved by the burgeoning Guadalajara consortium. Marijuana, opium, and heroin were also regional commodities that had long been produced in Sinaloa, but cocaine had been introduced as an import from the Andes and grew especially important after the DOJ began to clamp down on routes moving through the Caribbean. Among those three commodities, cocaine provided the most lucrative profit margins and represented the greatest enrichment opportunity for the drug barons who had begun their operations from within the Golden Triangle: they didn't have to worry about its production, only the transportation. In Sinaloa, each *animalito* had a master *wrangler*—Fonseca Carillo was the overseer of poppy and heroin production and to a lesser extent cocaine shipping; Caro Quintero was a master and genius at growing and distributing marijuana, especially the sinsemilla and *cola de rata* varieties; and Félix Gallardo would emerge as the most powerful godfather or el padrino, who oversaw the intricacies of cocaine importation and the creation of distribution networks that were protected from seizure by his personal contacts in high places in the PGR and even higher. There are literally dozens of authoritative books and documents describing the formative years of the Sinaloa Cartel, and all of those published before 2020 acknowledge that these three men were the central figures. And for the most part, they also describe Miguel Ángel Félix Gallardo as the key liason between the others and judicial officials and politicians in Sinaloa and in the capital, Mexico City.

Each crime boss oversaw an underground and subterranean network that was more deeply immersed in violence, co-optation, and bribery and that involved and corrupted most state institutions and local businesses. Félix Gallardo was especially skillful in the subtleties of narco bonding because of his personality and his extensive contacts from a former career as policeman and personal bodyguard to Governor Sánchez Celis. Holding everyone together as the consigliere was another man, Esparragoza Moreno, who developed a reputation for being the ultimate conciliator and wise adviser who kept disagreements from getting out of hand.

This trio of men eventually forged an alliance cemented by their shared origins and connections to the municipality of Badiguarato, Sinaloa. Their network grew larger and stronger by kinship, intermarriage, rituals of compadrazgo, mutual connections with public officials, and an increasingly complex partnership with traffickers from Durango and Chihuahua who transported their drugs further afield. Specifically, their connections to a regional cacique, Pablo Acosta of Ojinaga, Chihuahua, allowed them to ship contraband directly into the U.S. market.

Mexican journalist Julio Scherer García (2008) would later describe the connections among Félix Gallardo, Fonseca Carrillo, Caro Quintero, Esparragoza Moreno, and others together as a *narco society*. The folkways and patterns that regulated daily life in that isolated area of Mexico had gradually crystallized into a more formalized relationship regulated by its own norms and understandings. Sandra Ávila, the niece of Félix Gallardo and infamous La Reina del Pacífico, grew up in that narco society and described its power in an interview with Scherer thirty years after Operation Condor:

> Narco society is hard, cruel, and in its own way a society unto itself. There's
> no code that determines penalties during power struggles. Neither are there
> laws to resolve disputes, and I don't see any authority capable of intervening
> in the chaos that comes and goes, is always present and always on your mind.
> (Scherer García 2008, 99)

That narco society was firmly established by the time of Operation Condor, and arguably grew stronger afterward. As dominating as it was, it remained largely invisible to outsiders and even for the many who indirectly profited from its existence—a subterranean influence with tentacles holding many people in place. The invisibility of the connecting bonds allowed those men and a few others to establish a powerful presence with little fear of formal repercussion. And unless one was part of the network as Ávila was, it was hard to imagine that it even existed.

The three amigos (Félix Gallardo, Fonseca Carrillo, Caro Quintero) and others like Esparragoza Moreno grew enormously rich and powerful during their exile from Sinaloa because they had realized that they could expand their production of marijuana and opium, and that they now had significant power over the cocaine market. Operation Condor had arguably driven them to larger urban centers, where they were presented with opportunities to expand their global vision and formalize links to a transnational drug market and fortify the connections with corrupt government officials. But even as that happened, they never forgot their roots in rural Sinaloa nor neglected the local connections, and that had given them strength in a mutual quest. Their shipping routes and their products were still based and centered in Sinaloa and had not been disrupted by Operation Condor. Ironically, their strengthened partnership and organizational consolidation might never have reached the next level without that operation or developed by simple chance—it's said that Fonseca Carillo had selected Guadalajara as the destination simply because his girlfriend was from there and she was related to the state governor. No matter how it happened, the Sinaloans took advantage of a balloon effect and an opportunity that fell in their lap without forgetting that the source of their strength remained rooted in the Golden Triangle and the traditions of narco trafficking that had evolved and ruled in Sinaloa.[44]

Félix Gallardo became the first kingpin to dominate narcotic trafficking in Mexico and would greatly expand the routes within his country northward to the U.S. border.[45] He was also one of the first to formalize deals with the Medellín Cartel and other Colombian suppliers. He would come to be known as el padrino (the godfather) and considered Jefe de Jefes (Boss of Bosses), and it was he who would eventually oversee the structural reorganization of crime groups that would go on to dominate narco trafficking in Mexico between 1989 and 2000.

At the young age of seventeen, he was working for Sinaloa's corrupt state judicial police. His first assignment was to protect the family of Governor Sánchez Celis, whose term of office was from 1963 to 1968. Sánchez Celis remained the power behind the scenes well into the late 1970s; he introduced his protégé Félix Gallardo to businessmen, politicians, large landowners, journalists, judges, prosecutors, and members of federal law enforcement agencies. Another of Félix Gallardo's key mentors was Eduardo "Lalo" Fernández, who introduced him to the intricacies of the heroin trade.

Félix Gallardo was godparent to the governor's son Rodolfo Sánchez Duarte. As Sánchez Celis's righthand man, he began to accumulate the narco equivalent of a rolodex that would convert him into one of the nation's top drug dealers, cement important connections to Mexico's corrupt political establishment, and create the original covert netherworld of narco trafficking: "El Padrino ensured that the 'right people' up and down Mexico's Pacific coast were in his pocket, a diverse and extensive group that included businessmen, politicians and policemen" (Beith 2010, 41). Félix Gallardo also prospered without any setbacks under each of Sánchez Celis's successors: Alfredo Valdés Montoya (1969–74), Alfonso G. Calderón (1975–80), and especially the state government of Antonio Toledo Corro (1981–86).

Disaster: The Camarena Murder

In late 1984, several large marijuana plantations owned by members of the Guadalajara Cartel were in place across Mexico, with the explicit knowledge of the federal attorney general even though Mexico was officially destroying such operations under a joint program of eradication mandated by bilateral treaties and accords with the USA.

Enrique "Kiki" Camarena was a junior DEA agent who had been assigned to the Guadalajara region, and by all accounts he had been "very successful at developing contacts who provided information about Rafael Caro Quintero, Ernesto Fonseca, and other traffickers in the marijuana business" (Shannon 1988, 117). In May 1982, one of the DEA informants told Camarena and his fellow agents about a large plantation operating in San Luis Potosí State and also reported that it was jointly owned by Rafael Caro Quintero, Ernesto Fonseca Carrillo, and Juan José Esparragoza Moreno. That particular plantation extended over more than 220 acres, had built an elaborate irrigation system, and was using canopy covers to protect plants from the searing sun. That megaplantation was so large that it reportedly employed more than ten thousand workers. Camarena and his fellow DEA agents were skeptical about the accuracy coming from their source, especially because the fields were so large and because the Mexican government continued to insist that it was fully cooperating with the United States to eradicate marijuana. Elaine Shannon reported:

> The easiest way to find out what was going on would have been to fly over the place, but the DEA agents needed official escorts to do that, and they were not ready to tell the Federales what they knew. Kiki planted more informants inside the ring. According to Camarena's case files, those informants reported that a comandante of the Federales was protecting the plantation and had delivered arms there. (1988, 118)

Camarena's boss, James Kuykendall, went directly to U.S. State Department officials with the files describing those megaplantations, but they shrugged off his report and argued they did not want to alienate their Mexican partners in the War on Drugs. But Camarena independently obtained photos of the plantation and presented such irrefutable evidence that the PGR was left with no option except to follow through with a visible response. In September 1982, seven helicopters belonging to Mexico's Policía Judicial Federal (PJF) were reluctantly deployed to search and destroy that megaplantation.

Some weeks later, additional large plantations of sinsemilla were discovered and grudgingly destroyed by the Mexican army following orders issued by the PJF. In each instance, they also discovered that each plantation was under the protection of a *madrino*—a PJF comandante who provided cover and protection. Shannon also reported that Camarena was convinced that there were other plantations spread across the northern highlands, and each one was protected by Federales (the PJF and the DFS). Camarena decided to undertake his own reconnaissance mission and came up with a plan codenamed Operation Milagro.

In 1984 the DEA had gathered definitive proof that Guadalajara narco traffickers had formed an investment syndicate to finance thousands of acres of sinsemilla fields in Zacatecas, Durango, and Chihuahua. In violation of a formal agreement with Mexico that required cooperative investigation, Camarena had tapped into his own resources and hired a Mexican pilot named Alfredo Zavala Avelar to fly him over some of those fields located in Zacatecas State to gather the damning evidence in those files.

On February 7, 1985, Camarena and his pilot were simultaneously kidnapped in Guadalajara from different locations. In response to his disappearance, the American ambassador and the DEA chief immediately convened a press conference and emphasized that they would reveal the major discovery of marijuana megaplantations and evidence uncovered by American intelligence. The ambassador also reported that American field agents had provided concrete evidence that Guadalajara had become the center of a national and international drug-trafficking operation.

The Americans immediately initiated Operation Stop and Seize, which had an immediate effect on all border crossings. Given the absence of cooperation from Mexican authorities, the U.S. State Department had used that blockage of commercial traffic to strong-arm the Mexican authorities into immediately resolving Camarena's disappearance. Francis Mullen, the DEA chief, boldly accused DFS and PJF agents of having a direct involvement in the case. The pressure from the press conference and blocking of the border had an effect, and nearly one month after the kidnapping, two half-buried bodies with obvious signs of torture were found in Michoacán. They were the barely recognizable corpses of Kiki Camarena and Alfredo Zavala.

Because it had participated in Operation Condor, the Mexican government had earned the confidence of Washington and had been coasting along by carrying out a scaled-back eradication program that did just enough to demonstrate they were fulfilling a commitment to destroy crops. But the honeymoon that had emerged would turn into a nightmare for Mexico when DEA agent Camarena's body was found. Not even an elaborate and transparent attempt to offer up *chivos expiriatorios* made the Americans back down. Astorga describes this collapse:

> The Camarena case was a catalyst, a special occasion to show the level of corruption of Mexican police agents, and even politicians. Some agents and police commanders, accused of protecting Caro Quintero, were put in jail. DFS and Interpol-Mexico directors were removed. Caro Quintero was captured on April 4, 1985, in Costa Rica, and sentenced on December 12, 1989, to 92 years in prison. Fonseca Carrillo did not escape either. Félix Gallardo was caught in Guadalajara on April 8, 1989. In May 1994, he was sentenced to 40 years. (1999)

Enrique Camarena had been kidnapped on February 5, 1985, near the American Consulate in Guadalajara. Two gunmen working for Fonseca Carrillo had picked him up and brought him to a house in the Jardines del Bosque area of Guadalajara. Caro Quintero himself and the two gunmen tortured Camarena and demanded that he offer up names of those men who were working for him as informants and had leaked the details about the marijuana megaplantations. Fonseca Carillo was not present during that first day of beatings and torture but returned to the house on the following day and demanded to see Camarena. According to Mexican journalist Héctor Aguilar Camín (2009), Caro Quintero informed him, "You can't talk to him—he's dying."

Camarena had been severely beaten and tortured throughout the previous afternoon and long into the night. When Félix Gallardo learned about the kidnapping and torture, he was furious and immediately realized that it would bring down the sledgehammer upon the fledgling cartel. According to well-placed informants, he immediately made a decision that Caro Quintero must be sacrificed and turned over to the Americans. But it would not be enough, and Félix Gallardo would also end up also paying the price.

It didn't take long before Caro Quintero was arrested in Costa Rica thanks to the information that had been passed along to the DEA from Félix Gallardo, who had hoped to make his partner the high-level scapegoat for the Camarena fiasco. Fonseca Carrillo didn't get out of the country and was arrested three days later in Puerto Vallarta. Those two arrests did not let Félix Gallardo off the hook and in fact only unleashed bigger problems. Caro Quintero and Fonseca Carrillo were pressured into talking and apparently confessed almost immediately, and Félix Gallardo himself became the most wanted man in Mexico and subject of one of the largest manhunts ever undertaken—Operation Leyenda.

He managed to keep a low profile for a couple of years, until April 18, 1989. During that time on the run, he reputedly masterminded the reorganization of the cartel structure in Mexico. Reportedly, most of the details were negotiated at a meeting that resulted in the creation of three major plazas— the Juárez Plaza, the Tijuana Plaza, and the Sinaloa Plaza. The Arellano Félix family was assigned the Tijuana Plaza, Héctor Palma Salazar took control of the Sinaloa Plaza, and the Carrillo Fuentes family would control the Juárez Plaza. Furthermore, thirteen other smaller territories were identified, and regional lieutenants were named to direct each of those turfs.

The biggest winner of the shake-up would eventually be Amado Carrillo Fuentes. According to several reports, he was the first to fully understand the implications of the Camarena murder and to realize that the Guadalajara Cartel needed to disband. According to several observers with access to the full testimony eventually provided by protected witnesses, Carrillo Fuentes immediately set about to insulate himself from prosecution and consolidate his position in the confederation. For instance, the secret testimony of Tomás Colsa McGregor indicates that Carrillo Fuentes immediately arranged to bribe several Mexican federal officials in order to shield himself from prosecution.[46] Colsa was an important conduit in setting up meetings, and mostly importantly he paved the way for Carrillo Fuentes to bribe high-level officials using watches, diamonds, and jewels as currency. Carrillo Fuentes purchased diamonds and jewelry worth hundreds of thousands of dollars from Colsa and used the gems to pay off officials and make them part of the covert netherworld that was crystallizing into a new form. In the aftermath of the Camarena murder, the most important figure Carrillo Fuentes wanted to recruit was the head of the PGR antinarcotics division and head of Mexico's team involved in Operation Leyenda—Guillermo González Calderoni.

González Calderoni and Carrillo Fuentes then partnered to become the most important players during those formative years when the new federated cartel structure took shape and the covert netherworld cemented old and new connective links to legitimate government and business. González Calderoni would turn on his partner and be the one who eventually arrested Félix Gallardo in 1989 and would also lead the team that executedCarrillo Fuentes's major troublemaker and dissident narco lord operating on the northern frontier—Pablo "El Zorro" Acosta Villareal.

A Perfect Storm

Although there is no denying the criminal brilliance of Félix Gallardo or Carrillo Fuentes and the powerbase rooted in Sinaloa connections, the Guadalajara Cartel and its later incarnations might never have emerged were it not for the confluence of a perfect set of circumstances that turned Mexico into the ideal trampoline for delivering drugs to the American market. The DOJ and the DEA had been successful in their attacks on the Colombian cartels, and the Medellín and Cali Cartels had been greatly diminished by those interventions. The cocaine routes moving directly through the Caribbean to the port of Miami had been effectively closed down and interrupted. NAFTA had by then opened up commerce and trade routes to Mexico and created new opportunities for piggybacking the shipment of drugs using the same routes that legitimate commerce would follow.

For thirty years, the official narrative asserted that Camarena was eliminated because he had been responsible for the destruction of several megaplantations of marijuana. But a bewildering decision years later by a Mexican judge resurrected long-standing rumors that American agents had been directly involved in his torture. Claims about tape recordings made during Camarena's torture circulated in rumor mills for years, and those tapes purportedly indicated that CIA agents were present at his torture because they were worried that Camarena had also learned that CIA agents were working directly with Caro Quintero to supply arms to the Contras and that those agents had also turned a blind eye when cocaine was shipped to the United States.

The incident that triggered the revisitation to the Camarena murder was the unexpected release of Caro Quintero from Puente Grande prison on August 9, 2013, based on a judge's narrow and technical interpretation of

Mexican Constitutional law. The judge ruled that the Mexican government had originally prosecuted Caro Quintero based on a law that did not apply to his case, and that he should not have been found guilty of the murder of Camarena based on the specific statute that had been applied. The Supreme Court of Mexico quickly overturned the initial ruling, but by then Caro Quintero had vanished and has remained free ever since.[47] The unexpected release of Caro Quintero infuriated the directors of the DEA and raised the hackles of many in the DOJ and Homeland Security, but most importantly it caused several former DEA agents to come forward with angry denunciations about the entire Camarena affair and the failure to prosecute those who were actually responsible for killing him.

Specifically, retired DEA agents Hector Berrellez and Phil Jordan and a CIA contract pilot named Robert "Tosh" Plumlee were featured in a Fox News report (La Jeunesse 2013) denouncing CIA complicity in the kidnapping and murder; in that news report, they made the claim that the actual reason that Camarena had been murdered was because the information he had gathered about the Guadalajara Cartel exposed the cartel's involvement in the Iran-Contra arms deal overseen by CIA operatives. Those three witnesses were pointing to something that had grown increasingly obvious over time—that the CIA had contracted directly with Caro Quintero to ship illegal arms to Nicaraguan Contras from a landing strip in Veracruz State. Furthermore, Caro Quintero properties were used by dissidents for training in their hope to undermine and defeat the leftist Sandinista government of Nicaragua. As payment, Caro Quintero was allowed to ship drugs to the USA (specifically crack cocaine) on his own planes without fear of being detected.

The claims of CIA involvement in the murder of Camarena and Zavala were not loony conspiratorial fables and in fact had been revealed in Senate committee hearings chaired by Senator John Kerry. But the accusations were suppressed and buried quickly, in spite of compelling evidence compiled by journalist Gary Webb, who had published several lengthy investigative reports about those reputed links between the CIA and Caro Quintero. The U.S. Senate report on the Iran-Contra affair whitewashed all accusations of CIA complicity with the Guadalajara Cartel, and Webb was discredited and sadly committed suicide.

But rumor and speculation had not been completely suppressed, and the details gained new credibility following the unexpected release of Caro Quintero. Bill Conroy's widely read blog, *The Narcosphere* (2013b), had heavily promoted the investigative work of the late Gary Webb, and the entire sordid affair was thoroughly documented in the long epilogue of a book by Russell H. Bartley and Sylvia Erickson Bartley (2015).[48]

The complications of that putative CIA involvement are far too detailed for elaboration here, but it is important to stress that the operations of the CIA in Mexico and the illegal transportation of arms through Mexico support the narrative that a number of circumstances had converged to create opportunities for the Guadalajara Cartel to expand, and most certainly suggest its leaders had forged close working relationships with shadowy government officials in Mexico and elsewhere in a subterranean and covert netherworld. Those accusations also serve to demonstrate that the many truths about narco Mexico are buried in secret archives and have only been partially revealed in heavily redacted documents of several government agencies.

A Second Generation of Drug Dealers Takes Control

Even though they had left ancestral homelands and their rural communities years ago, families such as the Arellano Félix siblings and the Carrillo Fuentes family still maintained deep roots in Sinaloa State.[49] They became the principal beneficiaries following the reorganization of the Guadalajara Cartel in the aftermath of the Camarena murder. Their families had moved from overseeing relatively minor rural and micro businesses dedicated to drug running and had entered into a global world of international commerce and large-scale money laundering.

The Arellano Félix brothers and sisters—some with advanced university degrees in business management—had relocated to Tijuana, where they seized complete control of the lucrative narcotics routes feeding the Southern California market.

The Carrillo Fuentes family would prosper even more and soon emerged as the most dominant crime organization in the first few years following the Camarena affair. As a young apprentice and rising leader in the Guadalajara Cartel, Amado Carrillo Fuentes had been assigned to Ciudad Juárez to work alongside the charismatic, unpredictable, and notorious regional drug smuggler Pablo Acosta. The oldest Carrillo Fuentes sibling learned well and recognized that Ciudad Juárez was the key to distributing for drugs—especially cocaine.

By the mid-1990s, Amado Carrillo Fuentes became principal distributor and overseer of Colombian cocaine routes thanks to a fleet of special airplanes licensed to his private company, Taxi Aéro del Centro Norte. He began to purchase airplanes two years after the arrest of Miguel Ángel Carrillo Fuentes in the Operation Leyenda manhunt, and in so doing cemented his status as the emergent leader within a narco-trafficking federation that had risen from the ashes of the Guadalajara Cartel. He became so proficient at smuggling drugs that he acquired the famous nickname "El Señor de los Cielos"—The Lord of the Skies. Most importantly, he emerged as the principal purchaser, seller, and overseer of almost all cocaine moving through Mexico—allegedly 80 percent. His managerial and organizational skills led to the emergence of a powerful organization that controlled more than two-thirds of the country. He forged permanent links with government officials—especially within the PGR—that would protect the cartels from prosecution for decades to come.

Anabel Hernández's recent book, *El traidor* (2020), does raise several questions about the actual leadership and command structure overseeing those massive shipments of drugs in the 1990s. Her revelations from the diary of El Mayo Zambada García's son Vicente allege that many of those shipments of cocaine into Mexico were in truth being arranged and controlled by El Mayo, who had established the command structure of the Sinaloa Cartel while he was based in Los Angeles, in the aftermath of Operation Condor. It is entirely plausible that El Mayo also played a significantly large role in that covert netherworld of narco traffic and that Carrillo Fuentes was in reality a key lugarteniente (lieutenant) or perhaps co-leader alongside Zambada. Should future revelations prove that El Mayo was de facto head of the Sinaloa Cartel, that would not diminish the significant role that Carrillo Fuentes and his fleet of transport planes played in the emergence of Mexican drug cartels.

In spite of the persistent myth that Colombian cartels were directing the drug trade in the Americas, Carrillo Fuentes's Juárez faction and the Arellano Félix Tijuana faction had emerged as the principal operatives in the narcotics trade by the mid-1990s, and the Colombians had assumed the role of supplier. Although the Colombians produced cocaine, it was Mexicans who controlled shipping routes into Mexico and effectively delivered it to the United States. Furthermore, the Mexicans had the advantage of being diversified organizations that were not limited to a single commodity—they also controlled and oversaw marijuana production, opiate products, and eventually most variants of synthetic drugs that consumers demanded or could be convinced they needed.

The principal illegal drug market in the USA was estimated to have a potential annual value of more than $30 billion at the end of the 1990s. The DEA also estimated that 90 percent of all cocaine entering the U.S. market had springboarded through Mexico, and that a significant portion of all imports of marijuana and opium passed through the porous Mexican border. When drug war crackdowns on the U.S. side eventually focused on synthetic drugs, the cartels on the Mexican side developed new partnerships with previously subsidiary crime organizations in Mexico to work with global suppliers of precursors, especially the Chinese, to manufacture and feed as much as 85 percent of the American demand for amphetamines, ecstasy, and other synthetic drugs, including fentanyl. Those newly popular designer drugs eventually strengthened the bargaining power and influence of previously minor affiliates of the new federation and gave birth to the dangerous and lethal criminal syndicates that emerged after 2000 (e.g., the CJNG).

Amado Carrillo Fuentes was spectacularly successful at creating a stable delivery infrastructure to ship drugs on a global scale, and also a vast financial network that could launder the massive profits. He was a key figure in a criminal organization that U.S. agents began to refer to as the Federation, although that was not a name used within Mexico to describe the covert netherworld that had emerged. In fact, the more common label was the Juárez Cartel since most of the directives reportedly came from Ciudad Juárez, where the Arellano Félix family had established operations. *The Federation* was not routinely used as the label for criminal drug organizations in Mexico until first introduced by Colleen Cook in 2007 in an influential report prepared for Congressional Research Services (Cook 2007). In spite of the ambiguity surrounding the correct name for that covert netherworld, it is clear that there was an emerging and powerful drug network with three recognizable divisions operating cooperatively to move illegal drugs into and out of Mexico, and to move money and arms back into Mexico. It is also clear that the Juárez faction had emerged as the most influential and powerful faction under the guidance and direction of Carrillo Fuentes.

Marijuana and heroin production and distribution had allowed Carrillo Fuentes and his partners to establish a near permanent work force, create an efficient and focused division of labor to move product, and regularly meet payrolls and pay bribes to everyone connected in that expanding covert netherworld. The shift westward of Andean cocaine routes was equivalent to winning a lottery and represented the opportunity to corner the market on shipping that made the Juárez group and all Federation partners even more dominant. Under Carrillo Fuentes's influence and leadership, the Juárez faction grew to become the most dominant player in the post–Guadalajara Cartel era, and the border city where it was centered became the flagship plaza within a broader alignment of lateral partnerships that had initially included the Arellano Félix family in Tijuana and several other drug bosses based in Sinaloa.

Amado Carrillo Fuentes died in 1997—during an ill-advised attempt to disguise his identity through liposuction surgery—and the federated drug-trafficking organization he had nurtured would almost immediately disintegrate into three distinct and competing organizations wary of each other's actions. Amado's brother Vicente "El Viceroy" Carrillo Fuentes was weaker and a less inspiring leader and entrepreneur, and the power and influence that had accrued to Carrillo Fuentes's Juárez Plaza would gradually migrate toward directors of the Sinaloa Plaza, where it then remained solidly rooted for the next twenty-five years. The leadership of the Juárez Plaza was assumed by El Viceroy, but the overall direction of the expanding business in Mexico was now in the hands of men from the Sinaloa Plaza, such as El Azul Esparragoza Moreno, El Güero Palma Salazar, El Mayo Zambada García, Nacho Coronel Villareal, and El Chapo Guzmán Loera, who was still incarcerated in Altiplano at the time of Amado Carrillo Fuentes's death. The loosely organized but effective arrangements that had been forged under the leadership of Carrillo Fuentes fragmented amid persistent and ongoing arguments about turf and tolls, and arguably even more because of personal disputes between the entire Arellano Félix clan and the aggressive actions of El Chapo Guzmán. The Arrellano Félix family was the first to withdraw and assert independence, even though uncle and family patriarch Miguel Ángel Félix Gallardo had been the architect of the successful cooperative model that dominated throughout the 1990s. The family had locked down control of the lucrative Tijuana and Mexicali turf feeding Southern California and had decided that there was little point in working with others to manage routes that primarily ran through the inland states of Sonora, Chihuahua, and Durango.

The Gulf Cartel and Creation of Los Zetas

The history of narco trafficking up to this point has focused on Sinaloan roots, but another drug organization with a distinct history also emerged as a powerful force during the 1990s. One of its leaders created a powerful drug organization that would come to parallel the power and reach of the Sinaloa groups, and eventually one of its capos changed the face of narco trafficking after he created a paramilitary force. The nascent Cártel del Golfo emerged from a different tradition and context than that characterizing the cartels with Sinaloa origins. There were no dominant families with a long tradition of producing marijuana and heroin and links cemented over time by a powerful subterranean criminal code. Instead, a band of powerful individuals forged agreements to create a criminal enterprise in northeast Mexico that ruled over border cities south of Brownsville and Laredo, Texas, and expanded to interior cities connected by commerce and a history of smuggling illegal goods. The expansion into drug transportation began under the direction of Juan García Abrego, who recognized the business opportunity and created a drug-trafficking organization from scratch after the Rodríguez Orejuelas brothers from the Cali Cartel asked him to transport their cocaine. He created an organization and entered into an uneasy partnership with several other criminal groups and almost immediately emerged as a powerful figure in global narco trafficking. At the time, his organized crime group was often viewed as a *cártel consentido*—a favored cartel—during both the Ernesto Zedillo and the Vicente Fox administrations.

But arguably, the most radical impact on narco trafficking in Mexico happened after García Abrego had gone. A car mechanic and petty thief named Osiel Cárdenas Guillén brawled his way to the leadership of the Gulf Cartel through violence, betrayal, and terror and forced other Mexican cartels to respond in kind. One of his nicknames—"El Mata Amigos" or Friend Killer—was well deserved, and it encapsulated the dynamics that dominated the internal workings of an arriviste criminal enterprise whose connective bonds were rooted in fear, intimidation, and mutual avarice rather than trust and tradition.

An old-time regional cacique, bootlegger, and smuggler named Juan Nepomuceno Guerra was the original founder of the Gulf criminal enterprise, but it was his nephew Juan García Abrego who formed a criminal syndicate that expanded into drug trafficking and created the criminal group that eventually disintegrated to spin off more violent factions that were responsible for the worst violence that Mexico had seen since the revolutionary era.

By the time he died in July 2001 at eighty-six years of age, Nepomuceno had never been charged for any crime even though he had openly bragged that he began a lifelong trajectory on the edge of respectability while still a teenager involved in smuggling whiskey alongside his brother in the 1930s. By the 1970s and 1980s, he headed an underworld syndicate that smuggled goods of all types and was widely recognized as the most powerful cacique and fayuquero in northeast Mexico. His nephew diversified that smuggling empire by convincing his uncle to add cocaine, marijuana, and synthetic drugs to the repertoire. Nepomuceno reportedly agreed reluctantly to the expansion, as long as he personally could remain at arm's length from the new operations. Although he reportedly warned his nephew that drugs would bring the wrath of the DEA, he nevertheless allowed García Abrego to develop a network that would smuggle cocaine into the USA. But García Abrego would do much more than add Andean cocaine, and he eventually converted the entire fayuquero infrastructure into an efficient drug operation with several component parts that included marijuana and brown heroin (Guerrero Gutiérrez 2015a).

The Rodríquez Orejuela brothers at the head of the Cali Cartel were looking for new routes into the United States when the DOJ closed down its shipping routes through the Caribbean to Miami. They contracted with García Abrego to deliver Andean cocaine to the U.S. market. The contract with them was estimated to represent 15 to 20 percent of all the cocaine that reached the USA during the 1990s. In the beginning, García Abrego negotiated a flat fee per kilo (estimated to be $1,500) but eventually renegotiated a deal that allowed him to retain half of the shipped cocaine in return for the guaranteed delivery without charge of the other half into the U.S. market. The arrangement meant that García Abrego's organization—originally identified in DEA reports as El Cártel de Matamoros—had to purchase safe houses to stockpile cocaine, and it also made it necessary to beef up security teams and develop their own contacts for distribution of their half. Those contacts were forged through both bribery and threat and depended on buying off government officials in the Procuraduría de Justicia, in CISEN, in state police, and almost everyone in the municipal police. It also required the cooperation of customs and immigration officials on both sides of the border. But, most of all, it depended on the corruptibility of governors and politicians in Tamaulipas State. Quickly, the organization known then as the Cártel del Matamoros moved from being a regional player to a large-scale drug-trafficking organization and enterprise with a direct involvement in almost all stages of a drug business described in figure 3 earlier in this chapter. It had also established its own version of a covert netherworld in the northeast of Mexico. But the basis for the connectivity of component parts was radically different than that which had evolved organically within Sinaloa and within family-based enterprises such as those found in the Carrillo Fuentes or Arellano Félix crime organizations.

The Matamoros Cartel relied on a blatant plata o plomo model when negotiating with authorities and officials—and almost exclusively on bribes backed by serious threats of violence. It bought off everyone with relative ease because of the long history of government corruption in northeast states but also because it established an environment of explicit intimidation where power and brute force served as the primary bond holding everyone together in an alternate version of a covert netherworld. FBI documents revealed later that García Abrego's network of connections reached high into the upper levels of the Zedillo government, and that he had been equally successful at bribing officials on the U.S. side of the border—including many individuals working for Immigration and Naturalization Services (INS) and the Texas National Guard.

García Abrego maintained a volatile working partnership with several men who worked for him to move cocaine, and many of those partnerships proved to be unpredictable and eventually divisive. There were constant internal disputes and disagreements with aggressive partners and would-be challengers such as Salvador "El Chava" Gómez Herrera, Adán "El Licenciado" Medrano, Gilberto García Mena, and Hugo Baldomero "El Señor de los Trailers" Medina Garza. The enterprise may have been frequently unstable and routinely dependent on threats and brutality, but it was nevertheless incredibly successful: other criminal groups on Mexico's Atlantic side approached García Abrego to act as couriers, and the emergent Gulf Cartel soon became the principal distributor of marijuana provided by the Oaxaca criminal organization headed by the Díaz Parada brothers.

Within a short period of time, the flourishing Gulf Cartel was moving so much cocaine and marijuana that it attracted the attention of the DOJ, which reportedly assigned fifty agents and aggressively began a program to identify informers from within the criminal organization. García Abrego's uncle Nepomuceno had been justified with his concerns; a convincing legal case against García Abrego was easily made in the United States and quickly resulted in criminal indictments against García Abrego. In 1995 he was the first Mexican narco trafficker and kingpin placed on the FBI Top Ten Most Wanted list. He was arrested near Monterrey, Nuevo León; extradited immediately without Mexican government objection; brought to trial within eight months; and found guilty and sentenced to eleven consecutive life terms in a U.S. prison. For a period of time, he somehow managed to direct the Gulf Cartel from within the American prison, but that stopped when his lawyers were also charged with trafficking and laundering, and they could no longer relay messages.

The extradition and arrest of García Abrego set off a fierce battle for control of the Gulf Cartel. There was no family member to inherit leadership, but García Abrego had designated Óscar "El Licenciado" Malherbe de León to take over. He was arrested only four months after taking control. Without a clear leader, the Gulf Cartel began a descent into anarchy when several lugartenientes (subcommanders) began to operate autonomously and established private security teams to defend their strips of plaza: groups like Los Metros and Los Escorpiones emerged in Matamoros, Los Rojos in Reynosa, and Los Tangos and Los Sierras in Tampico; their clashes resulted in a horrific wave of violence across Tamaulipas. In the midst of that infighting, Salvador "El Chava" Gómez Herrera and Osiel Cárdenas Guillén emerged as the two most likely candidates to lead the Gulf Cartel.[50] El Chava realized that he could only retain a share of power if he was willing to reach an agreement with Cárdenas Guillén. But that was a fatal misjudgment; Cárdenas Guillén gained control and earned his notorious nickname, "El Mata Amigo," by ordering the execution of El Chava in 1999.

Cárdenas Guillén was unpredictable, prone to bouts of paranoia most likely fed by his prodigious cocaine habit. He trusted no one and was most likely justified to act that way, during an unpredictable period when the Gulf Cartel had descended into back-stabbing, chaos, and infighting. The members of the Gulf Cartel had been bound together by avarice and personal agendas rather than trust or family ties. Cárdenas Guillén's response to real and imagined threats had repercussions that would affect narco trafficking and change the dynamics of drug plazas; a decade of wars within cartels and wars between cartels was the result.

Cardénas Guillén asked his trusted personal bodyguard to recruit more deserters from the Grupo Aeromóvil de Fuerzas Especiales (GAFE) to serve as personal centurions and an armed wing and paramilitary force. That decision gave birth to Los Zetas—a violent group that would be front and center in most internal wars of cartels for the next decade. His bodyguard was himself a retired army lieutenant named Arturo "Z-1" Guzmán Decena, who lured an estimated twenty deserters to serve as Cárdenas Guillén's personal bodyguards.

The deserters were lured by high salaries and better living conditions than the army provided; many among them had received special training in antiterrorism tactics in Fort Hood, Texas, and were skilled in antiterrorism and the use of high-technology equipment and armaments. A recent Spanish-language novela describes the training regimen of those recruits, their initial days as praetorian guards for El Mata Amigo, and the expansion and eventual split of Los Zetas. The events portrayed in Ricardo Raphael's book are deeply rooted in truth and fact and present a history that is even more horrifying and frightening than most previous accounts of Los Zetas (Raphael 2019).

With the emergence of Los Zetas, the stage was set for a decade of violent clashes with the older organizations that had evolved in the Golden Triangle. That violence and those battles are described in the next chapter.

CHAPTER 5

Wars Within, Between, and Against Cartels

Meanwhile, Mexico remains a military oligarchy, and the army sucks up a fourth of the government's income. Soldiers are everywhere, and their only conceivable function is to hold down the restless populace, afflicted by hunger and choked by a prodigious birth rate, and ready to follow an impassioned orator who promises to lead them out of the wilderness.

Mother Mexico is not feeding her children.

—Lesley Bird Simpson, *Many Mexicos*, 1941

Period 3: Fragmentation, Wars Within Cartels, Wars Between Cartels

There were relatively few Mexican drug-trafficking organizations in the mid-1980s and only one—the Guadalajara Cartel—had a national and international reach. That first cartel came close to collapse in the aftermath of the Kiki Camarena incident but remerged as a federation and unity of purpose despite periodic disputes requiring *ajusticiamientos* that were inevitably violent. The factions were held together by a type of Pax Mafiosa and traditional codes that minimized and constrained the disruptive impact of disagreements. Equilibrium and balance were regularly restored whenever disputes and arguments threatened to undermine the business model. Distinct drug factions or syndicates ruled designated territories and regions where they had nurtured connections to local authorities and businesses—especially to police agencies and military officials. In those years, the hegemonic rule of the PRI was unassailable and remained a powerful driving and supportive force. Mexican drug syndicates progressively emerged as a global presence

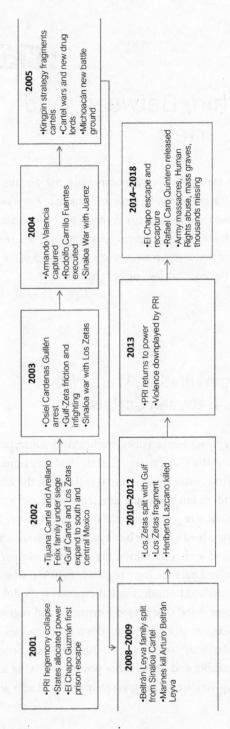

FIGURE 6 Cartel wars, 2001–2018. Graphic created by author.

2001
- PRI hegemony collapse
- States allocated power
- El Chapo Guzmán first prison escape

2002
- Tijuana Cartel and Arellano Felix family under siege
- Gulf Cartel and Los Zetas expand to south and central Mexico

2003
- Osiel Cardenas Guillén arrest
- Gulf-Zeta friction and infighting
- Sinaloa war with Los Zetas

2004
- Armando Valencia captured
- Rodolfo Carrillo Fuentes executed
- Sinaloa War with Juarez

2005
- Kingpin strategy fragments cartels
- Cartel wars and new drug lords
- Michoacán new battle ground

2008–2009
- Beltrán Leyva family split from Sinaloa Cartel
- Marines kill Arturo Beltrán Leyva

2010–2012
- Los Zetas split with Gulf
- Los Zetas fragment
- Heriberto Lazcano killed

2013
- PRI returns to power
- Violence downplayed by PRI

2014–2018
- El Chapo escape and recapture
- Rafael Caro Quintero released
- Army massacres, Human Rights abuse, mass graves, thousands missing

thanks to the powerful agents of the state who provided protection and, in all likelihood, authorized all business.

There are divergent views about who was specifically responsible for overseeing and administering the emergence of the cartels within the federal government, but it is certain that the chain of command and lines of authority passed directly through the corrupt DFS, which acted as the crucial nexus. Future access to documents and American court archives may eventually reveal which state agents were directly involved in creating the powerful Guadalajara Cartel and guiding its overall criminal infrastructure, but it's equally probable that archival evidence will show that the Guadalajara Cartel actually emerged organically by simply exploiting widespread corruption and gaps in governance. Although the specific role of government officials remains in the realm of rumor, the undeniable reality is that transnational narco trafficking took root in Mexico in the 1980s, and drug organizations emerged poised to become dominant powers in the Western Hemisphere and beyond by working hand in glove with government agents.

Growth and expansion were temporarily interrupted by the colossal blunder of brutally killing DEA agent Kiki Camarena. The economic power and antidrug dogma of the United States required the Mexican state to suppress the visibility of Mexican drug organizations. The outcome following Operation Leyenda was a restructuring and renegotiation of the terms of the Pax Narca between the state and the criminal organizations. That led to a temporary retreat into the subterranean world. The withdrawal was accomplished by a tripartite division of national turf and a negotiated agreement to operate by the same rules. It also included a shared understanding that drug operations would agree to federated and cooperative partnerships mediated by dominant jefes like Amado Carrillo Fuentes, Juan José Esparragoza Moreno, and others. Powerful officials within the PGR, Mexican intelligence agencies, and the PRI gave their blessing to the new arrangement and provided immunity as long as the new agreement held. It was inevitable that there would be grumbling, dispute, and disagreement among the partners, but in the aftermath of the Camarena murder, the commitment to a renegotiated Pax Narca was absolutely necessary because it staved off an international response—especially from the United States—but also prevented internal disputes from spiralling out of control.

The covert netherworld then focused on new opportunities that would come when the Carlos Salinas de Gortari government opened up Mexico and fast-tracked negotiations for NAFTA. For a few years, Mexico's underworld remained relatively peaceful and focused on taking advantage of the new economic reality and the increased access to the American market. That new trade agreement also created space for the Gulf Cartel to emerge as a powerful force and competitor to the older cartels.

The relative tranquility that dominated the 1990s was endangered when Vicente Fox Quesada and PAN ended the hegemonic rule of the PRI. The number of drug organizations mushroomed when the hierarchical model of governance and centralized federal power was supplanted by a decentralized version that shared power, authority, and even revenue with Mexico's thirty-one states and the Federal District. Simmering feuds erupted into violent confrontations when governance shifted to governors and as new routes and markets opened up because of NAFTA. But there were no major disruptions to the overall peace immediately, and the new millennium began with four powerful organizations in control of clearly demarcated plazas, and violence continuing its downward trend with the worst of it confined to a few states and municipalities in the northwest and along the northern border.

By the end of the first decade of the twenty-first century, the four criminal syndicates now competed with another ten that had emerged as powerful forces. Those fourteen organizations sometimes cooperated with each other but with increasing regularity challenged each other for dominance. More than a few were prepared to fight for the right to control established plazas and open up new ones. By 2008 three distinct but interconnected wars had erupted in Mexico and had generated the exponential increase in violence and death described in chapter 1. Several wars *within* cartels broke out when jefes challenged each other and ignored the traditional codes and shared understandings. Wars *between* cartels also erupted nationally when some organizations violently disputed control of existing routes and began campaigns to establish new ones in a period of expansion and diversification. And a disastrous war *against* cartels started in 2007 when the Felipe Calderón Hinojosa government sent the Mexican army to fight the cartels he identified as the most threatening.

The business model of global narco trafficking had also changed, and cartels began to look more like other global mafias: a perfect storm of circumstances had elevated Mexican crime bosses to become major players in global drug distribution and international money laundering, and all organizations—but especially those from the Gulf Coast—expanded their criminal involvement into areas far beyond the transport of drugs. The growth and expansion made Mexican criminal organizations the target of ever-watchful eyes within the DEA and FBI in Washington, D.C., who remained committed warriors in their four-decade-old global War on Drugs.

In 2007 a foolishly inept war against cartels was instigated by President Calderón and generated a spike in violence that soared to previously unimaginable levels. It was the beginning of a losing battle that would drag on for the next twelve years. He had committed the Mexican state to a narrow strategy focused on the capture and elimination of cartel leaders—a kingpin strategy—and did so by delegating the mandate to the military. Calderón's decision resulted in a fragmentation of criminal organizations and created new criminal groups led by bosses who were willing to do anything to achieve their goal.

Calderón ended his presidency as it began—with political controversy and minimal support of the nation. His term ended with him earning only a modicum of respect and applause from those who continued to believe in war as the solution to the drug problem, but his party and Mexican democracy suffered the consequences when the failure of his war paved the way for the PRI to rise from the ashes and return unexpectedly to power in 2012. PRI president Enrique Peña Nieto immediately moved to restore as much centralized power as he could seize; that new PRI government explicitly pursued security policies that deliberately targeted larger crime organizations for the purpose of fragmenting them into smaller groups. Peña Nieto believed smaller crime groups were more easily controlled, and over the course of his sexenio, the number of cartels and criminal groups exploded to reach a total of between sixty and eighty identifiable groups and left no state untouched by the impact of drug trafficking and violence. Those new groups are described in chapter 7.

Violence and the various wars on cartels are directly responsible for at least 60 percent of the 355,273 homicidios dolosos recorded by the Instituto Nacional de Estadística y Geografía (INEGI, National Institute of Statistics and Geography) between 2006 and the end of 2020.[1] Although this period has been variously called Mexico's never-ending war, a decade-long war, or the cancerous war, those descriptions oversimplify a complex history by treating them as one phenomenon (Editorial Nexos 2017). This was not an era of *one* war but in fact more accurately viewed as a tragic period when three simultaneous wars had broken out in Mexico—wars *within* cartels, wars *between* cartels, and a disastrous war *against* cartels waged by the military.

Each has a distinct trajectory, but there is absolutely no question that collectively those three wars were responsible for the surge in violence and the unimaginable bloodshed of the first two decades of the new millennium. The trajectory of each of those three wars is complicated, and the following pages will present a broad explanation for why each broke out and explore the connections between them.

Decentralization and Narco Politics

In the very first year of the new millennium, Partido Acción Nacional standard-bearer Vicente Fox was elected president and ended a seventy-one-year hegemonic reign of the Partido Revolucionario Institutional and what had been described as a "perfect dictatorship" by Carlos Fuentes. Mexico's constitutional limits on reelection had routinely generated instability and uncertainty during the final year of electoral terms, but the dramatic rejection of the PRI in 2001 had an earth-shattering impact on the Pax Narca and disrupted the equilibrium of the covert netherworld that had emerged under the PRI.[2]

During the seven-decade PRI domination, political power was exclusively hierarchical and centralized in Los Pinos (the Mexican equivalent of the White House); no decisions were made outside the purview of an imperial presidency and the oligarchical power linked directly to the president (Krauze 1997). That power included nominating successors via El Dedazo, and absolute control over cabinet, gubernatorial, justice, and judicial appointments.[3] Of course, there was also a widespread understanding that all negotiated arrangements with narco traffickers were centralized and that they reportedly reached into the highest levels of government.

PAN preferred decentralized governance and immediately instituted changes to allocate and share power with states—specifically, with the governors (see Jones 2016; Payan, Staudt, and Kruszewski 2013; Selee 2011). Under the hierarchical and centralized model of PRI governance, the links between narco traffickers and the state were located in Mexico City and situated specifically within the federal agencies, but in the decentralized model favored by PAN, governors' offices would become alternate loci of power—or at least parallel nexuses of dominance.

Most importantly, decentralization created opportunities for drug organizations to directly influence and control politics at the local level by funding local political campaigns and directly controlling parties at the state level:

the plurinominal electoral model that also applied to each state was easily manipulated and ripe for corruption. Drug organizations and entrepreneurial interests quickly adapted to the new governance framework and realized that the new political environment represented new opportunities for expansion through corruption. Making certain that governors and legislators were invited into the covert netherworld of illegality became the new mandate for cartels, and the decentralization of decision-making opened up new spaces for new and numerous criminal organizations. Although it is difficult to provide an exact figure, it is obvious that enormous sums of dark money were redirected toward the assurance of a regional influence. Bundles of cash made several corrupt governors extremely rich and left them sitting as important gatekeepers in the business of narco trafficking that was increasingly globalized. The negative poster boy for that new direction was Quintana Roo governor Mario Ernesto Villanueva Madrid, who was willingly corrupted when the Gulf Cartel expanded operations into his state to facilitate connections to Colombia and the Gulf Cartel's source of cocaine (originally, the Cali Cartel).

Not only state legislatures were targeted and enriched; municipal and state police were also targeted by the cartels (Ravelo 2007a). Some organizations immediately benefited from the change in overall governance: for example, the Gulf Cartel straightaway pursued and developed extremely profitable connections with state governors like Villanueva in Quintana Roo and Tomás Jesús Yarrington Ruvalcaba in Tamaulipas. In other states, the direct relationship between specific cartels and politicians were not as obvious at the national and international level, but they were definitely operating and recognized locally.

One change that came with the PAN administration initially seemed little more than a shift in presidential preference for stronger ties to the USA, but it triggered major disruptions in Mexican cartel organizations for years to come. President Fox had promised to eliminate barriers to Mexico's long-standing policy of no extradition—especially to the United States, which had aggressively pursued criminal activity across transnational borders. He promised to extradite criminals wanted by the DOJ and the U.S. Department of the Treasury, in particular the kingpins the United States had targeted in pursuit of its global War on Drugs. Fox promised to eliminate legal barriers in Mexican law even though there was a deep-rooted historical mistrust and fear of aggressive extraterritorial U.S. intervention in Mexican politics. As

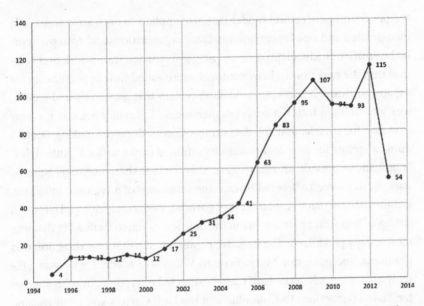

FIGURE 7 Extraditions from Mexico to the United States, 1995–2013. Reprinted from Clare Ribando Seelke and Kristin Finklea, *U.S.-Mexican Security Cooperation: The Mérida Initiative and Beyond* (Washington, D.C.: Congressional Research Service, 2014).

figure 7 shows, there were 920 extraditions to the United States from Mexico between 1995 and 2013, but only 56 of those happened before Fox took office (Ribando Seelke and Finklea 2014).

Extradition of drug lords and increasing dominance of the U.S. War on Drugs and reliance on a "kingpin strategy" grew under Fox's watch, even though that shift risked alienating Mexican nationalists who held strong objections to any bilateral agreement with the United States and to Mexican cooperation in the War on Drugs. Many Mexican intellectuals believed, rightly so, that Richard Nixon's global War on Drugs had been forced upon Mexico and was backed by aggressive U.S. foreign policy increasingly out of touch with global trends toward liberalization and decriminalization. Many argued that Mexico should develop a homegrown policy on drugs that was independent of the American intransigence and bullying that conveniently ignored the reality that its own citizens were the largest market for illegal drugs. There were also critics who argued that routinizing extradition would lead to the Colombianization of the U.S. War on Drugs and generate a violent backlash from cartels like those that exploded in Colombia when Pablo Escobar Gaviria and the Medellín Cartel created the paramilitary group

Los Extraditables to wage guerrilla warfare against the state. Judges and politicians were assassinated, and innocent civilians were murdered when Medellín Cartel paramilitary forces confronted the state directly and even planted a bomb on a passenger airline (M. Bowden 2001).

However, a paramilitary response from cartels and Colombianization did not occur in Mexico when extradition became certain. But there was a specific consequence that would have a long-lasting and bloody implication. Apparently worried about his own eminent extradition, El Chapo Guzmán Loera made his first escape from a maximum-security prison through bribery and collusion, and he fled to the welcoming terrain of the Golden Triangle, where he enjoyed the protection of local authorities and police (state and municipal) (see chapter 6). But it should be noted that Guzmán nor the Sinaloa Cartel responded to the arrival of extradition with paramilitary attacks; they seemed unconcerned that the federal government would actually consider pursuing El Chapo to the Golden Triangle, where he was protected by the fraternity of men and women and communities supportive of the Sinaloa Cartel.

The decentralization and allocation of powers to states, in fact, provided a safety valve that insulated El Chapo and other drug bosses from immediate prosecution and extradition initiated by federal authorities. Even though the federal policy seemed to represent a major shift and retreat from the implicit terms of a broader Pax Narca that had sheltered drug lords at the national level, the relief valve of power sharing with states had shifted enough influence on governors to serve as an alternate source of protection for drug bosses behind a powerful firewall now situated at the state level. Guzmán remained safe within the friendly boundaries of Sinaloa State and neighboring Durango. In fact, he went on to enjoy twelve years of freedom protected by governors, state legislatures, the military, and a corrupt Sinaloa state police. The violent backlash that had emerged in Colombia never materialized in Mexico in spite of the widespread fear that Fox's extradition policy would result in the Colombianization of Mexico's antidrug policies.

It was during the PAN government of Fox that the U.S. government and the DOJ and operatives in Mexico began to rely on two additional initiatives in pursuing the goals of the U.S. War on Drugs. Inadvertently, both of those policies also contributed to an increase in violence and eventually to the fragmentation of cartels. One policy was the introduction and full-blown application of the kingpin designation, and the other was a strategy employed by the DEA that sought to undermine criminal organizations by targeting lower-level operatives who could be made protected witnesses. The strategy was to gradually weaken criminal organizations from within by undermining them from below.

The Kingpin Act

The introduction of a kingpin policy provided the DOJ with a powerful tool to put pressure on drug organizations. It represented an attack on their money and businesses dependent on laundered funds. Sections from the DOJ press releases describing this policy are reproduced here at length:

> On December 3, 1999, the President signed into law the Kingpin Act (21 U.S.C. §§ 1901–1908 and 8 U.S.C § 1182), providing authority for the application of sanctions to significant foreign narcotics traffickers and their organizations operating worldwide. Section 805(b) of the Kingpin Act blocks all property and interests in property within the United States, or within the possession or control of any U.S. person, which are owned or controlled by significant foreign narcotics traffickers, as identified by the President, or foreign persons designated by the Secretary of the Treasury, after consultation with the Attorney General, the Director of Central Intelligence, the Director of the Federal Bureau of Investigation, the Administrator of the Drug Enforcement Administration, the Secretary of Defense, the Secretary of Homeland Security, and the Secretary of State, as meeting the criteria as identified in the Kingpin Act.
>
> On July 5, 2000, OFAC [Office of Foreign Assets Control] issued the Foreign Narcotics Kingpin Sanctions Regulations, 31 C.F.R. Part 598, which implement the Kingpin Act and block all property and interests in property within the United States, or within the possession or control of any U.S. person, which are owned or controlled by specially designated narcotics traffickers, as identified by the President, or foreign persons designated by the Secretary of the Treasury, after consultation with the Attorney General, the Director of Central Intelligence, the Director of the Federal Bureau of Investigation, the Administrator of the Drug Enforcement Administration, the Secretary of Defense, the Secretary of Homeland Security and the Secretary of State, as meeting the following criteria:
>
> • Materially assists in, or provides financial or technological support for or to, or provides goods or services in support of, the interna-

tional narcotics trafficking activities of a specially designated narcotics trafficker.

- Owned, controlled, or directed by, or acts for or on behalf of, a
  specially designated narcotics trafficker; or
- Plays a significant role in international narcotics trafficking. (U.S.
  Department of the Treasury 2014)

Under this designation, all assets of an individual or a family member identified as a kingpin could be immediately frozen—and much of that dark
money was systematically moving through U.S. banks and financial institutions, where it lay within reach of U.S. Treasury agents. Equally important,
the threat of being designated a kingpin became a powerful bargaining tool
and a sledgehammer that was increasingly used by U.S. agents who sought
out informants to build legal cases against narco traffickers much higher up
in the organizational chain. The act gave field agents a powerful lever that
could be used as a legitimate threat to "encourage" cartel operatives to provide evidence leading to the arrest of their business partners and associates
in return for being allowed to retain a portion of the proceeds gained from
the drug trade. In many cases, the arrangements involved the additional step
of granting protected witness status: that was done when a major narco-
trafficking figure could be arrested and extradited to the United States based
on the testimony of a witness who could gain immunity from prosecution,
retention of some of their savings, and a new identity.

This strategy had resulted in the takedown of major drug lords in Colombia, and how that unfolded was described in specific detail in *El Cártel de
los sapos*—an autobiographical book by a young Colombian who became an
informer (López López 2008; see also Birns and Sanchez 2007; Rueda and Congote 2008).[4] To this point in time, the most concise English-language description of how the DOJ relied on protected witnesses to build legal cases against
Mexican cartel capos is found in David Epstein's description of a DEA operation
that undermined and destroyed the Arellano Félix operation in Tijuana and
Baja California (Epstein and ProPublica 2016). Most recently, that strategy of
offering *protected witness status* was also described by Anabel Hernández in
her Spanish-language book *El traidor: El diario secreto del hijo del Mayo* (2020).

Paradoxically, both American strategies (extradition, protected witness
status) inadvertently strengthened the overall power and dominance of the
Sinaloa Cartel. Several reports and compelling evidence indicate that Sinaloa's

competitors were targeted more frequently for arrest, and consequently their organizations were badly weakened and left fragmented when leaders were extradited and left behind a leadership vacuum (see Burnett, Peñaloza, and Benincasa 2010 for an example): David Epstein's (2016) article in *The Atlantic* can also be read as a sad lament about how the arrests and extraditions of brothers in the Arellano Félix family directly resulted in the strengthening of the Sinaloa Cartel while it simultaneously granted immunity to brutal killers who received protective witness status.

Some statistical evidence supports the argument that the Sinaloa Cartel was relatively immune to prosecution and charges, at least during the sexenios of Fox and Calderón. During the Calderón sexenio, the Mexican army reported that it had arrested more than 41,000 suspects. An investigative team from National Public Radio (NPR) examined the profiles of 2,600 criminal defendants arrested between 2006 and 2011 and found that the Gulf-Zetas members represented more than 40 percent of the individuals arrested—more than 1,100 in all. The Sinaloa, Beltrán Leyva, and Tijuana Cartels each accounted for approximately 12 percent of the arrests. NPR also looked at arrests in the Ciudad Juárez area after March 2008, when the Mexican army arrived as part of the country's war against cartels. Up until 2010, the Mexican government had initiated criminal action against only *sixteen* Sinaloa Cartel members. In contrast, there were eighty-eight prosecutions of the Juárez Cartel reported (Burnett, Peñaloza, and Benincasa 2010).

It is impossible to definitively state why the Sinaloa faction was relatively successful in avoiding extradition and remained resistant to the fragmentation of its overall structure for years, but it is intriguing to speculate about the reasons for its permanence and long-standing success. Was it the result of direct government protection for a *cártel consentido*, or the result of the powerful bonds of social cohesion that linked members of the Sinaloa Cartel together, or simply the astute cleverness of a cartel sophisticated enough to engage in Machiavellian maneuvering?[5]

Or perhaps it was just a matter of waiting for a larger end point of U.S. policy to eventually run the entire course and complete a grander plan of action. The strategy of identifying protective witnesses very clearly began with lower-order members and pressured them to serve up the evidence implicating those higher up the pecking order. Perhaps the DEA and the DOJ actually do have a long-term plan to slowly move up the ladder, but it has to wait and build its case step by step by eliminating weaker links in the chain before it can bring down the most powerful.

The extradition and trial of El Chapo did not take place until eighteen years after his first spectacular escape in the first year of Fox's sexenio. The DOJ has given no indication that it now plans to stop attacking the Sinaloa Cartel even after the imprisonment of El Chapo. In the aftermath of his Brooklyn trial, U.S. justice officials released documents that signal their intent to pursue the prosecution of high-level government operatives and higher-placed intermediaries in a covert netherworld that disproportionately protected Sinaloa Cartel factions from prosecution. The first post-Chapo high-level target is none other than Mexico's former secretary of public security Genaro García Luna, who was initially held in a Texas prison to await a trial date and then shipped to Brooklyn, New York, at the beginning of 2021 (Angel 2019; Barragán 2020; Bojorquez 2019b; Estevez 2020b; Redacción Sin Embargo 2020).

It is also worth emphasizing that Vicentillo Zambada Niebla, the son of Sinaloa boss Ismael "El Mayo" Zambada García, was extradited and charged with international narco trafficking in a Chicago court; his principal line of defense was that he was actually an informant for the DEA and that he had evidence of that agreement with agents (Aristegui 2013; Vega 2014). Vicentillo further claimed that he had received both his father's and El Chapo's approval to accept that DEA offer because it not only allowed him an exit from the covert netherworld but would simultaneously weaken Sinaloa's competitors. The publication of *El traidor* (Hernández 2020) added support to the speculation of many who have long argued that the Sinaloa Cartel has always been the cártel consentido, which explains why it is the most stable criminal organization in Mexico. But it is especially important to note that El Mayo remains free, in spite of the claims found in Vicentillo's diary and Hernández's assertion that it is that very same El Mayo who is the *capo de tutti capos* and the person most responsible for overseeing the criminal underworld of Mexico for more than thirty-five years.

Wars Within and Between Cartels

El Chapo Guzmán's role has been elevated to mythical proportions and is greatly overstated (see chapter 6). Given the long history of narco Mexico and the nature of covert netherworlds, he alone could not be responsible for all the problems linked to the drug wars that erupted after 2004. But that does not mean he is unimportant nor that his role should be downplayed. In fact, he was directly involved in many incidents that were tipping points requiring a total restructuring and redirection of the cartel enterprise during the first decade of the new millennium.

Following his escape from Puente Grande in February 2001, he retreated to the Golden Triangle, where he reestablished a power base within the Sinaloa Cartel and the subterranean world of narco traffic with the specific support of El Mayo Zambada García and El Azul Esparragoza Moreno. Over the next decade, he was directly enmeshed and a prominent player in five actions that escalated the internal friction and led to fragmentation within the Sinaloa Cartel and resulted in direct attacks on and confrontations with several competitor cartels. His actions have triggered events that resulted in the wave of bloody violence described in chapter 1, but he cannot be held uniquely responsible for them.

Sinaloa Versus the Arellano Félix Family

Arguably, the first order of business for Guzmán Loera after escaping was to weaken and incapacitate the Arellano Félix operation based in Tijuana and controlling the Baja California routes. He was driven by a personal vendetta in targeting the Tijuana Cartel, ever since a feud with Ramón Arellano Félix resulted in his initial incarceration in 1993. But attacks on the Arellano Félix family represented much more than personal payback and *ajustes* or *ajusticiamientos* for old grievances: archival evidence from protected witnesses indicates that the fundamental reason that El Chapo Guzmán and the Sinaloa Cartel directly attacked the Arellano Félix Cartel was related to plaza disputes and unresolvable disagreements with the family over excessive tolls they demanded for access to their trafficking routes through Mexicali and other border crossings in western Arizona and eastern California.[6] Although there were violent confrontations between armed factions of the Arellano Félix and the Sinaloa factions, many of the attacks on the Tijuana Cartel were carried out indirectly by feeding incriminating information to the DEA. Those tips facilitated the arrests of the brothers and their eventual extradition to the United States. The information recorded on the DOJ indictments was provided directly from the Sinaloa Cartel and possibly El Chapo himself.

Many of those Machiavellian moves are described in an *Atlantic* article laying out the details of DEA operations targeting the Arellano Félix family (Epstein and ProPublica 2016). The DEA, the FBI, and the DOJ were responsible for eliminating the brothers who headed Sinaloa's competition in Baja California—the only exception being the direct killing of Ramón Arellano Félix after he set off on a misplaced and quixotic mission to personally execute El Mayo or El Chapo or both—only to be gunned down by a traffic policeman in Mazatlán, Sinaloa.

Sinaloa Versus the Carrillo Fuentes Family

While the DEA picked off the Arellano Félix family one by one, El Chapo and sicarios from the Sinaloa Cartel were busy on a second front challenging the Carrillo Fuentes family in order to undermine its control of Ciudad Juárez. Much of the dirty work and killing would be directed by El Chapo's longtime allies and childhood companions—the Beltrán Leyva brothers. But Guzmán's hands were not personally clean, and he played a direct role in issuing a command intended to send a message and weaken the Carrillo Fuentes family's control over the important border point of Ciudad Juárez. The Sinaloa faction was reportedly also unhappy with tolls on Sinaloa operators moving marijuana and cocaine through the important Juárez corridor but were especially angered by the strong-armed and arrogant tactics of groups working on behalf of the Carrillo Fuentes family. El Chapo was alleged to be personally responsible for ordering a team of sicarios to execute Rodolfo Carrillo Fuentes on September 11, 2004. The youngest Carrillo Fuentes brother, known as "El Niño del Oro," was gunned down along with his wife in a Cinépolis theater parking lot in Culiacán by commandos who were most likely state police officers on the Sinaloa cartel payroll or on retainers from them.

That cold-blooded execution was the initial salvo in what became a long, protracted, and especially bloody war between Sinaloa factions and Juárez factions within the Sinaloa Federation, and it immediately turned Ciudad Juárez into one of the most dangerous cities in the world as sicarios from both sides indiscriminately fought bloody battles in the streets and targeted anyone suspected of working for the other side. Often, they made mistakes and innocent civilians were caught in the crossfire (Guillermoprieto 2015). Mexico's homicide statistics show a sharp upward tick beginning in 2004 as a result of that specific dispute. Those battles between the Sinaloa faction and the Juárez faction are described more fully in four highly recommended English-language books by Malcolm Beith (2010), Ioan Grillo (2011), Ricardo Ainslie (2013), and Ed Vulliamy (2010). The brutality and viciousness of those years are described in another highly recommended biography of a sicario by Charles Bowden and Molly Molloy (2011).

Peace was eventually restored by a rumored high-level intervention and secret peace talks demanded by federal authorities. Those were overseen and arranged by intermediary Esparragoza Moreno, who had maintained strong ties to both sides in the dispute. The chaos and the brutality of that vicious war were also described by Bowden in his book *Down by the River* (2002) as well as in several other articles and books he authored (Bowden 1997a, 1997b, 1998, 2005, 2009).

Sinaloa Versus Beltrán Leyva Brothers

El Chapo Guzmán was also believed to be directly responsible for arranging the arrest of the youngest Beltrán Leyva brother—Alfredo—whose handle "El Mochomo" (Vicious Red Ant) was by all accounts an appropriate description of his unpredictable character. Arturo "El Barbas" Beltrán Leyva was the oldest of three brothers who had grown up with Guzmán near La Tuna in the sierra; there are unconfirmed reports that they are actually cousins. The young Alfredo had become a divisive figure in Culiacán because of his bullying and aggressive swagger; there were many complaints forwarded to Sinaloa Cartel elders that he was a loose cannon and abusively disruptive, and that he had finally gone too far in testing the patience of friends of the cartel in the capital city, Culiacán.

Whatever the reason, Alfredo was arrested by federal authorities on February 21, 2008, when his bodyguards failed to report for duty to his safe house in central Culiacán. Federal troops headed by Edgar Millán Gómez, the third-ranking member of Mexico's Secretariat of Public Security and the acting commissioner of the Federal Preventive Police (PFP), literally swooped in on PGR planes to arrest Alfredo and immediately fly him to Mexico City for arraignment. El Mochomo's older brother Arturo immediately blamed El Chapo Guzmán and wasted no time in declaring war against his erstwhile partners in the Sinaloa Cartel; he simultaneously issued a very public notification that he was now the Jefe de Jefes—Boss of Bosses.

His revenge began three days after Alfredo's arrest with the execution of five Federal Police sitting in a vehicle in the heart of Culiacán in the early morning hours. They were the first executions in what became a bloody war of attrition between Arturo's forces and the rest of the Sinaloa Cartel. Shortly afterward, El Chapo's son Édgar was executed by sicarios who blasted him to oblivion with a bazooka.[7] That internal war of Sinaloa members was largely responsible for the exponential increase in the number of homicides in 2008 and 2009; that no-holds-barred civil war continued even after Arturo Beltrán Leyva himself was literally cut to pieces by marine gunfire in Cuernavaca, Morelos, two years later on December 21, 2010.

Arturo Beltrán Leyva had been security overseer and the main recruiter of sicarios for the Sinaloa Cartel; in his position, he had trained several different fighting groups on behalf of the Sinaloa faction. His teams of armed killers remained intact and operated with semiautonomous permanence after his execution; his teams were eventually responsible for the violence that spread to Guerrero State, regions of Sinaloa in the north and the south, and especially into Mexico State. The killing that soon surged out of control in Guerrero and concentrated in Acapulco was also the direct outcome of that Sinaloa War Within Cartels between the Beltrán Leyva and Chapo Guzmán factions.

Sinaloa Versus Gulf Cartel and Los Zetas

El Chapo Guzmán and the Sinaloa Cartel directly confronted the Gulf Cartel and Los Zetas at different times and in many different locations across Mexico. Guzmán and others believed there was an opening to control the border communities that spread eastward along the northern frontier from Reynosa to Nuevo Laredo, and they hoped to seize turf that they had never directly controlled. The Sinaloa Cartel apparently believed that then Gulf capo Osiel Cárdenas Guillén had spread his resources too thinly when he sent his praetorian guards, Los Zetas, away from Matamoros on a mission to expand the Gulf reach into new plazas in Nuevo León, Michoacán, and further south into Veracruz and the Yucatán.

The Sinaloa perception that the Gulf Cartel had been weakened became more credible when Cárdenas Guillén was subsequently arrested and extradited to the United States—allegedly with the help of information fed to the DEA by Sinaloa operatives. El Chapo believed that the Gulf Cartel had been seriously compromised; he deployed newly created sicario teams called Los Pelones to Piedras Negras in Coahuila State on the edge of vast Pemex oil fields. The plan was to cut off the oil and gas revenue that paid for many Gulf operations and establish a front for direct attacks on Nuevo Laredo, which had by then become the largest transborder crossing on the U.S.-Mexico frontier.[8] The Gulf Cartel was not as weakened as Guzmán and others believed, and the borderlands erupted in all-out war. About the same time, Los Zetas began a break from the Gulf Cartel and independently created estacas (local teams of hit men) north of Angostura in Sinaloa; they entered directly into an alliance with the Arellano Félix brothers, who were still battling to retain control of Tijuana. The result was a bloody wave of violence that peaked in 2011 and 2012 and which also spread far inland from the initial battlefronts situated close to the American border.

Every one of those incursions and internal battles involving the Sinaloa Cartel requires an entire book to describe, but there is one general observation that can be made. The possibility for re-creating a unified and powerful cartel in Mexico had now disappeared, and the fragmentation of cartels that was triggered by the Fox regime was irreversible. What should also be emphasized is that cartel wars had spread violence to all parts of Mexico, and the displays of victims and violence had become brutal and wanton exercises in dramaturgy. Mass killing, decapitation, and mutilation had become the norm.

When Jean-François Gayraud wrote his influential book describing the major criminal organizations of the world in 2007, he did *not* include Mexican organizations. One reason may have been that international observers still held on to the view that the drug trade in the Americas was a Colombian enterprise, and they had not yet recognized that Mexican crime organizations had successfully seized control of cocaine shipping by the mid-1990s. The Gulf Cartel had reduced the Cali Cartel to supplier status, and its Colombian rival the Medellín Cartel was using Amado Carrillo Fuentes air routes according to terms that he had established. A perfect storm of events had turned Mexico into the preferred trampoline for drug transit, but the world was slow to notice that Mexicans had taken over the control and management of those routes.

But Gayraud was perhaps justified in not including the Mexican drug organizations in his list of the most important transnational syndicates because they were still unlike other mafias of the world. They were more specialized and narrowly focused on the movement of drugs during those years. There was little evidence during the early 1990s of any deep and extensive involvement in the diverse range of criminality typical of other global mafias that had their finger in everything, from trash collection to counterfeiting goods to human smuggling (Saviano 2015). However, the singular organizational focus on drugs began to change when the Gulf Cartel emerged as a powerful player, especially when it created Los Zetas as its armed wing.

The emergence of that paramilitary force in Tamaulipas, and the fierce internal competition to control northeast plazas, also meant that force and violence had become the primary instrument for enforcing compliance and maintaining control of territory. Furthermore, the cost of maintaining a paramilitary force required larger payrolls (*la nomina*) to keep so many on retainers. The result was an expansive diversification of criminal activity to include kidnapping, extortion, prostitution, trafficking in migrants, gambling, auto theft, and especially oil and gas theft as a necessary means to pay for the growing army of criminals now under the command of cartel bosses. It also meant that the production and distribution of synthetic drugs were on the table, and that required new partnerships with suppliers of precursor drugs from overseas and the creation of new routes and markets.

The first cartel to expand extensively into diversified areas of criminality was the Gulf Cartel. Expansion became the driving force of Los Zetas, who moved into new cities where they created criminal cells known as estacas under the direct control of one of the twenty original GAFE deserters. Each invasion involved the saturation of a target area with posters announcing the coming arrival of Los Zetas and a declaration that all criminal activity in that region was now immediately under their control. Local gangs were forcibly subsumed and their activities taken over by the lead Zeta and his estaca team upon pain of brutal execution. The demonstrable ruthlessness of Los Zetas preceded their arrival in new territories and spread fear and terror; theywasted no time in institutionalizing their reputation by carrying out brutal executions and staging public displays of the bodies of those who had resisted—and in some cases, Los Zetas thought that the execution of innocents would impose a compliance on everyone who was not a gang member.

That expansion and diversity of criminality was gruesomely choreographed by the display of bodies that grew increasingly violent and brutal after Los Zetas reached into Guatemala and invited an elite corps of trained brutal soldiers known as Los Kaibiles to join their ranks. Those foreign recruits had also been trained in counterterrorism techniques and the use of heavy armaments in the USA (Fort Hood), but in addition they were less constrained when they set about to sow terror through public displays of brutality, decapitation, and dismemberment. The recent book *Hijo de la guerra* (2019) by Ricardo Raphael hints at why the original Zetas were constrained to a degree that did not apply to Los Kaibiles, who served as mercenaries. All the original Zetas simultaneously retained official posts and were still being paid as Mexican army officers and agents of the PGR even while they worked on behalf of Gulf Cartel leaders Osiel Cárdenas Guillén and his brother Antonio "Tony Tormenta" Cárdenas Guillén. Los Kaibiles were outsiders with absolutely no ties or connections to the communities they brutalized, and they were not subject to the constraints that apply to fully integrated participants in the illicit netherworld that included local politicians and business entrepreneurs.

Gulf Cartel Versus Los Zetas

In 1996 the Gulf Cartel was left with no clear leader after Juan García Abrego was extradited to the United States.[9] Osiel Cárdenas Guillén seized control in 1999 when his personal bodyguard Arturo Guzmán Decena shot his rival Salvador El Chava Gómez Herrera in the head. Cárdenas Guillén almost immediately formed a paramilitary force of deserters recruited from Guzmán Decena's former military squadron—the Grupo Aeromóvil de Fuerzas Especiales. GAFE had been initially created when President Zedillo Ponce de León hoped to rebuild Mexico's intelligence and security system and replace the widely discredited federal police. Zedillo's overall strategy was to assign military officers to key positions in administrative security and intelligence where the federal police had previously been in charge, but many of those new placements proved no more trustworthy. Zedillo also arranged for select army officers to be sent to the United States for training at the School of the Americas.

Juan Nepomuceno Guerra's criminal organization had come to drug trafficking later than the groups based in Sinaloa or Oaxaca. Personally, the longtime bootlegger and smuggler had serious doubts about expanding in that direction because he believed it would attract attention from the DEA and FBI and put his overall enterprise at risk. He relented when his nephew Juan García Abrego proposed entering into a shipping agreement with the Cali Cartel to move cocaine, and gave his blessing as long as two conditions were met: first, he would not directly participate in negotiations with

Colombian cartels, leaving the new business to be supervised directly by his nephew; second, he allowed García Abrego to use only some factions of his smooth-running fayuquero organization—specifically, the existing smuggling routes and the associated government protection that operated smoothly through bribery.

That understanding meant that García Abrego could not use his uncle's organization or network to recover decommissioned drugs or track down drugs sidetracked during transport. In effect, the uncle forced his nephew to create a parallel organization that required safe houses, protective enforcers, and an even wider network of bribed officials. García Abrego launched the organization by expanding an incipient criminal network based in Matamoros. New operators and criminal groups were put in place, and all were directly responsible to García Abrego rather than Nepomuceno. The veteran criminal gradually stepped aside and retired from the smuggling business to never spend another day in prison.

The Matamoros criminal group moved from being a regional presence to one of the most powerful criminal organizations in the Americas during the final years of the Salinas sexenio. Many observers have argued that the direct support of the Salinas family (especially Raúl) made the Gulf drug operation of García Abrego one of the sexenio's favored cartels (cártel consentido) as a result of commercial expansion spurred by NAFTA.

There are at least three reasons that success came quickly to García Abrego and his Matamoros criminal organization: first, its geographic location gave direct access to four of the most important border crossings into the United States (Matamoros, Miguel Alemán, Nuevo Laredo, and Reynosa); second, it had already established deep connections to corrupt officials in both the Salinas administration and state governor offices; and third, cocaine shipping was essentially the only business that García Abrego managed, and he would not be sidetracked by complications related to marijuana or heroin production. His immediate success brought incredible wealth, but that led to increasing notoriety and raised warning flags in Washington, D.C.

Incoming president Ernesto Zedillo responded to pressure from the DEA. García Abrego was arrested on his ranch in Villa Juárez, Nuevo León, in January 1996 without shots being exchanged. His dual citizenship justified immediate extradition to the United States on the day immediately after his arrest: within eight months, he had been adjudicated guilty on eleven different indictments and sentenced to several consecutive life terms. García

Abrego had no family members to designate as replacement, but he named trusted lugarteniente Óscar "El Licenciado" Malherbe de León to take over the reins. The arrangement lasted only a few months, and El Licenciado was arrested in February 1997, leaving the Gulf Cartel effectively rudderless. Several subcommanders and regional bosses began to operate autonomously and created their own teams of bodyguards and thugs to defend their territories during that leadership vacuum. During 1997 and 1998, vicious bands of outlaws and criminals like Los Metros and Los Escorpiones emerged in Matamoros, Los Rojos terrorized Reynosa, and Los Tangos and Los Sierras battled for dominance in Tampico. Most of those groups have remained operational through 2021, and several of them have mistakenly been elevated to the level of cartel by journalists and casual observers even though they are actually bands of criminals for hire.

In the midst of the chaos, two lugartenientes emerged as more powerful than others, and a ferocious struggle for control of the Gulf Cartel began. Cárdenas Guillén challenged El Chava Gómez, who had been the head of sicarios for García Abrego. El Chava reportedly attempted to form a partnership with Cárdenas Guillen, but the latter did not trust him and responded by creating a private security team that would eventually morph into Los Zetas. His response had an impact that lasted far beyond the internal power struggle, and it eventually changed the face of narco trafficking in Mexico. The formation of a security team consisting of highly trained paramilitary forces soon transformed Tamaulipas, Nuevo León, Coahuila, Veracruz, Michoacán, Mexico State, and Jalisco into what Guerrero Gutiérrez (2015a) described as a dominion of fear.

Dominion of Fear

The battle for control of the Gulf Cartel took a bloody and complicated turn with the emergence of Los Zetas, and paradoxically much of it flew under the international radar for several years even though it affected a large swath of the busy international border and was happening in an area that the DEA and the FBI had been monitoring closely for at least a decade. Some observers argue that the DEA had let down its guard after it had successfully captured and prosecuted Juan García Abrego and that it mistakenly believed that it had won a decisive victory in its War on Drugs.

Osiel Cárdenas Guillén prevailed to seize control of the Gulf Cartel, and his most pivotal move turned out to be the appointment of Arturo Guzmán Decena as his chief of security in 1998. Guzmán Decena had been trained as a member of the Grupo Aeromóvil de Fuerzas Especiales (GAFE), and Cárdenas Guillén gave him the responsibility of hiring a team of sicarios who would counteract El Chava Gómez and his team of trained sicarios. Guzmán Decena had targeted thirty-four former members of GAFE to join the dark side by offering salaries three times higher than their army pay, better food, and much more autonomy to earn money on the side through involvement in prostitution, human smuggling, and other crimes: ultimately, he was successful in recruiting twenty-one, but the final number reduced to twenty when one of those recruits was reportedly killed for betraying the others (see Raphael 2019). The deserters had received specialized training in heavy armaments and counterterrorism, intelligence gathering, and advanced communication at Fort Hood in the United States and they were committed to a code of military honor that bound them together as a band of brothers.[10]

Guerrero Gutiérrez is one of many observers who argue that the emergence of Los Zetas forever changed the nature of narco trafficking in Mexico.

The rise of Los Zetas signified a paradigmatic change in the operations of criminal narco-trafficking groups, since it initiated a new phase where criminal forces were professionalized. Other cartels observed the development with fear and resentment and saw how Osiel Cárdenas had seized control, and used Los Zetas to easily push aside other groups in Tamaulipas, and forced his way southward to oust the Valencia family in Michoacán and opened up and controlled all of the routes joining the Pacific and Gulf coasts. (2015a)

Cárdenas Guillén's seizure of the Gulf Cartel did not go unnoticed by the Sinaloa Cartel and its leaders at the time—especially Arturo Beltrán Leyva. According to Guerrero Gutiérrez, Cárdenas Guillén's paranoia directly led to his downfall. He never slept twice in the same place, and he lived in constant fear and terror that those closest to him were plotting to oust him. Consequently, he ordered Guzmán Decena to unleash a reign of terror aimed at rooting out anyone who might betray him or was suspected of doing so. The best description of that paranoia and reign of terror is found in Ricardo Raphael's Spanish-language novela *Hijo de la guerra* (2019), which is actually based in fact and drawn from interviews with a prisoner claiming to be one of the original Zetas. Osiel and Tony Cárdenas Guillén also ordered Los Zetas to directly consolidate their government and police contacts and to guarantee full cooperation through an aggressive plan of plata o plomo, and they initiated a frightening campaign to threaten journalists. John Gibler (2011) and Alfredo Corchado (2014) are but two examples of U.S.-based journalists who were caught up in those threats from the Gulf Cartel that lasted long after the Cárdenas Guillén family had gone; those journalists survived to write about their threats from the Gulf Cartel and its volatile and unpredictable leaders. They were fortunate and were Americans. Many Mexican journalists paid with their life—132 have been killed since 2000—and northeast Mexico has remained the most dangerous place in Mexico to be a reporter (EFE 2020).

Osiel Cárdenas Guillén had converted the Gulf Cartel into a personal fiefdom and had done so almost exclusively by sowing fear through wanton violence to ensure compliance. Under his watch, Los Zetas grew more powerful: they further organized a number of small cells known as estacas, consisting of about twenty members who were given some freedom to act independently but required to respect the military hierarchical chain of command.[11] The leadership in Los Zetas created an estaca in municipalities or regions they had targeted for takeover, and a delegated commander posted signs announcing their coming. The Zeta in charge then approached local politicians and gangs to announce their arrival and demand cooperation. Those actions were the equivalent of placing the targeted territories under a sword of Damocles—*join us, or die* was the message. One of the implications of the expansion was that the Gulf Cartel and Los Zetas found it necessary to diversify criminal activity far beyond the shipment of drugs in order to continue feeding the bribery and its payroll (la nomina): kidnapping, extortion, and auto theft began to rise dramatically wherever Los Zetas estacas had been established. Los Zetas were responsible for unleashing a decade of tragedy that ranged from massacres to the burning of the Casino Royale in Monterrey when owners would not pay (de Mauleón 2017b). The Gulf Cartel and its armed mercenaries also began to systematically siphon off oil and gas from Pemex pipelines through force and through bribery of Pemex directors.

By 2002 the Gulf Cartel and Los Zetas controlled almost all criminal activity in Tamaulipas, Nuevo León, Coahuila, Veracruz, and Tabasco—

and they had made significant inroads into Guerrero, Michoacán, Jalisco, Colima, Nayarit, Sinaloa and Sonora, Durango and Baja California. Those states had become black zones of disinformation as newspapers and journalists were threatened or forced into silence. Even social media was not immune; prominent social influencers were threatened and some murdered (*Blog del Narco* 2013). The expansion of Los Zetas soon reached directly into Guatemala; deserters from Los Kaibiles, the elite military force trained in counterintelligence, were invited into their ranks. As many have noted, the recruitment of Guatemalan killers triggered a new phase in Mexico's drug wars: Los Kaibiles were more bloodthirsty and less sophisticated killers than were Los Zetas; they were directly responsible for escalating the level of violence in Mexico and descending to new levels of barbarism. Los Kaibiles were especially skilled in disseminating terror through mass *levantones* (forced kidnappings), torture, decapitation, and dismemberment—and staging public displays of their handiwork.

Osiel Cárdenas Guillén and the Zetas had transformed the traditional model of drug organizations in Mexico. The Gulf Cartel and Los Zetas were *not* organizations where power was cooperatively shared within families, where protection came at the hands of amateur gunman, or where they remained entrenched to operate from within their regional territorial base, nor had they limited their criminality to drug production and trafficking. Under Cárdenas Guillén and those who followed him, the Gulf Cartel had moved to employ only professionally trained armed wings, undertaken aggressive expansion, and diversified into a broad range of criminal activities. Not only was the Gulf Cartel focused on controlling specific points of a drug route or plaza, but it had also established an organization that could control an entire territory in order to minimize all risk and eliminate vulnerability from any point within its domain. It was a successful and terrifying model of dominance, and it changed the face of narco trafficking—but it also came with risks and instability. Unlike the other major cartels, there were few moderating factors such as family or community bonds to mediate the tension that was the foundation of the organization and was constantly reinforced. The connections between criminal associates were also rooted in fear and power, and the organization inspired a Darwinian version of *survival of the fittest* that was fixed in place by the discipline of a military code of discipline. In his novela, Raphael describes an incident where Los Zetas were gathered together by Tony Cárdenas Guillén to demonstrate their loyalty and commitment to the brotherhood after a betrayal and execution of one of their members. The remaining Zetas end by chanting an oath of loyalty in unison. The incident may be imagined, but it captures the commonly held belief that Los Zetas are truly a brotherhood of ruthless killers who are loyal to no one except their fellow Zetas.

> A brotherhood was born out of that betrayal, and it would endure. Think of
>   it as a ritual that will unite us forever.
> The blood that flows in our veins keeps us alert, more than any other drug.
>   On this day, a legion of soldiers disposed to do whatever it takes to sur-
>   vive has surged forth. With great enthusiasm, the boss asked:
> —And your Code, what is it?
> It was Decena who pronounced the first phrase:
> —Kill. God forgive!
> The rest of us completed it:
> The others, we complete them:
> your father, the nation;
> your mother, the flag;
> your wife, your pistol;
> your children, your bullets;
> For heaven, sea and land,
> Our only objective
> Is to give it to the enemy
> And win, or die in the intent.
> There are no friends, there is no family,
> And love doesn't exist.
>
>   (Raphael 2019, 24)

In March 2003, Cárdenas Guillén was arrested in Matamoros and imprisoned in La Palma, where he continued to control the organization and named his brother Antonio "Tony Tormenta" Cárdenas Guillén as his successor.

The Sinaloa Cartel mistakenly believed that the elimination of Osiel Cárdenas Guillén as the kingpin represented an opening into the northeast, and deployed a paramilitary force to attack Nuevo Laredo. The military discipline of Los Zetas had not collapsed amid Gulf infighting; they responded by defending the invaders and counterattacking traditional locations historically controlled by the Sinaloa Federation elsewhere. Violence escalated across the country; during 2005 the Fox government deployed troops to Tamaulipas in Operation México Seguro, which was successful to some extent in that violence declined around Laredo and Reynosa. But it popped elsewhere in a balloon-like effect as the expanding war *between* cartels shifted to different fronts.

The responsibility for the expansion of war has been attributed to the Zeta number 3—Heriberto Lazcano Lazcano. He had emerged as a unifying figure and was convinced that Los Zetas deserved more power and control. A split from the Gulf Cartel was the only way to achieve that. Guerrero Gutiérrez (2015a) succinctly states the implications of Lazcano and the split: with the split of Los Zetas from the Gulf Cartel, one of the most violent conflicts in the history of organized crime began almost immediately.

There were now several distinct battle fronts and war zones across Mexico—an ongoing war *against* cartels waged by the Calderón government with U.S. encouragement and support, wars *within* cartels fought over leadership and control of organizations, and several wars *between* cartels fought ferociously over turf (Gibler 2011). Initially, the most violent battlefronts were in Nuevo León, Tamaulipas, and Coahuila, where internal wars within the Gulf Cartel and invasions from Sinaloa were simultaneously being fought. Those confrontations soon expanded to several cities and left all of Tamaulipas in constant terror and the neighboring states in a condition of high alert.

Los Zetas gained the upper hand, and the Gulf Cartel leadership retreated to regroup in traditional stronghold cities of Matamoros and Reynosa. That move allowed the Gulf Cartel to continue operation as *casetas de cobro* (toll plazas), where the primary source of income was payment for the right of passage. Meanwhile, Los Zetas became more deeply involved in any and all criminal activity that generated the necessary funds to meet an expanding payroll—and kidnapping and extortion rose to the top of the list as the most lucrative. It was also during that initial period of wars within cartels and wars between cartels that the theft of hydrocarbons by so-called *huachicoleros* increased dramatically in areas near Tampico and Piedras Negras.[12]

The split between Los Zetas and the Gulf Cartel left several leaders dead, and furthermore, the leaders of both the Gulf Cartel and Los Zetas were then high-profile targets of the Mexican government and the USA. The deaths and the arrests eventually contributed to the weakening of both the remaining Gulf Cartel and the Los Zetas factions. The changes and fragmentation of both groups will be revisited in chapter 7 when the description focuses on describing the individuals within cartels and the groups working for them.

Escalating Violence

In Stephen Pinker's masterpiece *The Better Angels of Our Nature* (2011), he persuasively argues that violence has been declining around the globe. His observation also applies to Mexico—at least if the starting point is somewhere around 1990 and the end point is 2004. However, by 2005 a long downward trend had dramatically reversed and escalated rapidly upward until 2012, and statistics from the Secretariado Ejecutivo del Sistema Nacional de Seguridad Pública (SESNSP, Secretary General of National Public Security) indicated it had slowed for a short period, only to jump drastically once again and increase dramatically year after year. That continuing escalation of violence is the direct result of the simultaneous wars and battle fronts that are playing out across Mexico. Most of that violence is now the result and by-product of the wars between cartels and the wars within cartels.

This section briefly describes that rise in violence as measured by homicide statistics—specifically the total number of homicidios dolosos recorded each year.[13] Other obvious indicators of violence such as forced disappearances or specific manifestations of violence such as femicide will not be described here—even though they are important and critical measures of social disruption. The discussion here focuses on the broad trends of homicide and murder that are evident over the past twenty-five years.

Several detailed and sophisticated analyses of violence are available: in particular, an annual report on violence in Mexico from the Justice in Mexico Center at the University of San Diego is highly recommended for anyone interested in knowing more about the different ways of counting homicide and the distribution of violence in Mexico (Calderón et al. 2019; Heinle, Molzahn, and Shirk 2015; Heinle, Rodriguez Ferreira, and Shirk 2017). The Justice in Mexico project regularly publishes the most accurate information and detailed analysis of homicide and violence available to English-language readers. Within Mexico, reports and databases are made available annually through the INEGI and the SESNSP, and several nongovernmental reports are regularly released, such as those from Eduardo Guerrero Gutiérrez's consulting agency Lantia Consultores (see Guerrero Gutiérrez n.d.).[14]

Criminologists correctly preface their analysis of crime statistics with a routine cautionary warning that measuring changes or interpreting differences over time can result in competing explanations that are equally reasonable. Changes or variations in statistical patterns may be caused by three factors: (1) a true statistical change in the count or rate, (2) a change in recording practices, or (3) statistical error or manipulation. Although homicide statistics are generally considered to be one of the most reliable crime measures, that assumption may not be absolutely true for Mexico. In fact, the politics of counting homicide in Mexico has too often been heavy handed, and official statistical measures and reports must be viewed within a broad lens of skepticism. But in spite of this cautionary note, the general trends leave absolutely no doubt that the Calderón sexenio was violent and bloody, and that there was a stunning and precipitous reversal of a long-term downward trend in homicide. And there is absolutely no question that horrific violence persisted through the entire Peña Nieto sexenio and continued unabated over the first two years of the López Obrador era.

Figure 8 is a graphic representation of the trend in homicidios dolosos between 1989 and 2020. This graphic uses the *total number* of homicidios dolosos recorded each year and does not track annual *rates* adjusted for population, but comparable trend analyses using rates all show that there was a sharp upward trend after 2006. Furthermore, figure 8 also has a trend line for the *estimated* proportion of murders that can be reasonably attributed to criminal violence and drug wars from 2006 through 2020. The total number of homicidios dolosos recorded by the SESNSP is represented by the topmost trend line; a second trend line below it tracks the estimate of homicidios dolosos attributable to cartel ajustes and the various cartel wars. The distinction between *routine homicide* and *cartel-related homicide* in this figure represents an *educated guess* that is nevertheless based on a reasonable assumption that *at least 60 percent* of all homicides in one year are attributable to criminal violence and organized crime.[15]

Figure 8 indicates that there was an overall downward trend in violence from the late 1980s until 2004, when a sharp upturn began to be reflected in the official record. The increase at that time can be directly attributed to the wars within cartels and the outbreak of several wars between cartels—that is, battles for leadership within some organizations and for turf between different criminal organizations. On one front, the Sinaloa Cartel had triggered an internal war with the Carrillo Fuentes family by executing Rodolfo Carrillo

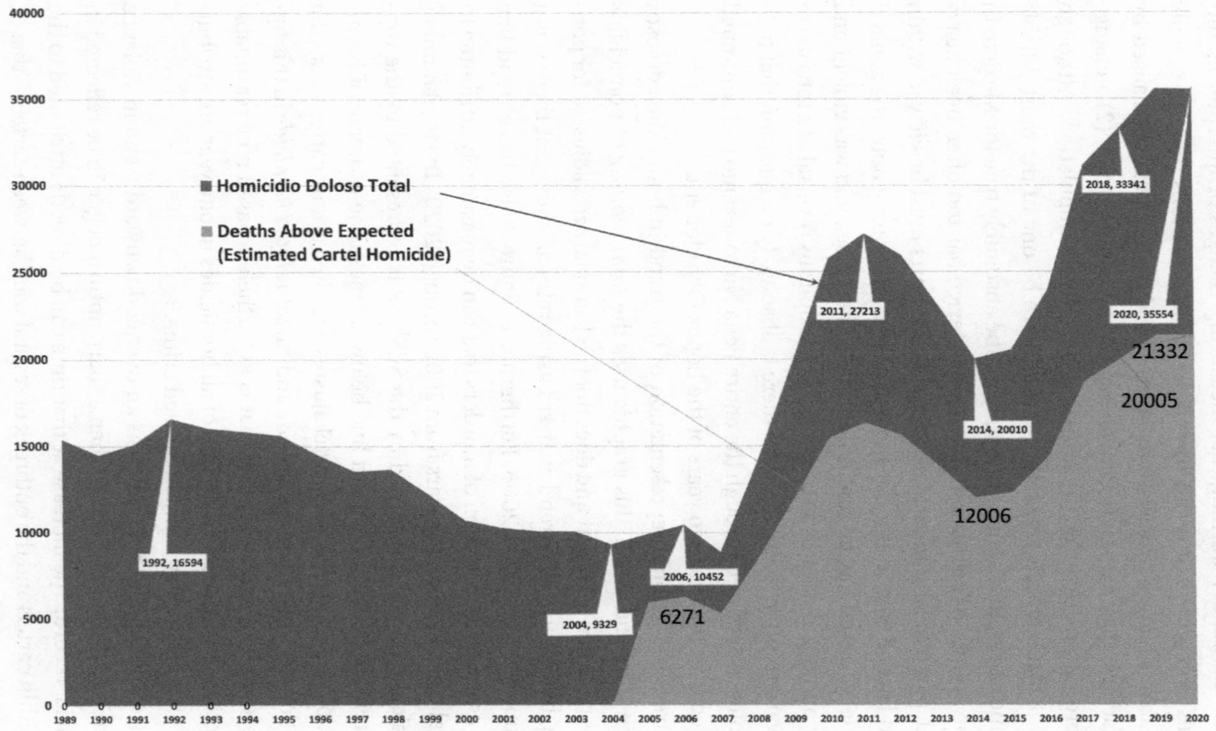

FIGURE 8 Homicides by year (total homicidios dolosos and estimated cartel killings), 1989–2020. Data from Secretariado Ejecutivo del Sistema Nacional de Seguridad Pública (SESNSP).

Fuentes in late 2004, and that led to a wave of killings and violence concentrated in and around Ciudad Juárez, Chihuahua. At about the same time, the internal battles for control of the Gulf Cartel and the expanding power of Los Zetas led to a generalized increase in violence throughout Tamaulipas, Coahuila, Nuevo León, Veracruz, and Michoacán. However, those internal wars were actually declining in ferocity and bloodshed around 2006 because some factions had clearly won the battle—specifically, Sinaloa in Ciudad Juárez and Los Zetas in the northeast and Michoacán—and because internal truces had been negotiated among the cartels through intermediaries hoping to restore a Pax Mafiosa (Ravelo 2007b).

In 2007 the official homicide totals represent the beginning point of a catastrophic rise. The increase in violence between 2007 and 2011 is attributable to three ongoing cartel wars—primarily Calderón's war *against* cartels, but the wars *between* cartels and wars *within* cartels were ongoing; even now in 2021, those cartel wars show no signs of ending (see figure 8). The wars escalated in intensity in 2008, when Arturo Beltrán Leyva declared war on his former allies in the Sinaloa Cartel. Contemporaneously, Michoacán blew up in chaos when Los Zetas arrived to encounter fierce opposition from the regional criminal syndicate with millenarian religious roots known as La Empresa, which later morphed into La Familia. Nuevo León and Veracruz exploded into violence when the sicarios of the Gulf Cartel and Los Zetas battled each other for supremacy, and as both groups turned their attention to harassing migrants moving up the eastern corridors toward the U.S. border.

Figure 8 also shows a brief drop in homicides *after* the PRI's return to power. But that would only be a short-lived flattening. Many observers suggest that SESNSP government databases were significantly manipulated in the initial years of the government of Peña Nieto in a misguided attempt to divert attention away from a violence narrative. The drop in the number of homicides over 2012–13 may represent an actual reduction in the number of homicides, or it could just as easily be the result of a counting error, the inability of medical examiners to do their job, or deliberate manipulation.[16] It is also very clear that Mexico's acknowledgment at that same time that there were at least 25,000 *desaparecidos* has significant implications for the degree of validity attached to these homicide data counts. Obviously, the trends would dramatically change if even a small proportion of missing persons had been victims of homicide and killed in the cartel violence.

Felipe Calderón's War Against Cartels

Perhaps the kindest thing that can be said about Felipe Calderón is that when he assumed office, he was immediately enveloped within a policy bubble that made it damn near impossible to view cartels as anything other than an enemy to be crushed through military force. The ideals of governance guided by rational policy making could not easily counteract the institutionalized *mano dura* views in his Consejo Nacional de Seguridad (CNS, National Security Council), and he did not have the foresight nor the character to break free of the constraints those hard-line views imposed. He was also working closely with and theoretically dependent on three men in his security directorate who clashed frequently and would later be accused of having close ties with cartel bosses in the covert netherworld—secretary of national defense, General Guillermo Galván Galván; secretary of public security, Genaro García Luna; and attorney general, Eduardo Medina Mora. But Calderón bought directly into the mano duro view, and even commonly wore a military outfit when he inspected bases or security teams. His affinity for war immediately came under question and became the source of much speculation.

First, his electoral win was extremely thin and there were ongoing massive protests questioning the legitimacy of that election. Second, he inherited an administration and security advisers who came from military backgrounds and whose voices dominated the CNS.[17] Third, several incidents of violent brutality had dominated newspaper headlines in the months leading up to his inauguration—for example, a horrific incident in Uruapan, Michoacán, where members of La Familia Michoacana rolled five heads across a crowded dance floor.[18] Fourth, there was no compelling evidence to believe that Mexico's 1,666 federal, state, municipal, and quasi-private police forces were actually competent enough to deal with the crime and the increasing possibility that organized crime groups had emerged.

The homicide patterns described in the following pages have been frequently used as a damning indictment of Calderón's decision to declare War Against Cartels and deploy the Mexican army. Vicente Fox had previously sent 20,000 troops to provide security in states that had been disrupted by the Gulf-Zeta expansion and eventual dispute, but Calderón almost immediately increased the number to 45,000 and deployed troops across the country in several major operations—beginning in his home state of Michoacán. Even if the military did not directly kill, it contributed to violence by fomenting conditions where other measures were downplayed and by creating power vacuums where cartels faced instability within which their leaders were attacked.

A short and widely read book—*El narco: La guerra fallida* (2010) by former CISEN director Rubén Aguilar V. and one-time external affairs minister Jorge G. Castañeda—argues that Calderón jumped into the drug war and relied on the army without understanding the situation on the ground, and with no consideration for immediate or long-term consequences of deploying troops in situations that typically called for a police operation and coordinated social-political strategy. Their arguments were widely echoed (Beittel 2015; Buscaglia 2013; Carrasco Araizaga and Castellanos 2009; Cook 2007; Grayson 2010; Hanson 2008; Hoffmann 2008; Ravelo 2007b; Sullivan, Cook, and Durand 2008).

Aguilar and Castañeda wrote that Calderón's rush to war against cartels happened in the absence of a clear delineation of the problem or a full consideration of alternate policy options—but their most damning criticism was that Calderón did not ask four fundamental questions that any head of state is obligated to answer before choosing a war option: make certain that your military has enough power to overwhelm and defeat the enemy, make certain that an exit strategy is in place prior to undertaking the war, have a clear understanding of what victory entails and how success will be defined, and make certain that the minds and the hearts of the people want that war.[19] In making his rash decision, the incoming president did not ask any of those questions or wait to evaluate the answers.

But as damning as those criticisms are, they do not address the fundamental question that should have been asked before even considering deployment—"What was the reason for going to war against the cartels?" Calderón ordered his generals to attack cartels without providing a compelling reason for why those actions were necessary at that point in time and without explaining how a military intervention could finally fix a problem that had endured for many years. In fact, he seemed to have conveniently forgotten that the military had once been assigned the same task and that it had failed and had been replaced by newly created police agencies (O'Day 2001).

In an ideal world, rational governance demands the extensive analysis of serious social problems and the reasonable evaluation of alternate remedies before attempting to intervene. Obviously, the real world is rarely rational, and political action most often reduces to the art of the possible—but citizens nevertheless expect their leaders to at least explore and define the dimensions of a problem beforehand. Nine years later, Calderón responded to a journalist's question about his lack of preplanning in his failed war by throwing back a question of his own to the questioner: "What would you have had me do? That I had greeted them? That I had invited them to spend time with me? That I had taken them for a coffee?" (Astorga Almanza 2015, Kindle Location 1592).

Obviously, that is not what people had expected or wanted from Calderón! The majority of rational citizens would have preferred that he address three very simple issues before he jumped precipitously into war: specifically identify the exact nature of the problem and consider all its dimensions; propose and lay out an instrumental solution that might be reasonably expected to address and remedy the problem identified; and before implementing his action plan, evaluate whether the proposed solution conformed to the fundamental ideals and values that are most important to the people. In retrospect, it is clear that none of those considerations were made—or if they were, the answers he received have never been made public.

What immediate and pressing problem demanded a precipitous blunt show of force from Calderón in 2006 and beginning in Michoacán State? Overall, violence had been declining, and the slight reversal in 2004 and 2005 was not increasing at a statistically significant level. Had other social problems emerged and become increasingly unmanageable during the Fox sexenio? Had drug abuse and addiction grown internally in Mexico, or had violence linked to trafficking increased far beyond the means of state security to control it? Had external political pressure from the United States made it imperative for Mexico to step up its level of interdiction and control at the source? Or had the corruptive influence of drug money gone beyond the tipping point and damaged any chance of rational governance? Or did the problem that Calderón saw reduce to something fundamentally venal and personal? Had he begun that war to strike at political adversaries and symbolically tie them to cartels, and would him acting like a general provide the legitimacy that had been questioned from the moment the election results were released?

There is little evidence that these things were explored or reviewed before Calderón's War Against Cartels began, and there is little evidence suggesting that military action was the only effective policy alternative that should have been on the table. But if success can be measured by the direct disruption of some cartels, then deploying the army undeniably had an impact and could theoretically be judged as having been successful: the Secretaría de la Defensa Nacional (SEDENA, Secretariat of National Defense) reported that between December 1, 2006, and December 2011 it had arrested 41,023 suspects and killed 2,321 criminals. George Grayson (2013) and his student Nicole K. Shuman identified ninety-eight high-ranking cartel leaders and bosses who were arrested or killed during the Calderón sexenio. Their list includes several important cartel leaders who were responsible for triggering Wars Within Cartels (e.g., Arturo Beltrán Leyva, Heriberto "Z-3" Lazcano Lazcano) or leading figures in the Wars Between Cartels (Edgar "La Barbie" Valdez Villareal). The army casualties were relatively low given the scale of confrontations, but there were nevertheless 267 deaths, 744 wounded, and 196 kidnappings during the Calderón sexenio.

Aguilar and Castañeda had argued that before starting a war, a leader should begin with a preconceived understanding of what can count for success. The number of casualties and the disruption of cartels can arguably be claimed as valid indicators for one type of success. But employing the military had consequences that were not anticipated, and which have now created a serious negative impact on Mexico. Of the three simple guidelines for devising a rational social policy to deal with social problems, it can be putatively asserted that steps one and two possibly occurred when the army was deployed. That is, cartels themselves were defined as the problem, and the army was the only available instrument to eliminate that specific problem. But there is also a third necessary element in all rational policy planning— the requirement to ensure that interventions and remedial actions do not contradict fundamental values and principles that are held as important to citizens. When the army was sent to deal with the cartels, it also meant that important social values and beliefs were pushed aside and ignored to allow the army and the marines to play the dominant role in setting policy and implementing justice. And far too often, that meant that the intervention came at the expense of protecting human rights and guarding civil liberties.

The dependence on the military during the Calderón presidency represented a major setback for the continued emergence of a democratic state and the establishment of functional institutions.[20] During the Calderón sexenio, the number of military officers who served directly at the head of federal, state, and municipal security institutions increased dramatically when they were specifically designated to replace civilian and even elected appointees.

Grayson (2013) identified forty-eight distinct and key security positions where army appointments had supplanted civilians under the direction of Calderón's secretary of national defense, Guillermo Galván Galván.

That quiet appropriation of all security did not attract much notice nor raise red flags or concerns as it slowly unfolded. In the idealized vision of justice in jurisprudence and sociology, the various components in a justice system serve as counterbalances and checks on other parts in order to avoid creating a situation where the investigation, prosecution, determination of guilt, and application of punishment are the responsibility of a single person or institution. Those higher-level ideals were not discussed or considered in Calderón's rush to war. But the role of the military and concern about its dominant role eventually did raise a great deal of concern and anger when blatant and abusive violations of civil rights were attributed to soldiers and marines over the course of fighting the War Against Cartels. And those concerns became even greater and evident during the sexenio of Calderón's successor, Peña Nieto.

Ordinary citizens and nongovernmental organizations increasingly demanded the removal of armed forces from the streets because of the abusive treatment of citizens during the frenetic efforts to find cartel members and kingpins. Nevertheless, 62 percent of respondents in public opinion polls applauded the use of military force and were content to give Mexico's presidents a free reign to intervene. But in the end, that public trust collapsed, and all hell broke loose after Calderón left office.

Ayotzinapa, Tlatlaya, *Autodefensas*, and Public Protest

Enrique Peña Nieto had sold a vision of saving Mexico when he ran for election as the PRI candidate. But his dreams for Mexico quickly descended into a horrible nightmare. His and Grupo Atlacomulco's vision of continuing to create a modern neoliberal state slithered down the vortex of violence and protest only a few short weeks after he had undertaken a global tour that boasted of major legislative reforms and Mexico's battle against cartels. The purpose of his European tour was to send out a message that Mexico was open for business and the world was invited to invest in the new Mexico. Peña Nieto was so confident that Mexico had turned the corner on violence that he even offered Mexican troops to serve as global peacekeepers during his stopover at the United Nations.

In retrospect, the signs of a bubbling discontent within Mexico were evident to anyone who had been paying attention, but most of those serious problems and dangerous hot spots had been constrained and controlled through the use of a long-proven three-pronged government strategy that included (1) obfuscation, silence, and disinformation—the tardy release of statistics about violence that may have been underestimated and the non-compliance with requests for information; (2) a well-orchestrated public relations campaign intended to convince the world—but primarily investors—that Mexico had turned the corner and things were under control; and (3) a security policy based on the targeted arrest of *well-known* crime bosses and a broader strategy that was intended to fragment large criminal organizations into smaller entities—or cartelitos.

By the end of September 2014, three seemingly unrelated crises converged to unleash a firestorm within Mexico that would enflame the wrath of ordinary Mexicans and leave the outside world questioning Peña Nieto's ability to deliver on his promise of building a modern Mexico. The military, which had assumed and been entrusted with so much power, was front and center in each one of those crises.

The first body blow came from the reports and photographs published by the Associated Press and *Esquire* magazine (Ferri Tórtola 2014). Those images provided irrefutable evidence that a squadron of the Mexican army had massacred twenty-two young people at Tlatlaya near Ecatepec in Mexico State. The articles and images were widely circulated by traditional media outlets and spread even more widely on the Internet; those reports documented a cold-blooded execution carried out by the military, and the ensuing deliberate manipulation of evidence to make it appear that it took place over a two-hour period. That was done in order to back up the specious claim that the army had been ambushed and forced to engage in a firefight with narco traffickers in self-defense.

The second blow to the administration emerged when student protests at Mexico's Instituto Politécnico Nacional (IPN, National Polytechnic University) exploded into something more than annual commemorative marches. Student leaders had been planning for a massive march to take place on the forty-sixth anniversary of the October 2 massacre of a previous generation of students at Tlatelolco. Previous marches had been peaceful and uneventful, but there were concerns that the 2014 version might escalate into more disruptive protests after IPN administrators imposed arbitrary changes to the curriculum and modified graduation requirements. Student leaders and professors argued that those modifications had been imposed to further a neoliberal vision of Mexico's future that had been dictated directly from Los Pinos. The IPN administration and Los Pinos became so concerned about potential violence in the upcoming march that interior secretary Miguel Ángel Osorio Chong took the nearly unprecedented step of agreeing to negotiate directly with student leaders.

The third crisis, and eventually the most incendiary and long lasting, was the execution of six young men in Iguala, Guerrero, on September 26, followed immediately by the disappearance and killing of forty-three student teachers from the Raúl Isidro Burgos Normal School located in Ayotzinapa. On the 26th, Iguala municipal police killed three students, two footballers, and another person when they machine-gunned a white minivan. The police claimed occupants had stolen the van and represented a threat to their safety. One of the dead was tossed face-up into the street and inhumanely desecrated—his skin peeled away from his head and eyes gouged out.

Early the next morning, at least fifty students marched in protest against the shooting, and mysteriously vanished into thin air. Video suggests that white unmarked vehicles sped away with young men visible in the cargo area. A few of the missing reappeared over the next few days and reported that local police or men dressed as military had forced their companions to march up narrow trails into the hills, where they were hunted like dogs (Matías 2014). Faced with a barrage of national and international outrage, the federal procurador, Jesús Murillo Karam, deployed a newly established Mexican police force (La Gendarmerie) and invited Argentinian forensics specialists to visit the area as investigators.

Four hillside grave sites (*las fosas*) were discovered shortly afterward, and seventeen bodies recovered from just one. Initial reports indicated that those victims had been shot in the head, thrown into a hole filled with branches, and incinerated with diesel fuel. An additional eleven bodies were located in three other graves, and all twenty-eight were sent to Mexico City for forensic testing. Later, there were many reports of new grave sites with mangled bodies and bones—but never any confirmation that any of those discovered remains actually belonged to the missing forty-three *normalistas*. In fact, most of those bodies belonged to other victims of cartel and gang violence. The fact that the remains are not the missing students provided little consolation—they were all unknown victims of horrendous killings who were unceremoniously discarded in a part of Mexico where there was little evidence of any government control or concern about reducing violence.

The mayor of Iguala, José Luis Abarca Velázquez, and his wife fled on September 27, and a massive Interpol manhunt began. Twenty-two police from Iguala and another eight from a neighboring town (Cocula) were arrested and charged with murdering the six young men on September 26 and for their suspected complicity in the disappearance of forty-three students on the twenty-seventh. At least one of the arrested led investigators to the grave sites in the hills, and others claimed that they were acting on orders of the mayor. Many of the arrested turned out to be halcones (spies) and sicarios (hit men) on the payroll (nomina) of Los Guerreros Unidos—a gang that was known to be working directly with the Beltrán Leyva Cartel to protect its dominance of an important drug plaza. Guerrero governor Ángel Heladio Aguirre Rivero himself had also been linked to the Beltrán Leyvas, and many believe that he was also directly involved in approving the disappearance of the forty-three normalistas.

Those incidents led to another round of massive protests at most Mexican university and preparatory schools, and eventually public demonstrations in more than fifty Mexican cities and seven different states. The world also took notice; unprecedented news coverage of the Tlatlaya and Iguala massacres endured throughout the entire Peña Nieto sexenio.

Instead of dealing with the murder of students and the disappearance of forty-three others head on, the Mexican government resorted to a traditional three-pronged strategy of containment—obfuscate, undertake public-relations blitzes, and arrange show-boat arrests. Peña Nieto said nothing substantive relating to the forty-three missing normalistas nor the massacre at Tlatlaya, and his silence became deafening (J. Ramos 2014). In the aftermath of unprecedented and enduring negative world press, the secretary of the exterior organized a campaign to minimize the impact by holding special debriefings for selective foreign press agencies and reporters in Mexican embassies and consulates around the world (Esquivel, Appel, and Alcaraz 2014).

Even the old-faithful strategy of arresting a big cartel boss was pulled out of the hat in an attempt to blunt the impact of the protests. But the idea to capture two big-fish capos failed to stem bad press, quell dissent, or control growing unrest; instead, it fed into a widespread public view that the government was the real problem. First the government countered by announcing the capture of Héctor "El H" Beltrán Leyva—the alleged leader of the notoriously violent Beltrán Leyva Cartel—in colonial San Miguel de Allende. But the credibility of the government was undermined because of the man who was arrested alongside Beltrán Leyva: El H was with Germán Goyeneche Ortega, who turned out to be the chief financial officer of the cartel. Goyeneche is not only the scion of an elite Aguascalientes family, but he was also an active member of the Partido Verde—a proxy and close political offshoot of the PRI. The arrest of Beltrán Leyva also brought down one of the PRI's own, and reminded the world that the wealthy and the elite are intimately involved in the drug trade and the covert netherworld of Mexican narco trafficking.

To counteract the bad press that had now specifically linked Mexico's elite to the cartels and violence, the PGR then captured a long-retired capo—El Viceroy Carrillo Fuentes—in a bloodless takedown in Torreón, Coahuila. Ten years earlier, that would have been major news, but informed insiders knew that El Viceroy's days as head of the Juárez Cartel were in the distant past and the cartel had been controlled by others for at least five years before he was arrested (*InSight Crime* 2017).

By the end of the Peña Nieto sexenio, it had become increasingly clear that violence in Mexico should not only be blamed on the cartels and their leaders. The government itself was violent, and the vision of a modern Mexico rooted in neoliberal economics was being promoted by individuals who were more interested in their self-enrichment. The previously beloved Mexican military had also become a big part of the problem. The line between the illegality of cartels and the elite had been blurred, and Mexicans now understood that the criminals and the government were made of the same cloth. Sadly, in many parts of the country, the people had come to trust the cartels for support and protection rather than the government, the army, or the police.

The reality of the situation hit them hard and portended the changes that were about to come in the national elections of 2018.

CHAPTER 6

The Mythological Life of El Chapo Guzmán

magic realism: noun (also magical realism); a style of writing that mixes realistic events with fantasy
—H. W. Fowler and Ernest Gowers, *A Dictionary of Modern English Usage*, 1965

In *One Hundred Years of Solitude*, Nobel laureate Gabriel García Márquez (2003) describes a "semi-surreal saga of a hundred years of life among the Buendías, a family of mythical achievements and absurdities in the mythical South American town of Macondo" (Kennedy 1973). His epic account of an imaginary family is the best example of "fiction that integrates elements of fantasy into otherwise realistic settings" (Fetters 2014). The factual basis of García Márquez's writing is often overlooked because of his emphasis on surreal yarns, even though he often insisted that his inspiration lay in real events: "in Mexico . . . surrealism runs through the streets. Surrealism comes from the reality of Latin America," he notably observed (qtd. in Kennedy 1973).

Likewise, the reporting of Mexico's century-long tradition of narco trafficking has become inseparable from the chronicles of individuals and families living in the remote hamlets and ranchos of Mexico's Sierra Madre Occidental that make up la cuna del narcotráfico (the cradle of narco traffic). The region, widely known as the Golden Triangle, is a special place exemplifying García Márquez's claim that surrealism runs through the streets of Mexico and underpins all reality.

Perhaps no one better exemplifies the unique character of individuals who inhabit such domains than Joaquín Archivaldo "El Chapo" Guzmán Loera. Just as the fictional Aureliano Buendía did, Guzmán moved away from his remote rancho to explore a wider world where he would achieve fame and notoriety during a forty-year saga that was filled with escapades, spectacular escapes, and close encounters with death. Even though El Chapo's notoriety would be magnified in the outside world, he would always remain rooted to that remote sierra where had been born. Guzmán's biography is not a fictional imagining—but it is muddled by fable, greatly distorted in the telling, and manipulated to suit political agendas. It was ultimately rendered ambiguous by an exaggerated overemphasis on his importance to the world of organized crime and narco trafficking—even after his life was unveiled for all to see in the Brooklyn courtroom where he was sentenced to life in prison.

His personal narco odyssey elevated Guzmán to super celebrity and global fame. He has been proclaimed to be the Jefe de Jefes of a global enterprise that generates billions of dollars in profit each year (Resa Nestares 2003). He has also been portrayed as a devil incarnate for his betrayal of longtime allies and attacks on upstart rivals (Rodriguez Nieto 2016). *Forbes* magazine contributed to his mythmaking by including him in its list of global billionaires between 2009 and 2013.

But there are also many other observers who are perplexed by the widely held assertion that Guzmán personally wields such a powerful influence. Undoubtedly, El Chapo is a violent and clever criminal, but there are many who argue it is unreasonable to think that he was uniquely responsible for the success of narco trafficking in Mexico and for the violence it has generated.

The myth of El Chapo has been embellished over the years by many claims that overestimate his significance within the drug-trafficking enterprise. Furthermore, the excessive attention directed toward him leaves the world with reductionist explanations about organized crime: too many have narrowly focused on Guzmán's individual exploits and have overlooked the broader sociopolitical context that elevated El Chapo to narco stardom. Guzmán deserves a prominent place on the scaffold of shame alongside other narco traffickers and criminals, but he doesn't sit there alone and could never have achieved that status without the complicity of corrupt politicians and an accommodating state security in the covert netherworld of narco trafficking. El Chapo's role in Mexico's narco-traffic history will be incompletely understood unless it can explain how he came to be anointed with the totemic and symbolic status of Jefe de Jefes, and how systemic institutional corruption placed him there.

The Legend of Shorty

Most of what we know about Joaquín Guzmán Loera's personal and criminal life is drawn from journalistic accounts, and many of those have been sensationalized to create the legend of Shorty. An inner circle of confidants has been largely silent in that world where the code of *omerta* (pain of death) rules and no one close to Guzmán has publicly revealed his enigmatic existence.[1] There were many blinkered circles of access surrounding El Chapo's family, and even family members were ordered to keep their distance (Hernández 2010, 2016c, 2016d).[2]

Prior to the showcase trial in a Brooklyn courtroom, legal dossiers revealed little about his personal life. With the exception of the charges related to the execution of Mexican cardinal Posadas Campos, the jurisprudential records in Mexico are shockingly sparse. Jorge Carrasco Araizaga describes El Chapo based on Mexican legal documents:

In spite of the allegations going back 20 years, Joaquín Archivaldo Guzmán Loera, El Chapo, has not been found guilty, up to this point in time, of one single conviction for narco trafficking. Moreover, he has been absolved or sheltered from prosecution for some twenty charges related to homicide, production and trafficking of marijuana and cocaine, charges related to endangering health, or possession of weapons reserved for the military. (2016)[3]

El Chapo was formally sentenced (*auto de prisión formal*) three times in Mexico—he was handed a twelve-year sentence for his part in the murder of Posadas Campos in 1994, a six-year sentence for criminal association in 1996, and a seven-year sentence for conspiracy and criminal association dating back to activity from 1997.[4] Over two decades, twenty criminal processes in Mexico ended up with Guzmán absolved or having charges stayed. Following his 2014 recapture in Mazatlán, twelve of twenty older criminal charges were reinstated, and another related to his 2001 escape from Puente Grande prison was tacked on. But details and evidence supporting those charges have never been fully revealed, and all thirteen legal proceedings remained pending at the time of his second dramatic escape in 2015, this time from Altiplano prison; nor were these charges addressed during his trial in Brooklyn in 2019. The only additional charge laid in Mexico after his 2016 recapture related to that second spectacular escape, in July 2015.

None of those charges have been specifically related to his alleged role as boss of Mexico's criminal underworld. Guzmán's prison dossier and the known *averiguaciones previas* (preliminary inquiries) represent a narrow, selective, and negotiated criminal biography as seen through the eyes of Mexican judicial gatekeepers: problematically, few Mexican documents related to El Chapo have ever entered into the public domain, and there are no public records to substantiate the claim that Guzmán is the Jefe de Jefes of drug trafficking.[5] Furthermore, it's doubtful whether the official record in Mexico can be trusted should it become available: in the Mexican judicial labyrinth, one should never discount the possibility that documents are routinely suppressed and falsified to promote the official version of the truth.[6]

Even though little information supports the claim, the endorsed narrative and the official stance of the Mexican government and the U.S. Department of Justice is that El Chapo Guzmán is public enemy number one and the most important Mexican drug cartel boss.

What we know of Guzmán's personal life is pulled from several biographical accounts and investigative reports that appeared in periodicals and Mexican newspapers. The most credible accounts available are those written by Anabel Hernández (2010, 2013), Diego Enrique Osorno (2009), José Reveles (2014), Ioan Grillo (2011), and Malcolm Beith (2010).

None of those descriptions of his life are based on direct contact with El Chapo or interviews with family members; there are only four known descriptions of him that are attributed directly to him or his immediate family. The first is a thirty-nine-second clip from 1993 when El Chapo was paraded before journalists in Toluca, Mexico State, as the putative head of the Mexican cartels: in it, he tersely claims to be a farmer growing corn and beans and that he had never used weapons (Anonymous 2014). In a second video, his mother, María Consuelo Loera Pérez, speaks at length of El Chapo's childhood, his character, and his dreams (Univision 2014a, 2014b). The longest statement directly from El Chapo is a seventeen-minute interview from October 2015, taped by him for actors Kate del Castillo and Sean Penn (Penn 2016) to provide background for a possible eponymous movie. The longest family interview about the details of his life was a four-hour interview that his common-law wife, Emma Coronel Aispura, gave to Hernández to denounce the administrative and human rights abuses in the aftermath of his 2016 recapture (Baumoel 2016; Hernández 2016c). There remains much speculation that Mexican actress Kate del Castillo had an agreement to produce an eponymous film of his life, but frankly, no one expects that a Hollywood account of the life of El Chapo Guzmán will serve as a definitive biography: nevertheless, such a film might provide more information than is currently available in the public record.[7]

Several biographical details have trickled out over the years, and Guzmán reaffirmed many of them in that interview he taped as a favor to del Castillo (*Rolling Stone* 2016). Joaquín Archivaldo was born in 1957 in a tiny mountain rancho called La Tuna in the rural Sinaloa municipality of Badiguarato. He completed third grade, although registries record only episodic attendance through grade 6. His lack of formal education is not an indicator of low intelligence, and many have described him as astute and clever: his inclusion on the *Forbes* list of billionaires maybe be exaggerated and questionable, but there is evidence that he is a successful financial entrepreneur and strategist (Volpi 2016).

He began working in marijuana fields by the age of fifteen, where he was initiated into narco trafficking under the tutelage of Miguel Ángel Félix Gallardo and most probably Pedro Avilés Pérez. He climbed the ranks of the nascent drug cartel based in Sinaloa and was later headquartered in Guadalajara. He grew up alongside many who would make up the central core of a powerful drug business with deep roots in the northwestern sierra: from childhood, he knew everyone in the Carrillo Fuentes family from Guamuchilito, Sinaloa, as well as working and reportedly even living with the Beltrán Leyva brothers from nearby Badiguarato. Initially, he worked with Héctor Palma Salazar, Ismael Zambada García, and Juan José Esparragoza Moreno shipping marijuana and opium into the United States from collector points in Sonora State—primarily from the area immediately south of Douglas and Naco, Arizona.

He was first arrested following the execution of Mexican cardinal Juan Jesús Posadas Ocampo and sentenced to a twelve-year prison term in 1993. On January 19, 2001, he escaped for the first time and eluded capture for thirteen years before a dramatic rearrest on February 22, 2014, in Mazatlán, Sinaloa. He was imprisoned once again in Altiplano (Federal Social Readaptation Center No. 1, Amoloya de Juárez), only to escape seventeen months later on July 12, 2015, via a 1.5 kilometer tunnel that directly connected his prison cell to a construction site. He remained free for nearly six months in his familiar home turf in the Golden Triangle, although he reportedly changed locations several times to keep ahead of the massive military operation that hunted him over a three-month period. He was finally recaptured following a violent confrontation with Mexican marines in Los Mochis, Sinaloa, on January 28, 2016.

Everyone, including his mother, calls him El Chapo—Shorty—in accordance with a rural informality that sees no harm or indignity in identifying people by a physical trait. He's about five feet five (1.68 m) and sixty-three years old, having been born on April 4, 1957, in the remote sierra north and east of Culiacán, Sinaloa. His home rancho, La Tuna, has changed little from his childhood and sits in a relatively remote area accessible only by secondary roads.[8] To this day, fewer than fifty houses remain scattered across a rise that sits 3,500 feet above sea level and in the shadows of nearby peaks laying east in Durango State. In the last census, La Tuna recorded 215 residents—almost the same number as when El Chapo worked the nearby marijuana and poppy fields four decades earlier.

One house is comparatively plush and home to his mother, María, although she sometimes occupies another compound in the Las Quintas area of Culiacán during family gatherings and religious holidays. The 2015 census indicates that only four homes in La Tuna had computers, and the mean education level remained low—slightly more than five years because of the tradition of leaving school around age fourteen or fifteen to work in fields or raise livestock. Although Guzmán's religion is presumed to be Catholic, his mother is a devout evangelical Christian rather than Catholic.

Between 2009 and 2012, *Forbes* magazine reported that El Chapo had moved far beyond the impoverished circumstances of his childhood to assume a place among the richest people in the world. Even if *Forbes* incorrectly guesstimated his worth, it's undeniably true that the boy known as Shorty had soared beyond circumstances that situated him among the lowest 0.1 percent to take a place among the economic elite occupying the upper 1 percent. According to his mother, he dreamed of fantastic wealth as a boy— and counted make-believe currency that he had arranged in stacks (Univision 2014b). His childhood fantasy came true, and the opium poppy fields that initiated him into the drug trade for a few years now belonged to him!

It was in that remote region that Guzmán first encountered and worked with men, women, and families who would remain at the center of Mexico's drug trade for the next five decades—the dozen siblings of the Carrillo

Fuentes family from Guamuchilito, the seven brothers and four sisters of the Arellano Félix family in Navolato, and the four Beltrán Leyva brothers from Badiguarato. Like most boys from the sierra, he was initiated as a fifteen-year-old *fresa*—a novice—and advanced in a burgeoning drug trade that was being forged by powerful narco bosses such as Miguel Ángel Félix Gallardo, Ernesto Fonseca Carillo, and Pedro Avilés Pérez. El Chapo's responsibility in that burgeoning Sinaloa drug cartel grew exponentially after Operation Condor—which saw some narco bosses relocate to the state capital of Culiacán, Sinaloa, and drove the most important members further afield to Mexico's second-largest city in Guadalajara, Jalisco, and others like El Mayo Zambada García north of the border to Reno, Nevada. In the early 1980s, Guzmán's name began to be mentioned as a *minor* operative in intelligence reports tracking cartel bosses and their efforts to expand cocaine operations; El Chapo was a very low-level operative compared to jefes such as Fonseca Carrillo, Félix Gallardo, and Caro Quintero.

Guzmán's connections to his childhood acquaintances (*cuates*) from the Golden Triangle and Badiguarato municipality provided him with an enduring legitimacy and allowed him to survive the many fluctuations within Mexican drug organizations that would take place over the next four decades. Successful businesses are always reduceable to four essential components—a desired product, efficient delivery of that product, the ability to adapt to changing market conditions, and firm and stable leadership—and each of those factors were found in abundance in that remote region of Mexico that was Guzmán's childhood home. El Chapo and other compañeros proved to be more than capable opportunists ready to exploit the easy access to profitable commodities—the prolific marijuana and opium crops laying within easy reach just south of the world's largest consumer market. When traditional Andes to U.S. shipping routes via the Caribbean were disrupted by the U.S. War on Drugs, the experienced narco traffickers from the Golden Triangle stepped in to provide alternate routes and efficient delivery models. Smuggling through mountain passes had been routine for generations and perfected by wizened pioneers like Avilés.

El Chapo has been married to at least four different women, although some observers have also written about additional *official* marriages.[9] By most accounts, he has fathered seventeen children, including ten within four recognized marriages, and seven children through common-law relationships referred to in Mexico as *parejas sentimentales*. One of those common-law relationships produced a daughter, Rosa Isela Guzmán Ortiz, who was born before he officially married for the first time.[10] The families and romantic liaisons of El Chapo were routinely monitored and tracked by intelligence agencies (CISEN and the DEA) and considered to be an important strategy for tracking his movements: those connections were also used to trace money-laundering connections to companies and property registered in the name of family members or paramours, or those who have served as proxy head of companies that he actually owned (*prestanombres*).[11]

In 1977 El Chapo married Alejandrina María Salazar Hernández in Sinaloa and fathered four children, who would remain closely connected to him—César, Iván, Alfredo, and Alejandrina Giselle. This specific relationship is often cited as an example of how intermarriage cemented narco bonds and forged new narco alliances among narco traffickers of northwest Mexico: Alejandrina was reportedly a close relative of Héctor Palma Salazar, who was El Chapo's primary business associate in the early years. Fifteen years later, and without having formally divorced Alejandrina, El Chapo married Griselda López in Culiacán in 1992 or 1993 and fathered Édgar, Joaquín, Ovidio, and Griselda. In some biographical accounts, Guzmán also entered into a marriage with a Nayarit bank clerk named Estela Peña while he was still married to Griselda López, but others suggest that this was not a formal arrangement and suggest no consensual enchantment: in fact, reports say that El Chapo kidnapped and raped Estela, and that she had two children who have remained anonymous.

Six years following his 2001 prison escape from Altiplano, at forty-nine years old, El Chapo married eighteen-year-old Emma Coronel Aispuro in an elaborate wedding ceremony a few short months after she won the Miss Coffee and Guava beauty contest in Angostura.[12] She has dual Mexican/American citizenship and is widely believed to be the niece of another of El Chapo's partners—Ignacio "Nacho" Coronel Villarreal—though Coronel Aispuro has vehemently denied this (Hernández 2016c).[13] She had maintained a residence in Culiacán while attending university, but he was never far away and he regularly moved among several safe houses in the nearby Golden Triangle. She was at his side in the Mazatlán condominium when he was recaptured in February 2014; she described that arrest in detail during the interview with Hernández (2016c). She also acknowledged living near Altiplano maximum security prison until shortly before Guzmán's spectacular prison escape in July 2015. Emma and Joaquín Guzmán Loera have twin daughters, María Joaquína and Emali Guadalupe, who are also American citizens since they were born in a Southern California hospital in 2011, thanks to Emma's dual citizenship (Wilkinson and Ellingwood 2011). Emma also emerged as an Internet celebrity when she regularly sat in the front row at the Brooklyn trial, where her husband was eventually sentenced to a life sentence in an American prison (BBC News Mundo 2018; Esquivel 2018; Garza 2019; Honan, Berman and Zezima 2019). Emma herself later pled guilty and was sentenced for money laundering, conspiracy to import drugs into the USA, and helping El Chapo escape from Altiplano (Hsu 2021).

Alejandrina, Griselda, Estela, and Emma are Guzmán's recognized wives, but he also had children with Lucero Sánchez (two) and Neri García (one). Although it did not result in children, El Chapo also had an ill-fated relationship with a prostitute named Zulema Hernández while both were imprisoned in Almoloya de Juárez (Puente Grande), Jalisco.[14] Anabel Hernández in her biographical and historical account *Los señores del narco* (2010) describes how Guzmán pursued Zulema with love letters and poetry and used her as his regular sexual consort.[15] Zulema was a hopeless drug addict and was provided unlimited access to drugs from the supply that El Chapo routinely imported into Mexico's most secure prison facility: she is by far the most tragic of Guzmán's conquests and was murdered and stuffed in a car trunk near Tlaxcala in 2007 by Los Zetas sicarios who had targeted her in retaliation for El Chapo's incursions into their northeastern plazas, and to avenge several attacks that he had orchestrated against their imprisoned companions-in-crime.

El Chapo, El Mayo, and the Paradox of Visibility

El Chapo Guzmán and El Mayo Zambada are veteran narco bosses who have been involved in the drug trade since the 1970s. They are also connected by compadrazgo, and supposedly share grandchildren through the marriage of Vicentillo Zambada García and Rosa Iselda Guzmán (Montenegro 2016). El Chapo and El Mayo are currently the narco elders in a bloody and unforgiving underworld where most jefes die young or are imprisoned early. Compared to other capos, these two remained relatively unscathed when survival, longevity, and wealth are used as the indicators of success.[16] Furthermore, their criminal enterprise—based in Sinaloa State—has suffered fewer setbacks than comparable Mexican organizations (Buscaglia 2013; Villareal 2014). Narco-enterprise success should never be solely attributed to particular men, but the leadership of El Mayo and El Chapo has been demonstrably critical to the success and longevity of the Sinaloa Cartel over two decades.

But unlike El Mayo, El Chapo became the universal face of narco trafficking and the totemic representation of all the harm that is caused by drugs and narco traffic. But Guzmán's fame poses a paradox since it contradicts the recognized pattern where traditional mafia bosses operate in anonymity and invisibility. With the possible exception of the Japanese Yakuza, global mafias have been most successful when their leaders have remained unknown outside the organization, and when they adhere to the criminal dictum that visibility attracts unwanted attention and reaction (Gayraud 2007).[17] Throughout his career, El Chapo has consistently remained in the spotlight, and the world has directed extraordinary attention to him while his allies have remained hidden and anonymous. El Chapo's narco stardom might signify something other than power, and might actually be a sign that Guzmán is less important than Zambada or than even more unknown others who have managed to remain invisible in the covert netherworld. In the dominion of organized crime, El Chapo's ultra-visibility is truly an exception, whereas El Mayo's invisibility fits more closely into the traditional pattern of a mafia boss. Visibility may be important at the street level where threat and intimidation generate fear, but most powerful mafia bosses have remained in the shadows, where they can exert control through implied threat, negotiation, and subtler forms of coercion.

El Chapo's visibility has been conflated with power. His larger-than-life presence has made El Chapo the focus of fables, tales, and rumors. Guzmán epitomizes the antithesis of ideal mafia leadership, and the inordinate attention directed toward him distracts from a closer examination of the structure of organized crime in Mexico. Guzmán's fame most likely explains why he has been incarcerated and is the focus of international attention, while El Mayo has avoided prison and still remains relatively unknown. El Chapo's hypervisibility might even have been encouraged by his partners to preserve their anonymity: the international focus on him allows others to remain in the shadows. Guzmán has been provocative because he has been the most visible narco and he became the symbolic representative of a shadowy criminal world where outsiders can only make guesses about organizational structure.

Zambada has been publicly profiled only once, in an interview arranged with a dean of Mexican journalism, Julio Scherer García (2010), shortly after El Mayo's son Vicentillo had been extradited to the USA. A respected observer of mafias, Roberto Saviano, describes the differences between the two veteran Sinaloan crime bosses:

"El Mayo" Zambada, [is] the brain and, probably, the [n]ew leader of the organization. In fact, if the Sinaloa Cartel has retained its position as the most powerful organization in Mexico, it's due to his very presence, far removed from the focus and attention at the international level. And even as the name "El Chapo" has become known and his pictures in extravagant shirts have gone viral in the world, few people know the name of his most important ally and even fewer would recognize his face. It's that invisibility that enhances the success of Ismael "El Mayo" Zambada and has cemented his position as the true pillar of the organization. (2016)[18]

In fact, the later publication of *El traidor: El diario secreto del hijo del Mayo* (Hernández 2020) stated it even more strongly and made the claim that Zambada has always been the leader of the Sinaloa Cartel and that it would not exist without him.

El Chapo's Significance?

Mexican journalist Anabel Hernández has been one of the most vocal skeptics about Guzmán's importance to the Mexican drug trade, and she has identified several incongruities regarding his enigmatic leap to prominence from his first known role as a subordinate to El Güero Palma Salazar. In *Los señores del narco*, she writes that Guzmán was a nobody in the early 1990s— an ambitious underling and lugarteniente working under Amado Carrillo Fuentes, who was at that time seen to be the main consolidating force of Mexican drug organizations following the reported demise of the Guadalajara Cartel.[19] Carrillo Fuentes was a visionary, and he operated on a different level than either El Chapo or El Güero, both of whom she characterized as violent ambitious men in search of money and power by means of aggression and overt confrontation. Guzmán and Palma Salazar were regional bosses operating from a provincial base and with a limited understanding of the big picture, but they nevertheless rose in the hierarchy of the narco-trafficking

world by belligerently challenging Manuel "El Cochiloco" Salcido Uzeta and
the Arellano Félix family to obtain a larger share of a Guadalajara franchise
(Hernández 2013, 23). El Güero and El Chapo were also linked to several
bloody attacks on enemies and were allegedly responsible for the kidnapping, torture, and murder of nine members of Félix Gallardo's family and
entourage in 1992. Palma Salazar and Guzmán also attempted to assassinate
Francisco Javier Arellano Félix by ambushing him in Acapulco at Discoteca
Cristina in November 1992 (Epstein and ProPublica 2016; Hernández 2016b).

El Chapo's ambition and his predilection for violence brought him notoriety; his actions exposed the narco enterprise to extreme risk precisely
when Mexican groups were ascending to global prominence. Confluent circumstances, centered around a U.S. clampdown on Andean cocaine routes
through the Caribbean, handed Mexican drug organizations a golden opportunity to become the dominant trampoline for moving drugs into the U.S.
market. While El Chapo and El Güero operated with brute force, other leaders within the cartel such as Amado Carrillo Fuentes and Ismael Zambada
were hypervigilant to the real danger posed by violence and visibility and
were committed to avoiding unnecessary attention.

In 1985 political machination, geopolitical manipulation, treachery, hubris,
and arrogance mingled and led to the downfall of the most powerful Mexican
drug lords in Guadalajara after they tortured and murdered DEA agent Kiki
Camarena. The most widely accepted narrative is that it was a revenge killing
after Camarena and his pilot, Alfredo Zavala Avelar, had discovered a major
marijuana plantation at Rancho Búfalo, resulting in the loss of millions of
dollars for Rafael Caro Quintero. However, that official narrative has been
substantially undermined with the appearance later of evidence that the CIA
was an active participant in the interrogation, torture, and murder because
Camarena had stumbled upon its complicity with the drug cartels in the complicated scheme to train and ship weapons to Nicaraguan Contras dedicated
to overthrowing the left-leaning Sandinista government (Bartley and Bartley
2015; Malone 1989; Shannon 1988).

Even though the evidence leads to the conclusion that the drug capos
were co-conspirators in the murder of Camarena, they would be the only
ones who paid the price. The three most important and powerful bosses of
the Guadalajara Cartel—Rafael Caro Quintero, Miguel Ángel Félix Gallardo,
and Ernesto Fonseca Carrillo—would be imprisoned in spite of their wealth
and power and importance in the covert netherworld. Nevertheless, their

personal misfortune did little to disrupt the connections to Andean cocaine sources or the operation of those new and lucrative routes into the USA: their incarceration simply meant that the baton had been passed to a new generation of leaders who set about to formalize operations and rationalize the enterprise they inherited.

The next generation of cartel leaders had learned an important lesson and understood the need to remain invisible even as they expanded routes and increased the importation and exportation of drugs. The new leaders were so successful that it would be several years before the outside world even realized that Mexican cartels were in charge of narco trafficking in the Americas, and that the Colombians had become suppliers. The new generation would eventually become identified as the Federation, and the most prominent director was Amado Carrillo Fuentes—The Lord of the Skies.[20] In the midst of exponential expansion and increasingly monopolization of the routes, Carrillo Fuentes managed to remain largely invisible even at the apex of his power and dominance. Charles Bowden was astounded by his obscurity and, in one of the first English-language reports highlighting the power of Mexican cartels, he drew attention to Mexican drug organizations and the incredible power of the new drug boss, Amado Carrillo Fuentes.

Bowden (1997a) lamented, "No one is certain what Carrillo looks like or how old he is or how well educated. Only four photographs exist, and they are nearly a decade old at best." Carrillo Fuentes would be murdered shortly after that article was published—during liposuction surgery—but even in death, his identify was not easily established. His invisibility had been so complete that his corpse remained temporarily unidentified until his own mother confirmed it was her son. His body was returned to Guamuchilito, Sinaloa, where a massive funeral attracted the elite and powerful of Mexico who certainly knew who he was and who recognized his powerful status.[21]

If Anabel Hernández is correct in her claim that El Mayo was actually the Jefe de Jefes, Bowden's lament about the invisibility of narco bosses has even more frightening implications. There were many other powerful leaders besides Carrillo Fuentes, and they worked unseen and unknown by outsiders within the covert netherworld that had emerged.

It was in that context that El Chapo Guzmán mysteriously emerged shortly afterward to be paraded before the world as the crime boss responsible for all narco trafficking in Mexico. He was insignificant and his name worthy of only passing references in intelligence reports tracking organized crime in Mexico, even though many rumors had linked him to the three original Guadalajara capos who were now jailed as a result of Operation Leyenda. It's conceivable that Guzmán played a part in the kidnapping, torture, and killing of Camarena in 1985, but that involvement is not indicated in reports that are currently available to the public. There is significantly more evidence that the CIA was involved than was El Chapo.[22]

Reorganization

The Guadalajara Cartel was reorganized in 1989, reportedly under the orders and direction of Félix Gallardo following the Camarena fiasco and immediately following the imprisonment of his partners Fonseca Carrillo and Caro Quintero. Three major plazas and three groups were carved out and conjoined into a cooperative business arrangement that would continue to move drugs into the lucrative U.S. market in a franchise model of distribution. Guzmán was not assigned the oversight of a plaza, even though there are some who write that he had expected to be granted a significant franchise because of his proven track record of exporting drugs across the border from points east of Sonora (Naco, Sasabe) and as far west as Mexicali, Baja California. Instead, El Chapo was designated to remain a subordinate (lugarteniente) to El Güero, who had been allocated leadership of the Sinaloa franchise. That Sinaloa division of the Guadalajara franchise controlled all shipments (imports and exports) moving through the Golden Triangle, Culiacán, and Guadalajara, and was directly involved in overseeing the production of marijuana and opium in the hills above Culiacán.

The Focus on El Chapo

Malcolm Beith's biographical account of Guzmán is titled *The Last Narco* (2010), but he has explained that using the descriptor "last" did not mean that El Chapo was irreplaceable; rather, he felt that El Chapo was the last of a specific generational breed of narcos, and would perhaps be the last of them to receive so much attention, and to openly benefit from support rooted in systemic and endemic corruption.

Popular narratives of organized crime in Mexico have narrowly focused on this one man—admittedly, an extraordinary and compelling figure. But the story of illegal drugs, violence, and corruption has too often been reduced to a fascination with El Chapo's character and his exploits. Guzmán's life and deeds are spectacular, astonishing, and even surreal—and it is understandable why many limit analyses to individual explanations and the improbable exploits attributed to this one man. Humans are amateur psychologists at the core and automatically focus attention on those who are unique and different.

But El Chapo is not unique! He is unusual given his endurance and permanence in the public view for much longer than the usual fifteen minutes of fame, but many audacious Mexican narcos and capos such as Rafael Caro Quintero, Ernesto Fonseca Carrillo, Juan José Esparragoza Moreno, Ismael Zambada García, and Amado Carrillo Fuentes also emerged in the last quarter of the last century.[23] Each of those men lived extraordinary lives that truly demand a suspension of disbelief when looking at their exploits. When El Chapo leaves the scene, another narco will take his place, but as Beith writes, it is unlikely that they will ever achieve the fame and visibility that surrounds Shorty Guzmán.[24]

The obsessive focus on Guzmán, his attributes, and his motivation have contributed to a generalized tunnel vision about narco traffic in Mexico, and many serious issues have been left unexplored. How was it possible for a semiliterate man from a peasant background to rise from dreaming about being a millionaire to actually becoming one of the wealthiest and most powerful men today? How did one man move all those commodities when the world's greatest superpower had declared a war on his business and been vigorously fighting against it for forty-five years?

Anabel Hernández provides the most comprehensive description of Guzmán's career; she has explored those questions listed in the previous paragraph. She has also offered an answer, and it is surprisingly simple and usually ignored—he is powerful because decay and corruption in Mexico allowed him to attain that status and thrive in a covert netherworld.

> The story of how Joaquín Guzmán Loera became a great drug baron, the king of betrayal and bribery, and the boss of top Federal Police commanders, is intimately linked to a process of decay in Mexico where two factors are constant: corruption and an unbridled ambition for money and power.
>
> Semi-illiterate peasants like Caro Quintero, Don Neto, El Azul, El Mayo and El Chapo would not have gone far without the collusion of businessmen,

politicians and policemen, and all those who exercise everyday power from behind a false halo of legality. We see their faces all the time, not in the mug shots of most wanted felons put out by the Attorney General's Office, but in the front-page stories, business sections, and society columns. All of these are the godfathers of Narcoland, the true lords of the drug world. (Hernández 2013, 6)

Rolling Stone magazine's seventeen-minute video of an interview with El Chapo was released less than two days following his recapture in Los Mochis, Sinaloa (January 12, 2016). The video shows Guzmán in a rural setting stiffly answering questions presented to him by an anonymous querist.[25] The questions came from American actor Sean Penn and were answered tersely by El Chapo, without inflection, and absent any follow-up probes or interaction with the interviewer. Guzmán appeared uncomfortable, and his answers were short and uninformative. His demeanor left few with the impression that he could possibly be the most powerful drug lord allegedly running one of the most sophisticated drug organizations in the world. El Chapo personally downplayed his role and power. When asked, "Do you consider yourself a violent person?," El Chapo simply answers, "No, señor." "Do you consider your activity, your organization, a cartel?" also draws a simple response: "No, sir, not at all. Because people who dedicate their lives to this activity do not depend on me."

Anabel Hernández was interviewed many years later, immediately after El Chapo was captured again, and she reflected on those early years when El Chapo first came to attention and was proclaimed to be the boss of a powerful underworld. In that discussion with Carmen Aristegui, she spoke of the gaping disconnect between the power that had been imputed to El Chapo and personal inadequacies.

For the first time, people can take measure of the size of Joaquín Guzmán Loera, his personality and can understand what I had written a long time ago, when I published the book *Los señores del narco*, that "El Chapo" Guzmán is a man who is considerably simple, primitive, and is a criminal who barely completed the third grade. He's not capable of articulating grand ideas according to people who knew him in Puente Grande prison, and he doesn't appear to have evolved much since then. . . . "El Chapo" cannot elaborate many ideas because he is not a man of ideas. (*Aristegui Noticias* 2016)[26]

The Mythology of El Chapo

Unlike others, El Chapo Guzmán Loera and El Güero Palma Salazar had few qualms about preserving anonymity, and they became entangled in a public and violent feud with the Arellano Félix family, which was in control of Baja California and major cities such as Tijuana and Mexicali: this personal vendetta threatened to expose the entire Mexican drug enterprise, even as most of its leaders were desperate to remain in the shadows following the Camarena fiasco (Castillo García 2016a).

Hernández describes the ongoing battle that Guzmán and Palma Salazar waged against the Arellano Félix family as a roiling feud akin to a schoolyard brawl where boys fight battles with machine guns instead of fists.[27] Most observers trace the origins of that feud to the beheading of El Güero's wife and the murder of his children by Miguel Ángel "El Padrino" Félix Gallardo (Castillo García 2016a, 2016b; Hernández 2016b) or alternately to ongoing jealousy, resentment, and envy resulting from the assignment of the Tijuana Plaza to the Arellano Félix family in the partition of the Guadalajara Cartel and assignment of franchises.[28] The evidence suggests that the blood feud with the Arellano Félix family was rooted in quarrels that predated the reorganization.[29]

Whatever the reason for the feud, in 1992 Guzmán, reportedly with El Güero's assent, authorized a homicidal attack on Ramón and Javier Arellano Félix when they traveled to Puerto Vallarta, Jalisco. Forty men in police uniforms ambushed them while they partied at the Christine Discotheque: Javier escaped in the initial chaos, while Ramón made an improbable escape through a small window thanks to his American bodyguard, David Barron Corona. Afterward, Ramón remained obsessed with making El Chapo pay the consequences for that attack.[30] His most outrageous plot brought disaster to himself even though it did result in the arrest of El Chapo. He flew a team of sicarios to Guadalajara intending to assassinate Guzmán but failed miserably. Instead of leaving El Chapo dead, Mexico's second-ranking Catholic prelate, Cardinal Juan Jesús Posadas Ocampo, was gunned down in the cross fire between Arellano Félix's men and El Chapo's bodyguards at Guadalajara International Airport. Posadas Ocampo lay dead, riddled by high-caliber bullets—allegedly mistaken for El Chapo Guzmán by Arellano Félix's hit men.

Ramón Arellano Félix fled back to Tijuana within the hour and spent the rest of his life hoping to convince his mother and others that he had not been involved in killing a cardinal and that he was not irrationally obsessed with seeking revenge on Guzmán. In the aftermath, El Chapo fled to Guatemala, where he was then captured by the Guatemalan army following a tip and handed back to Mexican justice officials at a border point in Chiapas. His whereabouts were reportedly revealed by his best friend, El Güero Palma Salazar (Hernández 2016b).

El Chapo's First Arrest

Anabel Hernández's description of El Chapo's 1993 arrest and capture clearly portrays him as a subordinate player within the Federation at the time of the cardinal's murder. The monetary reward offered for his capture was relatively small—significantly lower than those typically posted for senior drug lords like those offered in Operation Leyenda. The circumstances and details of his arrest in Guatemala and his immediate delivery to Mexican justice officials also signify that he was not considered an important figure: he was arrested without shots being fired, hooded, hands bound behind his back, and tossed onto a truck flatbed like some "poor devil" for delivery to Mexican justice officials without concern for legal niceties such as extradition treaties (Hernández 2010).

But astonishingly, between the moment he was loaded onto the Mexican government plane as a bedraggled prisoner and the plane's touchdown in Toluca (Mexico State), Joaquín Guzmán Loera had bafflingly been elevated significantly in status. He would somehow be dragged off that army plane as Jefe de Jefes of Mexico's drug world! Hernández describes that enigmatic transformation with understated irony: "On June 10, 1993, the Salinas government pulled out all of the stops to present to the public, a relatively minor drug trafficker converted overnight into the cream of crime bosses: El Chapo Guzmán. The scapegoat for the cardinal's murder" (2013, 40).[31]

The world's first glimpse of El Chapo Guzmán, newly designated Boss of Bosses at Mexico's Puente Grande prison, was on an elevated platform wearing a gray winter jacket and a tan ball cap. Responding to an anonymous journalist's question about his occupation, he uttered a few words that would be the only public statement he was known to make until Mexican actress Kate del Castillo and American actor Sean Penn recorded him twenty-two years later: "No, señor . . . Yo soy agricultor" (No, sir . . . I am a farmer) (Anonymous 2014). His appearance and nonthreatening demeanor gave little credence to the Mexican government assertion that the most important cartel leader was being paraded there on a raised platform before Mexico's press.

The execution of Cardinal Posadas Ocampo would be the first of many incidents involving El Chapo where multiple narratives would be floated as reasonable explanations of an event to purposely sow confusion, and it would not be the last time that one *preferred narrative* would be promoted as probable even when it directly contradicted equally believable alternatives. During his long career, El Chapo would often be at the center of contradictory and ambiguous narratives. Several versions of the shoot-out at Guadalajara International Airport would emerge to contradict the official version that Cardinal Posadas Ocampos simply arrived at the wrong place at the wrong time in a vehicle resembling El Chapo's. One competing narrative argues that Ramón had indeed sent a team of hit men but also claims he was not there personally. In another version, it is argued that Ramón had been lured to Guadalajara by Guzmán hoping to set a trap, ending with Arellano Félix taking the blame for the shoot-out: in that version, El Chapo's men are said to have accidently executed the cardinal as they ambushed Ramón, or had even killed Posadas Ocampo to deliberately frame Ramón. In yet another version, Ramón was allegedly bringing evidence to the cardinal describing narco connections between Guzmán and powerful officials, and that government assassins were directly or indirectly sent to stop this from happening. The execution of Posadas Ocampo is just one of many spectacular killings that has never been fully explained, and his murder remains unsolved in the realm of speculation and myth and even magic realism.

The events surrounding the assassination were further complicated by vociferous public denials from the Arellano Félix family, which denied any part in killing the cardinal; and the determination of the truth was further complicated by the haste of the Salinas government to offer up a scapegoat who would diffuse the international attention focused on Mexico exactly when it was negotiating a free trade agreement. The most convenient scapegoat was Guzmán—and the mythologizing of El Chapo as Jefe de Jefes was underway.

Hernández (2016b) reports that another powerful leader of the Federation, Amado Carrillo Fuentes, had made at least one earlier attempt to eliminate El Chapo due to his erratic behavior, drug use, and overt insubordination. El Chapo had become too visible and had attracted far too much attention in the aftermath of the Christine Discotheque shoot-out. That shoot-out had been widely covered in the press and drew international attention because of Puerto Vallarta's important place in tourism: Guzmán's conspicuous visibility represented a dangerous complication for an organization that was desperate to slink into the background of a covert netherworld. Hernández reports that El Chapo was summoned to meet Carrillo Fuentes with the intent of killing him, but Guzmán anticipated the danger and arrived with a contingent of heavily armed bodyguards. He survived that meeting, but the threat he represented became more urgently problematic following the Posadas Ocampo killing.

Unable to act directly, Carrillo Fuentes and Palma Salazar and perhaps Ismael Zambada likely offered Guzmán as the convenient *chivo expiatorio* (scapegoat) to take the full blame for the Guadalajara shoot-out, and they fed information to the Salinas government indicating that Guzmán was fleeing to Honduras by way of Guatemala and El Salvador. Palma Salazar was directly involved in betraying Guzmán, and observers suggest that it was his idea to have El Chapo take the blame (Hernández 2016b). The order to apprehend El Chapo came directly from Los Pinos and was delivered to the Guatemalan and El Salvadorian presidents: they were expected to intercept Guzmán without getting involved in any entanglement or messy requirement of extradition. El Chapo was arrested in Guatemala when El Salvadorian officials refused his entry and turned him away. He was seized and unceremoniously returned to Mexican authorities by Guatemalan officers who delivered him to the northern border with Chiapas and handed him directly to two Mexican generals sent from Mexico City to retrieve him.

From Poor Devil to Head of Cartel Within Two Hours

Procurador Jorge Carpizio deployed two generals and a backup team of sharpshooters to Chiapas to drag Guzmán back to the capital. A Guatemalan military captain unceremoniously turned over his bundled prisoner to General Jorge Carrillo Olea while General Guillermo Álvarez Nahara stood nearby. The officer had transported Guzmán tied up and bound like a sack of beans. Carrillo Olea's first reaction was that that he was being handed some poor devil, and it pained him that any human being was hooded and trussed with such indignity.[32] Carrillo Olea phoned his boss, Procurador Jorge Carpizio, to deliver the news that he had the "package in his hands" and would soon depart for Mexico City; Carpizio reportedly said, "What great news. I'll tell our boss" (Hernández 2010, 27).

During that two-hour flight from the Chiapas-Guatemala border to a PGR airport in Toluca, El Chapo was mysteriously and inexplicably transformed from some poor devil tossed onto a pickup flatbed into a significantly more important status of Jefe de Jefes of the Sinaloa Cartel and chief executive of a powerful narco Federation. When the plane landed, Guzmán was soon paraded before the world as the most important crime figure the Salinas administration had ever brought to justice.[33]

> Dozens of photographers turned up at the maximum-security prison in the State of Mexico for the show. El Chapo, head shaved, posed for them in khaki regulation pants and a thick nylon bomber jacket. There was a grin on his face. What did the rookie drug baron have to laugh about, with so many years in jail ahead of him? (Hernández 2013, 40)

That would be the last public comment made by El Chapo Guzmán for twenty-two years, until the seventeen-minute video from October 2015 was posted online by *Rolling Stone*. In 1993 Guzmán was most certainly lying when he claimed to be merely a farmer, but the Salinas government also used that public scaffold to foster an even bigger prevarication by presenting him as the man responsible for the murder of Cardinal Posadas Ocampo, and even more outrageously, as Boss of Bosses of the most powerful criminal drug organization in Mexico.

The myth of El Chapo was launched at that 1993 press conference, and the black legend (*leyenda negra*) of Shorty Guzmán would grow more notorious during the next two decades through an indiscriminate blending of fact and fable. Over the years, there would be further fabrications to magnify his folk-hero status and sprinkle reality with large doses of pure magic realism. The mythmaking was neither accidental nor arbitrary, and it served an important purpose—it shielded government officials from intrusive scrutiny and allowed the actual leaders of drug organizations to operate anonymously for years to come. Corruption and collusion were free to continue in the shadows after El Chapo Guzmán had been designated the face of narco traffic.

He was handed a twelve-year prison term to be served in Puente Grande (Federal Social Readaptation Center No. 2, near Guadalajara). On January 19, 2001, he escaped and eluded capture until rearrested thirteen years afterward, on February 22, 2014, in Mazatlán, Sinaloa. Meanwhile, he had moved about Mexico in relative freedom until finally being cornered following a massive manhunt involving hundreds of agents from Mexican intelligence agencies and Mexican marines working cooperatively with American intelligence teams. He was imprisoned once again in Altiplano (Federal Social Readaptation Center No. 1 "Amoloya de Juárez"), only to escape fifteen months later, on July 12, 2015.

Pax Narca and *Chivos Expiatorios*

The details of Guzmán's 1993 elevation to the status Boss of Bosses may never be clarified, but his arrest and the government's role in selling the myth of El Chapo followed a template that would see itself repeated many times over the years. The intent of the strategy is to divert public attention away from government corruption and its own complicity in the drug trade and covert netherworld while simultaneously protecting the routine business links that had been negotiated with criminal organizations in a covert netherworld of complicity. It was a marvelous Machiavellian scheme designed to maintain a Pax Narca and yet make it appear that the Mexican government was cooperating fully in a War on Drugs.[34]

The murder of Cardinal Posadas Ocampo represented a dangerous moment for the Salinas administration and demanded a swift and immediate response. The president had committed Mexico to a major neoliberal economic shift, and the North American Free Trade Agreement was the keystone initiative. But an official reaction against organized crime also required his constraint for two important reasons: the drug organizations funneled necessary funds into a fragile Mexican economy, and overreaction might result in embarrassing revelations about government corruption and collusion with organized crime. President Salinas could not push back too vigorously without jeopardizing the cash flow generated by narco traffic or releasing a flood of embarrassing revelations that would diminish the credibility of his government. His reaction required walking a fine line between demonstrating a commitment to law and order and secretly allowing the drug trade to continue. The rules delineating that balance between the impression of action and preservation of the status quo have been correctly and cynically described as Pax Narca and earlier in this book as a covert netherworld using the terminology of Alfred McCoy. The government reaction to the Posadas Ocampo murder was designed to preserve mutual arrangements, and it relied on a plan of action that would become a standard framework for response that would reappear many times in future narco crises.

The strategy for containment and protection involved four different stages of action.

1. The preferable response and initial adjustment would be left to drug organizations to handle extrajudiciously: inconvenient and embarrassing players had to disappear. Execution was the most expeditious option, with flight or disappearance as a second, albeit less desirable, alternative. A body was required for presentation to the world.

2. The saturation of the public domain with an official narrative accompanied by a campaign to sell the official truth. This would unfold even if cartel leaders had solved the problem internally (in stage 1) by eliminating a troublemaker or problem. An official narrative would be filtered through journalists who willingly spun the official line and in return would be compensated by placing them on government or cartel payrolls—often on both. The narrative would be reinforced via an intensive public relations campaign and through the unchallengeable power of a Televisa-PRI collaboration to ensure that official narratives gained the loudest voice and would be the only narrative repeatedly voiced. Well-placed journalists—on substantial retainers and pejoratively known as *chayoteros*—ensured that the official narrative circulated in print and was repeated on radio and in public forums.

3. This component was the most devious and reveals the sophistication of the Mexican government's ability to manipulate public opinion. It involved the systematic release of competing and contradictory narratives to sow confusion and justify government inaction. Officials would systematically release competing narratives that referred to new lines of investigation or point to new suspects who were allegedly the *intellectual authors* of a crime. Those competing, yet reasonable, narratives made it difficult to coalesce public consensus around one single explanation even when the facts were overwhelmingly supportive, and they justified a dawdling response from a government claiming it was bound by legal requirements to adhere to constitutional principles and explore all lines of investigation.[35]

4. A chivo expiatorio (scapegoat) would be presented along with convincing evidence to support the legitimacy of the official government narrative. A

confession would be provided wherever possible. It was also important to produce a "warm body" to parade in front of journalists. El Chapo's participation, unlike many future cases where the strategy would be used, did not involve torture.

El Chapo Guzmán became the sacrificial lamb only after Amado Carrillo Fuentes had been unable to silence him, deliver him to authorities, or personally arrange his killing. The Salinas government, abetted by compliant journalists, circulated several competing narratives about the murder of Posadas Ocampo and gave the government the freedom to argue it required more time and resources to investigate and comply with the requirements of law. The government then moved to muster the evidence that the El Chapo Guzmán narrative represented the most credible explanation of the murder, and simultaneously and improbably initiated a plan to persuade the world that this insignificant and uneducated man from Mexico's Western Sierra Madre was the most eminent boss of Mexico's most important drug cartel and responsible for much of Mexico's crime. A compliant or a manipulated press helped sell the vision and helped sell the first chapter in the legend of Shorty.

The fourth stage is more complicated than has been briefly summarized here; it involved negotiation and bargaining replete with expectations of trade-offs. One of Guzmán's greatest talents is his ability to anticipate the various options and negotiate from a position of strength that kept the government on edge and fearful of the blowback. That strength is not dependent on firepower and weapons, although that is certainly an important factor—it's based on Guzmán's knowledge of the connections and the specific arrangements between corrupt politicians and crime organization bosses in the covert netherworld that reigned supreme. Of course, it's also based on money and what it can purchase in a corrupt environment. Guzmán was able to use this information to create his own personal Pax Narca with terms satisfactory to both the government and other cartel bosses.

Secret Pacts?

Anabel Hernández uncovered documents implying that Guzmán had specific knowledge about the Iran-Contra scandal and the links between imprisoned Guadalajara Cartel bosses (especially Rafael Caro Quintero), the DFS, and the CIA. There are many well-respected observers who dispute her interpretation of those documents, but they offer a plausible explanation about the power of El Chapo's key bargaining chip. Literally, he could have been thrown out of that military plane that brought him back from Chiapas—but he wasn't. Hernández's line of reasoning might not be so far-fetched given the evidence magnificently presented by Russell Bartley and Sylvia Erickson Bartley (2015) in their investigation of the perverted institutional complicity of the CIA in the murders of both Manuel Buendía Tellezgirón and Enrique Camarena.

Over his long career, El Chapo developed a reputation for providing authorities with specific details and information to cripple competing criminal organizations and leave the Sinaloa group with a market advantage. But in 1993 it's unlikely that he had any important information about other organizations to use as a bargaining chip. Drug organizations were collaborating and broadly committed to developing a federated or cooperative business model that paralleled business franchises, and the Federation continued to be successful even as disagreements emerged. Guzmán's animosity toward the Arellano Félix family was personal rather than organizational, and furthermore, the Federation bosses had already mutually decided that El Chapo would take the blame for the Guadalajara shoot-out instead of the Arellano Félix family. Furthermore, it would have been difficult for Guzmán to transfer the blame to the Arellano Félix family given the deep connections between PRI party stalwart Carlos Hank González and the Arellano Félix family; both had mutual business interests with the Salinas family and with other high-ranking members of the PRI machine based in the Grupo Atlacomulco in Mexico State.[36]

In brief, the absence of alternative explanations for El Chapo's bargaining power make Hernández's theory about his knowledge of Iran-Contra links more compelling. He must have had a powerful card to throw on the table, because although he would ultimately be imprisoned, El Chapo managed to escape with his life, receive a relatively light sentence, retain his wealth, and enjoy a privileged existence in Centro de Readaptación Social Número 2 "Puente Grande" in Jalisco State, where he effectively ran a narco enterprise from behind its walls. It seems likely that he had negotiated a personal pact with the government and was suitably compensated, and yet somehow he managed to retain power and influence within the narco Federation that controlled the drug trade.[37]

El Chapo Guzmán's ritual elevation to Jefe de Jefes also served an important function for the drug bosses. The resolution of the Posadas Ocampos murder not only helped the government sell the free trade deal; it also mitigated the external pressure for it to deal with organized crime. It's almost certain that Guzmán also negotiated a payout or trade-off from other cartel leaders. He was owed a reward because he took the blame and neutralized the growing international fallout and pressure being directed at the Federation and its enterprise. Although loyalty may not have much value among thieves, it's important to remember that Guzmán was connected to a Sinaloan hierarchy since childhood by marriage and by the broader custom of compadrazgo (illustrated by the marriage of his own children to other narco juniors). The Sinaloans in the Federation still respected and honored that code of loyalty, and it remained strong throughout the 1990s.

Others have noted that El Chapo Guzmán was extremely resourceful and skilled at moving drugs, importing weapons, and retrieving payments from the USA. Specifically, he oversaw a tunnel system on the border for which he would become even more notorious after the 2015 prison escape.[38] In essence, Shorty Guzmán was a valuable asset even while incarcerated. Guzmán also had a personal network of contacts and support in the covert netherworld that remained loyal, and the Federation would have access to his assets only if he remained alive. Finally, the Federation was still apparently being directed by Amado Carrillo Fuentes until his death in 1997—that is, through the fourth year of El Chapo's imprisonment. Although it is unlikely that Guzmán was actually Jefe de Jefes when paraded as such in 1993, it is not improbable to believe that he ascended the leadership ladder once the Lord of the Skies was murdered; it's certainly not impossible to believe that his close allies had arranged for Carrillo Fuentes's death in surgery.

The First Escape

In 1993 Guzmán saved himself because he understood the code and rules of the Pax Mafiosa and the Pax Narca. El Chapo and others realized the world was changing, and that it had been dramatically altered after Vicente Fox Quesada ended PRI hegemony in 2000. The first prison escape was predictable following Fox's devolution of power to states and governors. Guzmán reportedly feared the consequences of extradition to the United States, but the 2001 escape was also made necessary by the reality that his contacts at the federal level had weakened by the downward shift to states, and it was necessary to be on the outside to rebuild the links that had been disrupted.

His remaining connections to powerful federal figures smoothed the way for him to walk out of prison in 2001, while his safety could be assured (Hernández 2010). Fox's election increased the likelihood of extradition to the United States, and it became time for Shorty Guzmán to call in favors as he reputedly bribed his way out with a rumored *golden kilo* to vanish into the underworld and reinforce his personal power base at the state and municipal levels.[39] His escape was the first step, and it eventually allowed him to become repositioned as a key player for the next thirteen years.

There is no evidence that El Chapo Guzmán immediately returned to lead the powerful Sinaloa faction of the disintegrating Federation after his first escape from Altiplano. In fact, he desperately required the protection of old friends—especially El Mayo Zambada and El Azul Esparragoza. They arranged hideouts and safe houses, provided security teams, and hid him from the Arellano Félix family, which was still hoping to get revenge for the Christine Discotheque attack and the Cardinal Posadas Ocampo disaster. El Chapo would gradually reestablish his place in the underworld hierarchy and go on to play a major part in restructuring narco Mexico.[40]

Shifting Plazas

Drug-trafficking organizations of Mexico do not fit into one singular monolithic and inflexible organizational model—a pattern described in the previous chapter. The Guadalajara Cartel and the Federation had gradually emerged into a limited hierarchical structure where many actions required horizontal lines of negotiation and partnership. It took that organizational form because it had organically emerged from links based on family relationships, traditions, and understandings that had evolved over decades in the sierra and later in Guadalajara. The cooperative and family business model was about to change—and perhaps had already shifted by the time that Amado Carrillo Fuentes made the Ciudad Juárez Plaza the most dominant franchise in the enterprise. At the end of the 1990s, there was one overarching federation, but within a few years three dominant divisions of the Federation would be operating independently and under different business models. In addition, a new challenger in the northeast had emerged to challenge the Federation and those three divisions located in Tijuana, Sinaloa, and Juárez.

The cartels of the new millennium have different organizational leadership structures than that of the 1990s Federation.[41] Its three dominant factions evolved in response to internal disputes, geopolitical factors, and changing market conditions while the emerging Gulf Cartel in the northeast was built on an entirely different basis. The Sinaloa faction retained many of the horizontal features of the Federation, whereas the Tijuana and Juárez factions became family business models. Each of those three groups depended on mutual cooperation and negotiation with the others, but the glue within each one was different: Tijuana remained a family business run equally by siblings, Juárez was a family business dominated by a patriarch, and Sinaloa managed as an enterprise among mutual partners—some of whom were related or connected by marriage and compadrazgo.

Many observers continue to think of narco trafficking in monolithic terms, but Howard Campbell correctly warned that rigid and unchanging constructions of criminal organizations would be "replaced by a more supple concept of cartels as shifting, contingent temporal alliances of traffickers whose territories and memberships evolve and change because of conflicts, imprisonment, deaths, changing political circumstances, etc., and whose fortunes and strengths wax and wane over time" (2009, 19).

Since 1990 there have been at least five transformational events changing narco-trafficking patterns and spurring organizational change, and El Chapo Guzmán and his allies in the Sinaloa faction were protagonists for each of those shifts—as either the instigator or the target. These shifts, briefly described in chapters 4 and 5 and explored again from a different viewpoint in chapter 7, are:

- A prolonged plaza war between the Sinaloa faction and the Arellano Félix family in Tijuana.
- A brutal and intense plaza war between the Sinaloa Federation and the Carrillo Fuentes family.
- Internal Sinaloa Federation quarrels and a brutal war with the Beltrán Leyvas.
- A Sinaloa hostile expansion into Gulf Cartel plazas.
- Organizational reaccommodations triggered by a government strategy to target kingpins.

Campbell wrote that internal conflicts were the principal reason that drug cartels changed; Guzmán's actions following the 2001 prison escape support this observation. El Chapo's conflicts with former allies and childhood friends triggered several shifts during the thirteen years that he remained free. For much of that time, he was focused on driving enemies, former childhood buddies, partners, and allies out of the narco business.

El Chapo: A Catalyst of Change

Only a few of El Chapo's personal relationships, such as those with El Mayo and El Azul, have survived the test of time because of their strong personal bonds, but also because both those men were willing to compromise and they recognized El Chapo's significant contribution to the business. Many other personal relationships degenerated into bitter and bloody disputes that led to the dramatic restructuring of Mexico's narco-traffic plazas between 2001 and 2012.[42]

El Chapo's first adult responsibilities in the Sinaloa Cartel involved moving marijuana and cocaine via mountain and water routes to the staging points in Naco, Sonora, in the east and Mexicali and Baja California in the west. In Mexicali, he moved drugs through tunnels initially carved out during the Chinese migrations from one hundred years earlier (Osorno 2009, 2015). Clearly, he was an important operative delivering drugs to markets during the 1980s—and his skill as an expeditor of shipments was a critical reason for success of the Federation and the Sinaloa faction. Guzmán would eventually become the catalyst for change—and frequently, trigger actions that ended with violent battles with childhood friends and former allies.

The Arellano Félix Feud

The disruption around 2002 involved the Arellano Félix family business, but it was not Guzmán alone who led that attack: Héctor Luis Palma Salazar, Ismael Zambada García, Juan José Esparragoza Moreno, and many others had grown weary of excessive tolls and violence linked to that family. Business deals involving the family were systematically and regularly leaked to the DEA and to the Mexican PGR. It led to the arrest of several brothers over a period of years (Epstein and ProPublica 2016) and the murder of Ramón Arellano Félix, El Chapo's old nemesis from the Guadalajara shoot-out. On the morning of February 10, 2002, a Mazatlán municipal policeman stopped a white Volkswagen Beetle driven by Arellano Félix. He emerged from his car firing at close range, and the traffic officer killed him. It was later reported that Arellano Félix had set off on a personal quest to seek revenge and assassinate a Sinaloa Cartel kingpin—reportedly, El Mayo.

El Chapo eventually forged an alliance with a former Arellano Félix enforcer and lugarteniente, El Teo García Simental, following Eduardo Arellano Félix's 2008 arrest, and as a result the Sinaloa Cartel had effectively assumed control of Tijuana and pushed aside the Arellano Félix family.

Feuds with the Carrillo Fuentes family

El Chapo Guzmán also feuded with the Carrillo Fuentes family controlling Ciudad Juárez and the U.S.-Chihuahua *frontera*. Guzmán triggered a bloody war with leader Vicente "El Viceroy" Carrillo Fuentes when he ordered the execution of the youngest Carrillo Fuentes brother, Rodolfo—El Niño del Oro. Rodolfo and his wife, Giovanna Quevedo, were gunned down by commandos in the Cinépolis movie theater parking lot in Culiacán on September 11, 2004. A prolonged period of violence and bloodshed followed, particularly in areas near Ciudad Juárez, after El Chapo and the Beltrán Leyva brothers sent teams of sicarios to target the gangs employed by the Carrillo Fuentes family. In the space of a few years, Ciudad Juárez became the most violent city in Mexico and identified internationally as one of the most dangerous cities on the planet.

The War with the Gulf Cartel and Los Zetas

El Chapo and the Beltrán Leyva brothers pushed into northeast border regions beginning in 2006. El Chapo Guzmán, El Mayo Zambada, and the Beltrán Leyvas launched attacks on competitors with the intent of controlling the border between Mexicali and Nuevo Laredo. A low-grade war emerged when the Gulf Cartel resisted the incursion, and Nuevo Laredo, Reynosa, and other cities in Tamaulipas became contested plazas and bloody battle zones. The Sinaloa intrusion into Mexico's northeast proved to be more difficult than the seizure of the Baja California Plaza when the Gulf Cartel and Los Zetas successfully defended the incursion and pushed the invaders back to the west. The Sinaloa Cartel was also maneuvered into pulling back forces when the Los Zetas paramilitary wing of the Gulf Cartel opened new battle fronts in previously uncontested Sinaloa territory: Sinaloa foot soldiers were withdrawn and redeployed to its suddenly and unexpectedly vulnerable strongholds in the Golden Triangle. Los Zetas moved southward into Nuevo León State and also made bold expansionary incursions into central Mexico, especially Michoacán State, where they seized control of synthetic drug production and the overland routes feeding the industrial port of Lázaro Cárdenas.

The Los Zetas strategy forced their Sinaloa counterparts to reorganize in order to protect their long-standing plazas—and that led to the rapid creation of new armed wings. The threat from the Gulf Cartel and Los Zetas also forced the Sinaloenses (El Chapo, El Mayo, and the Beltrán Leyvas) to reinforce and empower old connections such as that with the Milenio Cartel to counteract Los Zetas incursionary invasions into Jalisco and in Michoacán. That move resurrected the influence of the Milenio Cartel and eventually led to the emergence of another powerful group years later—the Cártel de Jalisco Nueva Generación. Inadvertently, the actions of the Sinaloa faction strengthened the position of the Milenio Cartel that would later emerge to challenge El Chapo, El Mayo, and El Azul for dominance. The violence and disputes soon spread to Guerrero, Jalisco, and Mexico State as the number of groups involved expanded, and violent hot spots emerged deeper into central Mexico and further from the border. Blockades created congestion in major cities like Monterrey and Guadalajara as the organizations engaged in major displays of turf protection.

Split with the Beltrán Leyvas

A fourth event was specifically attributed to El Chapo. It was the bloody split with childhood companions the Beltrán Leyva brothers. The specific catalyst is unknown, but the youngest brother, Alfredo "El Mochomo" Beltrán Leyva, was the focal point. Purportedly, Alfredo had become an inconvenient figure because of aggressive bullying and loose-cannon behavior within the city of Culiacán. His nickname refers to a querulous red army-ant that was a fitting representation for his uncouth swagger. His bad behavior and general unpredictability made him unwelcome within a cartel that prided itself on following a *civilized* code of conduct—especially on home turf Culiacán. The federal PGR received an anonymous tip about his safe house in Culiacán and assurances that his bodyguards (state police) would not appear. PGR forces were sent from the capital to seize him and bring him to Mexico City for trial and a speedy uncontested extradition to the USA.

Arturo, the oldest brother, fingered El Chapo for the betrayal and angrily split from the Sinaloa Cartel with a bold declaration of war, followed up by an immediate wave of violent reprisals.[43] He also began to refer to himself as Jefe de Jefes in a defiant gesture of power. His men brutally attacked and gunned down five federal police in Culiacán who he accused of defending Guzmán and unleashed several other shoot-outs and ambushes in the first ten days pursuant to Alfredo's arrest. Édgar Millán Gómez was the highly placed federal agent who arrested El Mochomo; he was assassinated soon afterward, as he entered his home in Mexico City, by a sicario who admitted his connection to the Beltrán Leyvas. The Sinaloa Federation and Beltrán Leyva split represented the most serious threat faced by the Sinaloa Cartel and resulted in internal disputes and battles that continued long afterward. The fracture was so bitter that not even the death of Arturo or the arrest of the remaining brothers stopped the violence. For the first time since the emergence of the Sinaloa Federation in the 1990s, Sinaloa was fragmented by warring factions battling for control of the Sinaloa faction. The traditional allies and directors retained control of central Sinaloa—including Culiacán—but the Beltrán Leyva faction, remnants, or allies control a sizeable region in the remote north and established strongholds east of Mazatlán.

Fragmentation: El Chapo the Hunted

For twelve years, Guzmán was instigator and provocateur while four major plaza readjustments unfolded. During that time, his notoriety and the legend of Shorty had grown. But in the final months of 2012, he became the hunted instead of the hunter. Enrique Peña Nieto reclaimed the presidency for the PRI and an Atlacomulco oligarchy that hoped to restore a centralized state. His election and any chance for restoring a federalist state hinged on his ability to renegotiate the terms of narco politics. Under PAN's decentralized vision of governance, Guzmán and the Sinaloa partners had encountered minimal interference from federal powers and had absolutely no opposition at the local level since they always had intimate ties to governors and mayors: El Chapo Guzmán's only real threat during his dozen years of freedom came from the other cartels, the occasional annoyance from DEA pursuits, and revenge-seeking former friends. In 2012 the new federal administration of Peña Nieto represented an unknown that left El Chapo feeling vulnerable.

President Peña Nieto planned to take a different approach to drug organizations; he appointed Colombian national General Óscar Naranjo Trujillo as his chief security adviser. Naranjo's strategy was heavily weighted to the fragmentation of larger organizations into so-called cartelitos. No criminal organization would be allowed to compete directly with the federal government as an alternate power, and in return the state would foster a climate of benign tolerance toward smaller organizations less likely to create international scandals or draw attention to government corruption at the national level. That strategy had been relatively successful in Colombia and in fact left the impression that the drug problem was under control. In fact, it was actually a shell game, and it simply demanded that the drug lords shift gears and operate without generating excessive noise or fostering violence.

Operation Gargoyle

El Chapo became the obvious target given his international profile, his continuing visibility, and his legendary reputation for instigating violence. Furthermore, it is highly likely that other partners and directors of the Sinaloa Cartel and its franchises had already negotiated a pact to work within Peña Nieto's new security framework during the Year of Hidalgo. Accordingly, Mexican security forces and CISEN were now specifically authorized to hunt down Shorty. Operation Gargoyle went into high gear shortly after Peña Nieto's inauguration—almost assuredly with the full blessing of leaders and partners of the Sinaloa Cartel who had long wearied of El Chapo's notoriety and the need to clean up his messes. A major reaccommodation within the Sinaloa Cartel was very likely negotiated in the background and covert netherworld *before* Guzmán was specifically targeted for isolation and removal through Operation Gargoyle. In fact, all the evidence points to the reality that the Sinaloa Cartel bosses had agreed to offer up El Chapo as the scapegoat to negotiate a new Pax Narca with the state.

The catalytic event leading to the restructuring and reaccommodation within the Sinaloa Cartel happened three years earlier. On March 19, 2009, El Mayo Zambada García's eldest son, Vicentillo Zambada Niebla, was arrested in the Pedregal district of Mexico City. Negotiations within the cartel and subsequently between its leaders and the federal government shifted into high gear when Vicentillo was extradited to Chicago in 2010 for arraignment on narco-trafficking charges filed by the DOJ. Vicentillo had been a close and trusted confidante to his father, an emerging key player within the Sinaloa Cartel franchise system, and was privy to information that touched upon every aspect of the narco-traffic business in Mexico. Vicentillo's capture and extradition provided an extraordinary opportunity for American authorities to untangle some of the darkest organizational secrets of narco and politico Mexico and to critically disrupt the entire enterprise.

But the DOJ did not anticipate the powerful bargaining chip that lawyers for Vicentillo threw onto the table. They claimed that both Vicentillo and El Mayo had been cooperating with the DEA for several years to leak details about narco-traffic shipments and drug traffickers (Radden Keefe 2014a). If true, this legal defense team claim made Guzmán the most vulnerable target because his trusted operatives—Pedro and Margarito Flores—had flooded the Illinois and Chicago market with Sinaloa opium and cocaine. The twin brothers had been the chief targets of the DOJ indictments, and they themselves were allegedly negotiating protected-witness agreements (Hernández 2020).

Other evidence suggests that Guzmán had grown increasingly isolated by late 2012; eventually that explained the reason for his recapture in Mazatlán, Sinaloa, after more than thirteen years of untouchability. The official narrative would have the world accept that Guzmán's capture on July 22, 2014, was the result of brilliant intelligence gathered by CISEN and due to the precision operation executed by marine commandos who cornered the major kingpin after years of near misses. Operation Gargoyle almost resulted in Guzmán's capture one week earlier in Culiacán, but he had avoided marines by running barefoot through Culiacán's storm tunnels. He made his way through those sewers by entering below an ingenious cantilevered tub located in one of his many safe houses in Sinaloa's capital city (Radden Keefe 2014b). Guzmán was most likely unaware that almost all his hideouts in Culiacán had been recently identified by either José Rodrigo "El Chino Ántrax" Aréchiga, who had been arrested in Amsterdam, or were more likely identified based on information provided to CISEN and the DEA by Vicentillo Zambada, who was then in a Chicago jail—or even by Vicentillo's father in Sinaloa trying to negotiate a deal for his son's release.

Guzmán's miraculous and ingenious escape in Culiacán only added to the legend of Shorty. But several important associates were arrested, and his circle of support was irreparably compromised. He left behind telephones and was unable to directly communicate with backup teams for fear that all communication links had been compromised during the raid. He was extremely vulnerable as he worked his way south to Mazatlán, where he arrived accompanied by a skeleton team of bodyguards. He was almost immediately tracked to a small condominium residence on Mazatlán's *malecón* and arrested early on a Saturday morning without a single shot fired.

A Mexican navy communiqué reports that Guzmán surrendered meekly while his wife Emma Coronel Asipuro pleaded with marines to spare his life. There was no bloody shoot-out like those in Al Pacino's *Scarface* nor the one where former ally Arturo Beltrán Leyva was cut to pieces by hundreds of rounds of .50 caliber bullets.[44] Rather, the arrest was portrayed as the meek surrender of a protective husband and devoted father apparently more concerned with the safety of his young wife and twin daughters in the adjoining bedroom. Skillfully orchestrated media coverage sold that version of an easy arrest by a government committed to battling organized criminals with efficiency and humanity.

In a later interview with Telemundo called "La reina de El Chapo" (see Baumoel 2016), Emma Coronel Asipuro claimed her husband had received instructions to work his way to Mazatlán to meet up with El Mayo Zambada at that specific condominium apartment on the malecón, and that her husband had expressed concern that El Mayo was actually plotting for his handover to the government in a very public place. Her comments make it clear that old friend El Mayo likely arranged for El Chapo's delivery to the marines.

Alternate Narratives of the Mazatlán Arrest

The official story of El Chapo's Mazatlán arrest was well scripted and credible—especially the version that was broadcast by Carlos de Loret Mola—a PRI favorite *chayotero* who had been given exclusive access to the capturing marines and to the hotel room. In Mexico, an obvious explanation is rarely the most truthful or accurate—especially when the government controls the creation of the narrative. Given the traditional fate of narco capos, one wonders why El Chapo surrendered without a shot or why marines did not kill him. The captured alive scenario and the perp walk to a waiting helicopter staged for the benefit of national and international media was a radically different outcome and fate than Arturo Beltrán Leyva's; he had been gunned down and his corpse displayed in humiliation (Guillermoprieto 2010). It was also high drama that would help raise the credibility of President Peña Nieto.

There are at least three alternate versions of that February arrest. One narrative—the *betrayal hypothesis*—asserts that the operation unfolded as described, but only because it used the inside information supplied by El Mayo. This asserts that Guzmán was betrayed by his longtime partner, compadre, and ally; Coronel Aispura's comments to Anabel Hernández lend credence to that betrayal narrative. However, a second narrative—a *negotiated pact* with government—also fits nicely: this second version asserts that El Chapo's Mazatlán arrest was a meticulous dramaturgical event staged for public consumption to allow El Chapo to retire from the business and for the government to save face. This second narrative might make more sense than the first: El Chapo escaped once again eighteen months later, exactly when the Mexican federal government seemed committed to extradite him to the United States in violation of any secret pact that might have been in place (Montenegro and Carrol 2016). A third narrative—the *retirement option*—suggests that El Chapo had simply grown tired of running and had negotiated surrender in order to shift his battles to the judicial arena, where he could threaten to expose everyone in the covert netherworld to the court of public opinion.[45] This final narrative seems less likely than the first two, except for the fact that this is precisely what Guzmán did two years later through the proxy voice of his wife Emma Coronel Aispuro, his sister, and his lawyers (Baumoel 2016; Montenegro and Carrol 2016).[46] And it is precisely what Vicentillo Zambada did when he met with Anabel Hernandéz to hand over his secret diary about the structure and operations of the Sinaloa Cartel. Reportedly, Vicentillo did so with the blessing of both his father and Guzmán (Hernández 2020).

The Great Escape

Guzmán was once again incarcerated in Altiplano prison in Almoloya de Juárez, Mexico, but escaped in spectacular fashion on July 11, 2015. About 9 p.m. on a Saturday evening, the concrete floor in his shower was air-hammered open from below to create an opening of approximately one square foot (30 × 30 cm) and access to a ladder that descended thirty feet into the abyss (10 m). Once he climbed down, he had access to a tunnel that was less than five feet (1.5 m) high and more than two feet (30 cm) wide and which ran in an impossibly engineered straight line for one mile (1.5 km). The tunnel had power, lighting, a fresh air supply, and a modified motorcycle sitting on a track that ran the entire length of the tunnel.[47]

Prison security video shows Guzmán changing shoes, stepping into the shower stall, and disappearing suddenly. He apparently descended the ladder into the tunnel and mounted the modified motorcycle to travel long enough to climb up another ladder into a room at a construction site one mile away. From there, he was transported to a nearby airport at San Juan del Río, where two planes were waiting. One was a decoy that headed directly to Sinaloa, but El Chapo allegedly boarded the other, flown by his regular pilot, Héctor Ramón Takashima Valenzuela, toward one of the hundreds of small drug landing strips located in the Golden Triangle. There was a considerable delay before prison staff noticed his disappearance and issued a general alarm. By that time, Guzmán was already across the state line and on his way to freedom near Cosalá— within a stone's throw of where he had started his career as a fresa narco.

The PGR released a professional-quality video laying out the precise details of the escape: that video reveals the sophisticated engineering required to build a tunnel and arrive exactly beneath a semiprotected shower area in his assigned cell. Later investigations established that it had been designed by a team of Italian engineers, and the construction had begun shortly after Guzmán had been returned to Altiplano from Mazatlán in early 2014 (Archibald 2015; Buchanan, Keller and Watkins 2016; Fiscalía General de la República 2016; Neuman, Archibald, and Ahmed 2015). If that timing is correct, it also lends credence to the theory that El Chapo had actually negotiated a formal departure or even retirement before his actual arrest in Mazatlán.

Guzmán fled to a region somewhere above Culiacán that stretched south and east from his birthplace of La Tuna, Badiguarato, toward Tamazula in neighboring Durango, and to the south and west toward the Pueblo Mágico of Cosalá in Sinaloa State.[48] That swath of land along the spine and perimeter of Mexico's Golden Triangle is dotted with small ranchos, and mountain trails invisible beneath dense forestation. The low population density and numerous plateaus hide many secret landing strips among opium and marijuana fields on the edge of those hillsides. The people who live there remain fiercely loyal to the Guzmán clan—and would remain stubbornly uncooperative with the security forces hot on the drug lord's trail.

A Major Embarrassment and Scorched Earth Response

It is an understatement of the highest order to say that the Peña Nieto government was embarrassed by the escape. In fact, the timing could not have been worse, since most of the Mexican cabinet had left Mexico for Paris the

previous day to begin a major trade initiative and pitch for European investment in Mexico. Peña Nieto had invited more than three hundred Mexican
officials and business men and women to accompany him and forty members
of his administration overseas (L. Flores 2015; Guevara 2015). The president
could only issue a statement from abroad decrying the deplorable escape,
but he sent his security minister and secretary of state, Miguel Ángel Osorio Chong, back to Mexico along with his attorney general, Arely Gómez
González, to handle the crisis and deal with the embarrassment.

Osorio Chong immediately authorized one of the largest deployments
of military forces and intelligence teams that has ever been unleashed in
Mexico in pursuit of one man. Thousands were assigned the specific and
dedicated task of locating Guzmán and recapturing him as quickly as possible. The campaign in the Golden Triangle would be the largest one Mexico
had undertaken since Operation Condor in 1976, and furthermore it would
employ the same scorched earth tactics that had been used forty years earlier.

Mexican marines were relentless in carrying out raids on villages and hell-
bent on shooting at buildings indiscriminately. The deliberate stormtrooper
approach was intended to undermine morale and intimidate people into
cooperating in the manhunt for one of their own. Hundreds fled from more
remote areas to relatively larger centers like Cosalá and even further afield to
Culiacán: the operation forced an internal displacement on a scale not seen
since the time of Operation Condor (Hernández Norzagaray 2015; Monjardín 2015). The strategy was different only in scale from the scorched earth
attacks unleashed by U.S. forces in Vietnam to intimidate and spread terror
in populations. Over a three-week period, Mexican marines swarmed the
region in a massive manhunt that drove residents away from communities
like Bastantitas de Abajo and many other small ranchos. But no one talked,
and El Chapo remained invisible to authorities, although there were many
who certainly knew his whereabouts.

How Could He Wander Freely?

A reductionist view argues that people cooperate with narco traffickers due
to the zero-sum strategy of plata plomo—bribes or brutality. But that bifurcated explanation is far too simplistic to explain why the Mexican government was unable to recapture Guzmán immediately after his escape, and
why he moved around in relative freedom for six months after that spectacular escape from Altiplano. Allegiance to El Chapo has roots in decades

of familiarity, friendship, intermarriage, and compadrazgo, and is further reinforced by a timeworn code in the sierra that the government is never to be trusted and loyalty to friends is always necessary for self-preservation.

Community recalcitrance did not weaken even in the face of the jack-boot tactics employed by the marines in pursuit of the drug lord; in fact, the tactics served to remind people of that invasion four decades earlier when Mexican troops displaced their grandparents, uncles, and aunts during Operation Condor. The scorched earth strategy and mano dura tactics favored by Mexican marines did little to weaken resistance and in fact contributed to an increasing alienation and belief that the Peña Nieto government had no interest in serving their common interest. How could a government be on the side of the people when it indiscriminately destroyed communities and displaced yet another generation of families from the hills of Mexico's golden triangle (Bojorquez 2015)?

While the marines carried out raids and invaded ranchos, government intelligence forces were at work looking for any information leading to El Chapo's hideout. Some searches bordered on the surreal, such as that focused on the movements of the pet monkey belonging to Emma Coronel Aispura's twin daughters.

On October 6, 2015, a security intelligence team was certain it had zeroed in on one of Guzmán's hideouts in a rancho near Tamazula, Durango. Pursuing clues worthy of magic realism, Mexican intelligence (CISEN) and DEA agents had identified a potential hideout by tracking the movements of a pet monkey named Boots (Botas). Some within the intelligence team believed that Guzmán had ordered the retrieval of Boots, who had been left behind when the drug lord's family quickly relocated a few days before the July prison escape in Jalisco. Guzmán's wife Emma Coronel Aispura and daughters Emaly Guadalupe and María Joaquína were nearby in Mexico State but left suddenly for Sinaloa just before the spectacular escape. In the haste, Botas was left behind, and reportedly the two girls pleaded that someone needed to retrieve their pet.

Mexican and American security agents engaged in a surrealistic game of fox-and-hound with Boots as a moving target. Emma Coronel Aispura had been under CISEN surveillance for some time, and agents knew of the children's attachment to their pet. When CISEN agents found documents and veterinary inoculation forms approving the air transport of a monkey to Culiacán, they believed they had caught a serendipitous break. However, either the paperwork was an elaborate ruse or someone short-circuited the arranged move when they recognized that CISEN was following the animal's paper trail. Someone in Guzmán's inner circle arranged to move the monkey overland, and Boots was transported in a late model red Mustang driven by El Chapo's brother-in-law Édgar Coronel Aispuro.

The mustang eventually made its way toward Tamazula, and audio intercepts indicated that El Chapo was nearby when a Secretaría de Marina (SEMAR, Naval Secretariat) helicopter assault descended on the small rancho of Bastantitas de Abajo. When the troopers arrived, Guzmán was already in full flight—reportedly suffering injuries to his leg and face while scampering down a hillside on an all-terrain vehicle in the company of a woman and children. Édgar Coronel Aispuro was arrested, but El Chapo had once again avoided capture. The attempt to track the pet monkey was reported in the reputable weekly *Ríodoce* but never confirmed by CISEN. However, agents have released reports that it had been monitoring the movements of several women and family members with the hope of locating El Chapo.

El Chapo's Achilles Heel

El Chapo is a serial womanizer—*un mujeriego*—and Mexican intelligence reports (CISEN) documented numerous visits from prostitutes and even released scurrilous reports implying a predilection for pubescent girls that was also made public after the Brooklyn, New York, trial. Diego Enrique Osorno visited CISEN and noted the emphasis on El Chapo's *mujerieguismo* (skirt chasing) and the widespread belief that it represented his Achilles heel and the key to his recapture. The historical record validates CISEN's emphasis: his rearrest in February 2014 followed a near-capture after visiting his former wife Griselda's Culiacán home, and the arrest in Mazatlán occurred while he was accompanied by his fourth wife. But wives were not the only women CISEN was tracking: during 2014 and 2015, two other women were closely linked to El Chapo, and their movements played a major part in tracking him down—a Sinaloa State congress member, Lucero Guadalupe Sánchez López, and the Mexican actress Kate del Castillo.

Prison Escape, and the Rearrest

The spectacular prison escape in July 2015 was facilitated by an intermediary named Lucero Sánchez López; Guzmán was tracked to the region of his penultimate whereabouts in the Golden Triangle, specifically Cosalá, by monitoring her activity (Nájar 2016; Osorno 2016).

Sánchez López was apparently a key player in Guzmán's escape from Altiplano prison through her role as a messenger and intermediary.[49] She acted as the courier in advance of the escape and allegedly coordinated Guzmán's instructions with the large team of tunnel builders, pilots, hideout logistics coordinators, and personal security forces. Later, Sánchez López allegedly was the principal coordinator for frequent moves between hideouts and safe houses while he roamed about in the Golden Triangle. To suggest that Sánchez López was another sexual conquest is speculative, but it is undeniably evident that she played a central role as an intermediary in his escape. And she would eventually be called as a prosecution witness in the Brooklyn trial after she had to bargain for U.S. asylum in return for testifying against El Chapo. Later, she attempted to cash in her offer to testify when she made a failed claim for asylum in the United States.

Sánchez López first surfaced as an unidentified female visitor to Altiplano a few weeks before the spectacular escape: a mysterious photo of an unknown female visitor was quickly identified by *Ríodoce* as the Sinaloa State deputy representing Cosalá, Sinaloa, as a proportionally designated representative; in the aftermath, she was designated by the nickname *la narcodiputada*. Initially, Sánchez López denied visiting the prison, but she finally claimed she was meeting with Guzmán in a legislative capacity allegedly as a representative of the Sinaloa State Partido Action National. PAN and other parties involved in a broad statewide coalition that backed the governorship for Mario López Valdéz denied knowledge and distanced themselves from her, and each party claimed the other coalition partner had placed her name on the list guaranteeing a seat based on percentage of votes cast. In Mexican legislative assemblies, there are two *levels* of representatives assigned seats: 60 percent are elected directly, and the remaining deputies are appointed from lists provided directly by officially recognized parties or formal coalitions of parties. Sánchez López was the deputy representing Cosalá as a plurinominal appointee; her name was selected from the pool of potential candidates established jointly by a broad coalition of state political parties.

Over time, it became clear that she was affiliated with a Sinaloa regional party called Partido Sinaloense (Sinaloan Party), which had been established as the personal power base for Héctor Melesio Cuén Ojeda, a Badiguarato native and former rector of the Autonomous University of Sinaloa. Cuén remains a controversial figure in Sinaloa due to credible allegations that he routinely diverted university funds for personal and political purposes. There are also long-standing rumors that he has close ties with important Sinaloa narco traffickers in the heart of the Golden Triangle and Badiguarato municipality. The fact that Sánchez López was an *appointed* deputy named by a coalition of parties simply reaffirms the deep narco-traffic entanglement with state, municipal, and even university politics in Sinaloa—and reveals the depth and extent of the links within the covert netherworld of narco trafficking (Milenio 2016).

Kate del Castillo, the Mexican telenovela star, was the second woman identified by CISEN as an important key to El Chapo's eventual recapture. She is an actress who starred in *La Reina del Sur*—the narco telenovela and Netflix series based on a best-selling novel of Arturo Perez-Reverte (2002). Guzmán, either mesmerized by her or hoping to establish a working relationship to produce his biography, made contact through his lawyers and exchanged messages with her that were sprinkled with sexual innuendo and blatant seductive endearments: "I will take care of you more than I do my own eyes," he wrote (qtd. in Jiménez Jaramillo 2016). Purportedly, the reason for making direct contact was to propose that she produce a movie about his life and the legend of Shorty, and it resulted in the secret meeting that eventually took place at an Autonomous University of Sinaloa biological reserve located just outside Cosalá—conveniently located on Deputy Sánchez López's home turf and on property owned by the university directed by ex-rector Cuén Ojeda, who had appointed her to that deputy position. Kate del Castillo and Sean Penn were invited to a clandestine meeting to discuss the proposition, although Guzmán was uncertain about any need to include Penn since he did not recognize the actor or know his work. Soon after that encounter with two actors on October 6, 2015, Guzmán sat down for the video interview to answer questions from a list hastily prepared by Penn. The resultant seventeen-minute interview quickly went viral, and the legend of Shorty had added another spectacular chapter.

Recapture

On January 12, 2016, El Chapo Guzmán was finally captured after six months of freedom and an extensive manhunt that involved hundreds of intelligence agents and as many as a thousand marines.[50] For some unknown and inexplicable reason, he left the relative safety of the Golden Triangle—specifically the region near Cosalá—to move three hundred kilometers north to Los Mochis, Sinaloa, just south of Sonora State. Even more inexplicably, this city was contested turf and largely controlled by his longtime bitter rivals—the Beltrán Leyva faction. He moved into a safe house that had recently been fortified in 2015 on his orders (Carroll 2016b). There are conflicting reports about how that specific house and his actual presence was identified, and even more questions about how Mexican marines came to launch an attack on it. In fact, evidence suggests that neither CISEN nor the marines were even aware that he was in Los Mochis until they found themselves embroiled in a skirmish after arriving by chance at that specific house.

Whatever the specific details of the final capture, the official narrative makes it clear that CISEN had been closely monitoring El Chapo's movements since the meeting with del Castillo and Penn in the southern part of Sinaloa near Cosalá. The official version asserts that SEMAR command knew of his movements but had decided to wait for the right time to act with minimum loss of life and lower risks of harm to innocent bystanders. Video evidence of marine activity around Cosalá and historical evidence undermine that supposed justification for restraint, since many Internet videos of the operation in the Golden Triangle show the marines had actually carried out a scorched earth strategy; furthermore, the historical record indicates that the Mexican military has rarely shown any restraint in carrying out its operations—the Tlatlaya massacre being only one example among many (Ferri Tórtola 2014). In fact, Mexican marines have a brutal reputation for ignoring human rights, and the Inter-American Commission on Human Rights specifically noted the excessive use of violence whenever they were involved in operations: data directly from SEMAR indicates that its elite marine forces kill roughly thirty combatants for each one they injure in their operations (Ahmed and Schmitt 2016; Ahmed and Villegas 2016; Open Society Foundations 2016). The claim that the marines were acting with restraint is also undermined by the reports that when they finally did move in to attack the house in Los Mochis (three hundred miles further north of Cosalá), they were not even aware that El Chapo was an occupant. One unconfirmed report indicates that marines had actually been alerted to strange happenings in the house by neighbors who grew suspicious when many strange men had suddenly appeared. In fact, that report specifically indicates that the most important clue that triggered the attack was the delivery of an extraordinarily large number of pizzas.

In any event, a relatively small team of marines (approximately twelve) stormed the house just before dawn and found themselves in the middle of a ferocious firefight with El Chapo's guards. When the ground level of the house had finally been secured, the marines shot their way to the second level and blasted through a security door, only to enter an empty room. A search, reportedly lasting almost two hours, eventually revealed an ingeniously engineered escape door hidden behind a mirror that led to a tunnel that fed directly into a Los Mochis drain system. The drain system was itself recently constructed and newly operational. At that point, Mexican marines issued a general alert and ordered that drain covers be removed in all the streets across a broad swath of the city.

An emergency-band call from *municipal* police alerted marines to an incident involving an unknown man who had been arrested by municipal police and was under custody at the nearby Hotel Doux—which coincidently was known as a tryst for adulterous affairs. Marines rushed to the hotel to find El Chapo meekly sitting on a bed in one of the rooms furthest away from the front and in a quiet area at the rear of the hotel. By the time they arrived, pictures of Guzmán in soiled clothes in the back of a police car and in the motel room had already been uploaded to the Internet and on their way to going viral.

Guzmán and his personal bodyguard Orso Iván "El Ivan" Gastélum Cruz had entered the storm sewer system when shooting began on the lower level of the safe house that the marines had attacked; he and El Chapo were working their way to freedom when the water level in those drains rose dramatically during a light rainfall and forced them to exit to avoid drowning. They used their only weapon, an AR-15, to prop open a drain cover and scampered onto a residential street from the manhole. At that point, they commandeered the older car of a man delivering morning newspapers, and it was he who called municipal police to report his stolen vehicle. Municipal police almost immediately intercepted Guzmán and Gastélum and placed them in the back of a squad car before receiving radio orders to take them to the Doux Motel. The Munis (municipal police) were holding the two men there when the marines arrived and demanded they hand them over.

Guzmán was immediately flown back to the same prison from which he had escaped and placed under a twenty-four-hour daily surveillance by guards accompanied by a German shepherd. He was moved to different cells on a rotating basis and allocated minimal privileges—including restricted access to lawyers or family.

El Chapo had regularly managed to avoid capture, escape close calls with death, and scurry away unscathed—even when the odds were improbable. He had twice escaped maximum-security prisons under improbable circumstances. He walked away unscathed from bloody shoot-outs where he had been specifically targeted for killing. His lifelong success in eluding capture and avoiding death can be attributed more to his preparation and foresight rather than good fortune: El Chapo always had safety outlets and a plan B at the ready, and his many hideouts (*las guaridas*) and safe houses (*los refugios*) were always innovative architectural masterpieces that required a small fortune to design and construct. Each incorporated defensive perimeters, accommodation for his ever-present armed guards, and even storage for a large fleet of fortified vehicles. Each hideout had an interior sanctuary that offered additional safety behind reinforced doors that also guaranteed precious time to flee through ingenious hidden exits feeding directly into tunnels and secret passages.

In spite of all those things being engineered and in place in Los Mochis, he was trapped—discovered because of a pizza delivery and being prematurely forced into an open space when the new storm sewers of Los Mochis flooded because they were incapable of diverting a light morning rainfall. He was trapped neither by intelligence nor military force but simply by chance. The accidental nature of his capture in a world where he was the most wanted man in the Americas would give anyone pause to reflect and think—even El Chapo himself.

Because of his historic importance, Guzmán's recapture will be accompanied by changes that may be much more consequential than seen following the capture of other capos. Whether he deserved it or not, El Chapo was the pre-eminent generational capo and the global emblematic personification of Mexican drug trafficking. The impact of his arrest and eventual sentencing in an American maximum-security prison will be far-reaching, but not necessarily in obvious or predictable ways.

Counterintuitively, the permanent collapse of the Sinaloa Cartel will *not* be one of the outcomes. But there will be, at least, four different consequences of his arrest: a restructuring within the Sinaloa hierarchy (which had already been underway), shifting alliances involving other groups and a period of intense disruptive violence, a shift in how Mexico addresses and sells the War on Drugs, and a move away from explanations rooted in charismatic leadership and toward those explanations that are more organizationally and institutionally based.

The fabled narrative of El Chapo had apparently come to an end, but the wars between, within, and against cartels continue. Needless to say, the U.S. War on Drugs will continue even though the DEA has worked hard to convince the world that it has just prosecuted and imprisoned the most important drug lord ever captured in the Americas.

CHAPTER 7

Fragmentation and Stabilization

cartel:

1 An association of manufacturers or suppliers with the purpose of maintaining prices at a high level and restricting competition.

"the Colombian drug cartels".

1.1 historical A coalition or cooperative arrangement between political parties intended to promote a mutual interest.

—Oxford Dictionary (online)

cartel:

1. m. Lámina en que hay inscripciones o figuras y que se exhibe con fines informativos o publicitarios.

2. m. Lámina con grandes caracteres que sirve en las escuelas para enseñar a leer.

cártel (al. Kartell):

1. m. Organización ilícita vinculada al tráfico de drogas o de armas.

2. m. Econ. Convenio entre varias empresas similares para evitar la mutua competencia y regular la producción, venta y precios en deter-minado campo industrial.

—Diccionario de la lengua española (online)

Cartel is now the English-language term that refers to all drug-trafficking and criminal organizations in Mexico, Colombia, and Latin America. It is an umbrella designation that is indiscriminately used to describe any criminal group irrespective of the vast differences in organization, authority struc-tures, bonds of commitment, criminal specialization, or the geographic reach among them. Cartel has become the cultural code word for all narco traf-ficking, even though such a broad use treats heterogeneous organizations as equivalent and leads to confusing narratives about crime and drug trafficking in the absence of critical reflection.

Unlike Spanish, English only occassionally pays attention to diacritical marks, and this has created some ambiguity about how the term *cartel* (without an accented *a*) is used as a universal English-language descriptor for organized crime in Latin America. The Spanish-language word *cartel*, without the accented *a*, refers to posters and charts; it is widely assumed that the first reference to drug cartels came when DEA agents in Colombia created broad organizational charts that linked key individuals involved in the production and distribution of cocaine. Those organigraphic descriptions of gang members gradually became the generalized shorthand term for drug organizations. The accented word *cártel* appeared in common Spanish-language usage later and is now commonly used to refer to criminal organizations as well as mutual industrial agreements.

Dictionary Definitions and Myth Reification

Standard English-language dictionaries were late to add criminal activity and drug trafficking as addendums or subsidiary definitions to an older traditional understanding of cartel—economic price fixing by conglomerates. Even when this happened, the English definition (as in the *Oxford Dictionary*) made only passing reference to crime organizations by inserting a short illustrative example of how the word has been used. In Mexico—now the major hub of criminal drug trafficking in the Americas—the *Diccionario del español usual en México* (L. Lara 1996) did not have an entry defining an accented *cártel*, and the unaccented entry *cartel* originally had no reference to criminal gangs or drugs. Several canonical sources that have described Mexican narco trafficking never used the term *cártel* as a descriptor. Luis Astorga's influential overview *El siglo de las drogas* (1996, 2005) made no reference to *cartel* with or without the accented *á*, and neither did the earliest popular English-language descriptions of narco trafficking in Mexico, such as Terrence Poppa's seminal work *Drug Lord: The Life and Death of a Mexican Kingpin* (1990, 1998) or Elaine Shannon's comprehensive *Desperados: Latin Drug Lords, U.S. Lawmen, and the War America Can't Win* (1988).

There is confusion and contradiction whenever the term *cartel* is broadly and indiscriminately used as the common and universal label for Mexican crime organizations. The standard English dictionary emphasis on economic price-fixing and mutual agreements between factions does not describe the

Mexican experience and has never been used in any description of a Mexican criminal organization. The popular culture understanding of a cartel has routinely incorporated inaccurate, stereotypical tropes about narco trafficking and organized crime in Mexico, and those perceptions have become fixed in the public mind as factual reality—especially in representations of criminal organizations now widely available through media streaming services like Netflix, Amazon Prime, and others. As this is being written, production has been completed for a third season of the popular series *Narcos: Mexico* on Netflix; the first two seasons were often accurate in their portrayal of narco history but were also riddled with many common and misleading representations about drug lords and cartels.

Price-Fixing

It is highly improbable that criminal groups identified as cartels have ever been dedicated to *price-fixing*, nor have they engaged in manipulations intended to drive up the price for consumers. Drug capos have no long-term or valid market incentive to cut back production or withhold distribution in order to drive up profit margin. In that sense, there is no compelling evidence that the street price of drugs has ever been fixed by crime bosses, and there is no documented evidence pointing to a collusion that limits production or slows down the distribution to deliberately create a shortage of supply. In fact, drug organizations are much more likely to flood markets than undertake any action that withholds product from consumers. The more drugs that are pumped out, the more income returns to the organization. And the more drugs shipped, the lesser the impact when authorities manage to intercept some of them. The more experienced crime bosses had also learned that destruction of crops or interdiction measures led to violence and loss in the absence of any backup product to replace that which was lost. In fact, street price *does* escalate when a product is scarce, but those shortfalls have never been *deliberately* instigated by organized crime bosses—they are the result of crackdowns and increased interdiction by authorities. Drug-trafficking organizations have no need to engage in conspiratorial acts to manipulate supply chains when there is an endless supply of users and an insatiable demand for their product. The drug trade is driven by a consumer market that always works to the drug lord's advantage in times of both surplus and shortage.

In short, suggesting that drug organizations operate like a *trust* to fix prices makes little sense in the case of Mexican trafficking organizations — and to hold such a perception incorrectly implies that criminal drug organizations operate in exactly the same ways as large-scale capital enterprises that collude to drive up prices and create a demand. Leave that type of action to oil companies and oil-dependent states; there is no evidence that it is a cartel strategy.

Associations or Trusts

The Spanish-language unaccented term *cartel* emphasizes the *cartelera* — an organigram of key figures linked hierarchally in organizations — without making any specific assumption about the nature of linkages connecting component parts or individuals. Drawing connecting lines between individuals on such organizational charts does not make assumptions or describe the nature of their relationships; on the other hand, the nature of those organizational links is specifically referenced in the secondary meaning of the accented term *cártel* with the reference to a *convenio* — an agreement or arrangement — among individuals. In the case of Mexico, the *nature* of those connections is critically important to understand since they led to the permanence and staying power of organizations and describe the important bonds that link its members. For instance, the Sinaloa Cartel is an organization conjoining specific members who were tightly bound together by tradition, historical codes of understanding, and directly by family ties and compadrazco.

Gangs and criminal groups cannot be easily classified and reduced to terms that conceptualize the gang as merely the cumulative acts of individual criminals acting independently, but instead any full understanding requires an explicit examination of the *contractual* terms and bonds that have interconnected the participants (Lyman and Potter 2007). Furthermore, the study of organized crime demands an explanation that accounts for the repetitive nature of criminal activity — that is, it must also consider the *institutionalization* of behavior that produces the continuity that outlasts one generation of criminals. Explaining organized crime demands much more than a focus on the individual causation of an *actor*; it demands an explanation for how different individuals have come together to engage in criminal acts in patterned and repetitive ways — and do so across generations.[1] The concept of cartel does not make any reference to anything that helps us understand the *permanence* and *continuity* of criminal organization.

Individual Agency

Academic criminology and psychology have proposed many distinct and competing theories of criminal causation; both disciplines have been prolific and often contradictory in proposing explanations for social connections that become institutionalized and emerge as organized and routinized patterns of behavior. But in their detailed consideration of gangs, academic theories have also vary widely and disagree on the fundamental reason that gangs have an attraction and pull for individuals: some theories emphasize the role of a power that *imposes* belonging; others emphasize the *persuasive* power of codes, values, or norms in socializing members and making them want to belong; other theories are much more basic and argue that shared acts are simply *utilitarian* and the result of instrumental rationality; and yet others propose that behavior can become *routinized* over time out of transient reciprocities and social exchanges; cultural theorists assume that socialization and membership is propagated by *transgenerational traditions* in specific geographic regions, social groups, ethnic or racial groups, or within families; and some explanations simply state that gang behavior is little more than patterned behavior that emerged over time or was reduced to a tribal pull. Such complicated and important considerations rarely appear in the popular narrative of cartels and gangs, and the casual observer has become accustomed to the notion that anyone who joins a gang is evil or in some cases is simply *conflicted* because they are caught between two competing worlds. But what *are* the bonds that connect criminals, and how do some of those bonds become permanent fixtures that allow cartels to emerge?

The Spanish meaning of *cartel* assumes that numerous individuals are connected and work together, but it makes no specific assumption about how they are connected. In the current common usage and application of cartel to drug organizations, the substantive nature of connections has not been explicitly identified and remains submerged in subtext and formed by culturally derived understandings. Two assumptions are most often made— one is based on the widely held perception that mob membership comes via *initiation*, and another assumes that all gang connections are fundamentally reducible to a *power relationship* within a hierarchical structure. The term *mafia*, and by extension *cartel*, thus incorporates a taken-for-granted assumption that a (gang) member must *earn* entry (often through violence), become a *made man* by taking an oath (usually sealed with blood), has progressed upward through an apprenticeship to occupy a specific role, and can *never leave* or discuss the group under pain of death (*omerta*). Such referents are routinely associated with the term *mafia* and widely popularized through cultural diffusion and media reinforcement. The emergence and widespread popularity of the term *cartel* is more recent, and any *cultural codes* or *initiations* attached to membership requirements have not yet been widely routinized in the general understanding: in fact, the current understanding of cartel membership is almost singularly influenced by moral campaigns—largely driven by U.S. views on drugs—that reduce the code defining membership to a oversimplifications. In general, cartel connections and the rules defining membership are essentially reduced to the assumed convergence of two factors: the leadership of ruthless kingpins and their unquestionable power of plata o plomo—the bribe or the bullet. Limiting cartel membership to either of those two motivational reasons—silver or lead—completely overlooks the historical reality of how criminal organizations emerged in Mexico and ignores the actual nature of bonds that hold members together in a loyalty that is unbreakable to the death. By all accounts, there are hundreds of thousands of people in Mexico who directly depend on cartels and the income they generate, and many more (millions?) who depend on the cartel to provide basic needs of community and life—paved roads, lighting, schools, and even support for the churches in which they worship.

In the case of Latin American cartels, those criminal links and cooperation have most frequently been explained by a reference to that oversimplified and bifurcated choice between plata o plomo (silver or lead): the common narrative built upon the assumption that anyone who works with gangs, or even chooses to look the other way, does so because they have been bribed or have acted defensively out of fear for their personal or family safety. That restricted and narrow view of motivation has recently been criticized for downplaying many other reasonable motivating forces that can explain cooperation with or support for narco traffickers: Gustavo Duncan (2014) argues that the narrower view based on bribes or bullets cannot possibly explain why businesses, governments, and many state agents are actively involved in narco trafficking. Nor can it explain why so many Mexicans place more trust in the cartels than they do in local police or their own government. Nor can it explain the routine traditions of corruption that have been institutionalized in the Year of Hidalgo or la hora de chapulines, described in chapter 3.

In Mexico, the social contract binding participants to a gang is not reduceable to an assumption that membership in a subterranean society narrative depends only on a bribery versus violence glue. There is little evidence that initiation rituals have played any major role in Mexican drug organizations, even though there are examples of ritual recruitment into some specific crime groups such as Los Zetas. A recent novela by Ricardo Raphael (2019) describes a *ritualized initiation* ceremony that was orchestrated by Osiel Cárdenas Guillén, his brother Tony Tormenta, Miguel Treviño, and Jorge Eduardo Costilla; those jefes had gathered the original twenty Los Zetas recruits together to affirm an oath that bound each one of them to a brotherhood. Those types of ceremonial initiations have not been described for other large cartels, but they are known to exist in lower-order gangs such as the Mara Salvatrucha, who are reported to orchestrate brutal initiation ceremonies that include beatings and killings, and then reward the initiates with a tear-drop tattoo (Logan 2009). Another notable criminal group, Los Caballeros Templarios, was committed to a specific set of beliefs and a commitment to an evangelical document and moral code based on aphorisms disseminated by its jefe Nazario Moreno González (Lomnitz 2016).

Other larger groups may be internally linked—at least at some informal level—by family or compadrazgo, but on the whole, the idea that gangs or cartels have a *formal social contract* bound by a set of rules or a charter or plata o plomo does not apply universally to Mexican drug groups. In fact, such codes are limited to the few mentioned above. It would also be misleading to believe that any glue binding cartel members to cartels can be reduced to a mutual agreement, such as that described in the English-language dictionary definition of cartel.

Subtext and Contradictions: A Linguistic Heisenberg Effect

There is a widespread acceptance of the term *cartel* and a shared understanding of what a cartel represents, but the concept is a confusing starting point for any formal study of narco trafficking or criminal organization in Mexico.

The term represents a restrictive and narrow vision of drug trafficking and organized crime, and the definitional dimensions it encompasses have promoted a broad and misleading perception of what Mexican drug-trafficking organizations actually do. Worse, it has narrowly restricted the scope of questions that have been asked due to the impact of linguistic blinders: once the dimensions and facets of a conceptual term have become reified in the public domain, the likelihood of later establishing more useful terms of reference for further examination are narrowed (see Alter 2013).

Contradictions are inherent in most popularized and common narratives of cartel—that is, there are many differences in what is intended by using the term or what is implied when it is used—especially when the term *cartel* is so widely used as the categorical descriptor for all organized crime in Latin America. For example, one narrative assumes that a cartel is always headed by a sophisticated criminal boss directing a powerful underworld: in that view, the cartel is treated as a parallel power to the state and is masterminded by a kingpin. A contrasting narrative—more common where organized crime groups are geographically based—downplays the premise that it is a competing power and instead acknowledges that it is rooted in cooperative and mutual links between criminals and the state.

That second conceptualization as a network linking criminals and the state in a criminal enterprise is captured perfectly by the covert netherworld conceptualization proposed by McCoy (see chapter 1). The total underworld of Mexican crime and drug-trafficking networks—the social milieu, the covert operations, and the illicit commerce—has never been comprehensively described in one English-language book, publication, or for that matter any academic studies of cartels in Latin America. In contrast to that academic treatment of cartels, the subculture and underworld of crime has been the *primary* focus of fictional accounts and popular entertainment that have increasingly used narcos, cartels, and Mexican criminal organizations as the malevolent and unpredictable violent protagonist. The popularity of *Breaking Bad* and *Better Call Saul*, or streaming series such as Netflix's *Narcos* and *Narcos: Mexico*, or best-selling novels such as Don Winslow's *The Border* has amplified the public awareness of Mexico's complex and largely invisible world of clandestine actors operating beyond the bounds of civil society. Nevertheless, those cultural representations are *fictionalized* and prone to borrow much more from fiction than they do from reality and fact. Narco Mexico and cartels have been heavily mythologized over time, and the public understanding of what they actually are and what they do has been largely distorted in the telling.

Cartel and Applications to Drug Trafficking

The term *cartel* is attributable to the DEA. Colombian cocaine-trafficking networks, such as Pablo Escobar Gaviria's Medellín crime syndicate, were the first to be labeled as cartels around 1980. Within a short decade, *cartel* had then entered into the lexicon and emerged as the common referent label for all criminal drug organization based in Latin America. Other terms for organized criminal networks—such as drug-trafficking organizations, trans-national crime organizations, criminal drug organizations, violent criminal drug organizations, and even the generic concept "mafia"—were used only within specialized contexts (for example, academic journals and legal indict-ments) and have rarely been applied to Latin American criminal organiza-tions that draw public attention.

The general consensus is that the etymological origins of *cartel* (without the Spanish version's accented *á*) lie in Colombia. From there its usage spread to South Florida and Miami during the 1980s crack-cocaine epidemic and during an escalation of the Nixon–Reagan War on Drugs. The most plau-sible explanation for its origin is that it was an anglicized appropriation of *carteleras*—the Spanish term for the bulletin boards where criminal inter-relationships were routinely arranged as posters and organigrams during police investigations.

A Generalized Model of the Division of Labor

A generalized and conjectural version of a cartel organizational structure is presented in figure 9. This organigram represents an idealized model of a Mexican criminal drug organization and many of its component parts.[2] Sociologists would describe this diagram as an *ideal* representation of a social organization since it is not intended to describe any particular cartel, and in fact it may not be applicable to every crime organization that has been called a cartel: too many crime groups are called cartels in spite of not having an organizational structure that comes close to approximating that

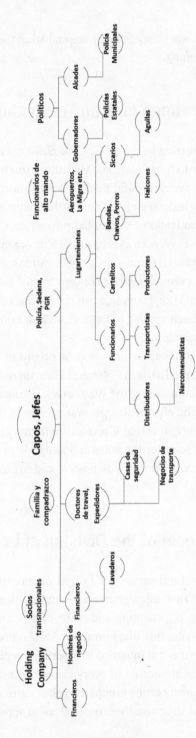

FIGURE 9 La cartelera: An idealized cartel organigram. It was initially inspired by a graphical report titled "Pelean cartels el control en México," *Reforma*, June 6, 2005, and modified by the author to include other sources.

represented in figure 9. It is presented here to make the point that drug cartels are actually *complex social organizations* with a sophisticated division of labor dependent on systematically interconnected parts such as jefes or capos (the cartel boss), financieros (financial officers), políticos (politicians), funcionarios de alto mando (high-ranking advisors and associates), jefe de seguridad (chief of security), operadores (operators), lugartenientes (subcommanders), lavaderos (money launderers), doctores de travel (expeditors, shippers), sicarios (hit men, killers, assassins), distribudores (distributors, mules), halcones (lookouts), productores (producers); narcomenudistas or puchadores (pushers), various justice agents located in SEDENA (military), policía (includes PGR, CISEN), estatales (state police), munis (municipal police), and other operatives managing financial and transnational connections and affiliations that are necessary for the success of the organization.

In popular discourse and narratives, the term *cartel* has been routinely applied to all criminal organizations in Mexico whether or not those groups have an institutional structure that approximates this idealized model. Too often, the classification *cartel* is incorrectly used to describe smaller gangs that are carrying out specific *sub-tasks* and performing *auxiliary roles* within a larger organization. Historically, a few drug-trafficking organizations in Mexico have developed a significant number of the linkages suggested by this ideal model of a drug organization, including the Guadalajara Cartel; the Juaréz Cartel of Amado Carrillo Fuentes; the Sinaloa Cartel of El Mayo, El Chapo, and El Azul; and perhaps early manifestations of the Gulf Cartel. And in mid-2021, it is arguably true that *only* the Sinaloa Cartel and the Cártel de Jalisco Nueva Generación should be conceptualized as comprehensive criminal organizations with a complex division of labor.

The diagram in figure 9 is nevertheless an *incomplete representation* of Mexican drug-trafficking organizations. In fact, the division of labor and organizational structure is much more complex than suggested by this organigram. To provide but one example, the Arellano Félix drug organization's lugarteniente responsible for security was Teodoro "El Teo" García Simental, and he supervised a complex team of hit men and gangs while infamously employing others with specialized skills such as making bodies disappear. One man he employed was the notorious soup maker known as "El Pozolero"—Santiago Meza López—who was disturbingly proficient in dissolving corpses of victims in acid (Tijuano 2013). Another example is the absence of a specific term in figure 9 for the sophisticated team of technicians and engineering units working on behalf of the Sinaloa Cartel: El Chapo Guzmán Loera and the Sinaloa Cartel routinely contracted European engineers to build tunnels, including the infamous 1.5-kilometer escape tunnel in July 2015, and they also employed a sophisticated team of IT software engineers and communications experts (see Feuer 2020).

Most English-language narratives do not view drug organizations within the organizational framework represented by figure 9.[3] Limited and specific aspects of cartel structure and organization have been emphasized and mythologized to the point where they are all that is noticed. Far too much attention is directed at drug lords and kingpins or to the brutal killers and hit men leaving bloodshed in their wake (e.g., Bowden and Molloy's [2011] description of sicarios; see also Bowden 1998, 2009). On the other hand, there are several wonderful untranslated Spanish-language books that have focused on the specific tasks and jobs required within the broad drug-trafficking enterprise: in particular, the award-winning Culiacán journalist Javier Valdez Cárdenas, who was gunned down outside his *Ríodoce* office, published several books and weekly columns that are marvelous *biographical profiles* of individuals such as the halcones and sicarios mentioned in figure 9 (2009, 2011, 2012, 2015); and Ricardo Ravelo has published several short books looking at the various ways that divisions within police departments were routinely and systematically corrupted to work on behalf of cartels (2006, 2007a, 2007b, 2013). Although there have been many who have pointed out how important it is to follow the money and focus on money laundering, there are only a few scholars or journalists who have actually done so: Edgardo Buscaglia (2010) has consistently focused on that theme of money laundering and corruption; and the late dean of Mexican journalism Julio Scherer García (2008) also wrote specifically about the extent and pervasive reach of money laundering through his exclusive interviews with drug personalities like Sandra Ávila Beltrán.

Roberto Saviano is an Italian journalist who has written widely about the mafias of the world and is much admired in Mexico; his book *Zero, Zero, Zero* (2015) focuses on the all-encompassing structure and organization of the Calabrian branch known as the 'Ndrangheta. Although prone to poetic description, he effectively relies on an extended metaphor of a large and ancient tree to present an overview of how Italy's powerful southern Italian mafia has reached into all aspects of life and how it has endured over time. Saviano also points out the strategic importance of the *expeditors and shippers* that he referred to with the term *doctors of travel* (doctores de travel in figure 9): those mafia figures are the key operatives who arrange all movcements of drugs and money and who play a crucial and absolutely essential role. Commodities would not move from point to point, nor arrive at market, unless someone with exceptional managerial and organizational skills was overseeing the delivery and arranging all steps of the process. In the global context of transnational drug shipment, a comprehensive drug-trafficking organization requires an expert logistics manager and a team of specialized experts to move products into Mexico, within Mexico, and across international boundaries close and distant.

Some of the most unique, insightful, and even shocking revelations about the Sinaloa Cartel in *El traidor: El diario secreto del hijo del Mayo* (Hernández 2020) are those long sections where Vicente Zambada describes how his father, El Mayo, moved drugs through Mexico. Much of the time, Ismael Zambada García operated as a broker who sought out investors to purchase lots or shares in cocaine futures. At other times, he made the purchases directly through his Andean contacts. But in all cases, he relied on trusted middlemen to move cocaine or other commodities on behalf of his investors or for himself. Dozens of pages of Vicente's diary are dedicated to describing the many sophisticated and creative ways El Mayo used to move drugs into Mexico, transport them through Mexico, and transfer those drugs on to others who moved them into the United States. The same expeditor, or doctor of travel, was often used to ship back money earned from those drugs and the arms purchased by others in the organization.

"El Macho" Prieto Inzunza was one of the important middlemen who worked directly with El Mayo to expedite the shipment of drugs through Mexico. Gonzalo Inzunza Inzunza was a high-level lugarteniente in the Sinaloa organization and responsible for two different tasks. On the one hand, he headed a gang of sicarios based in Culiacán that could be deployed as bodyguards or shifted to other regions to defend plazas when necessary. Simultaneously, he supervised an efficient organizational network that moved drugs, money, and arms on behalf of the Sinaloa Cartel. Inzunza oversaw the transportation of drugs to safe houses within Mexico as well as delivering product directly into the United States. He also moved cartel money and arms to many parts of Mexico where his operatives routinely bribed local officials and sometimes relied on weapons to safeguard the shipments from enemies or from seizure by federal forces.

Vicente Zambada told Anabel Hernández (2020) in great detail about one sophisticated operation that El Macho Prieto had arranged on behalf of his father. A shipment of cocaine had arrived from the Andes hidden in Pemex *buques* (ocean tankers), and El Mayo contracted with Inzunza to off-load it and then arrange to ship it across the country. The younger Zambada knew a great deal about the process because he personally had extensive dealings with many of the people working for el Macho Prieto, and more importantly because he also acted as the direct intermediary between his father and Inzunza when meetings were necessary to arrange the details of complicated operations.

Since about 2004, Inzunza had been using ingeniously modified tanker trucks for smuggling operations. On the outside, his fleet of a half-dozen trucks looked exactly like official Pemex oil tankers. But his *pipas* had additional compartments constructed inside the main tank and those were large enough to hold cocaine, money, amphetamines, and even arms. All operations managed by Inzunza relied on a skilled team working in sophisticated coordination, and Vincentillo described one of those operations to Hernández:

> The tanker trucks were brought to secret warehouses arranged by Gonzalo and his people. Gonzalo had a special team of workers responsible for opening and sealing those secret compartments. Gonzalo used to transport that special team from place to place in airplanes because they were the only ones who knew how to open them. The compartments needed to be opened with a blowtorch and then re-soldered shut. Consequently, the process to open and close the compartments was a dangerous business—especially since there was also gasoline in the cargo hold. (2020, 123)

But El Macho Prieto's operation was not limited to modifying those tankers and simply burying contraband in secret compartments for movement across Mexican highways—it was supported by a sophisticated cover operation and backup that was made possible because of endemic corruption in Pemex and other government agencies responsible for tracking shipping and monitoring highways. Inzunza's *pipas* actually shipped gasoline using the space around the secret compartment, and the driver for every shipment of drugs had official paperwork supplied by Pemex through bribery. And to guarantee that nothing went wrong during the transport, each tanker was followed by one or two cars of cartel operatives responsible for watching for Mexican government officials or military patrols along the route. One of the men in the car acted as a *banker* and paymaster with the responsibility for delivering bribes to government officials, police, and army personnel in each state or zone.

Vicentillo Zambada told Hernández that senior-level Pemex officials received a monthly retainer from Inzunza, and they were rewarded with a bonus for every vehicle that made it to its destination.

> Those government officials were paid monthly bribes and also a bonus payment for each trip that a tanker made through their zone or state. Those monthly payments and bribes always came to about 50,000 to 150,000 dollars. Once the tanker arrived at the final destination, the same team that sealed the compartment was transported there to open it up. The cargo removed was then hidden in warehouses or secure houses maintained by Gonzalo until it was time to move it to the next location. (2020, 124)

Vicentillo's diary provides several other examples of how drugs, arms, and money moved through Mexico. It has long been recognized that the Sinaloa Cartel has been especially successful at moving cargo, money, and arms, but not as much is known about how underworld experts arrange the logistics and bribe officials at each stage of the operation. The Sinaloa Cartel's sophistication and ingenuity is demonstrated in the example detailed here, and many times in the past, their shipping arrangements have been equally inventive and creative—building fiberglass submarines that are virtually undetectable, engineering sophisticated tunnels, shipping drugs in canned foods, and so on. But in spite of what Saviano wrote about the fundamental importance of expeditors who make those arrangements, the doctors of travel remain virtually unstudied and unknown to the outside world. It is also worth noting that those who are skilled in these tasks are apparently in touch with each other at a global level: Saviano reports that at least one of the cartels in Mexico (unnamed by him) had consulted with an Italian senior consigliore to improve and tighten up its organizational structure in order to improve its business model (Saviano 2014, 2015).[4]

The Sinaloa Cartel

The Sinaloa Cartel has an organic structure and a horizontal leadership; it depends on trusted lieutenants and subdirectors to execute specific operations that are necessary to its success. There is a hierarchy and a division of

labor, but not in any sense suggesting that the cartel has supervised employ-
ees on the payroll at each stage of the drug business. Unlike other drug-
trafficking organizations in Mexico, the Sinaloa group has nurtured direct
and indirect connections to every stage of the drug market from importation, to production, to delivery and cycling back funds for reinvestment
and security measures. In fact, most of those connections developed over
a long period of time through a complex combination of tradition, family
and intermarriage, compadrazgo, mutual enrichment, and of course via the
occasional use of the silver or lead—plata o plomo—strategy. Over decades,
the Sinaloa Cartel has become interlinked and deeply connected to Mexico's
economic elite, power brokers in the political structure, and to agents in
the criminal justice system; it is a prime example of a stable and successful
covert netherworld.

Earlier, figure 3 suggested that there are at least nine idealized organizational stages that are key divisional components of a large-scale drug enterprise. The Sinaloa Cartel has developed powerful organizational arrangements for each of those component processes of the drug trade but does not
have a hierarchical command structure. It operates as an organic model of
production and delivery that evolved by mutual agreement and the shared
understandings of many people across generations. It has been successful
for three principal reasons. First, it is a modern version of a tightly knit
tribal organization based on family and communal ties that reach back to
the 1940s. Second, it has retained control of key bottleneck and transition
points in the movement of drugs and money, and it has been innovative
and ingenious in keeping routes open. For instance, it introduced innovative
strategies such as building fiberglass submarines to import cocaine, and it
has constructed elaborate tunnels to distribute drugs to safe houses and to
return money and weapons to Mexico. Third, the Sinaloa Cartel developed
powerful and deep connections and allies at all levels of Mexico's oligarchy,
government, and politicians as well as to all agencies of the criminal justice
system and judicial officials.

The Sinaloa Cartel is not a monolithic structure but represents a stable and
long-lasting entity because it directly and indirectly manages those "shifting,
contingent, temporal alliances of traffickers whose territories and memberships evolve and change because of conflicts, imprisonment, deaths, changing political circumstances etc., and whose fortunes wax and wane or die out
over time" (Campbell 2009, 19).

The next section turns to describe a broad overview of the institutional-ization of narco traffic in Mexico, with a focus on the overall patterns and key moments during that evolution. Other sections of this book have pre-sented specific details about organizations and cartels as well as biographical portraits of some of the many key players occupying prominent roles within criminal drug organizations.

Narratives and Moral Viewpoints

There is no consensus about how *cartel* came to usurp other terms for orga-nized crime such as *mafia* or *transnational organized crime* but a reasonable conjecture is that it was popularized by the movie *Scarface* (1983) and by popular television series such as *Miami Vice* (1984–89) when they intro-duced DEA jargon and the narrative of drug wars to the general public. How-ever it came about, the reality is that the framework and dominant narrative of narco trafficking has now been dominated by a jargon of war and battles against drug cartels for more than thirty-five years. Because of those origins, the concept of cartel has almost exclusively been associated with organized *drug* trafficking.

Table 1 provides a generalized overview of the narratives that have been used to describe narco trafficking over the past 150 years. The table is also a synopsis of the historical trajectory of Mexican narco trafficking described in previous chapters. Although the *War on Drugs* is identified with Rich-ard Nixon's specific declaration of war in 1971, the narrative of war and the term *cartel* did not become dominant until Ronald Reagan doubled down on Richard Nixon and declared his own war on drugs in 1982 (Drug Policy Alliance n.d.). Furthermore, the idea of fighting wars against drugs cannot be said to have originated with Nixon, since it had roots in older moral crusades that first appeared in the 1930s. The *criminalization* of narcotic drugs and battles against drug dealers, especially in the USA, was first spearheaded by the Federal Bureau of Narcotics (FBN) and manifested in Harry Anslinger's crusades against marijuana and heroin (Hari 2015).

Table 1 indicates that the policies of narcotic control have not always been framed in terms of battles and war, and it further indicates that Mexico and the United States have not always been on the same page about addiction and drug use. But alternate narratives of narcotic use, especially those based

TABLE 1 Moral codes, social problems and government response

Time Frame	Moral Framework	Generalized Social Context	Government Reaction/Response
1880–1916 Roots of Mexican narco traffic	• Moral neutrality about narcotics—especially a broad tolerance of marijuana use • Racism: Chinese opium users targeted and viewed as a eugenic threat	• No legal impediments to producing marijuana, opium, heroin • Few restrictions on amapola production • Production by rural farmers in remote areas and distribution networks controlled by bandits	• Institutional neutrality • Invisible concern during Mexican Revolution • Personal addiction viewed as a health and medical issue rather than a crime • Banditry targeted by state agents—via ley fuga and Rurales • Chinese exclusion and expulsion
1917–1938 Borderland "Sin City" era	• Prohibition in USA makes Mexico a destination for alcohol sales • Prohibition had low priority in Mexico • Moral neutrality about narcotics in Mexico—especially for marijuana • Drug use considered a health matter in Mexico • Chinese remain selectively targeted for opium use	• Contraband smuggling groups grow in power • Bootlegging a profitable business • Personal addiction levels were high • Regional drug empires and caciques emerge • Corruption in police is widespread	• Harrison Act begins to introduce restrictions • Health policies to handle drug addiction are introduced in Mexico • Harry Anslinger and FBN initiate moral crusades against narcotics in USA

Period / Theme	United States	Mexico	Drug control measures
1942–1955 Political alliances and era of caciques	• Cold War—Fascism, Communism dominate global politics • FBI focuses on taking down organized crime groups like the Cosa Nostra • Benign neglect regarding drug use in Mexico • Corruption in Mexico remains widespread	• Bootlegging a profitable enterprise in Juaréz and northeast Mexico • Gomeros and gangsters in huaraches appear in Culiacán and Sinaloa • Heroin availability falls during World War II when Turkey joins axis • Sinaloa isolation and exceptionalism gives rise to proto-drug organizations • Era of traveling briefcase and beginning of DFS oversight of narco trafficking	• Drug control is assigned to the Procuraduría de la Republica (PGR) • Police and army oversight of narcotic production and distribution in Mexico (1947) • Eradication is the main goal
1969–1989 U.S. War on Drugs	• Criminalization of all drug use • Interdiction and elimination at source promoted by the USA	• Second and third generation of narco traffickers take over • Mexico becomes trampoline for Andes cocaine • Arms smuggling intensifies	• DEA advisors in Mexico • Operation Condor • Operation Intercept • DEA expansion in Mexico • Operation Leyenda takes down Guadalajara Cartel
1990–2004 Consolidation and expansion of production and distribution	• Crusade against drugs puts pressure on Mexico to conform	• Cartel power and influence expand • Plaza wars • Synthetic drugs expand • Narco politics and corruption	• Plan Mérida • Eradication • Interdiction • Favored groups • Kingpin strategy • Extradition
2005–2018 Drug war kingpins	• Crusade against drugs • War on Terror takes precedence in USA • Anti-migrant rhetoric	• Decentralized state • Cartels, cartelitos • Violence escalates	• Police unification • National Guard established • SEDENA and MARINA given responsibility for cartel control

on a medical model of treatment, were eventually superseded by a powerful hegemonic vision emanating from the United States—specifically, that war is *necessary* to eradicate the drug problem. The dominant American perspective of criminalization and war was the end result of what American sociologist Howard Becker (1963) would have described as successful *moral entrepreneurship*—in this case the impact of two presidential declarations and the ongoing efforts of the DEA to sell a narrative of dangerous drug cartels. That is, the DEA and the USA managed to impose moral viewpoints about a drug problem upon other nations through a persistent drumbeat of war and arguments that cartels were responsible.

There are a couple of well-known examples where moral perspectives have diffused into the public domain to become the dominant perspective after government officials convinced enough people that there was a problem in need of a solution; those agents did so by creating a demonizing label for the problem, while simultaneously arguing that they had the skill and the strategy to eliminate the problem they identified. In many respects, the DEA has simply been following the model of other American agencies when it promotes and reminds people of the danger of drug cartels. J. Edgar Hoover's lifelong campaign (Burrough 2004) to legitimate and defend his agency (the FBI) and to sculpt a heroic public role for its agents is one illustrative example of how bureaucracies had previously created or even *invented* issues that led to expansion and growth of a government agency.

Hoover's ongoing entrepreneurial efforts to promote his heroic agents popularized terms like *gangster, organized crime,* and *G-men* (Burrough 2004), but more importantly it convinced the public and the government that the FBI was performing an essential, unique, and necessary task on behalf of society. Another well-documented example is the unwavering *moral crusade* that was waged by Harry Anslinger over decades to demonize drug users and criminalize all narcotics and stimulants (Hari 2015). Crusades like Hoover's and Anslinger's not only convinced the public that there was a problem—they *legitimated* the need to hire *experts* capable of identifying and constraining that problem they had personally identified.[5]

The promotion of the idea that there were dangerous *drug cartels* legitimated the DEA's unique role within the Department of Justice. The pursuit of *drug traffickers* was specifically assigned to the DEA when it was created in 1973, and drug control has remained its fundamental mandate even after the newly created Homeland Security repurposed security priorities in 2001.

Under the Homeland Umbrella, the DEA has remained responsible for one primary target—*the organized trafficking of drugs*. It was assigned that specific institutional turf, while other security agencies and departments were allocated different areas of responsibility: the Border Patrol and Immigration and Customs Enforcement (ICE) handled illegal migration; the Bureau of Alcohol, Tobacco, Firearms and Explosives (ATF) monitored the flow of firearms; the CIA focused on terrorists and alien threats; and the FBI investigated organized crime and violations of federal codes.

The complex organizational structure of Homeland Security illustrates how security and justice have become so complicated that they led to the creation of specialized bureaucratic subunits with specifically delineated mandates.[6] But as Max Weber (1958) noted, that specialization and rationalization in bureaucracies also introduces an incentive to carve out a bureaucratic niche and protect agency turf; paradoxically, the specialization intended to create efficiency also introduced the possibility of dysfunction if subunits operate in isolation or are forced to compete with other units for resources. The overall result is commonly referred to as a *silo effect* or *silo mentality* (Lencioni 2006).[7]

In principle these independent agencies are expected to work cooperatively, but in the modern iron cage of bureaucratic reality, each of those subunits is actually competing for recognition and for funding. Each agency must justify its existence every time broad national security mandates shift or when public opinion and community tolerance fluctuate and demand new priorities; in the aftermath of 9/11, *terrorism* became priority number one—and in fact led to the creation of the umbrella agency Homeland Security that then imposed a new mandate on all agencies. Most recently under the Trump xenophobic agenda, immigration and border security concerns emerged as the putative national priority number one, and that resulted in a shift of resources within Homeland Security, the unprecedented expansion of the Border Patrol, and a new rhetoric and focus on a border wall that left other agencies such as the DEA scrambling to justify funding allocations (Miller 2014).[8]

The DEA has been largely responsible for the widespread popularity of the term *cartel*, and because of that there is a common perception that organized crime in Mexico is *largely limited to drug trafficking*. Nothing could be further from the truth, and Mexican criminal organizations are deeply involved in a wide range of illegal and criminal activity that has been assigned as the organizational mandate to several other Homeland Security and U.S. agencies. Besides drug smuggling, Mexico's organized crime groups are smuggling migrants, engaged in human trafficking, moving firearms and weapons across the border, laundering money and extorting businesses (including American enterprises), to identify just a few of the many types of organized crime. It should be obvious that several of those organized criminal acts are the specific responsibility of agencies other than the DEA; the tracking of firearms is the responsibility of ATF, migration is the responsibility of ICE, human smuggling the responsibility of the FBI, and money laundering and extortion the responsibility of the U.S. Treasury and agencies like the FBI and even the CIA.

The DEA is required to demonstrate to Homeland Security overseers and to Congress that it continues to meet its mandate and that the problem it has been assigned still exists; most recently it has been required to do this in a climate where most attention has been refocused on terrorism and migration—and where the public tolerance of drugs has led to more liberalized views. In order to survive, the DEA must remind politicians, bureaucrats, and the general public that the threats from organized gangs and dangerous kingpins are real—basically that cartels exist and that those cartels are powerful. Historically, support for the DEA peaked following the Kiki Camarena murder in 1985; subsequent to his kidnapping and torture, the DEA encountered few strong organizational demands to justify its value, but national priorities dramatically shifted following 9/11 and the DEA became one of fourteen distinct agencies now charged with fulfilling a security mandate—and not necessarily responsible for a security mandate that everyone believed remained crucial.

In addition to defending its turf against thirteen other departments requiring funding, the DEA mandate has arguably been undermined by changing community norms that question the hard-line approach to drug policies. Support for legalization has grown enormously, and the War on Drugs has increasingly been called into question—even within the United States. Perhaps this context explains why the DEA seized the opportunity to vociferously remind Congress and the public about Kiki Camarena's murder and continuing cartel power when the Mexican Supreme Court released Rafael Caro Quintero in 2013 based on a dubious legal technicality (see Watkins, 2018).

Furthermore, the DEA produces and releases dramatic reports and graphics warning that Mexican cartels are a growing threat across the United States.

The most recent reports have focused on the relatively malignant target of Mara Salvatrucha (MS-13) gangs—even though the Maras fall far short of being an organized crime syndicate. In spite of the alarmist tone in many recent DEA reports and speeches, there is little data to back up the claim that Mexican organized crime has made significant inroads into the United States (DEA 2015).

During the turbulent presidency of Donald J. Trump, the dominant narrative of the border was dramatically hijacked by his insistence on using xenophobia and racist values in the absence of factual evidence. The enemy at the southern border became the *migrant* more so than narco traffickers. The Border Patrol became the largest agency within the entire Department of Justice and increasingly received a *disproportionate* share of resources. More than one-third of all federal agents employed by the DOJ are from the Border Patrol (Graff 2020). The events and political shifts during the Trump administration had pushed the DEA further down the pecking order of institutional relevance, and the heads of the DEA and the DOJ seized the opportunity to showcase the El Chapo Guzmán trial because it allowed that agency to return to a spotlight from which it had been displaced by the rabid xenophobia of a racist president and his nonsensical border rants.

What Is Unexplained by the Term *Cartel*?

None of the above is intended to argue that drug-trafficking organizations do *not* exist, that they are imaginary organizations, or that they pose no real harm or threat. It is simply intended to illustrate how and why the popular conceptualization of organized crime has been framed by a DEA interpretation that is specifically focused on drug trafficking, and why many other dimensions of organized criminal activity have not been routinely studied or analyzed.

Cartel is a term widely used to describe narco trafficking and the transport of drugs by organized gangs in Mexico, and by extension other Latin American countries. *Cartel* is now firmly entrenched in the English-speaking world even though it provides only a *nominal* classification for any type of drug gang. Its parameters are extremely broad, can describe several distinct types of organization, gangs of all sizes, and any group involved in any manner of narco trafficking and criminal enterprise. *Cartel* does not take into account the complex and unseen dimensions of organized criminal activity that have been described in this book and characterized as a covert netherworld.

El Narco

El narco, another term that is widely used to describe organized crime in Mexico, better captures the extent of narco trafficking, the organizational complexity, and the contamination resulting from its diffusion into all other institutions in society. *Narco* is commonly used as both a noun and a powerful prefix to many nouns. But compared to cartel, *el narco* represents a more comprehensive picture of organized crime and recognizes the extensive connections of narco trafficking.

El narco acknowledges that the tentacles of organized crime have seeped into all levels of society, from the backstreets and alleys to the offices of government and those of the privileged and financial movers and shakers. As Ioan Grillo (2011) notes, the noun *narco* is used to describe both a person and the organizational enterprise in which that individual operates. The prefix *narco* is even more common and powerfully descriptive of the reach and extent of drug activities into all realms. It has been attached to a countless number of terms and in doing so reveals an insidious spread of a criminal enterprise touching all areas of social existence.

Mexican Organized Crime: Cartel Discourse

The dominant public perception is that all organized crime in Mexico is tied to the drug trade and controlled by cartels. Luis Astorga has described how that perception of organized crime in Mexico has come to be shaped by American narratives—and in particular by the DEA protecting its mandate in the War on Drugs.

> Last, but not least, the U.S.A. government discourses (both those made by McCaffrey, the U.S.A. drug *tzar* [sic], and the DEA) on drug issues in Mexico, and in many other countries, have succeeded in imposing a kind of symbolic domination. They have become, more than the Mexican government discourse on the same subject, the official versions of what has to be perceived and believed by the public opinion about the Mexico case. (Astorga 2002a)

Controlling the discourse means much more than seizing the power to name a problem. It also validates a specific moral framework and shapes the parameters of acceptable societal response. This requires power, but other benefits accrue from waging moral campaigns—the discourse is legitimated, and its proponents are anointed and ordained to remain in charge of shaping the societal response. Astorga observes that the Mexican narco-traffic discourse has been fixed by drug control agencies situated in the United States and controlled from there by virtue of moral campaigns: the analysis of drug trafficking in Mexico cannot be made without reference to the dynamics of the U.S.-Mexico relationship and to role of the DEA (Astorga 1995, 1999, 2002a, 2002b; Astorga and Shirk 2010; Astorga Almanza 2005, 2007).

Drug production and distribution networks have been part of the landscape in Mexico for at least 150 years, but earlier eras were dominated by different discourses prior to the emergence of the cartel narrative and the invention of a War on Drugs model by the Nixon administration. Drug production and transportation had different unique names over the years and were situated within different moral contexts. The current DEA discourse and narrative of drug cartels have been dominant for approximately forty years and have achieved a near hegemony in the years immediately following the Camarena murder in 1985.

The Institutionalization of Mexican Drug Cartels

Cartels and criminal organizations in Mexico have been traditionally identified using two broad conventions for naming: a name referring to the regional or geographical base of operations, and a categorization of the organization by using the name of its criminal boss. In the past, both conventions appeared interchangeably—for example, the Tijuana Cartel was also known as the Arellano Félix Organization (AFO), the Juárez Cartel was identified as the Carrillo Fuentes Organization (CFO), while the Sinaloa Cartel was sometimes called the El Mayo Zambada–El Chapo Guzmán–El Azul Esparragoza Organization.

Those names have been useful but may have outlived their purpose since Mexican criminal organizations have spread far beyond their original territory or birthplace; furthermore, the most successful have actually morphed into leadership structures that share responsibilities and are horizontally distributed rather than hierarchically based. In addition, many of the organizations have fragmented and have renamed their component factions to reflect a division. Increasingly, focusing on giving a name to a specific organization downplays the reality that the criminal organizations are only one component of a larger and hidden covert netherworld where many parts operate together as part of a broader and extremely successful enterprise.

Only a few organizations have successfully expanded their geographic reach and established a powerful presence in many states and regions across Mexico. In fact, the most successful have also developed a strong international presence and operate beyond Mexico's borders (Rosenberg 2015; Saviano 2014, 2015). Although the naming convention based on origin serves as a useful tag, it does not mean that organizational activities are limited to a specific or narrow geographical area. Furthermore, it is more difficult to identify one leader or determine the specific role played by one individual within a criminal organization because the decision-making of some groups has been structured more to resemble a *holding company* managed by the equivalent of a board of directors (see Emmot 2010; Fernández Menéndez 2001). The leadership of organizations has regularly been in flux because of the U.S. emphasis on a kingpin strategy over the past fifteen years. The U.S. Congress and the DEA and Mexican authorities have targeted leaders they have designated as kingpins, only to see fractures emerge and equally capable substitutes take over. It has become similar to a game of whack-a-mole where organizations pop up under a different name and regularly reappear in two different places under different names. While it is undoubtedly true that many ruthless and charismatic personalities have dominated Mexico's narco landscape, it is much too simplistic to conclude that Mexico's entrenched criminal drug problem has been simplistically caused by individuals and their specific criminal proficiency.

Narco trafficking in Mexico is profoundly institutionalized and intertwined with legitimate institutional arrangements. It involves an ongoing symbiotic relationship with the state and its institutions; this interconnection explains the cartels' ongoing success and the difficulty in eradicating their presence. Criminal gangs specializing in drug production emerged more than a century ago, but their success and wealth escalated dramatically when their unique traditions, distinctive regional values, and specific norms of cooperation formalized about five decades ago. Furthermore, Mexico's criminal organizations and narco traditions emerged along different trajectories: some grew through the sheer force of threat, power, and intimidation, targeting anyone standing in the way; others developed gradually and organically based on specific norms of reciprocity and the gradual institutionalization of routine interactions that crystallized into mutual and ongoing benefits for the participants; and yet other groups emerged because corrupt government agents directly intervened to organize and supervise distribution networks that would deliver commodities to consumers and to markets.

The history of drug trafficking in Mexico must take into account the reality that some groups achieved institutional permanence and lasting success and have been the beneficiaries of a relative immunity from punitive sanctions. Additionally, any comprehensive explanation must explain why some specific organizations grew prominent and retained their power over extended periods, while others seemingly achieved a momentary success only to see it disappear, decline, or be snatched away by others. In almost every way, the Sinaloa Cartel is the most stable organization that has emerged; it remains situated in a powerful position of permanence that makes it difficult to break. The prosecution of its putative boss, El Chapo Guzmán, did little to undermine its overall power and weaken the influence it has accrued over decades. Sentencing one man to a life term in an American prison has not destroyed the organization he was accused of leading.

How Many Cartels?

There is disagreement and even confusion about how to categorize and count drug-trafficking cartels and criminal organizations in Mexico. In 2021 it has become increasingly evident that there remain only two groups in Mexico organized enough to be described as cartels—the Sinaloa Cartel and the Cártel de Jalisco Nueva Generación. Those are the only two that have a national and international reach, and the only two with an organizational complexity that involves all different dimensions and processes of the idealized drug trade model described in figure 3 or the organizational structure described in figure 9.

All other large organizations and factions that were described in the chronology of narco Mexico have fragmented into smaller parts or have assumed roles that are limited and specialized in the overall production and distribution of drugs. It cannot be said that they have disappeared or that they have been defeated and crushed. Rather, they are now focused on providing specialized services and performing tasks as contracted providers within a larger subterranean economy.

The overall focus on kingpins and the strategy that deliberately led to the fragmentation of larger cartels have been largely responsible for this outcome. But undeniably, the wars within cartels and the wars against cartels also contributed to the current reality, and many internal readjustments and redistributions of power over time have created two dominant organizations and more than eighty distinct criminal groups of varying size that perform specialized tasks within a vast subterranean network. In 2021 we should no longer be asking, "How many cartels are there in Mexico?" but focus on two different questions—"How many different crime groups emerged in the aftermath of the three wars that raged across Mexico since 2004?" and "What is the relationship of each specific criminal group to the two larger entities?"

Chapters 3 through 6 presented a chronology that described how one unified cartel first emerged in the 1980s, only to fragment into distinct factions before reforming as a unified federation during the 1990s. That second Federation collapsed into competing powerful factions, and simultaneously new organizations emerged in an era of expansion that brought chaos and violence to all Mexican states; by 2010, as many as nine or ten large-scale organizations were competing.

Between 2004 and 2014, the geographic distribution and reach of several of the larger organizations expanded beyond their place of origin. By the end of 2014, at least twenty-three states in Mexico reported a significant cartel presence. Only four of those twenty-three jurisdictions were dominated by a single criminal organization, whereas nineteen others reported at least two different cartels competing within their boundaries. Figure 10 describes the radiographic change across sexenios and uses shading to graphically display the number of cartels operating within each of the subnational political jurisdictions. During the extended period of stability between 1976 and 1994, cartel activity was identified in, *at most*, thirteen of Mexico's thirty-two regional jurisdictions (thirty-one states and one Federal District).[9] Most significantly, a *single* organization had seemingly established dominant control within twelve of those states through 1988 and thirteen by 1994.[10] But after 1994—not coincidentally the year of NAFTA's introduction—cartel presence had doubled and expanded to twenty-six states, and *at least* two organizations competed for dominance or operated in parallel in thirteen of those

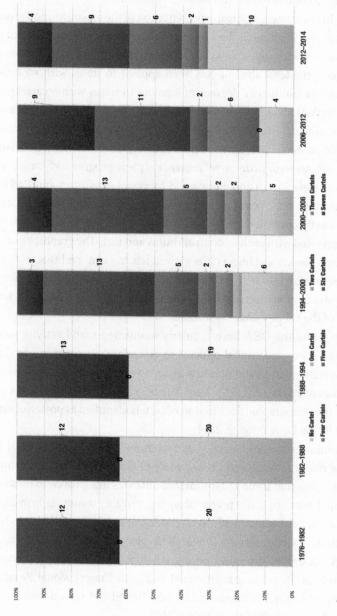

FIGURE 10 Cartel expansion, competition, and reach by sexenio. Graphic by author based on data from *Animal Político*. https://www.animalpolitico.com/root/diez-de-guerra/index.html.

states. Even more disturbingly, six states by then had three or four cartels competing to control routes and establish domination.

Figure 10 is a statoc graphical representation of the expansion and growth of cartels across sexenios.[11] The specific numbers inside the graphic are the count of states with only one cartel, states with three cartels, and so on. For instance, the least shading has been applied to states with *no known cartel presence* and higher degrees of shading to states with a cartel presence; the darkest shading is applied to states where several different cartels were operational. Between 1976 and 1988, there were twenty states *without* any significant cartel presence. In the following years, the lightest shaded category—*states with little cartel presence*—grew progressively smaller as more states were increasingly impacted by cartel expansion and had cartels operate into their boundaries. At the same time, more Mexican states became heavily contested plazas where as many as five to seven different cartels competed with each to control routes and turf. The graphic contains progressively darker shading as it is viewed left to right, and that indicates both an expansion into more states and an increased competion for plazas. Figure 10 also demonstrates that the expansion of cartels peaked in the waning years of the Felipe Calderón sexenio.

The DOJ and the DEA have regularly monitored cartel activity inside Mexico and presented annual updates to Homeland Security and to Congress in specific reports and updated summaries prepared by the Congressional Research Service (CRS). Map 2 is from one of those resports and describes the radiographic distribution of cartels identified as powerful organizations by the DEA through 2014.

The number of groups classified as cartels by the DEA and the DOJ has *fluctuated* over the years and the accuracy of the count is further complicated by the fact that some groups formed alliances that proved to be short-lived. Map 2 was originally prepared by the private consulting firm Stratfor Global Consulting and made available in the public domain through its reproduction in Congressional Research Service reports. The image reproduced here describes the cartel presence across Mexico as it was thought to exist in 2014; it was first reproduced in a 2015 Congressional Research Service report (no. 41576) authored by June Beittel and reproduced in several revised versions since then (Beittel 2020).

Map 2 identifies *eight* major organizations operating in Mexico in 2014 that were being tracked by the DEA: the Sinaloa Cartel, the Juárez Cartel, the

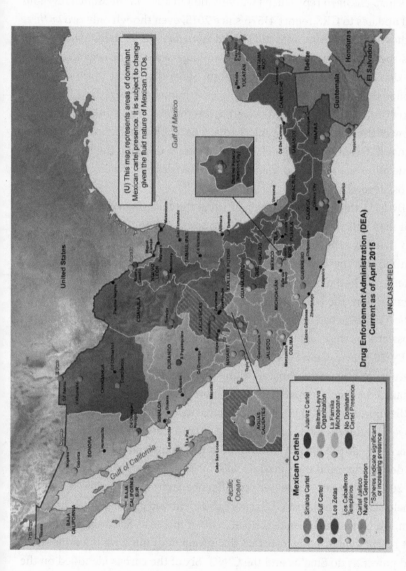

MAP 2 Cartel presence at the end of 2014, according to DEA, April 2015. Reprinted from Congressional Research Service R41576 · VERSION 34 · UPDATED.

Gulf Cartel, the Beltrán Leyva Organization, Los Zetas, La Familia Michoacana, Los Caballeros Templarios, and the Cártel de Jalisco Nueva Generación.
This map has been reproduced without modification in the annual revisions
and updates to CRS report 41576 since 2015, even though only *two or three*
of those organizations were still viewed as *major organizations* in later years;
this specific map represents the *apex* of large-scale crime organizations in
Mexico during the Peña Nieto sexenio. Since that point in time, several
groups that were once considered large criminal organizations have split
into distinct and smaller parts—*perhaps* as many as eighty in total, and only
a few of those fragmented gangs had a geographical presence that reached
across different states.[12] Later in this chapter, I describe the emergence of
some of those groups and their affiliation with larger criminal organization
across several sexenios.

By 2014 the DEA was no longer using the term *cartel* in the same way
that the public had come to understand and use it; the common perception
was that *any* crime group in Mexico was a cartel, but the DEA clearly recognized that there were major differences among those groups. That reality
is reflected in the names that were used in 2014 to categorize the different
organizations the DEA had been closely tracking. The referent term *organization* was attached to only *five* of those groups at that time and indicate that
those groups were larger and more powerful than the others.

By 2019 it was obvious that the DEA and the DOJ no longer believed
there were nine or ten organizations that should be considered mafias or
organized crime groups. Map 3 is a more recent map reproduced from a
CRS report (Beittel 2020); it indicates that *at most* there are *three* dominant
players, and most likely only *two*—the Sinaloa Cartel, which was also being
referred to as the Sinaloa Federation in this graphic and elsewhere as Cártel del Pacífico; and the Cártel de Jalisco Nueva Generación (CJNG), which
by 2019 had greatly increased its influence and power to rival that of the
Sinaloa Cartel. The latest CRS report also identified a Tamaulipas Organization, which was has been described in other places as El Cártel del Noreste,
but recent evidence suggests that that group does not have the same reach
and power as do Sinaloa and the CJNG. Six of the cartels identified on the
2014 map had declined significantly in both reach and power and were now
being referred to as organized crime *remnants*—at least in the categorization
of organizations recognized by the DEA. One organization, the CJNG, had
emerged from what had been a relatively minor status to become a major

MAP 3 Regions of Mexico and cartel presence in 2018. Data from U.S. Department of Justice, Drug Enforcement Administration, and Stratfor Global Consulting. Reprinted from June Beittel, "Mexico: Organized Crime and Drug Trafficking Organizations" (Congressional Research Service, July 28, 2020), 8. Reprinted with the permission of Statfor, a RANE company, a leading global geopolitical intelligence and advisory firm.

player and an extremely dangerous foe of the state and a major challenger to the Sinaloa Cartel.

The government strategy to fragment large cartels, specifically during the Peña Nieto sexenio, did have an effect, but it did not eliminate gangs and it left sixty or more smaller ones in place; furthermore, it left two powerful competing organizations standing. The CJNG is one of those two large groups, and it is an interesting case because it seemingly rose from the ashes to become one of the two most powerful cartels in Mexico by 2021.

There have been a few times in the annals of Mexican drug history that a criminal group has supposedly been suppressed only see it reappear later. One farcical example was the case of La Familia Michoacana; it was once thought to have collapsed when its delusional but charismatic leader, Nazario Moreno González, had been declared killed in a Mexican military operation, only to be discovered two years later that he was very much alive and *killed a second time* while leading an offshoot group renamed Los Caballeros Templarios.[13] The Moreno González "resurrection" from the dead is merely farcical compared to how the Valencia Cartel arose from the ashes to reform as the powerful Cártel de Jalisco Nueva Generación with a national and international presence.

Many believed that the Valencia Cartel (Milenio Cartel) had permanently faded into the background before it reemerged as two distinct and competing factions around 2009. Those two groups emerged in Jalisco State following the arrest of Orlando "El Lobo" Nava Valencia, who had headed a relatively subservient component of the larger Sinaloa Cartel known as El Cártel de Milenio. El Lobo's organization had begun to assume an increasingly larger role in the Sinaloa enterprise when the production and distribution of synthetic drugs grew more important as a source of income. Amphetamines and other synthetic drugs became increasingly profitable commodities after crackdowns in the United States shifted production south of the border and into the hands of the Valencias (Fierro 2015; U.S. Department of the Treasury 2015). El Cártel de Milenio controlled the Guadalajara and Jalisco plazas that became the central hub for the importation of precursors and the manufacture and distribution of synthetic drugs.

Following El Lobo's arrest, the struggle for leadership and control of the Valencia group grew complicated and happened independently of Sinaloa control because Mexican marines had earlier killed Ignacio Coronel Villareal, who had been the powerful intermediary linking the Valencias to Sinaloa jefes and the larger enterprise. Coronel Villareal was coincidently the reported uncle of El Chapo's wife Emma Coronel Aispura. In the aftermath of El Lobo's arrest and the death of Coronel Villareal, two factions competed for control of the remnants of the Valencia organization—Los Cuinis, led by Abigael González Valencia; and the CJNG, led by Nemesio "El Mencho" Oseguera Cervantes (Eells 2017).

El Mencho eventually won control of that synthetic drug empire that extended into Michoacán, Guerrero, and Mexico City. And then under his leadership, the CJNG expanded its presence to control Nayarit, Colima, and Guanajuato. El Mencho was not averse to carrying out audacious displays of power and force, and he authorized bold and brutal attacks directly against

Mexican soldiers and marines using military-grade armaments he had stock-piled (Guerrero Gutiérrez 2015b). CJNG power increased exponentially during the first two years of the AMLO sexenio and it is now the dominant criminal cartel in Guanajuato State, Mexico State, and CDMX; its dominance of CDMX was never more obvious than when it deployed a heavily armed team of sicar-ios in a failed attempt to assassinate Mexico City's secretary of security Omar García Harfuch (González Diáz 2020; Raziel and Montalvo 2020).

In launching that attack, El Mencho was doing what he had always done—going back to the years when he was a lugarteniente commanding sicarios for the Sinaloa Cartel. He and his killers had *routinely* resorted to displays of brutal and inhumane ferocity in his battles against Los Zetas. In fact, he had created a group of sanguine sicarios known as Los Matazetas—Zeta killers—so-named for their specific target but also because they regularly employed .50 caliber military-grade bullets. Los Matazetas and El Cuini were responsible for several horrific massacres, such as the stacking of thirty-five decaying bodies of supposed Zetas in the back of cattle trucks left on the main highway passing through Boca del Río, Veracruz. El Mencho and the CJNG had also routinely uploaded videos via YouTube that display the tor-ture and mutilation of anyone who dared to cross their path or interfere with their business (see *InSight Crime* 2020b).

Flexible Leadership

Some historically entrenched criminal organizations, in particular the Sinaloa Cartel, have consistently demonstrated great adaptability in replacing lead-ers without skipping a beat or diminishing their entrenched influence and power; it has regularly and successfully experienced organizational restruc-turing even when Mexico's security strategy and international scrutiny had intensified. The Sinaloa organization and its leaders have occasionally with-drawn into obscurity and seclusion but remained ready to reemerge when market and political circumstances proved more promising.

Anabel Hernández's book *El traidor* (2020) makes a convincing case that the DOJ's successful prosecution of El Chapo Guzmán has done little to affect the overall leadership of the Sinaloa Cartel. If she is right in her claims, and more and more people are convinced she is, the actual leader of the Sinaloa Cartel is El Mayo Zambada García, who remains free. Events such as El Culiacanazo in late 2019, where the army meekly retreated from the attempted arrest of Ovidio Guzmán López, is a stark reminder that the organization is still incredibly powerful.

Sinaloa Leadership

The reality is that the actual leadership structure of the Sinaloa Cartel is unknown and remains the subject of rumor and speculation. One intriguing and illustrative example of guesswork involves the current role of Rafael Caro Quintero. He was a petty hoodlum who became a jefe within the first generation of narco traffickers located in Sinaloa. He was also a dominant boss within the Guadalajara Cartel when it grew incredibly rich in the years following Operation Condor. After he was sentenced to life imprisonment for his role in the murder of Kiki Camarena, most observers believed that the subsequent division of the Guadalajara Cartel into three factions had *excluded* Caro Quintero from any ongoing leadership role in any of Mexico's remaining plazas.

But unexpectedly in 2013, he emerged from obscurity after being unexpectedly released him from prison in August (Beith 2014). Instead of serving the final years of his long sentence, he was mysteriously allowed to vanish into the underworld, to the surprise and anger of many—especially veterans of the drug war who worked with the DEA. Perhaps Caro Quintero's unexpected release represents nothing more than his personal good fortune and the legal maneuverings of a skillful team of lawyers, but one should never discount the possibility that the surprise outcome is linked to organizational rearrangements within the Sinaloa Cartel and a rumored restructuring of cartel leadership following the 2013 arrest of El Chapo—who at the time was widely assumed to be Boss of Bosses within the Sinaloa Cartel.[14] Caro Quintero had long been relegated to a background role and forgotten by most, but now there are some who believe that he may have reappeared to play a significant role in a reorganized Sinaloa Cartel as a senior advisor, consigliore, or even as one of its senior jefes.[15]

Auxiliary Gangs, Armed Wings, and Subordinate Factions

Mexico has always had a significant number of dangerous criminal gangs and regional groups that were subsidiaries or specific offshoots of the larger criminal organizations. A full understanding of narco traffic in Mexico requires a systematic description of how those groups are connected to larger organizations and how they are related to each other on a regional or micro level. Most of the violence and brutality within the drug trade is attributable to the actions of auxiliary gangs, armed wings, and factions of the larger cartels. In the wars between cartels, some of those groups had became so powerful that they became dangerous threats in their own right. The best example of that is Los Zetas.

Overall, there is little evidence that armed wings, hit men, or auxiliary gangs in the service of cartels represented a strategic component of the drug trade during the first twenty-five years following Operation Condor. The first major gang that was specifically *recruited* and directed by another cartel was Los Zetas; they did not appear until the final years of Ernesto Zedillo Ponce de León's presidency. At that time, the Gulf Cartel had recently emerged as a national presence alongside the Sinaloa, Juárez, and Tijuana Cartels when its mercurial and certifiably paranoid leader, Osiel Cárdenas Guillén, recruited Los Zetas to provide personal protection during his battle for control of the Gulf organization with Salvador Gómez Herrera (Ravelo 2009). It is worth noting that semiautonomous gangs appeared first within the Gulf Cartel—an organization that had expanded into narco trafficking almost three decades later than the Sinaloa, Juárez, or Tijuana organizations.

Two broad takeaway observations can be made regarding the recruitment of Los Zetas. First, unlike the other narco-traffic organizations, the Gulf Cartel was an upstart organization compared to the Sinaloa Cartel. The linkages that were formed among partners were based much more directly on instrumental and financial transactions rather than having evolved out of historical friendships or traditions. Furthermore, the Gulf Cartel had more ambiguous connections to regional elites and power brokers after the death of its legendary longtime leader, Juan Nepomuceno Guerra. Although his nephew Juan García Abrego undoubtedly inherited some of his uncle's goodwill and old alliances, he was beginning from scratch to build his own connections to power through bribery and corruption. When García Abrego was arrested, the organization fell into the clutches of unpredictable thugs like Cárdenas Guillén, who sat even further outside the perimeters of local power brokers and was personally inclined to employ brutality and thuggery than were the leaders of other Mexican cartels who had maintained close connections to the halls of power over long periods. The Gulf Cartel, in the absence of established connections and networks, depended more directly on force and bribery to achieve compliance and cooperation with both local authorities and the communities. Second, the formation of armed wings, teams of hit men, and auxiliary gangs became a model that was almost immediately imitated by the older established cartels (Sinaloa, Juárez, Tijuana).

In other words, expansion into new plazas demanded that the major cartels follow the example of the Gulf by recruiting auxiliary groups in order to remain competitive. The Sinaloa Cartel and jefes like El Chapo Guzmán had little need for diverse and complex auxiliary groups before 2003 or 2004, but the Sinaloa decision to challenge shipping routes and border points from Ciudad Juárez to Nuevo Laredo made it mandatory for the Sinaloa Cartel to create its own auxiliary groups and recruit semi-independent groups such as Los Pelones to serve as their armed enforcers. In response to the threat of both Los Zetas and Sinaloa, Vicente Carrillo Fuentes also escalated the militarization of Ciudad Juárez by creating his own group of hit men—La Línea—who were primarily ex-convicts and members of existing armed gangs located in both Ciudad Juárez and El Paso, Texas.

By the end of Zedillo's sexenio, and at the start of the Fox sexenio, the Gulf Cartel had been the first to establish an auxiliary semiparamilitary force of trained armed killers. But by the midpoint of the Fox sexenio, both the Sinaloa Cartel and the Juárez Cartel had established their own armed wings and provided them with training and heavy armaments. El Teo García Simental, head of security for the Arellano Félix family in Tijuana, also expanded his personal team of thugs and hit men and prepared them for battle. By the time the Sinaloa Cartel made its expansionary moves on the Carrillo Fuentes domination of Ciudad Juárez, there were two powerfully armed groups in place to fight each other in a war for drugs—Los Pelones and La Línea (figure 11).

Cartels and Armed Wings—2006 to 2012

The number of cartels and armed gangs exploded exponentially during Felipe Calderón Hinojosa's sexenio, and at least sixty different armed wings, gangs of thugs, and subordinate factions emerged as auxiliary forces linked to the eight distinct cartels operating at the midpoint of his presidential term. The expansion in the number of auxiliary gangs was the result of at least four factors that emerged during the Calderón presidency. First, two of the largest

Sexenio	Cártel	Armed Wings
Ernesto Zedillo P 4 Cartels, 1 Armed Wing	Sinaloa	
	Juárez	
	Tijuana	
	Gulf	Los Zetas
Vicente Fox Q 3 Cartels , 3 Armed Wings	Sinaloa	Los Pelones
	Juárez	La Línea
	Tijuana	
	Gulf	Los Zetas

FIGURE 11 Zedillo and Fox sexenios: Armed wings and auxiliary gangs. Graphic created by author.

cartels—Sinaloa and the Gulf—had each split into two factions following bloody internecine struggles; in 2007 and 2008, four powerful groups were aggressively searching for recruits to expand their numbers. Second, the Sinaloa Cartel and its now bitter rival Beltrán Leyva faction were in a bloody competition to hold on to existing plazas and gain footholds in new ones. Third, Los Zetas and La Familia, which had already claimed plazas, recruited more foot soldiers to meet the threat of the Sinaloa and Beltran Leyva forces. Fourth, several of the plazas plagued by the internecine battles within cartels were simultaneously invaded by federal security forces deployed by Calderón in the ill-advised war against cartels. The emergence of three simultaneous wars—wars *within, between,* and *against* cartels—spurred the creation of new armed wings and the intense recruitment of footsoldiers.

Initially, there was no shortage of bodies available to serve as cannon fodder. High unemployment levels and a downturn in the economy on both sides of the border meant there was a large pool of potential recruits. The United States directly contributed to the pool of would-be killers by deporting large numbers of prisoners from American prisons during cost-cutting measures.[16] Within Mexico, men who had served in either the army or police forces were specifically targeted for recruitment to the emerging paramilitary units and gangs: the Mexican army had unusually high numbers of desertions because of low pay and low morale (estimated to be more than 120,000 by some accounts), and most army deserters had few options for legitimate work within Mexico. At the same time, several police forces had been decimated and even eliminated when the Partido Acción Nacional (PAN) and Partido de la Revolución Democrática (PRD, Party of the Democratic

Revolution) governors and mayors took office and replaced many commanders and agents with their own preferred candidates.

At first the pool of recruits was older, but as casualties mounted, the armed wings focused on the recruitment of younger boys from among the millions of youth known as NINIs—those neither in school nor employed (*ni estudian ni trabajan*).

Figure 12 identifies sixty armed wings that had emerged by the time Calderón's sexenio ended. Some of those groups had long-standing connections to larger organizations, where they had previously operated as lower-level street gangs before transforming into more militarized gang organizations toward the end of the Fox presidency between 2004 and 2006. Some of those gangs had little presence or operated independently before they were recruited.

Most of the criminal organizations in this list first became visible or were initially tracked by intelligence reports only *after* Calderón decided to deploy military troops in his opening salvo against drug cartels in his native state of Michoacán. There are many who convincingly argue that the Michoacán armed wings became more organized only after Calderón recklessly decided that military intervention was necessary; before the military intervention, those gangs represented little more than local nuisances.[17] Even if those groups were disorganized criminal nuisances at the beginning of Calderón's sexenio, several of them would become increasingly militarized and remain a serious threat by the time Enrique Peña Nieto became president. Arguably, the level of threat that they represented escalated to extremely dangerous levels when assault weapons became more readily available after 2004.

During Calderón's presidency, Michoacán had been invaded by advance teams of Los Zetas, who at the time were still working directly for the Gulf Cartel. Those invaders hoped to establish a foothold in both the heroin and marijuana trade—both of which were produced in remote regions of Michoacán. They also hoped to control the shipping routes important for the Gulf Cartel's burgeoning synthetic drug trade that was situated in the west coast port of Lázaro Cárdenas. The United States had cracked down on synthetic drug production within its borders, and that opened up a new opportunity for production that was recognized by members of the Gulf Cartel. Michoacán's own in-state criminal gang, La Familia, also emerged in that period. It had evolved from a tradition of crime associated earlier with La Empresa, and Nazario "El Chayo" Moreno González emerged as the self-appointed

Felipe Calderón H 8 Cartels with, 60 Armed Wings	Sinaloa, 12 Armed Wings	Gente Nueva, Jalisco Nueva Generación, La Cabrera, La Barredora, El Comando del Diablo, Cártel del Poniente, Cártel de la Laguna, Los Mata-Zetas, El Aquiles, El Tigre, Los Artistas Asesinos, Los Mexicles
	Beltran-Leyva, 20 Armed Wings	FEDA, El Chico Malo, El H2, Los Mazatlecos, Los Tigres, El 2 mil, Los Granados, Los Rojos, Morelos Unidos, Nuevo Cártel de la Sierra, Los Pineda, Los Zafiros, Cártel del Pacífico Sur, La Oficina, La Mano con Ojos, El Mosco, Los Gilos, El Tigre, Los Ardillos, Los Arturos
	Juárez, 2 Armed Wings	La Línea, Los Aztecas
	Tijuana, 14 Armed Wings	Don Balas, El Mario, El Melvin, El Chan, El Jorquera, Grupos dirigidos por García, Grupos dirigidos por Barranco, Pelioni, El Kieto, Chikaka, El Bibi, El Licenciado, El Turbo, Los Zamudio
	Gulf, 2 Armed Wings	Los Pelones, Metros
	Familia-Michoacana, 5 Armed Wings	Guerreros Unidos, La Resistencia, Champis Crew, Brown Side Family, La Empresa
	Zetas, 3 Armed Wings	Los Talibanes, Los Legionarios, Los hijos del diablo
	Caballeros-Templarios, 2 Armed Wings	Guardia Morelense, Los Troyanos

FIGURE 12 Calderón sexenio: Armed gangs and auxiliary wings. Graphic created by author.

defender of Michoacán State from the invasionary teams of Los Zetas and later the Beltrán Leyvas.

Elsewhere, the most aggressive recruitment and creation of groups happened within the Sinaloa Cartel, especially under the direct leadership of Arturo Beltrán Leyva and his brothers, who had long headed the enforcement wing of the Sinaloa Cartel. It was also during the first few years of the Calderón presidency that a major arms race began within the cartels;

there was also an unprecedented stockpiling of military-level armaments and equipment. At first, almost all Sinaloa troops created by the Beltrán Leyvas were trained as *invasionary forces* for deployment directly into plazas originally allocated in the 1990s to Tijuana (Arellano Félix family) and Ciudad Juárez (the Carrillo Fuentes family) in the reputed deal brokered following the Guadalajara Cartel collapse. But there were also other Sinaloa paramilitary forces created specifically to defend traditional Sinaloa turf from invasionary thrusts coming from Gulf Cartel and Los Zetas mercenaries: in particular, Sinaloa gangs were created to counteract the serious threat posed by Z-3 Lazcano Lazcano. The armed wings, military forces, and associated gangs of both sides fought brutal battles against each other in several cities and regions stretched along the border such as Tijuana, Ciudad Juárez, Nuevo Laredo, Reynosa, and Matamoros.

In 2008 Arturo Beltrán Leyva had angrily split from the Sinaloa Cartel and triggered a violent and bloody internal war among former brothers-in-arms. New groups formed, and each of the established armed wings became cannon fodder in a confusing war that pitted former allies against each other and even family against family. Beltrán Leyva had created many armed groups and gangs that remained loyal to him after the split; he also established new ones—assisted by mercenary subcommanders such as La Barbie Valdez Villareal. Some armed wings remained loyal to El Chapo Guzmán and El Mayo Zambada; meanwhile, those two capos continued to recruit, organize, and arm sicarios to defend themselves and their historical plazas.

During the Calderón presidency, the Gulf Cartel and Los Zetas had also undertaken an aggressive period of expansion into the states of Coahuila, Nuevo León, Michoacán, Veracruz, and some regions of Guerrero (Acapulco): on several occasions, the Gulf mercenary force Los Zetas engaged in wild shoot-outs with armed groups from the Sinaloa Cartel forces aligned with the Beltrán Leyva family or those created by La Familia (*InSight Crime* 2013; Tuckman 2011). In Michoacán, Los Zetas were challenged and met with forceful resistance from Michoacán armed groups and the revitalized La Familia that flourished as a formally organized group after the deployment of Mexican armed forces to Michoacán. Michoacán descended into even further chaos when La Familia fragmented and reincarnated or morphed into Los Caballeros Templarios. The situation in Michoacán became unequivocally explosive and unpredictable when the Cártel de Jalisco Nueva Generación intervened as a proxy force for the Sinaloa Cartel and provided direct support to some of the regional *autodefensa* units that had pledged to expel Los Zetas and Los Templarios.

A separate wave of violence also broke out in Tijuana and Baja California when armed groups working for the Tijuana Cartel defended the Arellano Félix Plaza against aggressive Sinaloa incursions and simultaneously from direct attacks from Mexican armed forces and an aggressive and authoritarian municipal police force headed by Julián Leyzaola (Finnegan 2010). The Arellano Félix family would eventually lose control due to the destabilization of its leadership, and many among its armed groups switched allegiance to the Sinaloa side. Some defections came from senior lieutenants, including the chief enforcer El Teo García Simental, whose newfound allegiance to El Chapo Guzmán expedited the demise of the Tijuana organization. Many armed wings that García Simental had created as the chief of security for the Arellano Félix family also switched sides and joined him in the Sinaloa Cartel.

The Peña Nieto Presidency: Shifting Hot Spots and Auxiliary Gangs

The landscape of cartels and the number of recognized auxiliary wings fluctuated widely during the first three years of the Enrique Peña Nieto presidency—creating a great deal of confusion or disagreement about the actual number of cartels and auxiliary gangs in operation: there is ambiguous information and conflicting details about the total number of armed wings and even less information about who pays the salary for members of those gangs. The DEA drug threat assessment reports identified eight major cartels operating in 2014 (see figure 13), but in reality, there may have been as few as three or somewhere between seven and nine—depending on how each cartel was defined and of course dependent on the accuracy of intelligence and information fed to the DEA. Some changes showing a reduction of large cartel activity during the Peña Nieto presidency are undoubtedly real and represented permanent changes in a shifting narco landscape, but others may have simply been an artifact of the Peña Nieto government's blatant attempt to stage manage its international image (Conroy 2013a; El Sabueso 2015).

In specific terms, the Tijuana Cartel was weakened but still recognized as a major criminal organization at the time of the Peña Nieto inauguration, but it had disappeared entirely from the list of major groups by the end of

Sexenio	Cártel	Armed Wings
Enrique Peña Nieto 9 Cartels with, 42 Armed Wings. NOTE: during 2013-14 CJNG and Los Cuinis were identified by the DEA as distinct cártels	Sinaloa, 8 Armed Wings	Gente Nueva, Los Cabrera, La Barredora, Cártel del Poniente y de la Laguna, El Aquiles, El Tigre, Los Artistas Asesinos, Los Mexicles
	Cartel de Jalisco Nueva Generación	Unknown affiliates, Under direct control of Nemesio "El Menco" Oseguerra Cervantes
	Los Cuinis	Unknown affiliates, Under direct control of Abigael Gonzalez Valencia
	Beltran-Leyva, 7 Armed Wings,	Los Mazatlecos, El 2 mil, Los Granados, Los Rojos, La Oficina, Los Ardillos, Cártel Independiente de Acapulco
	Juárez, 2 Armed Wings	La Línea, Los Aztecas
	Tijuana, 3 Armed Wings	El Chan, El Jorquera, El Kieto
	Gulf, 12 Armed Wings	Metros, Rojos, Grupo Lacoste, Grupo Dragones, Grupo Bravo, Grupo Pumas, Grupo de Apoyo Ceros, M3, Los Fresitas, Los Sierra, Los Pantera, Ciclones, Los Pelones
	Zetas, 8 Armed Wings	Sangre Zeta, Grupo Operativo Zetas, El Círculo y El Extranjero, Unidad Zetas, Néctar Lima, Grupo Delta Zeta, Los Negros, Fuerzas Especiales Zetas
	Familia-Michoacana, 2 Armed Wings	Guerreros Unidos, La Empresa

FIGURE 13 Peña Nieto sexenio: Armed wings and auxiliary gangs. Graphic created by author.

his third year (Epstein and ProPublica 2016). Perhaps more ominously, new and powerful threats had also appeared with the addition of the leaders of the Cártel de Jalisco Nueva Generación and its closely affiliated partner Los Cuinis to the U.S. Treasury list of organized crime kingpins. In effect, at least one cartel—CJNG—with two factions had emerged by the third year of the Peña Nieto presidency and came to be identified as powerful forces by security officials in the USA and in Mexico.

One fact is indisputable: the number of reported armed groups recognized and being tracked appears significantly lower—down by at least eighteen—during the first three years of Peña Nieto's presidency. The reduction can possibly be explained by the shifting narco landscape, in which some contested plazas had cooled down significantly through an internal cartel negotiation of peace, by the victory of one faction over another, or possibly because of the success attributable to a national security strategy that focused on reducing violence specifically along the northern frontier. No matter why it happened, the Peña Nieto government was quick to wage an aggressive campaign to convince the world that the PRI government had the situation under control.[18]

The rumored cartel truce and the federal security policy were driven by an economic motivation and attempt to reduce costs by both the government and the cartels. The Wars Between Cartels (internal plaza wars) had drained resources and were disastrous for the bottom line of the cartel bosses, and the extreme violence represented a serious impediment to Peña Nieto's broad goal to encourage global investment in Mexico and foment the impression of stability. The lowered level of violence on the border in 2012 and 2013 and the federal government's success in targeting some violent factions and capturing key leaders—specifically Los Zetas and the Arellano Félix family—were emphasized in public relations campaigns undertaken by the government.

The Juárez Cartel was also seriously diminished by the weakness in its leadership, the arrest of several of its major operators, and most likely because the Sinaloa Cartel was finally emerging as a unified power after a long war waged against the Carrillo Fuentes family and against the Beltran Leyva faction. Meanwhile, the Arellano Félix family was decimated following several years of arrests and extradition of family members. Fourteen of the gangs that had been previously known to work for the Tijuana Cartel had disappeared or greatly diminished in power and influence. Los Zetas had also been severely weakened following the assassination and arrests of leaders and because it had stretched its resources too thin by waging battles and plaza disputes in disparate regions. Notably, Lazcano Lazcano died in a shoot-out with marines one month before Peña Nieto assumed office. Los Zetas remained under attack on all fronts from government forces and many enemies within the Sinaloa Cartel, the Gulf Cartel, and Los Caballeros Templarios.

The reduction in the number of armed wings and gangs did not mean that national violence significantly decreased. In fact, the changes produced something that has been called a displacement effect—something that Mexicans had seen before and had been referred to as the balloon effect (see chapter 4). The battle fronts simply shifted to different regions, sometimes involving the same actors but just as often involving new combatants. Significantly, most violence and disputes migrated to central and southern Mexico and away from the border region, and the major fronts and confrontations relocated to central states and regions around the capital. In some cases, the confrontations that festered from late 2013 to the end of 2016 represented the continuation of older simmering disputes such as the Sinaloa versus Beltrán Leyva war, or the Gulf versus Los Zetas internal readjustments. But in other locations, the situation became much more chaotic; armed gangs and divisions are engaged in disputes and battles that share more in common with those infamous gang wars typified by Bloods–Crips disputes in many U.S. urban centers.

At least fifteen armed wings continued to challenge each other in a simmering internal dispute between the Sinaloa Cartel and the remnants of the Beltrán Leyva cartel, headed by Fausto "El Chapo" Isidro Flores. Most Sinaloa versus Beltrán Leyva confrontations broke out in the north of Sinaloa and southern Sonora where the narco-trafficking routes into the USA remain important and irreplaceable; hostile battles sporadically burst out further south in sections of the sierra region above Mazatlán, Sinaloa, and the immediate environs of Acapulco, Guerrero.

Michoacán, Guerrero, Mexico State, Jalisco, and the Federal District came to be the most dangerous killing fields and battlegrounds. Although the major cartels continue to have a hand in fomenting and feeding that violence, much of it has become decentralized and initiated directly by affiliate groups and warring factions who are committed to establishing their dominance in a localized plaza. In particular, Guerrero State and its border regions with Michoacán and Mexico State have been brutalized by battles and violence that are more like tribal warfare than battles to serve the broader instrumental purposes of narco trafficking. It has become impossible to determine who is in charge and whether anyone is directing confrontations to meet a specific end.

CHAPTER 8

Transformation or Perdition?

Te la canto.
Me canso ganso
dijo un zancudo
cuando volar no pudo
una pata se le torció
y la otra se le hizo nudo,
luego le dio laftosa y hasta se quedó mudo.
Y ya mejor no le sigo porque luego yo sudo.

—Lyrics to "The Lost Child," 1947

"Me canso ganso" literally means "I'm tired goose." It is a Mexican colloquialism that is virtually impossible to translate outside its cultural context. It became a popular idiomatic expression after comedic idol Tin Tán (Germán Valdés Castillo) popularized it in the 1947 movie *El niño perdido* (The lost child). His character was a normal adult only until 7 p.m., when he reverted to childlike behavior owing to permissive upbringing by two women. In *El niño perdido*'s iconic scene, Valdés and his companion (Marcelo Chávez) can't pay a bill at a chic restaurant and, it being after 7 p.m., Tin Tán naïvely begins to perform to pay for supper and croons a nonsensical English song, "Chickory Chick" by Del Webb. Guitarist companion Chávez castigates him and says that the English words make no sense and reproaches Tin Tán for not knowing the meaning. Undeterred, Tin Tán aggressively asserts he certainly does—only to warble a nonsensical Spanish riff beginning "Te la canto. Me canso ganso dijo un zancudo" (I'll sing it—I'm tired goose said a mosquito).[1]

The phrase "me canso ganso" became a 1950s popular catch phrase roughly translatable as "Hey, don't worry—I've got it covered" or "Hey, trust me, I can do this." During the first one hundred days of the new Morena sexenio, Tin Tán's phrase became a viral expression when President Andrés Manuel López Obrador routinely repeated it in policy pronouncements and offered other assurances that the Fourth Transformation would really happen. Me canso ganso soon went viral via social media and was even commodified by fashionistas (*Indigo* 2019).[2]

López Obrador, who often uses colloquial phrases, relied on that specific Tin Tán catchphrase several times whenever he made making keystone promises (*El País Verne* 2018; R. Lara 2019). It was first used during a campaign promise to construct a tourist train around the Riviera Maya, and he emphatically inserted it the inaugural address when he spoke of economic development along Mexico's Pacific Coast. He continued to use it, and two months later he specifically incorporated it as an oath of affirmation to end corruption when he spoke in front of thousands in his native state.

> "I'm not going to destroy the name of Tabasco, *we are going to end corruption and privilege—impunity is going to end—me canso ganso*," affirmed the president of Mexico, Andrés Manuel López Obrador, during the initiation of the program Sembrando Vida in the community C-27 of Cárdenas, Tabasco.
>
> In an event attended by more than 10,000, the man from nearby Mascupana affirmed: "now we have begun—now is the time to be held accountable. Those on the top grew accustomed to not paying taxes and having money returned—that is over [*se acabó*]." (Pérez Magaña 2019, emphasis added)[3]

Chapter 6 made reference to Gabriel García Márquez's observation that magical realism runs through the streets of Mexico, and AMLO's use of that Tin Tán catchphrase typifies how easily fable and reality can still blend seamlessly with everyday occurrences and appear in unexpected ways—even in politics. The phrase "me canso ganso" quickly became a key metaphor symbolizing the carne y hueso of that pivotal moment of change in Mexico.[4]

López Obrador remained immensely popular in the postelectoral period and throughout the first three years of his sexenio. Polling data do show that Mexicans had confidence in him and most people continued to believe he was speaking honestly whenever he made statements such as "Trust me, I've got this under control."[5] In spite of AMLO's promising words, there was no end to insecurity following the December 2018 inauguration; violence continued in several states and homicides climbed to record-setting levels throughout the first three years of his sexenio; as reported in chapter 5, the year 2019 saw the highest level of homicide ever reported in any year of the modern era and 2020 fell just short of matching that record level of violence.[6] And new outbreaks of violence had spread to states that had not previously been hotspots during the Peña Nieto presidency: to cite one example, the Morena administration efforts to stop illegal siphoning of gasoline from Pemex pipelines created nationwide shortages and triggered a violent spike in violence in Guanajuato State when huachicoleros from the Cártel de Santa Rosa de Lima battled with El Mencho Oseguera Cervantes and the Cártel de Jalisco Nueva Generación over those Pemex pipelines (Dávila and Espinoza 2019). Even more tragically, mob panic sparked a horrific tragedy in Tlahuelilpan, Hidalgo, and eighty-five people burned to death when a pipeline ruptured during one misguided attempt to steal gasoline from the Pemex lines.

Although the Morena government moved quickly to create a new National Guard to deal with the violence, it also entrusted the command of the battle against cartels and violence to army generals and marine admirals whose predecessors had been directly linked to massacres and human rights abuses during the Peña Nieto and Calderón Hinojosa sexenios—and who were leaders in a military that had been known to work directly with drug cartels in the past (O'Day 2001). In the face of vociferous criticism and negative press about his continued reliance on military personnel, AMLO waved aside his critics and confidently assured the country that things would be different because he *personally* was not a corrupt politician and that the people had his personal guarantee that abuses would never happen again.

President Andrés Manuel López Obrador guaranteed that the National Guard will not violate human rights in security matters and there will be a change of direction in the work of the Armed Forces so that "they will assist us with their professionalism and their honesty to confront insecurity and violence without violating human rights. We are going to guarantee at the same time security and life." . . .

"When the Mexican army has not acted in a correct manner, when it has not followed rules, it was because of orders from a civil authority, especially in that infamous and sad time of the repression of students in 1968. It was then—and something that we must remember—an order given directly by the President of the Republic (Gustavo Díaz Ordaz) and executed by the Presidential Secret Service—an elite body directly linked to the Presidency and which owed its allegiance to the government." (Muñoz, Urrutia, and Olivares Alonso 2019)[7]

Prospects for Peace

There is absolutely no question that López Obrador had inherited a massive security deficit when he assumed office in December 2018. During a visit to Mexico three months into the new sexenio, the UN High Commissioner for Human Rights, Michelle Bachelet, observed that the Morena government had been handed control of a country plagued by extreme violence, and she voiced her personal astonishment at seeing a staggering number of violent deaths that were more typically recorded in countries at war—more than 284,000 homicides since 2006. She also expressed her horror upon learning about other statistics that measured violence's impact on society and recorded the degree to which human rights were violated.

> There was a surprise that I did not expect to see. Undoubtedly, I knew about the case of Ayotzinapa. But not about the 40,000 disappeared and 26,000 unidentified human remains or the nearly 10 women murdered each day.... I certainly knew about the violence—that I knew very well—but I did not have any idea about the dimension of those large number of cases indicating the violation of human rights. (qtd. in *Aristegui Noticias* 2019)[8]

The magnitude of that insecurity deficit was also cataloged in the World Peace Index Mexico Report for 2019 released shortly after AMLO's first one hundred days in office.

> Peace in Mexico declined by 4.9 percent in 2018, with ten states improving in peacefulness, while 22 states deteriorated. The major driver behind the deterioration was an upsurge in the homicide rate, which increased by 14 percent. Mexico's 2018 homicide rate reached historically high levels, at 27 deaths per 100,000 people, or over 34,000 victims. This level of violence surpasses the prior peak of 2011. The rise in the homicide rate in 2018 was accompanied by a substantial increase in the rate of gun violence, which rose by 16 percent, with 24 of the 32 states reporting escalating rates of firearms crimes.
>
> The main finding of this year's report is that government is underinvested in the justice system, given the high level of violence. Currently, government spending on police and the justice system is just half of the average for other members of the Organisation for Economic Co-operation and Development

(OECD), as a percentage of gross domestic product (GDP). And yet, only seven percent of crimes resulted in a criminal investigation in 2017 and less than three percent resulted in a conviction, leaving an impunity rate of 97 percent. (Institute for Economics and Peace 2019)

Such statistics and objective evidence are depressing, but Mexico's people nevertheless remained hopeful in spite of the negative evidence, and there were also many people in high places who remained confident that AMLO would ultimately be successful and restore security. For instance, the UN High Commissioner for Human Rights expressed confidence that Mexico is fully aware that it is a crucial moment and that it was prepared to act.

It is a moment of transformation and opportunity that has opened up since the new government has arrived in power. President López Obrador has expressed his willingness to implement a change of paradigm—one that places human rights at the center. I not only recognize this determination, but I show my willingness and that of my Mexico Office to support it. (qtd. in *Aristegui Noticias* 2019)[9]

But realistically, the challenges that AMLO and Mexico faced are enormous, and the fact is that those problems will never be solved by the repetitive restatement of hopeful promises and slogans. Unless AMLO's messages of optimism and hope are eventually accompanied by a specific plan of action, his continued use of phrases like "me canso ganso" will inevitably become just a sad and tragic symbol of ineptitude and amateurishness instead of a source of inspiration. This is a critical point in Mexican history and in the battle against cartels, and the integrative and symbolic power of words and rhetoric are *not* enough to end the power of criminal organizations, end violence, or break the hold that the covert netherworld has on Mexico. A multidimensional plan of action must be put in place and all of Mexico's security institutions must be strenghtened as soon as possible. And, most importantly, the enforcement of law can not be entrusted to the military alone. *All* of Mexico's institutions must contribute to the massive rebuilding that is necessary, especially those that will eradicate inequality and poverty, educate its citizens, and provide for the social welfare of all. Words matter, but ultimately they are no match for guns.

Framework and Transformations?

Real change will require at least a full generation to bring about, and it must organically emerge from the empowerment and rebuilding of all of Mexico's institutions.[10] Mexico's broken social fabric will not be repaired in another way, and certainly will not be permanently enacted by repeating promises.[11] In spite of broad and rhetorical assertions from AMLO and Morena that they remain committed to the task of restoring security and eliminating violence, there is no concrete evidence in 2021 that they have come forward with a realistic agenda and proposed a rational framework to end the violence and break the power of the cartels and destroy their corruptive influence.

Immediately after Morena won the election and during the lead-up to the December inauguration, AMLO and his advisors circulated a framework of action and announced a team of competent and qualified security advisors that would be appointed to implement it. López Obrador announced that he would create a central administrative structure, the Secretariat of Public Security and Citizen Safety, and it would be assigned the task of integrating the army, the marines, and the federal police, and establishing a new National Guard under one command that would report directly to him: "The president will be the commander in chief of the armed forces and I will not delegate responsibility for this conspicuous issue" (Lafuente 2018). The appointees to that security oversight committee were well qualified and familiar with Mexico's security deficit: Alfonso Durazo Montaño was appointed civilian chairman, and he would be advised by a team that included Alejandro Gertz Manero, Loreta Ortiz Ahlf, and Manuel Mondragón y Kalb; a secretary of national defense, Luis Crescencio Sandoval; and a secretary of the navy, José Rafael Ojeda Durán (Molina 2018). The four civilians in the security team (Durazo, Gertz, Ortiz, Mondragón y Kalb) had previously worked with López Obrador during his term as Mexico City mayor, where they had overseen several positive changes in policing that both addressed social issues and protected human rights; under their direction, Mexico City was relatively untouched by the violence that had afflicted the rest of the country during the two previous presidential sexenios.

In the final days of November, López Obrador's transition team also released a broad philosophical statement titled "Plan Nacional de Paz y Seguridad 2018–2024" that specifically identified eight mandates or framework principles that would guide security measures in the new sexenio: (1) erad-

icate corruption and reactivate the justice system; (2) guarantee of employment, education, health, and well-being; (3) full respect and promotion of
human rights; (4) a regeneration of societal ethics; (5) reformulate the battle
against drugs; (6) initiate the construction of peace; (7) recovery and dignity
of prisons; and (8) public security, national security, and peace (President
Elect Transition Team 2018).[12] The authors (primarily Durazo Montaño)
deliberately made it much more sweeping in scope and language than found
in the security plans of previous administrations, explaining, "What we are
announcing is a paradigm of security that is radically different than those
that have guided the previous presidential terms."[13]

There is absolutely no doubt that this National Plan for Peace and Security
was radically different in tone from the security plans of previous administrations, especially in its emphasis on *broad principles* rather than delineating a long list of desired goals and targeted actions and even the date for
completing those goals. In many ways, the ideals expressed in this Morena
document could replace the introductory chapter of a modern criminological textbook that is used to teach students about the root causes of crime. In
contrast, Calderón issued several statements addressing security, including
one named Operation Cleanup (Operación Limpieza) and another called We
Are All Juárez (Todos Somos Juárez), which listed specific objectives (large
and small) and borrowed heavily from the law-and-order perspective and
war-on-drugs mentality fostered in Latin America and the world by the U.S.
administrations through its old BNDD and its successor DEA (see Gobierno
Federal de México 2010)

The majority of framework statements are reassertions of AMLO's visionary themes of a Fourth Transformation and his hope to create a new moral
constitution. The eighth principle specifically called for the creation of a new
national guard that would assume all national responsibility for reducing
violence and instituting crime prevention. Mexico's Morena legislators in
fact made it a priority, and Mexico's organic law was modified to allow the
creation of that new police force under the direction of military personnel.[14]
The Guardia Nacional was formally established in February 2019. On the one
hand, it was immediately besieged by critics as potentially dangerous and
counterproductive to AMLO's originally stated goal and promise to protect
human rights (number 3 priority), even as he offered many assurances that
he would directly oversee its mandate and that there was a five-year window
to review its effectiveness (Semple and Villegas 2019). On the other hand,

the newly created National Guard also had many prominent defenders who argued that violence must be *immediately* addressed to reverse the cycle of bloodshed that turned Mexico into a giant national graveyard, but the voices of concern remained loud and prominent (Bojorquez 2018b; Luengo-Cabrera 2018; Meyer 2018; Ravelo 2018; Ríos 2018; Ríos and Wood 2018; Rodriguéz García 2019; Rosagel 2018; Sicairos 2018).

Will AMLO's long-term framework to address security and the creation of the new police force be enough? No definitive answer is offered here in the final pages and paragraphs of this book! Only time will tell, but the indications from the first three years of AMLO's sexenio are not encouraging.[15]

This book has described the reality of Mexico today and hopefully has provided insight to anyone seeking an understanding about how organized crime and criminal organizations have become deeply engrained in the very fabric of Mexico. The links of corruption must be shattered, and cultures and subcultures of criminality must be disrupted and redirected into positive channels of action. The ongoing horrific violence demands immediate attention, but that is also a specific criminogenic factor that can be addressed with proven policies and strategies that have been implemented in other countries—but always through a comprehensive plan of criminal justice that involves a holistic model of reform of policing, courts, and prisons. Above all, the eradication of violence must never be accomplished using tools or measures that undermine long-term solutions that attack the *root* causes that allowed violence to run rampant over the first two decades of this new millennium. Eliminating violence must be accomplished without ever losing sight of Mexico's deep, entangled roots of narco history, the social context that supports it, and the internal and external conditions that created the perfect storm allowing it to thrive for five decades. Above all, it must recognize that violence and chaos have been the product of a covert netherworld that must be destroyed.

Crime and violence statistics rarely reflect the social consequences, and almost never provide a meaningful picture of how killings and forced disappearances affect children and destroy innocence, but Mexican authors such as the late Javier Valdez Cárdenas have tragically described in detail how narco cultures and narco wars affect children and rip apart the social fabric to the degree that the only hope or option for some children is to work for cartels and brutal gangs (Valdez Cárdenas 2011, 2012, 2015, 2016).

Mexico has a rich tradition of memorable fables and myths about innocent children being harmed and lost to tragedy, but it also includes many fables about how innocence brought about change and eventually produced a transformation. Spanish missionaries taught Mexico's Indians about the never-ending battle between good and evil by using morality plays based on medieval classics such as *The Castle of Perseverance* or *El niño perdido*. Even the now classic Disney movie *Coco* from 2017 is an epic story of redemption brought about by an innocent and earnest child. Those themes of innocence and tragedy and salvation have endured and are reflected in cultural tropes such as the weeping woman, "La Llorona," and the legend of "La Calle del Niño Perdida" (Cisneros 2018), and are reflected in music such as the Banda Recodo classic version of "Niño perdido," whose lyrics lament, "I am just a lost child, there is no one else, they say that after an injury there is no going back, let yourself go, let yourself go."[16]

Mexico has suffered a grave harm, and there is no going back. It will bequeath that tragedy to future generations unless it breaks the cycle. Its people have overwhelmingly decided to place their trust in a leader who reassures them that all will be fine, and their children will inherit a better Mexico. "Me canso ganso," their president says, and they follow him in the dance.

But where will that dance end? In a transformed Mexico, or in the same lost and sad place?

The first three years of the AMLO era are ending as these words are being written, and the preliminary conclusion is that Mexico is tragically still a lost and sad place.[17] The journalist Ricardo Ravelo has covered cartels and crime in Mexico for thirty years, and his column from January 2021 appeared just as I was drafting this chapter. His assessment is disheartening: crime and its major manifestation—narco traffic—have been unstoppable; the majority of municipal police departments in Mexico have been co-opted by criminal groups; a wide swath of the country is now threatened by two large criminal syndicates and heavily armed regional groups that continue to murder, kidnap, and demand the right of passage with impunity; and no authority, federal or local, has been able to bring an end to those disturbing trends (Raziel and Montalvo 2020).

Two criminal syndicates remain powerful and dangerous in 2021 and a lesser one is still a major threat—the Sinaloa Cartel; the Cártel de Jalisco Nueva Generación; and the Cartel of the Northeast (Noreste), which is less organized than the first two and made up of former members of the Gulf Cartel and Los Zetas. Those three cartels have been relatively untouched, especially Sinaloa and the CJNG: the new Guardia Nacional created by AMLO and Morena has had almost no success in reigning in their power, and none of their capos or jefes have been arrested or killed. In the spring of 2021, there were at least seventeen other dangerous criminal groups operating as subordinate gangs in the service of those big three. Twenty of the twenty-seven Mexican states that still had a major cartel presence continued to see dramatic increases in the level of homicide and violence, with the most seriously impacted being Guanajuato, Michoacán, Guerrero, Estado de México, Sinaloa, Sonora, Quintana Roo, and Baja California. But violence is not the only indicator of the persistent cartel reach and power within the country. The cartels and gangs have diversified and are now directly active in more than *twenty distinct criminal activities*—for example, the theft and resale of oil and gas from Pemex pipelines that run across the center of the country from Tampico to Guanajuato.

During the first three years of the Morena government, Mexican cartels have also expanded their transnational reach to Argentina, Uruguay, Brazil, Chile, Costa Rica, Guatemala, Spain, Italy, the UK, Asia, Africa, and arguably into the USA. In spite of undeniable evidence of that global reach, the Mexican government has not taken major strides to cooperate with other countries or the United Nations to address the issue of organized crime. In fact, in the aftermath of the General Salvador Cienfuegos Zepeda incident (detailed in chapter 3), the Mexican government passed a law curbing the operations of foreign security agents (de Córdoba and Pérez 2020).

Chapter 6 described violence in Mexico and attributed almost all of that violence to the impact of four distinct wars. The killing and bloodshed in 2019 and 2020 are not caused by wars, but have climbed because of different reasons. The Mexican army and marines are evidently not at war with cartels, in keeping with AMLO's abrazos no balazos strategy; they reported fewer recorded skirmishes and confrontations, and furthermore the dominant cartels (Sinaloa, CJNG, Noreste) have seemingly been operating under a new understanding among their jefes—possibly even a codified Pax Narca—and they have been involved in major armed battles among themselves. But in spite of those changes, homicidios dolosos still reached record levels. What explains that continuing violence if there are no longer cartel wars? I cannot say with certainty, but what does seem to be uniquely different is that the larger cartels—specifically Sinaloa and the CJNG—have increasingly and aggressively targeted and suppressed and attacked regional gangs in order to force them under their umbrella, to eliminate competitors or simply take over the criminal enterprises that those gangs had developed. Perhaps the most obvious example is illustrated by events in Guanajuato State, where the Cártel de Jalisco Nueva Generación targeted the regional Cartel Santa Rosa de Lima, which had been involved in the black market oil and gas theft known as huachicolero (Alvarado 2019; Calderón et al. 2019; Dávila and Espinoza 2019). Similar patterns of low-grade warfare and attacks, where a much larger group targets a smaller group, have increasingly disrupted Mexico City and Mexico State and caused mayhem and chaos when the CJNG exerted its power.

What is most disturbing at the halfway point of the Fourth Transformation is that the covert netherworld remains entrenched and immutable. A mid-sexenio election took place on June 6, 2021, and as had happened regularly over the years, narco traffickers and their partners in the covert netherworld participated in la narcopolítica to back some candidates, financed campaigns with laundered money, pressured hundreds of administrative *grasshoppers*, and distributed funds to eager party officials, state and municipal police who had been recruited to work with them. However, in 2021, the cartels, especially the Sinaloa Cartel and the CJNG, overtly pushed beyond the traditional corruptive electoral routines, and unleashed what Eduardo Guerrero Gutiérrez (2021) described as a new level of direct electoral interference. It is clear that 2021 remained an election cycle where the bullet component of the *plata o plomo* equation played an oversize role in the heated competition where tens of thousands of candidates challenged for fifteen gubernatorial elections and the more than twenty-one thousand posts at play at federal, municipal, and state levels (Nacár 2021); Noria Research reports that many as one hundred candidates were murdered in the run-up to that midterm election while scores of other candidates were threatened, kidnapped, or went into hiding (Ernst 2021; Martínez Trujillo and Fajardo Turner 2021; Velasco 2021).[18] But *direct* violence was not the most disturbing feature of that electoral cycle, and several journalists reported that there was a significant increase in overt and organized *suppression* of voting by cartel operatives; the beneficiary was almost uniformly AMLO's Morena and its leftist candidates, and the targets of suppression were the right-leaning PRI-PAN-PRD opposition.

Guerrero Gutiérrez (2021) described how the Cártel de Sinaloa intervened in new ways to guarantee that victory for Morena even though polling had led most pundits to predict that there would be a competitive race between Morena and candidates representing the PRI-PAN-PRD coalition in Sinaloa. But instead of the anticipated narrow finish, when the final votes were tabulated, Morena's candidate for governor, Rubén Rocha Moya, won decisively by more than twenty-five percentage points and his fellow Morena candidates won in all seven electoral districts of the state and in seventeen out of its eighteen municipalities. Before 2021, Sinaloa had *never* elected a leftist governor and it had consistently remained a stronghold of either the PRI or PAN or coalitions of the two parties. The outcome changed dramatically because the Cártel de Sinaloa, and in particular the faction linked to Los Chapitos, intervened directly in an overt display of strength to squash any chance that the PRI-PAN-PRD coalition would win. In a coordinated operation that was reminiscent of El Culiacanazo in October, several PRI party leaders were approached by cartel operatives and warned against mobilizing party activists on election day or engaging in any of the usual electoral manipulations. And to guarantee that they remained on the sidelines, some of the party directors were kidnapped and sequestered a few days before June 6 and held in locations where they were unable to coordinate party workers who would normally engage in such practices such as intimidating voters at the voting station, stuffing ballots, or vote buying.[19]

Sinaloa is just one state—and unique in many ways because of its history as the birthplace of narco trafficking—but the influence of the covert netherworld and la narcopolítica has extended far beyond its borders. In the 2021 election, there is strong evidence that organized crime was directly active in influencing the elections in other states like Sonora, Guerrero, Jalisco, Nuevo León, Guanajuato, San Luis Potosí, and Michoacán—especially at the municipal level (Guerrero Gutiérrez 2021).

I wrote in chapter 3 that the nation was joyful on the day that Andrés Manuel López Obrador became president and that few celebrants remembered Octavio Paz's cautionary words about the inevitable outcome of all previous transformations in Mexican history. He had written that the winners of all transformations were those who were already winners in the old system, and that those who were at the apex *always* found a way to remain there after transformations (Paz 1970, 1978). Power remains permanently attached to those who already have it, even as it takes new forms and expresses itself in alternate ways. The pain of previous transformations rarely affected the elite and was exclusively felt by "the Other"—and the cost of any change was paid with their blood. A powerful covert netherworld emerged after Paz wrote his cautionary words a half century ago, and those new arrangements allowed criminal and clandestine actors to take their place inside the halls of power and alongside Mexico's traditional elite. If Paz was right, and if the lessons of previous transformations continue to be true, it seems inevitable that those individuals in the covert netherworld—the crime bosses, narco traffickers, politicians, and entrepreneurs operating beyond the bounds of civil society (McCoy 2018, 2)—will remain the winners and that "the Other" will continue to pay the cost. And the 2021 midterm elections seem to be demonstrating that things have not changed at all and that the netherworld is still in charge.

Increasingly, it is more and more apparent that the Fourth Transformation is leading Mexico further down a road to perdition, and sadly the global pandemic makes that outcome even more predictable. In the absence of a comprehensive security plan and a commitment to destroy the covert netherworld, it is inevitable.

ACKNOWLEDGMENTS

It is impossible to personally thank everyone who has influenced me while writing this book. I apologize in advance to those I have not mentioned by name and hope that they recognize that I am deeply grateful for their encouragement and support. Thank you to everyone who helped me refine my ideas and provided feedback for those many preliminary drafts.

Like many in my generation, my career trajectory was more often the outcome of accidental choices rather than a preordained journey guided by rational choice and planning. And this is especially true with respect to my interest in Mexico and twenty-five-year-long fascination with narco trafficking and drug cartels. As an undergraduate student, naïve idealism brought me to the Sierra Huasteca of Mexico, where I learned rudimentary Spanish and developed a deep respect and admiration for its people as a volunteer in a group called the Conference on Interamerican Student Projects (CIASP). That experience also brought me into contact with many whose ideas and philosophy influenced me and guided me throughout the rest of my life, and in particular Ivan Illich at his CIDOC center located in Cuernavaca, Mexico. Marriage and family brought me to the University of Arizona, where I came to appreciate the beauty of the desert borderlands and began to understand the deep connections border cities had with Mexico. And much later, a chance encounter led to my appointment as a visiting professor in Culiacán, Sinaloa, and the opportunity to learn much more about the birthplace of narco traffic over a fourteen-year stretch.

There are a few whose support and help must be specifically acknowledged. I am grateful for the financial and academic support that was provided by University of Alberta in Edmonton, Canada. The collegiality at the U of A resulted in many friendships and allowed me to work alongside knowledgeable and supportive colleagues in the Department of Sociology and other academic disciplines in the Faculty of Arts. My fellow academics and all of the non-academic staff were unflinchingly supportive and encouraging over the three decades I was privileged to work in Alberta as a professor and teach more than fifteen thousand students in my classes. Everyone's kindness, warmth, and generosity at the University of Alberta belies a common perception that universities are filled with many people who specialize in petty quarrels. I am especially thankful to my fellow criminologists who taught me a great deal about all matters of crime and justice. And the simple fact is that this book would never have had a beginning without the financial support provided by a sabbatical year that allowed me to travel to Mexico City and spend my time interacting with the scholars at El Colegio de México.

I arrived in Mexico City in 1996, post-NAFTA, during the waning years of PRI hegemony, and I lived there for almost a year while a shadowy Mexican criminal Federation began to emerge as the dominant power in transnational crime and drug exportation. Dr. Jorge Padua Nesrala, a University of Alberta graduate and COLMEX sociologist, arranged for me to have full access to the wonderful resources at El Colegio de México and helped me navigate my way around that sprawling, chaotic, and amazing metropolis of Mexico City. He was a gracious guide and host, my personal Spanish teacher, my protector, and a wonderful facilitator in introducing me to the many incredible scholars working at El Colegio. Mexico City was also where I first met my friend Dr. Julian Castro Rea, who taught me so much about the intricacies and cynical intrigues of Mexican politics; Julian was also personally responsible for arranging my appointment as a visiting professor to the Autonomous University of Sinaloa in Culiacán in 1998. Julian simply said, "I've arranged with my colleagues for you to work as a professor at a new program in American and Canadian Studies that will begin in Sinaloa next year." There was no option of refusal. "Why should I do that? I don't know anything about Sinaloa," I said. He answered, "Don't worry, you will like it and they will welcome you with warmth and gratitude." Truer words were never said!

That's how my journey deep into the world of Sinaloa and the cradle of narco traffic began in 1998. I was invited to offer one of the first seminars in a new program that Dr. Guillermo Ibarra Escobar and Dr. Ana Luz Ruelas Monjardin had established at the Autonomous University of Sinaloa in Culiacán. Their innovative program accepted its first cohort in 1998 and scheduled a number of creative seminars for a master's program that would be offered by an international team of professors from Canada, the United States, and Mexico. That original program soon expanded and emerged as a full-blown Faculty of International Studies and Public (FEIyPP), where more than seventy graduate students took seminars with me over a fourteen-year period. I am very proud that those students and the faculty of FEIyPP consider me to be one of the founding members of their faculty. Most importantly, the professors, non-academic staff, and students of la UAS-FEIyPP became my supporters and close friends. I have remained in touch with dozens of them over the years. I would like to name them all, but will acknowledge only one by name—Perla Lizet Vega Medina, who was tragically murdered and is one of the hundreds of victims of femicide. The honest truth is that every one of the graduate students I met at la UAS contributed to this book through their feedback, and I am forever grateful for their lessons and for their continuing friendship.

I met many wonderful Sinaloanses who helped me during my time in Culiacán and Sinaloa, but I want to especially acknowledge sociologist Dr. Jorge de la Herrán Garcia and Dr. Beatriz Yasuko Arita, who went out of their way to chauffer me around Culiacán and teach me a great deal about the sierra; they also made certain that I experienced the wonders of fantastic Culichi and Sinaloense cuisine. I also acknowledge that they always looked out for my safety and made certain I never put myself unknowingly in danger; I frequently received phone calls from them during my sojourns warning when things had heated up on the streets.

Much of the material in this book saw first light of day in senior undergraduate seminars that I was privileged to teach in the Department of Sociology and Anthropology at the University of Guelph between 2006 and 2017. It was a wonderful experience to be allowed to offer small classes and interact with the enthusiastic and bright students who served as sounding board and intellectual critics for the material that eventually appeared in these pages. Their curiosity and enthusiasm left me with much hope that our future is in good hands.

I also want to acknowledge the support and encouragement of the late George Grayson of William and Mary College. George encouraged me to write this particular book, and I deeply regret his untimely passing before we could complete another book that we had begun to write together. George and I disagreed on many things, especially politics, but he was a wonderful colleague and possessed of remarkable knowledge about Mexico and its political intrigue.

The editors and team at the University of Arizona Press are largely responsible for forging this book into something that is much better than the original manuscript I first sent to them for review. I would like to specifically acknowledge Kristen Buckles, because her careful vetting of my original manuscript pushed it in a direction that I had originally resisted. Without a doubt, the copyediting of Sheila McMahon has greatly improved the final product and helped me eliminate many mistakes and omissions. Many academics will complain about the vagaries of the formal review process, but I will not join their ranks. The comments and the feedback that I received from anonymous reviewers made this book much better and assured that I have stayed on point and focused on important issues. I am grateful for the help and support from everyone else who contributed to the production of this book at the University of Arizona Press. I am proud to have worked with them and appreciate their hard work and professionalism and thank them for bringing this book to completion.

NOTES

Introduction

1. The two Spanish-language authors are from Culiacán. Luis Astorga earned a PhD at the Sorbonne and wrote authoritative books and articles about drugs and cartels. I have cited his work extensively in the chapters that follow, and I learned much from him over the years. Leonides Alfaro is a mainstay and key figure in the thriving arts community in Culiacán, and his short novel was eventually recognized as a classic description of narco-culture and widely reprinted and eventually honored with a distinguished award in Spain. Charles Bowden is also cited extensively in the chapters that follow.

2. "Mientras el obispado local estaba más interesado en prohibir el uso de vestidos escotados y el mambo. Sinaloa es descrito como 'un estado muy rico, muy agricultor y, con pena hay que expresarlo, tierra donde el pistolero y su dama, la goma, es la pareja que anda del brazo y por la calle.' Ser sinaloense es casi sinónimo de ser gomero, aunque no necesariamente en el sentido estigmático: por ejemplo, una nota beisbolística señala que los gomeros pierden su tercera serie al hilo al frente al equipo del Hermosillo. Se dice que la colonia Tierra Blanca 'es el centro de operaciones de coyotes y gomeros,' que es un 'nido de gomeros' donde reinan 'el vicio y el desenfreno' y 'abundan los armados,' que es el 'refugio de más de un gomero,' que es un 'paraiso del vicio.'"

3. During my yearlong sabbatical in Mexico City, my friend and mentor Julian Castro Rea recommended that I pay attention to columnists writing in weekly magazine *Proceso* and Mexican dailies like *La Jornada* and *Reforma* to learn about corruption in Mexican politics and the pervasive links to crime. The journalists writing for those magazines and papers regularly published articles about corruption and narco Mexico, but very few are known in the English-

language world except in rare translations. Also, I began to pay attention to corridos and narcocorridos from groups like Los Tigres del Norte or Los Tucanes, who were explicitly blunt about the power of the narco subculture that had infiltrated the highest reaches of respectable politics, culture, and the economy. English speakers are generally not familiar with the enormous popularity and influence of groups like Los Tigres del Norte, and even those who have heard of them are unlikely aware that their songs speak to the truth and reveal the degree to which narco-culture has extended into the highest levels of power.

4. Obviously, the United States is not the only source of drug-use data. In fact, there are many international sources that academics consider reliable and valid measures of drug addiction and for monitoring the transactions of transnational crime. Specifically, the United Nations Office on Drug Control (UNODC) releases annual reports that are mandatory reading for anyone monitoring transnational drug crime (United Nations 2020). My point is not that the DEA and the U.S. DOJ have the "best reports" but that those DEA reports have had an undue influence in shaping public and even academic views of organized crime and drug cartels in the Americas.

5. In 2020 there were approximately fifty DEA agents still assigned to the Mexican office.

6. The use of surveillance technology is described in much more detail in two recent books: *El Jefe: The Stalking of Chapo Guzmán* (Feuer 2020) and *Hunting El Chapo: Taking Down the World's Most Wanted Drug Lord* (Hogan and Century 2019). Alan Feuer's book is highly recommended; it describes how electronic surveillance was instrumental in locating and extraditing El Chapo Guzmán to Brooklyn, New York. It also describes the complexity and difficulty of using surveillance on a group that was skilled at evading electronic monitoring. Before 2012, international law made it almost impossible to access electronic surveillance, but that problem was removed when Research in Motion and Blackberry servers were finally relocated to Texas.

7. The case of Osiel Cárdenas Guillén is an excellent example. His court records are sealed (McKinley 2010).

8. For example, programs included Operation Intercept, Operation Stopgap, and two operations code-named Condor. For a general overview, see Drug Policy Alliance n.d. Alternatively, for detailed descriptions, see Grayson 2010, 2014.

9. See Foreign Narcotics Kingpin Designation Act. Pub. L. HR 3164 IH, 113 Stat. 1626, 21 USC 1901 Title VIII, Public Law 106–120 (1999).

10. The CIA has also been implicated in participating directly *or* being complicit in the kidnapping and torture of Camarena. This is elaborated in chapters 4 and 6.

11. More than 80 percent of the newly formed Guardia Nacional has a military background as opposed to a policing background.

12. In 1996 I began to routinely collect citations and electronic copies of documents. The entries were stored in an EndNote archive that I have maintained

since. At the time of writing, there are more than sixteen thousand entries in those personal archives stored in a personal EndNote library.

13. The ASC was my formal academic reference point during an academic career as sociologist and criminological researcher. I attended and participated in most annual meetings over my professional career. I regularly presented papers at those meetings, including three that specifically addressed narco-crime issues in Mexico that are elaborated in this book (Creechan 1997, 1999, 2005, 2014).

14. Counting by retricting to "conference session" underestimates how many research reports are actually presented at the annual meeting. Some sessions typically have three to six unique papers presented.

15. The specific number of homicides refers to the years 2007 to 2017, my reference period for analysis of the ASC program. In several places in this book, there are different and seemingly contradictory counts for the homicide level in Mexico. This is because there are varied ways to count homicide and available statistics are notably unreliable. However, I have taken care to identify the source of all data when they are used throughout this book, and I have often explained the context for interpreting that data.

In spite of the name the *American* Society of Criminology, it is the largest global association of academic criminologists. Mexico is poorly represented for many reasons, but there are hundreds of international scholars who belong to this academic association. In 2007 one presentation focused on police in Michoacán State. In 2008 Mexico was mentioned in one paper analyzing domestic violence. In 2009 one session out of more than six hundred on the program specifically focused on Mexican gangs and border violence—and those gangs were based in the United States rather than in Mexico. In 2010 there was no reference to cartels, but there was one academic session describing violence along the border on the American side. In 2011 the first specific reference to "cartel" was made in a session examining organized crime in Mexico. The 2012 ASC meetings were in Chicago and perhaps unsurprisingly scheduled twenty-three sessions on organized crime but only one specifically focused on cartels: that was in reference to the use of Twitter to track hot spots and identify danger in northeast Mexico. During 2013, 2014, and 2015, there were no sessions making any reference to "cartel," but there were two distinct sessions focusing on fear of organized crime in Mexico in 2015. In 2016 there was a specific roundtable where the discussion was Mexico as a "failed state," and in 2017 one session described how tunnels were used to smuggle drugs at the border. To review, criminologists and sociologists had been exposed to information about Mexican crime in only ten academic sessions of the more than six thousand sessions presented at the annual meeting of academic criminologists over a ten-year period.

16. Colombian cartels are a different matter; there are a few books recognized as legitimate inside accounts. The best example is *El cartel de los sapos* (López López 2008).

17. It is my opinion that the history of narco Mexico cannot be understood with-
     out reference to the research and investigations of Luis Astorga. As a young
     scholar, his Spanish-language publications identified him as "Luis Astorga." In
     later years, he wrote in both English and Spanish under his full name, "Luis
     Alejandro Astorga Almanza." References to him will use the name that he used
     on a specific publication—that is, either Astorga or Astorga Almanza.

18. The National Institute of Mental Health project MH22350, "Community Toler-
     ance and Measures of Delinquency," was directed by lead researcher Dr. May-
     nard Erickson of the University of Arizona, and later co-directed by his col-
     leagues Dr. Jack Gibbs and Dr. Gary Jensen. My research assistantship was an
     assignment to this project alongside Dr. Grant Stitt and Dr. Karen Wilkinson.
     The three of us served as the senior researchers over three academic years
     during which we collected data and supervised ongoing research in Southern
     Arizona and along the border region.

Chapter 1

1. Epigraph: "Me, I like corridos / Because they're about things important to us.
    / And yes, I also like them because / They are songs rooted in truth." Lyrics by
    Teodoro Bello et al. 1997.

2. Chapter 1 of Turner's work (first serialized beginning in 1909) is titled "Los
    esclavos de Yucatán."

3. The term *científico* describes the bureaucratic class and the educated elite com-
    mitted to the economic ideas of liberal philosophy and modernization during
    the Porfiriato, especially its final years. Although there are key differences, the
    term parallels the modern idea of technocrat. Carlos Salinas de Gortari is argu-
    ably the Mexican president who was most committed to a neoliberal model,
    and his bureaucracies and advisors came to be disparagingly referred to as tech-
    nocrats who were concerned only about economic advance.

4. Demographers struggle with calculating the actual toll of the Mexican Revo-
    lution. Their estimates of total losses range from 1.9 to 3.5 million casualties
    (McCaa 2003).

5. Murder has always been tragically high in Mexico compared to Canada and
    the USA, but not murderous to the degree that most people think. And there
    is strong empirical evidence that the long-term homicide trend had followed
    the same long-term downward trend for violence in countries. The web portal
    Our World in Data (https://ourworldindata.org) includes a graphical repre-
    sentation of the homicide trend in Mexico between 1955 and 2010 that clearly
    demonstrates a steady downward decline that came to a halt in 2004 (Global
    Change Data Lab n.d.). Additional evidence for the long-term decline was been
    provided by Pablo Policzer (2019), who used judicial statistics going back to
    the late nineteenth century: he reported that the Ciudad de México (CDMX,
    Mexico City) had an average rate of 46 homicides per 100,000 between 1885

and 1871; 31 per 100,000 in 1909; a rate of 37 per 100,000 in 1930; and then it consistently declined until hitting a low of about 9 per 100,000 in 2004.

6. The total number of homicidios dolosos recorded by the Secretariado Ejecutivo del Sistema Nacional de Seguridad Pública (SESNSP) between 2001 and 2020 is 404,983. The yearly totals are available online from its website. This book's references include two different years of reports by the SESNSP (2019, 2021), but earlier years were also consulted. The number reported here is taken from a personal Microsoft Excel data archive.

7. Corruption is a major theme in political science texts (Bailey 2014; Grayson 2010; Morris 1991), and it has been routinely decried and documented in annual reports by international watchdog agencies. In its 2019 report, Transparency International ranks Mexico 130th out of 180 countries and indicates that 90 percent of citizens believe that corruption in government is a major concern. Inefficiency in policing, the courts, and penitentiaries is arguably recognized as Mexico's major failure in governance. With the possible and now diminishing exception of the military, no criminal justice institution has ever inspired confidence and trust among Mexican citizens. In fact, every justice institution is routinely viewed with fear and mistrust rather than respect. Finally, criminal organizations in Mexico have created havoc for at least 150 years, and even the powerful Sinaloa Cartel can be traced back 50 years. But things were never this violent. Corruption, institutional inefficiency, and organized crime are all linked to violence, but it is only recently that they have been linked together in explaining the bloody surge of violence that was triggered early in the twenty-first century.

8. The concept of *vacíos de poder* is difficult to translate literally. Specifically, the word *vacíos* refers to a vacuum, but Edgardo Buscaglia uses it in a wider sense that also incorporates the idea of gaps, failings, deficiencies, or simply absence. The term *vacíos* does not seem to translate directly into an English word that captures the full meaning intended by Buscaglia. A literal translation might be *vacuum*, but this implies a complete absence of structure. It's probably more correct to refer to a turbulence of power or an institutional weakness of the state: those ideas come much closer to describing the reality of gaps and cracks in the governance structure. Denise Dresser (2013) summarized Buscaglia's argument as follows: "La delincuencia—en México y en muchas partes del mundo que Buscaglia ha estudiado—florece en contextos de debilidad institucional. En donde persisten los vacíos generados por sistemas judiciales disfuncionales. En donde prevalece la corrupción gubernamental a todos los niveles. En donde no existen sistemas de control patrimonial. En donde no hay mecanismos de prevención social de los delitos."

9. For more about corridos and narcocorridos, see Edberg 2004; Pérez 2012; Wald 2001; Willkinson 2009.

10. Long after the links between the state and the cartel could no longer be dismissed as myth, Los Tigres were still banned from performing "La Granja" at concerts. That corrido was inspired by George Orwell's *Animal Farm* and the

lyrics described the impact on cartels and government officials after Vicente Fox Quesada won the presidency (Ramirez 2019; Willkinson 2009). *Jefe de Jefes* was rereleased as a limited vinyl collector's edition in late 2019. The first three stanzas in their allegorical song "La Granja" make reference to the election of Fox in 2000 and the beginning disintegration of social arrangements that had kept narcos in check. Los Tigres make reference to a grandfather who serves as the proxy for the hegemonic PRI governments that kept narco traffic constrained through co-optation and reciprocal arrangements. The fox in their lyrics refers to PAN president Vicente Fox, who unleashed the farm dogs who are proxies for the cartel jefes. The piggies in the lyrics refer to politicians who hoped to profit from the chaos when the narcos were unleashed, and the animalitos in their song refer to the three dominant drugs that were the initial source of Mexican cartel wealth (heroin, marijuana, and cocaine).

11. Many readers of this book are undobutedly knowledgeable about Mexican history, but there may be some who are unfamiliar with basic concepts and terms. The notes of this book regularly provide descriptions or definitions that might not be familiar to some. The PRI had governed Mexico for seventy-one years continuously until it was finally defeated in 2000 by Vicente Fox and the Partido Acción Nacional.

12. This is not an argument that all the changes after 2002 were uniquely caused by the appearance of Los Zetas. The history is much more complex than reducing it to this one factor. The emergence of Los Zetas was only one factor in what many have described as a perfect storm of events (see Hope 2013; Payan 2014). The impact of Los Zetas is described in a broader context in chapter 2 and elsewhere. See the section in chapter 2 titled "Wars Between Cartels," which describes the cartel violence during the Vicente Fox sexenio.

13. The roots of those social bonds within cartels are described in much more depth in chapters 4 and 5.

14. "La prioridad de este texto es documentar el fenómeno de la narco-insurgencia" (Cedillo 2018, Kindle Location 79).

15. For instance, Osiel Cárdenas Guillén, leader of the Gulf Cartel, was found guilty in 2010 by a U.S. court, but many documents were sealed and unavailable because they were part of ongoing investigations (U.S. Attorney's Office 2010).

16. "En pocos años el portal se convirtió en un archivo fundamental para escribir la historia del narcotráfico en México, gracias a la gran cantidad de confesiones que se rinden en los juicios y se documentan ahí."

17. Durazo resigned in late 2020 to campaign for the governorship of Sonora State, which he won.

18. This cell-phone conversation between Ovidio and Iván was livestreamed and quickly went viral.

19. There were apparently thirty-five prospective members for desertion. According to Ricardo Raphael (2019), high-ranking Mexican military officials had identified an elite group of thirty-five candidates to be sent to Fort Hood for

training. Fourteen of them are later untraceable (Raphael speculated that some were killed), but twenty-one were initially recruited directly to become the armed wing of Cárdenas Guillén's Gulf Cartel. One of the original Zetas was apparently assassinated for being untrustworthy, leaving the original twenty to remain as the core.

Chapter 2

1. Chapter 7 explores how the term *cártel* was introduced to describe Latin American transnational crime organizations. But it is worth noting that international experts on mafias, organized crime, and/or transnational crime rarely considered Mexican organizations to have the same degree of criminal power and reach as traditional mafias. For instance, Gayraud's prominent 2007 book on organized crime did not include Mexican organizations in the list of great mafias of the world.

2. The DEA was created by a presidential executive order in July 1973. It replaced the older Bureau of Narcotics and established a role for the DEA as the lead agency in the War on Drugs alongside the FBI and Border Patrol.

3. The beginning of the drug war and cartel narrative was directly layered onto hierarchical conceptions of criminality that had governed Mexico for centuries, and unsurprisingly reinforced dominant conceptions that a deviant underclass was responsible for all crime. Mafias and narcos were also seen through the restrictive lens of race and class and emerged as the modern equivalent of bandits and outlaws on the fringes of civilized Mexico. This hierarchical and class-based view of drug organizations prevailed from the start of the narrational shift: the origin of the Guadalajara Cartel has usually been described as a fortuitous tale of unsophisticated country bumpkins inadvertently stumbling into incredible wealth after being driven from remote ranchos by the DEA-backed Operation Condor (Shannon 1988).

    Symbolic interactionists assert that power is rooted in the naming and tagging of deviant acts, and it would fall to the DEA to champion the concepts of narco and cartel through the demonization of a covert underclass: their skill in managing that claims making allowed it to buttress a privileged status in the DOJ pecking order. The popular understanding of narcos and mafias has been directly and indirectly filtered through a DEA lens, and the trajectory of Mexican cartels has been made visible through intelligence the DEA gathered over five decades of America's longest war.

4. The thirteen groups identified by the DEA are Milenio Cartel, Oaxaca Cartel, Colima Cartel, Beltrán Leyva Cartel, Jalisco New Generation Cartel, Guadalajara Cartel, Sinaloa Cartel, Juárez Cartel, Tijuana Cartel, Gulf Cartel, the Zetas, the Family of Michoacán, and the Templar Knights.

5. The Milenio organization was more commonly referred to as the Valencia Family Cartel. It fell off the DEA radar and was no longer viewed as a large cartel by

about 2006. The Valencia family operation had been absorbed into the Sinaloa Federation under the direction of Ignacio Coronel Villarreal, but a power vacuum occured when several of its leaders were killed in plaza disputes involving Los Zetas. Smaller factions remained operational, including La Resistencia, headed by Ramiro Pozos El Molca, and the nascent Jalisco New Generation Cartel (CJNG), headed by Nemesio "El Mencho" Oseguera. Following Coronel Villareal's death in 2009, those two factions continued to operate as operatives of the larger Sinaloa Federation, primarily as hitmen and sicarios. Eventually, El Mencho would emerge as a powerful boss at the head of the CJNG in the last few years of Calderón's presidential term (see chapter 3). A more detailed description of the Milenio Cartel is found in Guillermo Valdés Castellanos's book *Historia del narcotráfico en México* (2013), beginning at Kindle Location 3807.

6. The *Diccionario del español usual en México* defines a cacique as a regional leader who exerts despotic and arbitrary control over a community (L. Lara 2009).

7. Sicilia was once considered the most important narco trafficker in Mexico, and he notoriously had mysterious ties and links to the CIA. His connections to Mexican high society and government officials were documented in *The Underground Empire* (1988), a classic early book by James Mills describing the development of narco Mexico.

8. He was much more than a bodyguard. He was a trusted confident and godfather to Sánchez Celis's children.

9. Established in 1947 by Miguel Alemán Valdés to guard the internal stability of Mexico against all forms of subversion and terrorist threats, the DFS was merged into the Centro de Investigación y Seguridad Nacional (CISEN, Center for Research on National Security) in 1985 after the Camarena murder. According to Peter Dale Scott, "the DFS was in part a CIA creation," and "the CIA's closest government allies were for years in the DFS." Mexican journalist Manuel Buendía Tellezgirón was alleged to have been murdered by members of the DFS for reporting on Mexican high-ranking officials' corruption, and their relation with the CIA and drug trafficking. The U.S. Senate hearings on the Iran-Contra affair identified DFS director Miguel Nazar Haro as a CIA asset with the nom de plume LITEMPO-12.

10. Both sentences were successfully appealed, and both men were released. Zuno Arce was then retried and resentenced.

11. Rumors about the actual location of the high-level meeting were clarified through the evidence used at El Chapo's trial in Brooklyn, New York. The meeting actually took place in Mexico City, according to El Mayo's brother, Jesús Reynaldo. That same claim of a Mexico City meeting was made in Hernández's recent book, *El traidor* (2020).

12. Season 2 of the Netflix series *Narcos: Mexico* offers a different and unsubstantiated interpretation. In this fictional version, there was a rebellion of the factions

and Félix Gallardo was squeezed out of his powerful leadership. I have seen no written reports indicating that this actually happened.

13. In the case of Juárez, the arrival of the Carrillo Fuentes family was described as an invasion of "barbarians" (Tercero 2011b).

14. Palma Salazar completed his sentence in an American prison in May 2021 and was eligible for release and expulsion to Mexico. A judge in Jalisco declared that since he had completed his sentence and that no additional charges were pending in Mexico, he would be welcomed back (Fuentes López 2021).

15. "El verdadero jefe del Chapo es Ismael Zambada. El verdadero instrumentador de todo es el Mayo. Él y el Chapo se conocían, tenían amigos communes, pero al principio no trabajaban juntos. El Mayo siempre ha sido independiente, es gente de temor, gente de mucho respeto. El Mayo cuando mata, mata, pero entonces las reglas de los narcos eran distintas. Eran incapaces de atentar contra la población civil."

16. There are many accounts of his presidency, including his own biography. But one of the first and still accurate descriptions was provided by Julia Preston and Samuel Dillon in chapter 7 of *Opening Mexico* (2004).

17. The routes and process for shipping would not be fully understood until much later. For instance, Hernández (2020, 123–26) relies on the diary of Vicente Zambada Niebla to describe how El Mayo shipped cocaine through Mexico. He would arrange to fly cocaine to various collection points, where he would warehouse it until he had gathered large amounts that he would offer for sale to anyone who would pay the asking price. El Mayo would deliver it to those buyers using vehicles and routes that he had established. According to Vicentillo, some Pemex oil tankers had been modified with special compartments for shipping to the middlemen or buyers.

18. El Chapo would remain at the center of all speculation during this time. There are those who vehemently argue that he was the mastermind of the execution of Carrillo Fuentes and others who argue that he was merely one pawn in a more complex and elaborate shuffle.

19. My formal academic training is in sociology and criminology, and cognizant of the problems with official crime statistics. However, there are good reasons to trust the overall pattern and trends of Mexican homicide statistics. The precision and exact count may be questionable, especially in some states—but the patterns are reliable indicators.

20. Mexico City was a Federal District and not a state at the time. It became a state known as Ciudad de México (CDMX) in 2018.

21. Guzmán was not the first narco trafficker to escape from prison by digging a tunnel. For instance, Sicilia made a spectacular prison escape through a tunnel in the mid-1970s.

22. This perfect storm included, among other things, the transition to democratic government in Mexico; the weakness and corruption in government and local police; the U.S. removal of the ban on assault weapons; the decision to target

capos; the U.S. deportation of prisoners to Mexico; the emergence of a nativist closed border movement; a perception of increased violence, and increasing brutalization of violence; and the cycles of unification and fragmentation of cartels.

23. In 2020 the Secretariat of Public Security reported that more than 1,300 bodies had been recovered from 1,027 graveyards in 614 different parts of the country over the previous two years (Redacción Animal Político 2020).

24. According to INEGI (2019), the total number of recorded homicides from the beginning of 2007 until the end of 2018 was 278,050. INEGI numbers are usually higher than the numbers reported by SESNSP (2019).

25. An article by David Epstein and ProPublica (2016) provides intriguing details about how this cartel was targeted and weakened.

Chapter 3

1. "Year of Hidalgo" was used in reference to the figure of Father Miguel Hidalgo y Costilla on the obverse of Mexico's five-peso coin.

2. It is important to recognize that the elections scheduled for June 6, 2021, will be the first in recent history that do allow "reelection" to congressional, senate, governorships, mayoralties, and state-level positions. The impact on Mexico is potentially radical (Cervantes 2021). Overall, I see it as a promising development, but it is far too early to know what impact it will have on the convert netherworld and narco politics.

3. A popular graphic book, *Qué tanto es tantito* (Rocha and Pulido Jiménez 2018), catalogs the corruption charges against eighteen governors. Mexican journalists exposed their corruption.

4. One graduate student registered in my seminar at the University of Sinaloa described his encounter with a narco trafficker who came to offer him a bribe. At the time, the student was a town councillor in a smaller community bordering Culiacán, and there were plans to create a park across from the house of a well-known cartel member. Ricardo received a visit from the trafficker, who expressed concerns that the park would leave him exposed to surveillance and monitoring, but all the subsequent discussion was indirect and moved forward in terms of "what if." It was clear money was on the table, but at the same time the narco trafficker had turned attention to pictures on the student's wall and interspersed the discussion with questions such as "Is that your family?" and "Where do they live now?" All questions implied an indirect threat. The narco trafficker then offered to underwrite the cost of the park if it were located elsewhere (a site that the narco trafficker identified). In that particular instance, the student managed to extract himself from potential danger after the mayor withdrew the proposal for the park (personal conversation, August 2009).

5. El Mayo Zambada's brother testified that the cartel offered more than $50 million to bribe the government of President Calderón. He also claimed that sev-

eral million dollars was given to a representative Mexico City mayor, Andrés Manuel López Obrador. Alex Cifuentes, a former high-ranking Guzmán aide, testified that the cartel sent $100 million to then Mexican president-elect Peña Nieto to protect Guzmán from capture (Winslow 2019a).

6. United States of America Against Salvador Cienfuegos Zepeda, Article MPR: CRH/RCH F. #2018R01833/ODDETF #NYNYE-801 (2020).

7. There were several governors implicated, including Roberto Sandoval Castañeda of Nayarit, Eruviel Ávila Villegas of Mexico State, and Quirino Ordaz Coppel of Sinaloa. The documents also indicated that there were specific connections at the federal level, such as Miguel Ángel Osorio Chong, who was secretary of state in the Peña Nieto cabinet until he resigned in the blowback from the Ayotzinapa massacre (Esquivel 2021). It is relatively important to note that the H-2 Cartel was a remnant group of the weakened Beltrán Leyva Cartel. In DEA documents, the H-2 Cartel is not recognized as one of the major cartels of Mexico, and its leader, Juan Francisco Patrón, was known as H-2. The group largely flew under the radar of U.S. surveillance and operated in Nayarit (*Insight Crime* 2020). The "relative" anonymity of the group does raise serious questions about how General Cienfuegos was "fingered" and identified as corrupt.

8. Copies of the SMS messages are included in a letter from Timothy Shea to Marcelo Ebrard Casaubón, secretariat of foreign affairs, October 29, 2020, available at https://www.gob.mx/cms/uploads/sre/informacion_recibida_por _la_sre_sobre_el_caso_del_general_retirado_salvador_cienfuegos_zepeda.pdf.

9. Esquivel (2021) has reported that there are at least seven sealed indictments that go back to the Camarena case and Operation Leyenda. Several prominent politicians, such as Manuel Bartlett, are reportedly named in those files.

10. "Ante este panorama, la regeneración moral es al mismo tiempo un medio y un propósito de la Cuarta Transformación. Más allá de encargar la redacción de una Constitución Moral que proponga nuevas actitudes en la relación entre individuos y entre éstos y el colectivo, además de enfatizar la cultura cívica y ética en los programas de estudio y en la comunicación oficial, la regeneración ética será la intención ejemplificante de un ejercicio de gobierno austero, honesto, transparente, incluyente, respetuoso de las libertades, apegado a derecho, sensible a las necesidades de los más débiles y vulnerables y pendiente en todo momento del interés superior; será, asimismo, una convocatoria permanente a toda la sociedad para retomar principios gregarios y remontar el grave deterioro del tejido social."

11. As the respected journalist Héctor de Mauleón (2019) explains: "Al México del horror, ahora se agrega un canal convertido en fosa. Un catálogo de cuerpos descompuestos, un desfile de familias destrozadas. Una serie de preguntas hundidas en la nada" (In the Mexico of horror, we can now include a canal transformed into an anonymous graveyard. A catalog of decomposed bodies and a parade of destroyed families. A string of hollow questions that lead nowhere).

12. Bojorquez is the cofounder and a current senior editor of *Ríodoce*, based in Culiacán, Sinaloa. His partner Javier Valdez Cárdenas was gunned down in front of the magazine offices in 2016 by order of a cartel sicario. *Ríodoce* won several journalism awards, including the prestigious Maria Moors Cabot Prize.

13. AMLO emphasized that theme in his inaugural address and in his report of the first one hundred days in office (Unidad de Investigación Aplicada de MCCI 2019). Morena also refers to a brown-skinned person—almost always in positive terms.

14. Many social thinkers ask the question "What connects a person to society?" Durkheim's ideas were influential among liberal thinkers at the time of the Mexican Revolution, and he specifically wrote about "moral society." His ideas were known in Mexico and throughout Latin America. For instance, the Brazilian national flag incorporates a phrase from Durkheim—"Order and Progress" (Durkheim 2011, 2013, 2014).

15. During most of the twentieth century, the patriotic heroism of the army was continually reinforced in schools, history lessons, tales of heroic child soldiers, and countless public ceremonies reminding citizens that the Mexican state was forged out of military valor and the generals' willingness to step aside for the sake of public governance at the end of the revolutionary war.

16. The expression literally refers to living ten years like a good ol' boy rather than forty years as a donkey. There are several versions of this refrain. The implication in this sentence is that there are too many people who know that life is short, and that it is better to seize any opportunity, however dangerous.

17. Some argue that there was a deliberate strategy to fragment cartels, but there is no specific evidence that Fox or Calderón did so as part of a broader policy plan. Peña Nieto actually did appoint a security director who had used that strategy in Colombia. But the cartels were already fragmented by the time Peña Nieto assumed office.

18. His electoral victory was controversial, and his own party (PAN) did not win a majority in Mexico's House of Representatives. The House of Deputies was blocked by protestors, and Calderón had to enter by the back door to quickly take the oath and assume the ceremonial sash. His exit was equally quick. His campaign did not focus on law and order nor specifically target criminal cartels. In fact, there are many who are convinced that Calderón began the war as a means of legitimizing his presidency. The electoral margin was razor thin, and it was not accepted by his opponents. Lopéz Obrador claimed that he was the "legitimate president" and Calderón the usurper.

19. The intervention was purportedly requested by the leftist PRD governor Lázaro Cárdenas Batel. There had been an upsurge in violence during the last two years of the Fox presidency when Guzmán broke ranks with Carrillo Fuentes in late 2004. An internal war within the Sinaloa Cartel led to a sharp jump in violence.

20. Most charges would eventually be dropped, and Calderón's decision to begin the War Against Cartels in Michoacán would be identified by critics as the first

of many missteps. Michoacán would prove to be an albatross around his neck, and the subsequent rise of La Familia Michoacana and the Caballeros Templarios contributed to the first major escalation in violence. Michoacán came to symbolize the capricious failure of Calderón's war: "A lo largo de los meses y los años, el estado de Michoacán, emblema de la 'guerra' calderonista contra el narco, cobró la forma de una caprichosa e inacabable síncopa de violencia, concomitante a los fracasos del gobierno federal en esta y otras entidades" (Carrasco Araizaga and Castellanos 2012).

21. "Como las bestias de arar, con tapaojos para no mirar hacia los lados" (Bojorquez 2017).

22. Furthermore, desertions from the Mexican army escalated during this period. Many Mexican soldiers had been recruited from rural villages, and the cartels actively encouraged desertion. Charles Bowden explained in a personal conversation that there were about 130,000 deserters from the army at the beginning of the Fox presidency.

23. Many of those trusted lieutenants would later rebel against their drug lord boss, most notably Arturo "El Barbas" Beltrán Leyva, who split from the Sinaloa Cartel.

24. "La fiera de la delincuencia organizada sintió el pinchazo en el lomo y desde entonces no ha dejado de dar coletazos."

25. Cartels and affiliated gangs are described in chapter 7.

26. "¿Qué querían que hiciera? ¿Que los saludara? ¿Que los invitara a pasar? ¿Que les llevara un café?" Luis Astorga Almanza's (2015) critical book analyzing Calderón Hinojosa's war takes its title from the first part of this statement. According to the publisher's description (www.megustaleer.com.mx): "¿Qué querían que hiciera? analiza diversos aspectos de la política de seguridad, dentro de la que se ubica la política de drogas, durante el sexenio de Felipe Calderón, así como en qué consiste la delincuencia organizada en México. Por el autor de El siglo de las drogas, Luis Astorga."

27. This observation will be elaborated in later chapters. Basically, most observers argued that there was a hierarchical control of the underworld by operatives in the Federal Police, and that control of plazas was assigned and purchased from Mexico City in return for a system of paybacks that were governed by the rule of thirds—one-third of the drug profits stayed with the cartels, one-third went to the plaza boss, and one-third went back to the federal source.

28. "With congressional approval, he placed the Secretariat of Public Security (including the federal police) and intelligence functions under the authority of the interior ministry. That ministry now coordinates security efforts with the military and state and municipal authorities. It also commands the new militarized police entity within the federal police, the national gendarmerie" (Ribando Seelke 2021).

29. By far, the majority of homicides are directly linked to the drug trade and narco trafficking. A reasonable estimate is 60 percent. See figure 8 in chapter 5.

30. "Por eso insisto. El distintivo del neoliberalismo es la corrupción. Suena fuerte, pero privatización ha sido en México sinónimo de corrupción. Desgraciadamente casi siempre ha existido este mal en nuestro país, pero lo sucedido durante el periodo neoliberal no tiene precedente en estos tiempos que el sistema en su conjunto ha operado para la corrupción. El poder político y el poder económico se han alimentado y nutrido mutuamente y se ha implantado como modus operandi el robo de los bienes del pueblo y de las riquezas de la nación."

31. AMLO's five immediate predecessors (Peña Nieto, Calderón, Fox, Zedillo, Salinas) governed guided by a neoliberal narrative committed to globalization. Before them, Mexico's other modern presidents (de la Madrid, López Portillo, Echeverría, Gustavo Díaz Ordaz) used the narrative of development: *desarollo*.

32. "En otras palabras, como lo hemos repetido durante muchos años, nada ha dañado más a México que la deshonestidad de los gobernantes y de la pequeña minoría que ha lucrado con el influyentismo. . . . Esa es la causa principal de la desigualdad económica y social, y también de la inseguridad y de la violencia que padecemos."

33. Even though he had immediately resigned as ambassador to India following the 1968 Tlatelolco massacre, Mexico's future Nobel laureate was shunned by many student leaders after publishing *Posdata*.

34. There are many excellent analyses examining the rise of Mexican cartels. The theme will be reviewed in much more detail in chapters 4 through 7. Some of the factors that converged to create a nurturing context include the transition to a democratic government in Mexico; the dilution of control; the weakness and corruption of government and local police; the U.S. loosening of rules to sell high-power weapons and arms; the policy decision to combat the drug issue as a war and to hunt down "capos"; the U.S. policy to deport criminals to Mexico; the close-the-border movement; the culture of violence and violent protest; the perception of an increase in violence, and the brutalization of violence; the cycles of unification; and the fragmentation of cartels.

Chapter 4

1. B. Traven was a pseudonym, and the author's real name most likely was Ret Marut (see Rohter 1990). His biographical history is another amazing example of how Mexico is truly a place where magic realism and unbelievable events turn out to be reality.

2. For a clip of the famous scene from *The Treasure of the Sierra Madre* where Humphrey Bogart and Alfonso Bedoya discuss "badges," see Movieclips, YouTube, February 5, 2014, https://youtu.be/4OcM23Hbs5U.

3. Most of the filming was done on site rather than in a studio. In Mexico, the sites included Bavispe, Sonora (just south of Agua Prieta), Jungapeo, and San José Purua in Michoacán and near Highway 15—which ran from the hills in central Mexico to the Pacific Coast before heading northward up through Nayarit,

Sinaloa, and Sonora—and in the turbulent cities of Acapulco, Guerrero, and Tampico, Tamaulipas. Coincidently, Mexico's secretary of security, Alfonso Durazo Montaño, was born there. In 2019 there was a horrible massacre of the children of an extended Mormon family caught in the cross fire between two armed wings of cartels. It remains a lawless area (Sáinz Martínez 2019; Ureste 2019).

4. "Traveling suitcase" refers to an organized system of bribery that would eventually evolve in Mexico. A federal police officer (most often in the DFS) would bid to be assigned to a specific plaza, often in a bidding war. Once that agent purchased the right to manage a plaza, a direct system was institutionalized wherein one-third of the proceeds of a drug transaction would remain with the trafficker, one-third would be passed upward to superiors, and one-third would remain with the DFS officer who had purchased rights to the plaza.

5. I would argue that criminal groups had such a degree of control and influence that it is accurate to describe them as *total institutions*. That is, they were the dominant social organizational entity of a region and they established the norms and values that pervaded all social interactions in the area: a culture of banditry, as it were.

6. This is the same Cosalá where El Chapo was hiding just prior to his recapture in 2016. Los Mochis is where he was captured after emerging from the sewers while fleeing from Mexican marines. See chapter 6.

7. Obviously, this is a superficial summary of the outcome of the Mexican Revolution. The viewpoint here has been informed by Mario Vargas Llosa and his observation that Mexico and the PRI represent a perfect dictatorship: "es la dictadura camuflada" and "tiene las características de la dictadura: la permanencia, no de un hombre, pero sí de un partido. Y de un partido que es inamovible" (*El País* 1990).

8. Julia Lovell (2014) describes how the opium trade became established and operated in China in the early nineteenth century. The model described in figure 3 would also apply to the development that she describes.

9. A holding company is generally understood to refer to the investors in an enterprise rather than the managers or operators.

10. The links to legitimate institutions were primarily with the state, and the official patronage of the drug trade meant that organized crime was partner and collaborator with the state rather than its competitor.

11. Those linkages and the corruption are gradually being revealed and explored in much more detail. One recent example is *Eclipse of the Assassins* (Bartley and Bartley 2015).

12. Maiz is obviously an ancient Mexican staple, but an increase in production of corn exclusively for ethanol has been controversial. Other crops such as eggplant and lychee have been introduced almost exclusively for foreign export.

13. Highway 24 is the only highway that connects the coast to Parral in Chihuahua, and it is not a route for the fainthearted. It is also virtually impassable in winter months.

14. This has the same name as a larger operation known as Operation Condor. But these are two distinct Operation Condors even though the CIA was involved in both. Both are drug eradication programs. The larger operation was based in the Andes and South America in 1985, where the DEA, the CIA, and the Guardia Civil began working together. Reputedly, it was the Colombians and Peruvians who code-named it Operación Condor.

    Mexico's Operation Condor is more curious. It was a key operation in a drug eradication program targeting Mexico that began in 1975 and continued through 1985. Mexico's DFS chief, Miguel Nazar Haro, was a known CIA asset who was also taking money from Mexico's drug barons but nevertheless worked with the Americans to eliminate drugs from a specific area of the Golden Triangle around Badiguarato. The Mexican government contracted with Evergreen International Aviation, which had CIA connections too numerous to count, to undertake herbicidal spraying. Evidence links the contract to two CIA operatives, and the spraying was overseen by the narcotics office at the U.S. State Department, but it became such a boondoggle that Mexico refused to let the United States fly over the spray zones to verify eradication. See Russell Bartley and Sylvia Erickson Bartley's (2015) book on the CIA involvement in Mexico.

15. Sinaloense is the common nickname for a person from Sinaloa. A person from Culiacán is known as a Culichi, and a person from Mazatlán is a Mazatleco(a).

16. Angostura is part of the municipality of Culiacán de Rosales. Towns and municipalities a bit further up Highway 15 are also important drug plazas—and Guasave and Los Mochis represent the most important points on the Sinaloa side.

17. A more detailed chronology of key events is available online as Jim Creechan, "Appendix A: Significant Events in the History of Cartels and Narcotraffic," 2016, https://www.academia.edu/43409279/Appendix_A_Significant_Events _Cartels_and_Narcotraffic_for_Mexico_Between_1969_and_2015.

18. Lovell's (2014) history of the Opium Wars suggests that they were triggered by a shortage of silver and the complications of depending on silver as the monetary basis for trade in China. At the time, the largest production of silver in the world was in Mexico, and it was moved to the Philippines and the Far East from ports in Acapulco and Ixtapa. It is just as probable that opium moved back to the Americas on those same vessels that transported silver to the east.

19. Mexico had a strong tradition of undertaking botanical surveys of its flora and fauna, and there were many studies and investigations inspired by Linnaeus dual classification taxonomy. The protomedicato model can be roughly thought of as a precursor to local health boards, and there is a very interesting history of how these boards retained their power during many political shifts in Mexico between Federalist and Decentralist movements. The local autonomy was retained until José Venustiano Carranza managed to impose a federal law on all states in 1916.

20. This section relies on an excellent book by Isaac Campos, *Home Grown* (2014).

21. The mistrust of the police is not only a modern phenomenon. Porfirio Díaz's Rurales were intensely disliked and feared. A little bit later, that dismissal of the character of soldiers was clearly evident in the common views about José Victoriano Huerta Márquez's soldiers.

22. It didn't matter that Chinese laborers were the ones who were disproportionately affected by the downturn in the economy caused by the overthrow of Porfirio Díaz, the violence of the Mexican Revolution, and the loss of confidence of foreign investors.

23. Anti-Chinese movements grew more powerful in Sonora and Sinaloa by 1915 with the support of powerful politicians such as future national presidents Plutarco Elías Calles and Emilio Portes Gil—the latter Sonoran governor and supreme court justice at the time. *Antichinismo* expanded and was justified by pseudoscientific ideas of social eugenics about racial purity and views that Chinese men had corrupted and abused Mexican women. Howard Campbell (2009) provides one of the best descriptions of how Chinese gangs had originally dominated the opium trade and established criminal traditions in Ciudad Juárez before being displaced by Mexican and Anglo gangs later in the 1920s and early 1930s. The 1906 San Francisco earthquake triggered another dispersion and exodus to those same borderlands, and veterans from the San Francisco underworld and Chinese triads fortified their numbers. Campbell specifically refers to an online article titled "La leyenda negra" (Linares 2010).

24. There is very little documentation describing those early Chinese gangs and their modus operandi. Recently, there have been passing comments and observations suggesting that Guzmán actually learned a great deal about smuggling from his knowledge of the Chinese tunnels in Mexicali and that his rise to prominence in the Sinaloa faction was directly related to his familiarity with those early tunnels.

25. The claim here is based on indirect evidence and documentation from elsewhere. For instance, Canada's first legislation on narcotics was introduced as a result of claims filed by Chinese merchants whose opium dens were burned to the ground in riots. The future prime minister of Canada was sent to Vancouver to investigate; he documented a great deal about the "opium culture." Similar details were incorporated in a book by an antidrug crusader (Murphy 1922) that became a best seller. The point is that the opium-smoking habit of Chinese migrants was well documented and also became linked to eugenicist movements that supported laws of exclusion.

26. Defined as habitual users of drugs as specified in the existing health code in sections 198 and 199 (Astorga 1996, 43).

27. Sinaloa, Sonora, Durango, and Chihuahua were not mentioned among the states where plantations should be destroyed.

28. Doctor Salazar Vieniegra, a director of the Departamento de Salubridad, had been the principal proponent.

29. "In the end, 'the only result obtained by the application of the modified rules of 1931, has been an increased and excessive value of illegal drugs, and because of this it provided a great windfall to the traffickers'" (Astorga Almanaza 2005, 47).

30. The story appears in several novels, but Astorga argues that he has never seen documentation in U.S. Department of State files. The tale has become quite elaborate over the years, and it includes many details about Luciano's motivation and even his anger at being deported back to Sicily even though he had done this for his adopted country. He has also repeated his observation to me several times in personal conversations.

31. Astorga describes its importance in the 1940s the following way: "During the 1940s, the northwest of Mexico, especially the State of Sinaloa and particularly Badiguarato Municipality, indisputably established itself as the region with the largest cultivation of poppies and production of opium" (Astorga Almanza 2005, 61).

32. Astorga Almanza has a full description of these events in *El siglo de las drogas* (2005), especially in the chapter "Los años cuarenta." El Gitano would serve a jail term and eventually be released, and served later governors and politicians as a bodyguard.

33. Astorga Almanza (2005, 86) notes that the term *narcotraficantes* first appeared in 1956 and was used in national newspapers to refer to the drug trade in Sinaloa.

34. Dan Baum was writing a book about the politics of drug prohibition; during an interview with John Ehrlichman, he asked about the War on Drugs. According to Baum (2016), Ehrlichman dismissed his questions with the following statement: "'You want to know what this was really all about?' he asked with the bluntness of a man who, after public disgrace and a stretch in federal prison, had little left to protect. 'The Nixon campaign in 1968, and the Nixon White House after that, had two enemies: the antiwar left and black people. You understand what I'm saying? We knew we couldn't make it illegal to be either against the war or black, but by getting the public to associate the hippies with marijuana and blacks with heroin, and then criminalizing both heavily, we could disrupt those communities. We could arrest their leaders, raid their homes, break up their meetings, and vilify them night after night on the evening news. Did we know we were lying about the drugs? Of course we did.'"

35. Of course, the counterargument is that drug production had increased so greatly that the number of seizures would go up by default. Since there is no accurate estimate of drug production, there is no resolution to this argument.

36. Reorganization Plan No. 2 of 1973 became effective on July 1, 1973, and among other things established a Drug Enforcement Administration in the Department of Justice. The Office for Drug Abuse Law Enforcement (established pursuant to Executive Order No. 11641 of January 28, 1972) and the Office of National Narcotics Intelligence (established pursuant to Executive Order No. 16676 of July 27, 1972) were, together with other related functions, merged in the new DEA. Drug Enforcement Administration, "The DEA Years," July 2018,

p. 34, https://www.dea.gov/sites/default/files/2018-07/1970-1975%20p%2030 -39.pdf.

37. "The long, proud, and honorable tradition of federal drug law enforcement began in 1915 with the Bureau of Internal Revenue. In the following decades, several federal agencies had drug law enforcement responsibilities. By the 1960s, the two agencies charged with drug law enforcement were the Bureau of Drug Abuse Control (BDAC) and the federal Bureau of Narcotics (FBN)." Drug Enforcement Administration, "The DEA Years," 30.

38. "By 1972, the quantity of brown heroin from Mexico available in the United States had risen 40 percent higher than the quantity of white heroin from Europe. Traditional international border control was no longer effective against the problem, and in 1974, the Government of Mexico requested U.S. technical assistance. On January 26, 1974, Operation SEA/M (Special Enforcement Activity in Mexico) was launched in the State of Sinaloa to combat the opium and heroin traffic. One month later, a second joint task force, Operation End Run, began operations in the State of Guerrero, concentrating on marijuana and heroin interdiction. Meanwhile, a third effort, Operation Trident, focused on controlling the traffic of illegally manufactured dangerous drugs produced in Mexico. Despite the fact that law enforcement in Mexico had some successes, these early efforts did not, in the long term, prevent the development of powerful drug trafficking organizations based in Mexico." Drug Enforcement Administration, "The DEA Years," 36.

39. Hernández had a major part in the 1968 student massacre at Tlatleloco and remained tainted with the disgrace of having been involved.

40. An argument can be made that the Sinaloan drug lords had actually planned to move before Operation Condor, and there is the possibility that President Echeverría's authorization of the operation was part of an elaborate plan to pave the way for that expansion into the cocaine trade.

41. Félix Gallardo "surgió en el negocio de las drogas en Sinaloa en los años sesenta y poco a poco su estatura de capo comenzó a hacer historia. Proclive al consenso, más que a la beligerencia, logró llegar a la cúspide de poder pocos años después y con el apoyo de importantes políticos y empresarios escaló posiciones que lo distinguieron como un fino director de empresas que se codeaba con la alta sociedad" (Ravelo 2006, 79). Two associates of Pedro Avilés Pérez, the regional powerful drug lord Ernesto "Don Neto" Fonseca Carrillo and Rafael Caro Quintero, and a fellow Badiguarato native named Juan José "El Azul" Esparragoza Moreno had entered into a loose partnership with Félix Gallardo in his Culiacán base.

42. As this is written, Fonseca Carillo is eighty-nine years old and is still in a Mexican prison. His mausoleum has already been constructed in Badiguarato beside a church that he has donated to the city.

43. There are differing interpretations about this connection to Matta Ballesteros. The most intriguing one argues that both were CIA assets.

44. "Balloon effect" describes the "relocation" of the drug trade when pressure is applied to one area. The pressure simply leads to a bulge elsewhere (Bagley 2012, 4–7). Ironically, in 2020 Bruce Bagley pled guilty for money laundering on behalf of cartels.

45. This description of Félix Gallardo is based on notes sent to me by the late George Grayson. It has been extensively edited, but the overview is inspired by his observations.

46. Colsa was "the jeweler" to the rich and famous of Mexico, including many capos. He turned state's witness after the death of Carrillo Fuentes (in 1997) and provided a detailed accounting of major events from 1982 onward. He was assassinated two weeks after he left protective custody.

47. He has occasionally resurfaced in periodic interviews, in which he continues to proclaim innocence and that he has no money and cannot afford to pay the legal fees required to oppose his extradition to the United States for charges stemming from the time of the Camarena murder (Heath 2020; *El Universal* 2019; Vega 2019, 2020). But more evidence suggests that he is actually the head of one of four factions within the post-Chapo era of the Sinaloa Cartel.

48. *The Narcosphere* blog posts may not be directly accessible online excepting some cases where the original posts by Bill Conroy have been reposted or excerpted by others. Conroy stopped posting to *The Narcosphere* after its main funding source, the Fund for Authentic Journalism, was plagued by financial and legal troubles. Conroy's *Narcosphere* blogs were originally posted to the *Narco News* site, an Internet portal founded by Al Giordano. Conroy was not implicated in the scandal, but his blog was affected by it. See SAJ Truthtellers 2018.

49. This section relies heavily on notes and draft shared with me by Grayson. Sadly, he died before he was able to compile his notes into a manuscript.

50. Cárdenas Guillén had been brought into the cartel by Jorge Eduardo "El Coss" Sánchez.

Chapter 5

1. INEGI figures for the number of homicidios dolosos per year: 10,452 (2006), 8,867 (2007); 14,006 (2008); 19,803 (2009); 25,757 (2010); 27,213 (2011); 25,967 (2012); 23,063 (2013): 20,010 (2014); 20,525 (2015); 23,953 (2016); 31,174 (2017); 33,341 (2018); 35,588 (2019); 35,554 (2020). The overall total for those years is 352,273 homicidios dolosos.

2. As mentioned in chapter 3, the final year of a sexenio is still referred to as the Year of Hidalgo in reference to the ten-peso coin that contained an image of Miguel Hidalgo. It was a year for everyone to grab their share of the public funds and enrich themselves. The final year and months before an election have also seen increases in the number of politicians and political appointees who retire early and seek new positions in other jurisdictions. The phenomenon has

also been referred to as the hour of chapulines (grasshoppers) because they jump from opportunity to opportunity.

3. El Dedazo refers to pointing the finger at the successor. The finger was on the hand of the president in power.

4. Slang for informant is *sapo* (toad). The term *soplón* is also used very widely, especially in narcocorridos.

5. The NPR investigation also looked at how bribes were used in Ciudad Juárez and Chihuahua. Its report "also analyzed cases that involved charges of cartel bribes of public officials. . . . Municipal officials were involved in most of the cases. The data suggest that bribes by the Sinaloa cartel focused on federal and military officials. Out of 19 cases, 14 of them involved federal and military officials. The Juárez cartel was charged with bribing 10 officials, and nine of them were municipal" (Burnett, Peñaloza, and Benincasa 2010).

6. An ajusticiamiento is an execution or the equivalent of a mob hit. An ajuste is a lesser response.

7. Édgar Guzmán López was murdered near the Tres Ríos development in May 2008. Other prominent Sinaloa Cartel juniors also died. Mario Antonio Meza, the son of El Mayo's former girlfriend and cartel money launderer, Blanca Margarita "La Emperatriz" Cázarez Salazar, was also gunned down. The killings have long been attributed to Arturo Beltrán Leyva, but there have also been unconfirmed rumors circulating that El Mayo was the one who was responsible.

8. An average of 8,000 tractor trailers a day were crossing there.

9. The material in this section depends very heavily on the work of Eduardo Guerrero Gutiérrez (2015a), but it is also informed by Ricardo Ravelo (2006, 2007a, 2013), Diego Enrique Osorno (2012), and George Grayson (2008a, 2012, 2014).

10. Ricardo Raphael (2019) devotes several chapters of his novela to descriptions of that torturous training. His book is marketed as a novel, but it is also based on meticulous research.

11. This organizational model appears to be very similar to the structure of the N'Drangheta. Roberto Saviano describes that model of organized crime in his book *Zero Zero Zero* (2015; see also Saviano 2014).

12. *Huachicoleros* is another unique Mexican slang word for robbery of gasoline and gas. It has an older meaning that referred to the watering down of alcohol— especially tequila. The origin lies in street slang where the prefix *guachi* is a Spanish equivalent of the English *watch*.

13. Homicidio doloso is effectively equivalent to intentional homicide and first-degree murder.

14. INEGI is the Mexican government agency responsible for tracking, recording, and generating all socioeconomic measures of societal well-being. A statistical measure for the cause of death is one vital statistic that has been compliant with international conventions for more than ninety years. In Mexico, as in most international jurisdictions, a medical examiner is the chief recording officer responsible for classifying cause of death. Homicide statistics are published

regularly by the SESNSP, but various measures of murder have also been regularly and systematically reported in additional sources: counts of homicides in national newspaper chains such as *Reforma, El Universal,* and *Milenio* often include finer distinctions and breakdowns into categories of homicide.

15. There are logical reasons supporting this estimate of 60 percent. It is a reasonable estimate of the overall cartel violence since 2004, and probably a low estimate. For instance, the overall numbers generated by this estimate are comparable to counts reported in sophisticated methodological and statistical studies, such as Guillermo Trejo and Sandra Ley's (2020) analysis of violence and politics in Mexico. Further, the usefulness of a measure such as *deaths above expected* has been demonstrated when it entered the public lexicon during the COVID-19 pandemic. Using historical data, I calculated a least-squares estimate of where the homicide total would have arrived if that historical trend had continued. The regression projection was that there would have been about 10 homicides per 100,000 by 2005. Instead, actual rates jumped and dramatically peaked at about 25 per 100,000 by 2012. Stated otherwise, Mexico's homicide rate during the cartel war era was at least 15 points higher than the "expected and predicted rate" of 10 per 100,000. Effectively, that is 60 percent of all homicidios dolosos recorded by SESNSP.

16. The president personally acknowledged that some parts of Mexico are beyond the control of government: his statement implies that the *recording* of vital statistics has been affected in some regions of Mexico and has lower reliability.

17. Implementing a security strategy was complicated by the internal dynamics of the CNS. This body consisted of twelve cabinet directors, including those within Secretaría de Gobernación (SEGOB), Francisco Ramírez Acuña, who was soon replaced by the president's chief of staff, Juan Camilo Mouriño Terrazo; Procuraduría General de la República (PGN), Eduardo Medina Mora; Secretaría de Seguridad Pública (SSP, Secretariat of Public Security), Genaro García Luna; Secretaría de la Defensa Nacional (SEDENA), Guillermo Galván Galván; and Secretaría de Marina (SEMAR, Secretariat of the Navy), Mariano Francisco Saynez, as well as the head of CISEN (Valdés Castellanos 2013).

In addition, the CNS embraced the Secretaría de Hacienda y Crédito Público (SHCP, Office for the Treasury and Public Credit), Secretaría de Relaciones Exteriores (SRE, Secretariat of Foreign Affairs), Secretaría de la Función Pública (SFP, Secretariat of the Civil Service), and Secretaría de Comunicaciones y Transportes (SCT, Secretariat of Communications and Transportation). The technical secretary was Dr. Sigrid Arzt Colunga until she left the post in April 2009 and was replaced by Jorge Tello Peón.

The entire body was also hamstrung by the sharp clashes over turf, resources, leadership, and policy between García Luna and Medina Mora—even though it was clear that García Luna was more often heard. García Luna raised hackles by reinforcing his office with officers recruited from the PGR's Agencia Federal de Investigación (AFI), Mexico's version of the FBI. He brought many of its best agents into the SSP before the force was abolished in mid-2009.

18. On September 6, 2006, three months before Calderón's inauguration, unknown men burst into the Sol y Sombra nightclub in Uruapan, Michoacán, fired shots into the air, ordered revelers to lie down, ripped open a plastic bag, and lobbed five human heads onto the dance floor. The men, who belonged to La Familia Michoacana, left behind a note hailing their act as *divine justice*, adding, "The Family doesn't kill for money; it doesn't kill women; it doesn't kill innocent people; only those who deserve to die, die. Everyone should know this; this is divine justice." The day before the macabre theatrics in Uruapan, the killers had seized their victims from a mechanic's shop and hacked off their heads with bowie knives while the men writhed in pain (Grayson 2008b). George Grayson also shared his working notes about this incident with me.

19. These criteria were proposed by U.S. secretary of state Colin Powell and used by him as a rationale for invading Iraq.

20. Calderón wasted no time in courting the armed forces and being guided by their advice. Within ten days of taking office, he dispatched nearly seven thousand federal police and military personnel to fight gangs that were active in Michoacán. Calderón even visited the Forty-Third Military Zone in Apatzingán, Michoacán, where he donned an olive-green field uniform emblazoned with five stars and the national shield—to symbolically emphasize his status of commander in chief and underscore his solidarity with the federal forces assigned to confront drug traffickers. His government initiated a public campaign to praise the armed forces through television commercials, and he appointed even more military personnel to important posts within and outside the country. Calderón's deference toward the military and use of troops to combat drug violence temporarily boosted his personal approval rating.

Chapter 6

1. The operative word in this sentence is "publicly." I would never discount the possibility that there is documentation provided by informants who have been granted protected witness status, or information collected from wiretaps or extracted from computers and documents seized in raids. Emma Coronel Aispura referred to the code of silence in an interview with journalist Anabel Hernández: when asked about a possible DEA presence, Coronel Aispura said, "I believe that what's most important to the DEA is to have contact with people who can bring them things [information], that is to point the finger at others, and they know perfectly well that this would never happen" (Hernández 2016c, 21).

2. One relative of Guzmán once told me about a phone call to him from El Chapo. The message was clear and simple: "Be careful . . . watch what you say." I was

also told by him that most family members were ordered to avoid using drugs and to stay away from the business (anonymous, personal communication in Culiacán, May 2012).

3. "Pese a las acusaciones en su contra desde hace más de 20 años, Joaquín Archivaldo Guzmán Loera, El Chapo, no ha recibido hasta ahora ni una sola sentencia condenatoria por narcotráfico. Es más, ha sido absuelto o amparado en una veintena de casos con homicidios, producción y tráfico de mariguana y cocaína, delitos contra la salud o portación de arma reservada a las Fuerzas Armadas." There were eighteen charges laid, and two instances of preliminary investigations recorded; all were set aside until twelve of those were "refiled" after his 2014 prison escape.

4. His sentence for the cardinal's murder was later reduced to seven years upon appeal.

5. Mexico's Instituto Nacional de Transparencia y Acceso a la Información Pública y Protección de Datos Personales (INAI, National Institute for Transparency, Access to Information and Personal Data Protection) has the authority to determine what information is released to the public and the right to place embargos on the release of some information. For instance, an embargo was placed on many documents related to El Chapo Guzmán's 2015 escape from Altiplano prison. Those documents will not be available in the public domain until 2028 (L. Flores 2016).

6. The most thorough and complete documentation of how Mexican institutions pervert and thwart transparency and openness is described in *Eclipse of the Assassins* by Russell Bartley and Sylvia Erickson Bartley (2015). They spent three decades trying to unravel the assassination of Mexican journalist Manuel Buendía Tellezgirón and were thwarted by trails of deception and misdirection at every turn. Their work, specifically chapter 10, "Secret, NOFORN," should be required reading for investigative journalists who seek to learn the truth from Mexican archives.

7. El Chapo, through one of his lawyers, lent credibility to the claim that a biography is in the works when there were reports that a lawsuit would be filed if a biography was produced without making a payment to Guzmán (L. Martínez 2016).

8. A satelite photo of La Tuna is available as of June 2021 at http://mexico.pueblos america.com/fotos-satelitales/la-tuna-11.

9. One must take into account the aspects of marriage and relationships that distinguish Mexico from the United States, Canada, and Europe. First, a formally recognized marriage in Mexico is a *civil matter*, and registration of marriages has historically been the responsibility of the state. A couple may also have a *religious marriage*, but that has generally been relegated to a ceremonial status because of Constitutional restrictions limiting the role of the church. There remains a cultural tradition among wealthy men of maintaining *una casa chica*—a second house where a longtime lover lives: I don't want to exaggerate

this idea, but this aspect of machismo has been frequently linked to the narco trade and in fact played a role in the capture of major figures in the narco-traffic business.

10. Rosa Isela was born in Zapopan, Jalisco, before El Chapo married Alejandrina Salazar. Rosa Isela would enter into prominence in March 2016 through a profile in *The Guardian* in which she claimed that her father had been betrayed by the government and that he was a scapegoat. It is also believed that she had two children fathered by Vicentillo Zambada Niebla, the oldest son of El Mayo (Montenegro 2016; Montenegro and Carrol 2016).

11. In Spanish, the term *prestanombre* refers to someone whose name is used to register goods or properties on behalf of someone else and with the intent of hiding the true ownership.

12. Beauty contests have an important place in the subculture of northwest Mexico and are especially important within Sinaloa and specifically in Mazatlán Spring Carnivals. Any discussion of the importance would require a lengthy and tangential description that is best left to another work. But the interested reader should consult at least two books by Sinaloa authors: *Miss Narco* (Valdez Cárdenas 2009) and *Morir en Sinaloa* (Santamaría Gómez, Martínez Peña, and Brito Osuna 2009).

13. In her interview with Hernández, Coronel Aispura describes how she came to be born in Santa Clara, California. She reports that it was during a time her mother was working as an illegal immigrant (*mojada*). She spent most of her childhood in Durango and felt that Angostura was her home. She also told Hernández that she spent at least one year of high school in the United States but felt uncomfortable and missed Durango (Hernández 2016c).

14. Mexican pentitentiaries have often changed names, and this creates confusion. El Chapo Guzmán was initially incarcerated in a federal prison located near Toluca, Mexico State. At the time, that prison was known as El Penal de Máxima Seguridad Número 1 "Almoloya de Juárez." It was also known as La Palma, after the rancho located nearby. When Mexico began naming its prisons Centros Federales de Readaptación Social (CEFERESOs), the prison near Toluca was renamed Centro Federal de Readaptación Social Número 1 (CEFERESO #1), more commonly known as Altiplano. In 1995 El Chapo was transferred from Almoya de Juárez (CEFERESO #1) to the Centro Federal de Readaptación Social Número 2 "Puente Grande" in Jalisco, from which he escaped in early 2001. When Guzmán was recaptured in 2014, he was incarcerated in Mexico State at Federal Social Readaptation Center No. 1, which by then was commonly referred to as Altiplano. The architectural plans and design of both prisons are essentially the same, and El Chapo's familiarity with the layout of Puente Grande (Jalisco) was a valuable resource when his team planned the spectacular tunnel breakout from Altiplano (Mexico State). It was announced in October 2020 that Puente Grande would be shut down (*Mexico News Daily* 2020), but that had not yet occurred as of this writing.

15. El Chapo's relationship with Zulema Hernández is documented in his psychological dossier from Puente Grande. The relationship was apparently invigorated by contraband shipments of Viagra that Guzmán had delivered to the prison.

16. Both men lost family and children as a consequence of the drug war. El Chapo's son Édgar was murdered during his war with the Beltrán Leyvas, and his brother Arturo was killed by hit men of the Arellano Félix brothers in Puente Grande prison. El Mayo's son Vicente was arrested and extradited to the United States. Two other children were arrested crossing the U.S. border and are awaiting trial.

17. Sean Penn's (2016) description of his meeting with El Chapo is the best reflection of this. His account repeats many absurdities and misconceptions, to the point where it can be reduced to a comical interpretation of organized crime.

18. "'El Mayo' Zambada, el cerebro y, probablemente, el Nuevo líder de la organización. De hecho, si el Cártel de Sinaloa se ha mantenido como la más poderosa organización en México se debe a su propia presencia, lejos de los focos y la atención a nivel internacional. Si en cualquier lugar es ahora conocido el nombre de 'El Chapo' y sus fotos con camisas extravagantes han dado la vuelta al mundo, pocas personas conocen el nombre de su socio más importante y menos aún conocen su rostro. Es esta invisibilidad la que ha hecho la suerte de Ismael 'El Mayo' Zambada y lo ha convertido en este último período en el verdadero sostén de la organización."

19. "En aquella época, Joaquín El Chapo Guzmán—miembro de la organización criminal comandada por Amado Carrillo Guentes, major conocido como El Señor de los Cielos—era casi nadie, casi nada en su actividad como narcotraficante" (Hernández 2010, 20).

20. The Federation was the name that the U.S. justice agencies would apply to the emerging organization that was headed by Carrillo Fuentes. The most reasonable estimate is that this name first appeared in a Congressional Research Services report in 2007 (Cook 2007).

21. The DEA provided information allowing the Mexican government to identify the body, and Carrillo Fuentes's mother claimed the body. In the aftermath, there are many who believe that Carrillo Fuentes had faked his death in order to retire to an unknown location in South America.

22. The murder of Camarena remains shrouded in mystery and arguably deliberate obfuscation. Some of the documentation has been sealed and subject to court challenges seeking the release. The most contentious claim is that members of the CIA were involved and present, and that there are audiotapes that have never been released.

23. Very few drug lords and senior bosses have careers that take them into their forties or beyond. In fact, one of the cultural codes within the Mexican drug trade makes reference to this idea of a short and spectacular career.

24. In the *Rolling Stone* interview, El Chapo himself makes the point that another narco will take his place (Penn 2016).

25. Penn prepared a list of twenty-two questions in English and asked Kate del Castillo to translate them into Spanish. In the actual taping, the interviewer poses approximately forty questions (Draper 2016).

26. "Por primera vez, la gente puede ver el tamaño de Joaquín Guzmán Loera, su personalidad y puede entender lo que he escrito desde hace mucho tiempo, desde que publiqué el libro *Los señores del narco*, que 'El Chapo' Guzmán es un hombre bastante simple, primitivo, es un criminal que apenas estudió hasta tercero de primaria. No es capaz de articular grandes ideas de acuerdo a gente que lo conoció en el penal de Puente Grande, no parece haber evolucionado mucho.

    . . . . "'El Chapo' no puede elaborar muchas ideas porque no es un hombre de ideas', señaló."

27. "Los pleitos entre los Arellano Félix, Guzmán Loera y su amigo Héctor El Güero Palma eran como de chichos preparatoria con metralletas" (Hernández 2010, 21).

28. Guadalupe Leija was decapitated in 1988 in her home in San Francisco, California. Her head was sent in a cooler with a message to El Güero Palma Salazar. A little later, four-year-old Natalie and five-year-old Héctor were found dead in a 150-foot-deep gorge outside Caracas, Venezuela, where they had been delivered to the care of a relative of Guadalupe Leija.

    The division of the Guadalajara Cartel is described in chapters 4 and 5. The generally accepted view is that Félix Gallardo arranged for a *convenio* (meeting) of lugartenientes and other bosses (widely reported to have been in Acapulco), and the Federation was subdivided into the Tijuana Plaza, the Juárez Plaza, and the Sinaloa Plaza. Although it is impossible to authoritatively verify, it was obvious that many individuals and factions within the Sinaloa group had serious problems about the allocation of Tijuana and Baja California exclusively to the Arellano Félix family. Those frictions would escalate into vicious plaza disputes and unimaginable bloodshed that played out over a fifteen-year period and did not calm down until the Arellano Félix family had been expunged of exclusive control of Baja California and the California access corridors at the end of 2012. El Chapo Guzmán occupied a central role in those wars and bloodshed, and his direct involvement would become more central as the dispute boiled over.

29. The complete description of the origins and events of the feud would require an entire chapter, or perhaps even a book. But briefly, El Güero played a major role in removing a violent narco named Manuel "El Cochiloco" Salcido Uzeta, who had hijacked a shipment of cocaine. He apparently felt that he deserved to be assigned at least part of the Baja California Plaza, specifically that around Mexicali. It did not happen, and he had running battles and disagreements with the Arellano Félix family for years after Félix Gallardo seemed to have favored his family with the partition of plazas. One of the most notorious incidents in the feud involved the seduction of Palma Salazar's wife by a Venezuelan cocaine dealer; she fled to South America with the man who seduced her and took

Palma Salazar's children. Her decapitated head was sent back to Palma Salazar, and his children were thrown to their deaths from a bridge in Venezuela.

30. "In November 1992, Ramón and Javier Arellano were at the Christine discotheque in Puerto Vallarta when 40 assassins posing as policemen burst in shooting. They'd been sent by El Chapo. One of Ramón's bodyguards, a preternaturally poised man named David Barron Corona, shot and killed a gunman, then picked up the man's AK-47 and held off the attackers while shoving Ramón and a top lieutenant into a bathroom. From there, he pushed them through a window and onto the roof—an arduous task, because Ramón was obese. The men clambered down a tree. On the ground, an assassin was waiting with a machine gun, but Barron killed him with his last bullet and all three escaped. Javier got away too, via a different route" (Epstein and ProPublica 2016).

31. "El 10 de Junio de 1993 el gobierno de Carlos Salinas de Gortari presentó con bombo y platillo al capo de capos creado de la noche a la mañana: Joaquín *El Chapo* Guzmán" (Hernández 2010, 78).

32. "Me dio pena, después de todo se trataba de un ser humano" (Hernández 2010, 26).

33. Could El Chapo Guzmán Loera really have been the most important leader in an enterprise that employed an estimated 450,000 people in agricultural production, shipping, and security (Ríos and Sabet 2008)? There are some who would argue that the narco enterprise is even bigger than these numbers suggest. The narco business is also cash driven. Even the most expensive commodities, such as homes or automobiles, are sold *d'efectivo*—or on a cash basis. On paper, bank records and transitions suggest that Culiacán is one of the poorest states in Mexico. And yet the number of luxury cars, spectacular mansions, and upscale restaurants contradict such banking evidence: for instance, many of the luxury cars sold in *narco cities* have underwritten the success of car dealerships in cities such as Culiacán, Sinaloa. Luxury car dealerships are located on Pedro Infante Boulevard, but many locals refer to the area with a slang term—El Narco Corredor. For many years, this relatively insignificant urban area of Culiacán (less than a million residents) supported a Hummer dealership that was a global leader in sales of that high-end vehicle, and jewelry and art remain hot commodities.

34. Pax Narca is admittedly a neutral term that understates the degree to which crime organizations and governments are connected and codependent. For an excellent description of the deep connections between government and narco traffic, see Grayson (2010, 2014).

35. *Eclipse of the Assassins* (Bartley and Bartley 2015) documents many examples of this strategy. In one instance, the special investigator assigned to the Buendía murder was dealing with forty-seven different logical possibilities to explain his killing.

36. Carlos Hank González would later serve as the mayor of Tijuana and governor of Baja California. The ties with the Arellano Félix family would become more apparent over time. The campaign to expose those links made Jesús Blancor-

nelas a heroic figure and resulted in *Zeta Seminario* emerging as a major independent source of news and investigative journalism.

37. Hernández describes Guzmán's privileges in *Los señores del narco* (2010). The most blatant privileges between 1993 and 2001 are found in Penal Process 16/2001. That legal document describes the charges that were filed by Attorney General Rafael Macedo de la Concha; they never reached the prosecutorial stage, but were reinsteated following his second escape in 2015 (thirteen years after his first escape). A partial list of his privileges includes bribery of prison personnel to obtain unlimited communication with the outside world, contact with his criminal associates, unchallenged and systematic introduction of illegal substances into the prison, access to women and electronic devices, access to restricted areas at all hours, authority over other prisoners, and the organization of parties complete with musical groups (Carrasco Araizaga 2016).

38. Although they are not all attributable to Guzmán, since 2000 there have been 2,178 tunnels discovered along the northern border (Becerril 2016).

39. A *golden kilo* was the cost of bribing Guzmán's way out of prison: either in the laundry cart as widely reported or by walking out the door dressed as a federal policeman as asserted by others.

40. There are emerging accounts about those early years on the run after his escape. One unverified story places him in an indigenous area where he apparently encouraged Huichol communities to grow amapola (Partida 2016).

41. The clearest and simplest overview of this idea was presented in an eighteen-minute TED video by Rodrigo Canales (2013). He compared the business models of the Sinaloa Cartel, the Gulf Cartel and Los Zetas, and La Familia Michoacana.

42. The Brooklyn trial of El Chapo Guzmán was heavily focused on the years between 2008 and 2012; most of the incrimating evidence covered crimes committed between the years 2010 and 2012, a period in which the DEA and the FBI had managed to turn several protected witnesses and also capture audio recordings of El Chapo.

43. I happened to be in Culiacán teaching at the Faculty of International Studies and Public Policy at that time; at one point I was on lockdown in my hotel near the site where five state police were ambushed and killed by El Barbas.

44. Several biographies of other drug bosses suggest that there is a cultish devotion to *Scarface*. Terrence Poppa's (1990, 1998) wonderful book about Pablo Acosta Villareal refers to the iconic shoot-out scenes.

45. El Chapo would not hesitate to take advantage of corruption and weakness in Mexico's courts, where his legal team could negotiate *favors*. He had powerful bargaining chips: he could threaten to expose his *invisible* collaborators, and if that failed, he could resort to plata o plomo. Collaborators were not the only targets of retaliation—their families were also at risk.

46. It would also involve the appearance of his never-before-identified eldest daughter, Rosa Isela Guzmán Ortiz, who made the bold claim that Guzmán Loera had a pact with agents, and that the government had violated it.

47. Not surprisingly, there are some Mexicans who believe that El Chapo never entered that tunnel and instead just walked out the door.

48. The term *Pueblo Mágico* is used by Mexico tourism officials to identify unique Mexican locations that are architectural and cultural examples of historic Mexico.

49. A longer description of her role in his escape is available in a report published by Juan Omar Fierro (2016) of *Aristegui Noticias*.

50. The details of his recapture are from several sources, but a very good English-language overview is in a *Guardian* report by Rory Carroll (2016a).

Chapter 7

1. To put these ideas in simpler terms, there are three focal points for studying organized crime—the reasons an individual acts, the dynamics that emerge when more than one individual acts to engage in crime, and the reasons for the institutionalization (organization) over time.

2. This is a modified version of one that I initially presented at the Seventeenth World Congress of Sociology (Creechan 2014). The organigram was inspired by several different informational and interactive graphics that had been published in various Mexico City newspapers over several years (primarily *Reforma* and *El Universal* in CDMX).

3. When the War on Drugs was declared, funding was made available to establish intelligence gathering and archives such as the El Paso Intelligence Center (EPIC). Agencies and intelligence groups have likely gathered information and identified individuals and likely have created organizational structures similar to figure 9. The general portal for EPIC at https://www.dea.gov/what-we-do /law-enforcement/epic is accessible, but full access is restricted. That information is not generally available to the public. See also DEA, "Intelligence," accessed May 10, 2021, https://www.dea.gov/law-enforcement/intelligence.

4. The range and scope of Saviano's work is impressive (see especially Saviano 2007, 2014). He has been accused of plagiarizing parts, and there is a fierce debate about the originality of his work. Saviano defends himself by arguing that his material comes from original court documents and that those alleging plagiarism have used the same documents without citation (Flood 2015).

5. The bureaucratic process of carving out specific responsibilities and assigning people to new tasks does not necessarily involve ideological or malicious manipulation—and instead may simply be a manifestation of what Max Weber (1958) called the *iron cage of rationality*: that is, modern bureaucracies are encouraged to maximize efficiency, rationalize control, and then employ specialized terms and agents to make it happen.

6. Homeland Security has the powerful mandate to monitor all security threats and has done so by allocating specialized tasks to each of the 187 agencies and 14 departments under its umbrella. A specific list of all units that currently make up the Department of Homeland Security can be found at "Opera-

tional and Support Components," accessed May 10, 2021, https://www.dhs.gov
/operational-and-support-components.

7. *Silo effect* is a term that has been used in business and manufacturing for about
thirty years.

8. Todd Miller (2014) reports that the Border Patrol grew from 4,000 agents in
1994 to 8,500 in 2001 and to 21,000 by 2013. Immigration reform bills envision
40,000 agents as the target. The data Miller uses is taken directly from the official web pages of the U.S. Border Patrol. Strangely enough, the Border Patrol
also provides specialized security for all NFL Super Bowls.

9. In 2016 Mexico City and the Distrito Federal were elevated to statehood.

10. In fact, it is likely that there was really only one true cartel operating in Mexico up until 1985—the Guadalajara Cartel. After 1985 and until 1994, there
were three (Sinaloa, Tijuana, Juárez) that operated in a Federation or cooperatively negotiated arrangement. The Gulf Cartel also emerged in the early 1990s
during the Salinas sexenio. This history is described in several places in this
book.

11. This graphic is a static representation of change, and the reader may find it more
helpful to visit the *Animal Político* graphic and website mentioned at the end of
chapter 1, https://www.animalpolitico.com/root/diez-de-guerra/index.html.

12. The number eighty has been floating in the public domain since an interview
with then Mexico attorney general Jesús Murillo Karam in 2012. He said that
he believed there were between sixty and eighty criminal groups operating in
Mexico. An English report of Murillo Karam's press conference had the header
"Mexico Has 80 cartels: Attorney General." There were certainly *not* eighty
organizations large enough to be considered a mafia (cartel), and the attorney
general also offered a "range between 60 and 80." But that number—eighty—
has been reproduced widely and was even cited in CRS report 41576 for many
years. I have never seen a full list of the number of gangs actually operating in
Mexico and believe that the number eighty is a guess.

13. A more complete and nuanced description of the Knights Templar is available
(see Bunker and Keshavarz 2019).

14. There are three possible reasons for his release: he provided evidence about the
existing structure and leaders of the Sinaloa Cartel, he threatened to release
incriminating evidence about key government individuals or agencies, or it was
arranged as a power move by the government to disrupt the leadership of the
Sinaloa Cartel.

15. Conroy (2014) has frequently written about how the outside world does not
know about the leadership structure of cartels. Consider the following observation he made: "Folks should keep that in mind now with Chapo—oh, and
capo Caro Quintero as well, who may well be having tea somewhere in America
with his old buddy Chapo—as both were part of the same team back in the
days when Chapo was a low-level player in the Quintero, et. al, Guadalajara
'Cartel' [the grandfather organization]—and when murdered DEA agent Kiki

Camarena became a footnote in the cover up of the arms-for-drugs Contra scandal—another story not covered, in the main, by the MSM [mainstream media]—despite the efforts of real journalists like Gary Webb and Chuck Bowden, who are sorely missed now."

16. This was also the period when Central American prisoners were deported and went home to form MS-13 and MS-18.

17. This issue was addressed elsewhere in the book. But the argument of many people is that Calderón required a defining issue to legitimate his presidency. The popular vote count was challenged by López Obrador. The declaration of war against cartels became a major symbolic statement, but the attack on Michoacán was puzzling to many who knew that the serious cartel problems were in Tijuana, Ciudad Juárez, and Sinaloa. Michoacán was off the radar in terms of major cartel presence, even though it had a long history of marijuana and heroin production in remote areas of the state.

18. This was done through the deliberate manipulation of crime statistics and by hiring a public relations firm to sell Mexico to the World (see Hernandez 2014).

Chapter 8

1. *Indigo* magazine in Mexico describes the origin of this phrase used by President López Obrador and its connection to the film (*Indigo* 2018).

2. T-shirts with the phrase were sold internationally on Amazon.

3. "'No voy a ensuciar el nombre de Tabasco, vamos acabar con la corrupción y con los privilegios, se va acabar la impunidad, me canso ganso,' así lo afirmó el presidente de México, Andrés Manuel López Obrador, al poner en marcha el programa Sembrando Vida en el poblado C-27 en el municipio de Cárdenas.

   "En un evento en el que más de 10 mil personas se dieron cita, el macuspanense afirmó: 'ya empezamos, ya se están dando cuenta. Estaban acostumbrados los de mero arriba a no pagar impuestos, luego se les devolvía y eso se acabó.'"

4. The use of catchy phrases is viewed as shallow by many people. For instance, journalist Léon Krauze (2019) critically demeaned AMLO's folksiness as "voluntarismo magico."

5. Going into the June 6, 2021, mid-sexenio elections, AMLO was still polling at 62 percent popularity (Espino 2021).

6. INEGI, "Homicidios a nivel nacional Enero a junio, 1990 a 2020," accessed June 22, 2021, https://www.inegi.org.mx/contenidos/programas/mortalidad /doc/defunciones_homicidio_2020_nota_tecnica.pdf.

7. "El presidente Andrés Manuel López Obrador garantizó que con la Guardia Nacional no se violarán los derechos humanos en materia de seguridad, pues se dará un giro a la labor de las Fuerzas Armadas para que 'nos ayuden con su profesionalismo, su honestidad, para enfrentar la inseguridad y la violencia, sin violar derechos humanos. Vamos a garantizar al mismo tiempo la seguridad y la vida.' . . .

"Cuando el Ejército mexicano no ha actuado de manera correcta, cuando se ha desviado, ha sido por instrucciones de la autoridad civil, de manera destacada y dolorosa durante la represión de 1968 a los estudiantes. Es entonces, el algo que debemos de revisar, la orden 'la dio el Presidente de la República (Gustavo Díaz Ordaz) y la ejecutó el Estado Mayor Presidencial, un cuerpo de élite vinculado a la Presidencia,' el cual indicó que se suprimió al inicio de su gobierno."

8. "'Fue una sorpresa lo que he me llevado. Sin duda, el caso Ayotzinapa lo conocía. Pero el número de 40,000 desaparecidos o los 26,000 cuerpos sin identificar o las casi 10 mujeres asesinadas cada día . . . Yo sabía de la violencia sin duda, eso lo sabía muy bien, pero no tenía impresión de la dimensión de estos casos de violaciones de derechos humanos,' aceptó en una conferencia de prensa."

9. "Es un momento de transformación y de oportunidades que se ha abierto desde la llegada al poder del nuevo gobierno. El presidente López Obrador ha expresado su voluntad de implementar un cambio de paradigma: uno que asume la centralizada de los derechos humanos. Yo no sólo reconozco esta determinación, sino que muestro mi voluntad y la de mi Oficina en México de apoyarla."

10. Radical change must especially occur in the justice institutions such as the Attorney General's office (PGR), long a source of cronyism and inefficiency (see Overa 2019b).

11. Alfonso Durazo Montaño, secretary of security, admitted this in a series of tweets in April 2019 (Redacción Sin Embargo 2019).

12. (1) Erradicar la corrupción y reactivar la procuración de justicia; (2) garantizar empleo, educación, salud y bienestar; (3) pleno respeto y promoción de los derechos humanos; (4) regeneración ética de la sociedad; (5) reformular el combate a las drogas; (6) emprender la construcción de la paz; (7) recuperación y dignificación de las cárceles; (8) seguridad pública, seguridad nacional y paz.

13. "El que se enuncia un paradigma de seguridad pública radicalmente distinto al que ha sido aplicado en los sexenios anteriores." One example of the difference is illustrated in a document, "Todo Somos Juárez" (Gobierno Federal de México 2010), issued during the Calderón sexenio. This was a specific plan to reduce violence in Juárez; it listed broad goals but more specifically listed more than one hundred specific targeted actions known as *compromisos* and the date by which that promise would be completed.

14. General Luis Rodríguez Bucio was appointed the first director of the National Guard (Carrillo 2019; Pantoja 2019).

15. One excellent analysis is E. Flores 2019.

16. "Sólo soy un niño perdido, No hay nadie más, Dicen que después de la herida, No hay vuelta atrás."

17. Many of the observations that follow have been influenced by and taken from a 2021 column by Ricardo Ravelo. I have read his work for many years, beginning with his reports in *Proceso* and then much later in many of his books.

18. The number of candidates murdered or kidnapped was not especially large, and in fact represented a decline from the election year where Enrique Peña Nieto won (Nacár 2021).

19. Guerrero Gutiérrez (2021) also wrote that Ismael Bojorquez from *Ríodoce* described how two PRI offices were barricaded by Sinaloa Cartel opertatives because those locations had stockpiled money to buy votes. That money was not available to pay party activists or be used to bribe voters or polling station officials.

REFERENCES

Acemoglu, Daron, and James A. Robinson. 2012. *Why Nations Fail*. New York: Random House.

Ackerman, Edwin F. 2019. "Mexico's Fourth Transformation." *Jacobin*, February 11.

Aguayo, Sergio. 2001. *La charola: Una historia de los servicios de inteligencia en México*. Mexico City: Grijalbo.

Aguilar Camín, Héctor. 2009. "Narco Historias extraordinarias." *Nexos*, January 1.

Aguilar V., Rubén, and Jorge G. Castañeda. 2010. *El narco: La guerra fallida*. Mexico City: Punto de Lectura.

Ahmed, Azam. 2020. "Mexico's Former Defense Minister Is Arrested in Los Angeles." *New York Times*, October 16.

Ahmed, Azam, and Eric Schmitt. 2016. "Body Count Points to a Mexican Military out of Control." *New York Times*, May 26.

Ahmed, Azam, and Paulina Villegas. 2016. "Investigators Say Mexico Has Thwarted Efforts to Solve Students' Disappearance." *New York Times*, April 23.

Ainslie, Ricardo C. 2013. *The Fight to Save Juárez: Life in the Heart of Mexico's Drug War*. Austin: University of Texas Press.

Alfaro B., Leonides. 1997. *Tierra blanca*. 2nd ed. [Mexico City]: Fantasma Editorial.

Alter, Adam L. 2013. *Drunk Tank Pink: And Other Unexpected Forces That Shape How We Think, Feel, and Behave*. New York: Penguin.

Alvarado, Enrique. 2019. "'Marro' contra 'Mencho': Los cárteles quieren Salamanca, y no sólo para vender huachicol . . ." *Sin Embargo*, February 3.

Andrade Bojorges, José Alfredo. 1999. *La historia secreta del narco: Desde Navolato vengo*. Mexico City: Oceano.

Angel, Arturo. 2019. "Una relación de 17 años con el narco, testimonios y sobornos: Las claves del caso contra García Luna." *Animal Político*, December 11.

Angel, Arturo. 2020. "Crimen y violencia en México: La guerra que no acaba." *Animal Político*, April 22.

Angulo, Sharay, and Anthony Esposito. 2018. "Mexico New President Vows to End 'Rapacious' Elite in First Speech." Reuters, December 1.

Anonymous [director]. 2014. "Entrevista a El Chapo Guzman en 1993 (Resuvido—2014)." YouTube, Febuary 25. https://www.youtube.com/watch?v=y5-N1IefRuQ.

Archibald, Randal C. 2015. "Mexico Officially Declares Missing Students Dead." *New York Times*, January 28.

Aristegui, Carmen. 2013. "La DEA, 'cómplice' de narcotraficantes, señala en EU defensa del 'Vicentillo' Zambada." *Aristegui Noticias*, October 13.

Aristegui Noticias. 2016. "No es el fin del cártel de Sinaloa, ni de 'El Chapo': Anabel Hernández en CNN." January 12.

Aristegui Noticias. 2019. "'México tiene cifras de muertes violentas propias de un país en guerra': Bachelet." April 9.

Astorga, Luis. 1995. *Mitología del "narcotraficante" en México*. Mexico City: Universidad Nacional Autónoma de México and Plaza y Valdés Editores.

Astorga, Luis. 1996. *El siglo de las drogas*. Mexico City: Espasa-Calpe Mexicana.

Astorga, Luis. 1999. *Drug Trafficking in Mexico: A First Assessment*. Management of Social Transformations: MOST Discussion Paper 36. Paris: UNESCO.

Astorga, Luis. 2002a. "The Field of Drug Trafficking in Mexico." In *Globalisation, Drugs and Criminalisation: Final Research Report on Brazil, China, India and Mexico*, edited by UNESCO/MOST, 6–22. New York: UNESCO.

Astorga, Luis. 2002b. "The Social Construction of the Identify of the Trafficker." In *Globalisation, Drugs and Criminalisation: Final Research Report on Brazil, China, India and Mexico*, edited by UNESCO/MOST, 39–55. New York: UNESCO.

Astorga, Luis, and David Shirk. 2010. *Drug Trafficking Organizations and Counter-Drug Strategies in the U.S.-Mexican Context*. Working Paper Series on U.S.-Mexico Security Cooperation. San Diego, Calif.: Trans-Border Institute, University of San Diego. Washington, D.C.: Mexico Institute, Woodrow Wilson International Center for Scholars.

Astorga Almanza, Luis Alejandro. 2003. *Drogas sin fronteras*. Mexico City: Grijalbo.

Astorga Almanza, Luis Alejandro. 2005. *El siglo de las drogas: El narcotráfico, del porfiriato al nuevo milenio*. Mexico City: Plaza y Janés.

Astorga Almanza, Luis Alejandro. 2007. *Seguridad, traficantes y militares: El poder y la sombra*. Mexico City: Tusquets.

Astorga Almanza, Luis Alejandro. 2015. *"¿Que querían que hiciera?": Inseguridad y delincuencia organizada en el gobierno de Felipe Calderón*. Mexico City: Penguin Random House Grupo Editorial México. Kindle edition.

Bagley, Bruce. 2012. *Drug Trafficking and Organized Crime in the Americas: Major Trends in the Twenty-First Century*. Washington, D.C.: Woodrow Wilson International Center for Scholars, Latin American Program.

Bailey, John. 2014. *The Politics of Crime in Mexico: Democratic Governance in a Security Trap*. Boulder, Colo.: FirstForumPress.

Baltazar, Elia. 2017. "Sicarios dejan Sinaloa y forman su cártel en Edomex, de nombre rimbombante: 'Nuevo Imperio.'" *Sin Embargo*, October 15.

Barragán, Daniela. 2020. "García Luna, tres sexenios: Creció con Fox; fue intocable con FCH y con Peña se volvió 'empresario.'" *Sin Embargo*, January 3.

Bartley, Russell H., and Sylvia Erickson Bartley. 2015. *Eclipse of the Assassins: The CIA, Imperial Politics, and the Slaying of Mexican Journalist Manuel Buendía.* Madison: University of Wisconsin Press.

Baum, Dan. 2016. "Legalize It All." *Harper's*, April 16.

Bauman, Zygmunt. 2017. *Wasted Lives: Modernity and Its Outcasts.* Cambridge, UK: Polity.

Baumoel, Stephanie. 2016. "'El Chapo' Guzman's Wife, Emma Coronel Aispuro, Speaks for the First Time About Her Husband in a Telemundo News Exclusive on Sunday, February 21." Broadcasting + Cable, February 19.

BBC News Mundo. 2018. "Quién es Emma Coronel, la esposa del Chapo que acompaña al capo durante su juicio." *Animal Político*, November 19.

Becerril, Andrea. 2016. "Solicita la Permanente a la PGR informe sobre acciones para eliminar narcotúneles." *La Jornada*, June 12.

Becker, Howard S. 1963. *Outsiders: Studies in the Sociology of Deviance.* New York: Free Press.

Beith, Malcolm. 2010. *The Last Narco: Inside the Hunt for El Chapo, the World's Most Wanted Drug Lord.* New York: Grove.

Beith, Malcolm. 2014. "The Narco of Narcos: Fugitive Mexican Drug Lord Rafael Caro Quintero." *InSight Crime*, April 14.

Beittel, June S. 2009. "Mexico's Drug-Related Violence." Congressional Research Service, R40582, 7–5700. May 27. https://fas.org/sgp/crs/row/R40582.pdf.

Beittel, June S. 2011. "Mexico's Drug Trafficking Organizations: Source and Scope of the Rising Violence." Congressional Research Service, R41576, 7–5700. April 15. https://www.refworld.org/pdfid/519cb92b4.pdf.

Beittel, June. 2015. "Mexico: Organized Crime and Drug Trafficking Organizations." Congressional Research Service, R41576, 7–5700. https://digital.library.unt.edu /ark:/67531/metadc743581/m1/1/high_res_d/R41576_2015Jul22.pdf.

Beittel, June S. 2020. "Mexico: Organized Crime and Drug Trafficking Organizations." Congressional Research Service, R41576, 7–5700. July 28. https://fas.org /sgp/crs/row/R41576.pdf.

Bello, Teodoro, Jessie Armenta, Francisco Quintero, Enrique Valencia, and Paulino Vargas. 1997. "Jefe de Jefes." *Jefe de Jefes.* Menlo Park, Calif.: Fonovisa. CD.

Berrellez, Hector. 2021. *The Last Narc: A Memoir by the DEA's Most Notorious Agent.* Los Angeles: Renaissance Literary & Talent. Kindle edition.

Birns, Larry, and Alex Sanchez. 2007. "The Government and the Drug Lords: Who Rules Mexico?" Council on Hemispheric Affairs, April 10. https://www.coha.org /the-government-and-the-druglords-who-rules-mexico/.

Blog del Narco. 2013. *Dying for the Truth: Undercover Inside the Mexican Drug War.* Port Townsend, Wash.: Feral House.

Bojorquez, Ismael. 2015. "El Chapo, persecución y circo." *Ríodoce*, December 27.

Bojorquez, Ismael. 2017. "Hace lustros los narcos invirtieron la ecuación." *Ríodoce*, November 6.

Bojorquez, Ismael. 2018a. "Andrés Manuel y sus líneas sobre seguridad." *Ríodoce*, January 11.

Bojorquez, Ismael. 2018b. "No se combate al narco con abrazos." *Ríodoce*, August 19.

Bojorquez, Ismael. 2019a. "Crecen los homicidios; los narcos no saben de la 4T." *Ríodoce*, January 29.

Bojorquez, Ismael. 2019b. "García Luna y una lección para Sinaloa." *Ríodoce*, December 22.

Bowden, Charles. 1997a. "Amado Carrillo Fuentes: The Killer Across the River." *GQ*, April.

Bowden, Charles. 1997b. "Chuy Carrillo Is Dead and Living Somewhere Far, Far Away." *Esquire*, October, 11.

Bowden, Charles. 1998. *Juárez: The Laboratory of Our Future*. New York: Aperture.

Bowden, Charles. 2002. *Down by the River: Drugs, Money, Murder, and Family*. New York: Simon & Schuster.

Bowden, Charles. 2005. *A Shadow in the City: Confessions of an Undercover Drug Warrior*. Orlando, Fla.: Harcourt.

Bowden, Charles. 2009. "The Sicario: A Juárez Hit Man Speaks." *Harper's*, 44–53.

Bowden, Charles, and Molly Molloy. 2011. *El Sicario—the Hitman*. North Sydney, N.S.W.: Random House Australia.

Bowden, Charles, and Molly Molloy. 2014. "Blood on the Corn." Medium, November 17–18. Part I, https://medium.com/matter/blood-on-the-corn-52aC13f7e643; Part II, https://medium.com/matter/blood-on-the-corn-part-ii-b4f447d70a8c; Part III, https://medium.com/matter/blood-on-the-corn-part-iii-b13f100cbf32.

Bowden, Mark. 2001. *Killing Pablo: The Hunt for the World's Greatest Outlaw*. New York: Atlantic Monthly Press.

Buchanan, Larry, Josh Keller, and Derek Watkins. 2016. "How Mexio's Most-Wanted Drug Lord Escaped from Prison (Again)." *New York Times*, July 13.

Buffington, Robert M. 2000. *Criminal and Citizen in Modern Mexico*. Lincoln: University of Nebraska Press.

Bunker, Robert J., and Alma Keshavarz, eds. 2019. *Los Caballeros Templarios de Michoacán: Imagery, Symbolism, and Narrative*. Bethesda, Md.: Small Wars Journal—El Centro eBook. https://www.academia.edu/38806893/Los_Caballeros_Templarios _de_Michoacán_Imagery_Symbolism_and_Narratives?email_work_card=view-paper.

Burnett, John, Marisa Peñaloza, and Robert Benincasa. 2010. "Mexico Seems to Favor Sinaloa Cartel in Drug War." *All Things Considered*, May 19. http://www.npr.org /2010/05/19/126906809/mexico-seems-to-favor-sinaloa-cartel-in-drug-war.

Burrough, Bryan. 2004. *Public Enemies: America's Greatest Crime Wave and the Birth of the FBI, 1933–34*. New York: Penguin.

Buscaglia, Edgardo. 2010. "México pierde la guerra." *Esquire*, March 1.

Buscaglia, Edgardo. 2013. *Vacíos de poder en México: Cómo combatir la delincuencia organizada*. Mexico City: Random House Mondadori.

Calderón, Laura Y., Kimberly Heinle, Octavio Rodríguez Ferreira, and David Shirk. 2019. "Organized Crime and Violence in Mexico: Analysis Through 2018." Justice in Mexico. Department of Political Science and International Relations, University of San Diego, May 22.

Campbell, Howard. 2009. *Drug War Zone: Frontline Dispatches from the Streets of El Paso and Juárez.* Austin: University of Texas Press.

Campos, Isaac. 2014. *Home Grown: Marijuana and the Origins of Mexico's War on Drugs.* Chapel Hill: University of North Carolina Press.

Canales, Rodrigo. 2013. "The Deadly Genius of Drug Cartels." Video transcript, October. https://www.ted.com/talks/rodrigo_canales_the_deadly_genius_of_drug_cartels?language=en.

Carrasco Araizaga, Jorge. 2016. "Justicia burlada por 'El Chapo.'" *Proceso*, February 28.

Carrasco Araizaga, Jorge, and Franciso Castellanos. 2009. "Michoacán: La pesadilla de Calderón." *Proceso*, edición especial 25, July 15, 22–26.

Carrasco Araizaga, Jorge, and Francisco J. Castellanos. 2012. "Michoacán bárbaro." *Proceso*, January 15.

Carrillo, Emmanuel. 2019. "Aún tengo dudas sobre mi encomienda: Comandante Rodríguez Bucio." *Proceso*, April 12.

Carroll, Rory. 2016a. "Blood, Mud and Lube: How El Chapo's Luck Came Up Short in Small Town Sex Motel." *The Guardian*, January 10.

Carroll, Rory. 2016b. "El Chapo's Lair: The Secluded House at the Heart of Mexico's Drug War." *The Guardian*, January 12.

Castillo García, Gustavo. 2016a. "Con El Güero Palma se rompió la regla de que la familia era introcable entre narcos." *La Jornada*, April 10.

Castillo García, Gustavo. 2016b. "Traición de El Güero Palma cambió código del narco." *La Jornada*, June 12.

Castillo García, Gustavo 2021. "La FGR exonera a Salvador Cienfuegos." *La Jornada*, January 15.

Cedillo, Juan Alberto. 2018. *Las guerras ocultas del narco / The Hidden Drug Wars.* Mexico City: Grijalbo.

Cervantes, Jesusa. 2021. "Sufragio efectivo, sí reelección." *Proceso*, January 2, 23–25.

CFR.org Editors. 2017. "Mexico's Drug War: Backgrounder." *Foreign Affairs*. https://www.cfr.org/backgrounder/mexicos-drug-war.

Cisneros, Stefany. 2018. "La leyenda de la Calle del Niño Perdido." *México Desconicido*, October 31.

Cohen, Stanley. 1972. *Folk Devils and Moral Panics: The Creation of the Mods and Rockers.* London: MacGibbon and Kee.

Cohen, Stanley, and Jock Young. 1981. *The Manufacture of News: Social Problems, Deviance and the Mass Media.* London: SAGE.

Conroy, Bill. 2013a. "Mexican President Peña Nieto Enlists US-Based PR Firm." *The Narcosphere*, November 23. Accessed November 24, 2013. http://www.narcosphere.com.

Conroy, Bill. 2013b. "Release of DEA Agent Kiki Camarena's 'Murderer' Is Game Changer for CIA." *The Narcosphere*, August 10. Accessed November 24, 2013. http://www.narcosphere.com.

Conroy, Bill. 2014. "Narco-Villain 'El Chapo's' Arrest Packaged for Media Consumption." *The Narcosphere*, March 1. Accessed November 7, 2015. http://www.narco sphere.com.

Cook, Colleen W. 2007. "Mexico's Drug Cartels." CRS Report for Congress, October 16. https://fas.org/sgp/crs/row/RL34215.pdf.

Corchado, Alfredo. 2014. *Midnight in Mexico: A Reporter's Journey Through a Country's Descent into the Darkness*. New York: Penguin.

Correa-Cabrera, Guadalupe. 2017. *Los Zetas Inc.: Criminal Corporations, Energy, and Civil War in Mexico*. Austin: University of Texas Press.

Craig, Richard. 1980. "Operation Condor: Mexico's Antidrug Campaign Enters a New Era." *Journal of Interamerican Studies and World Affairs* 22 (3): 345–63.

Creechan, James. 1997. "The Difficulties of Conducting Research on Crime in a Comparative Context: The Example of Mexico." Roundtable presentation at the annual meeting of the American Society of Criminology, San Diego, Calif., November.

Creechan, James. 1999. "The Crisis of Law and Order in Mexico: The Influence of Sociological Thought on the Construction of Justice in the USA, Canada and Mexico." Presentation (Powerpoint) at the American Society of Criminology Annual Meeting, Toronto, Ont., November 18.

Creechan, James. 2005. "Without God or Law: Narcotrafficking and Belief in Jesús Malverde" Presentation (Powerpoint) at the American Society of Criminology Annual Meeting, Toronto, Ont., November 16.

Creechan, James. 2012. "Civic and Organizational Response to DTOs and Narco-Violence in Mexico." Paper presented at the Meeting of the Canadian Association for Latin American and Caribbean Studies, University of British Columbia of the Okanagan, Kelowna, B.C., May 19.

Creechan, James H. 2014. "Cartels, Gangs, Near-Groups and Mobs: Organizational and Institutional Patterns in Mexican Mafias." Paper presented at the Seventeenth World Congress of Criminology, Monterrey, Nuevo León, Mexico, August 13.

Creechan, James, and Jorge de la Herrán Garcia. 2005. "Without God or Law: Narco-culture and Belief in Jesús Malverde." *Religous Studies and Theology* 24 (2): 5–57.

Cruz, Francisco. 2020. *García Luna, el señor de la muerte*. Mexico City: Planeta México.

Dávila, Patricia, and Verónica Espinoza. 2019. "Correrías del cártel huachicolero que presuntamente amenazó a AMLO." *Proceso*, February 2.

DEA (Drug Enforcement Administration). 2015. "(U) Mexico: Updated Assessment of the Major Drug Trafficking Organizations' Areas of Dominant Control." DEA Intelligence Report, November 27.

DEA (Drug Enforcement Administration). n.d. "El Paso Intelligence Center." Accessed May 10, 2021. https://www.dea.gov/what-we-do/law-enforcement/epic.

de Córdoba, José, and Anthony Harrup. 2021. "Mexican Former Defense Minister Cleared of Drug Allegations." *Wall Street Journal*, January 15.

de Córdoba, José, and Santiago Pérez. 2020. "Mexico Passes Law Curbing Operations of Foreign Security Agents." *Wall Street Journal*, December 16.

de Mauleón, Héctor. 2017a. "Así trabaja el cártel más violento de todo México." *El Debate*, March 15.

de Mauleón, Héctor. 2017b. "Esta década de sangre: Episodios de una tragedia." *Nexos*, January 1.

de Mauleón, Héctor. 2019. "En el México del horror." *El Universal*, March 21.

Devereaux, Ryan. 2017. "Three Years After 43 Students Disappeared in Mexico, a New Visualization Reveals the Cracks in the Government's Story." *The Intercept*, September 7.

DOJ (Department of Justice). 2019. "Joaquin 'El Chapo' Guzman, Sinaloa Cartel Leader, Convicted of Running a Continuing Criminal Enterprise and Other Drug-Related Charges." Press release 19–108, February 12. https://www.justice.gov/opa/pr/joaquin-el-chapo-guzman-sinaloa-cartel-leader-convicted-running-continuing-criminal.

Draper, Robert. 2016. "The Go-Between: The Mexican Actress Who Dazzled El Chapo." *New Yorker*, March 21.

Dresser, Denise. 2013. "Vacíos de poder." *Reforma*, December 2.

Drug Policy Alliance. n.d. "A Brief History of the Drug War." Accessed May 27, 2021. http://www.drugpolicy.org/issues/about-drug-war.

Duncan, Gustavo. 2014. *Más que plata o plomo: El poder político del narcotráfico en Colombia y México*. Bogotá: Debate.

Durkheim, Émile. 2011. *Moral Education: A Study in the Theory and Application of the Sociology of Education*. [Whitefish, Mont.]: Literary Licensing.

Durkheim, Émile. 2013. *Suicide*. n.p.: Snowball Publishing.

Durkheim, Émile. 2014. *Essays on Morals and Education*. Edited by W. S. F. Pickering. Cambridge, UK: James Clarke.

Edberg, Mark Cameron. 2004. *El Narcotraficante: Narcocorridos and the Construction of a Cultural Persona on the U.S.-Mexico Border*. Austin: University of Texas Press.

Editorial Nexos. 2017. "La guerra de diez años." *Nexos*, January 1.

Eells, Josh. 2017. "The Brutal Rise of El Mencho." *Rolling Stone*, July 11.

EFE. 2016. "Presentan archivo digital de masacres en México." *La Opinión*, October 12.

EFE. 2020. "Ong alerta por la normalización de la violencia y la falta de seguridad para periodistas en México." *Sin Embargo*, July 16.

El País. 1990. "Vargas Llosa: 'México es la dictadura perfecta.'" August 31.

El País Verne. 2018. "'Me canso ganso': López Obrador revive una frase de 'Tin Tán.'" December 18.

El Sabueso. 2015. "Sabueso En Vivo: ¿La violencia está disminuyendo como dijo el presidente?" *Animal Político*, September 3.

El Universal. 2019. "Caro Quintero estuvo 28 años preso, pero tiene 500 mdd; su círculo íntimo creó 30 empresas: El Universal." *Noroeste*, November 20.

Emmot, Robin. 2010. "Cartel Inc: In the Company of Narcos." Reuters, January 14.

Epstein, David, and ProPublica. 2016. "How DEA Agents Took Down Mexico's Most Vicious Drug Cartel: And How This Helped Give Rise to the Criminal Empire of Chapo Guzmán." *The Atlantic*, January/February, 35.

Ernst, Falko. 2021. "Violence Erupts as Mexico's Deadly Gangs Aim to Cement Power in Largest Ever Elections." *The Guardian*, April 20.

Escalante Gonzalbo, Fernando. 2009. "Homicidios 1990–2007." *Nexos*, September 1.

Espino, Luis Antonio. 2021. "Opinión: ¿Por qué López Obrador sigue siendo tan popular en México?" *Washington Post*, May 26.

Esquivel, J. Jesús. 2018. "El juicio al 'Chapo', el narcoespectáculo día por día." *Proceso*, November 17.

Esquivel, J. Jesús. 2021. "Estados Unidos enfurece y amenaza con reanudar la cacería contra el general." *Proceso*, January 18.

Esquivel, J. Jesús, Marco Appel, and Yetlaneci Alcaraz. 2014. "Descrédito mundial . . . y contraofensiva diplomática." *Proceso*, October 12.

Estevez, Dolia. 2020a. "García Luna enfrentará la furia de Fiscalía de EU: No hay acuerdo. Y será juicio cortito: 2 a 3 meses." *Sin Embargo*, October 6.

Estevez, Dolia. 2020b. "García Luna está 'aterrado.'" *Sin Embargo*, April 21.

Federal Judiciary. n.d. "Pacer: Pubic Access to Court Electronic Records." Washington, D.C.: United States Courts. Accessed August 16, 2020. https://www.pacer.gov.

Fernández Menéndez, Jorge. 2001. *El otro poder: Las redes del narcotráfico, la política y la violencia en México*. Mexico City: Aguilar.

Ferri Tórtola, Pablo. 2014. "Exclusiva: Testigo revela ejecuciones en el estado de México." *Esquire Latinoamérica*, September 17, 3.

Fetters, Ashley. 2014. "The Origins of Gabriel Garcia Marquez's Magic Realism." *The Atlantic*, April 17, 3.

Feuer, Alan. 2020. *El Jefe: The Stalking of Chapo Guzmán*. New York: Flatiron Books.

Fierro, Juan Omar. 2015. "Tan violentos como 'Los Zetas' o 'Templarios.'" *El Debate*, December 17.

Fierro, Juan Omar. 2016. "Aun sin fuero, la 'chapodiputada' podría no llegar a la cárcel." *Aristegui Noticias*, June 14.

Finnegan, William. 2010. "Silver or Lead." *New Yorker* 86 (15): 39.

Fiscalía General de la República. 2016. "Labores de inteligencia relacionadas con la captura de Joaquín Guzmán Loera." YouTube, January 26. https://youtu.be/XSijBk9xGn8, https://www.gob.mx/pgr/videos/labores-de-inteligencia-relacionadas-con-la-captura-de-joaquin-guzman-loera.

Flood, Alison. 2015. "Roberto Saviano Dismisses Plagiarism Claims over Latest Book." *The Guardian*, September 28, 2015.

Flores, Efrén. 2019. "Los 6 meses de la 4T dejan ver 5 retos de alto riesgo y donde se juega su éxito o fracaso político." *Sin Embargo*, May 31.

Flores, Linaloe R. 2015. "Fuga del 'Chapo' Guzmán marca en 2015 el ayuno de credibilidad en el gobierno." *Sin Embargo*, December 24.

Flores, Linaloe R. 2016. "¿Cómo le hizo 'El Chapo' para fugarse? Esa 'verdad histórica' no se sabrá hasta 2028." *Sin Embargo*, May 9.

Fowler, H. W., and Ernest Gowers. 1965. *A Dictionary of Modern English Usage*. New York: Oxford University Press.

Fredrick, James. 2018. "Mexico's New President Has a Radical Plan to End the Drug War." *Vox*, August 15.

Fuentes, Carlos. 1973. "Mexico and Its Demons." *New York Review of Books*, September 20.

Fuentes López, Guadalupe 2021. "'Padres fundadores' y herederos del narco van quedando libres, uno a uno. Aquí, pero más en EU." *Sin Embargo*, May 6.

Gándara, Sugeyry Romina. 2020. "Un año después del juicio a 'El Chapo,' todo está igual: El cártel intacto, la corrupción también." *Sin Embargo*, February 12.

García, Jacobo. 2020. "López Obrador admite que ordenó la liberación del hijo del Chapo Guzmán." *El País*, June 19.

García Márquez, Gabriel. 2003. *One Hundred Years of Solitude*. Translated by Gregory Rabassa. New York: HarperCollins.

Garza, Roberta. 2019. "El Chapo En Brooklyn, I." *Nexos*, February 1.

Gayraud, Jean-François. 2007. *El G 9 de las mafias en el mundo: Geopolítica del crimen organizado*. Translated by Amelia Ros García. Barcelona: Tendencias.

Gibler, John. 2011. *To Die in Mexico: Dispatches from Inside the Drug War*. San Francisco, Calif.: City Lights Books.

Global Change Data Lab. n.d. "Homicide Rate, 1955 to 2010." Our World in Data. Accessed May 4, 2021. https://ourworldindata.org/grapher/homicides-per-100 000-people-per-year?country=~MEX.

Gobierno Federal de México. 2010. "Todos Somos Juárez: Estrategia Todos Somos Juárez, Reconstruyamos la Ciudad." February.

Goldman, Franciso. 2015. "Mexico's Missing Forty-Three: One Year, Many Lies, and a Theory That Might Make Sense." *New Yorker*, September 30, 16.

González Díaz, Marcos. 2020. "Quién es Omar García Harfuch y por qué fue objetivo de un atentado de violencia sin precedentes en Ciudad de México." *BBC News Mundo en México*, June 17.

Graff, Garrett M. 2020. "The Story Behind Bill Barr's Unmarked Federal Agents." *Político*, June 5.

Grayson, George W. 2008a. "Los Zetas: The Ruthless Army Spawned by a Mexican Drug Cartel." Foreign Policy Research Institute, May 13.

Grayson, George W. 2008b. *Mexico's Struggle with "Drugs and Thugs."* New York: Foreign Policy Association.

Grayson, George W. 2010. *Mexico: Narco-Violence and a Failed State?* New Brunswick, N.J.: Transaction.

Grayson, George W. 2013. *The Impact of President Felipe Calderón's War on Drugs on the Armed Forces: The Prospects for Mexico's "Militarization" and Bilateral Relations*. Carlisle Barracks, Penn.: Strategic Studies Insitute, US Army War College.

Grayson, George W. 2014. *The Cartels: The Story of Mexico's Most Dangerous Criminal Organizations and Their Impact on U.S. Security*. Santa Barbara, Calif.: Praeger.

Grayson, George W., and Samuel Logan. 2012. *The Executioner's Men: Los Zetas, Rogue Soldiers, Criminal Entrepreneurs, and the Shadow State They Created*. New Brunswick, N.J.: Transaction.

Grillo, Ioan. 2011. *El Narco: Inside Mexico's Criminal Insurgency*. New York: Bloomsbury.

Grillo, Ioan. 2012. *El Narco: En el corazón de la insurgencia criminal mexicana*. Barcelona: Tendencias.

Guerrero Gutiérrez, Eduardo. 2015a. "El dominio del miedo." *Nexos*, July 1.

Guerrero Gutiérrez, Eduardo. 2015b. "El nuevo enemigo público." *Nexos*, June 1.

Guerrero Gutiérrez, Eduardo. 2017. "Un decenio de violencia." *Nexos*, January 1.

Guerrero Gutiérrez, Eduardo. 2021. "La operación electoral del 'Cártel de Sinaloa.'" *El Financiero*, June 21.

Guerrero Gutiérrez, Eduardo. n.d. "Asociados individuales: Eduardo Guerrero, Latnia Consultores." Accessed May 7, 2021. http://consejomexicano.org/index.php?s=contenido&id=421.

Guevara, Miguel. 2015. "El Chapo Escape Destroys Peña Nieto's Credibility." *Al Jazeera*, July 13. http://america.aljazeera.com/opinions/2015/7/el-chapo-escape-deals-new-blow-to-mexicos-credibility.html.

Guillermoprieto, Alma. 2010. "Killing Arturo Beltrán." *New Yorker*, January 6.

Guillermoprieto, Alma. 2015. "Mexico: The Murder of the Young." *New York Review of Books*, January 8.

Gutiérrez-Romero, Roxana, and Alessandra Conte. 2014. "Estimating the Impact of Mexican Drug Cartels on Crime." EQUALITAS Working Paper No. 25. http://www.equalitas.es/sites/default/files/WP%20No.%2025.pdf.

Hanson, Stephanie. 2008. "Backgrounder: Mexico's Drug War." Council on Foreign Relations, November 20. Accessed May 12, 2021. https://stephaniehanson.com/2008/11/20/mexicos-drug-war/.

Hari, Johann. 2015. *Chasing the Scream: The First and Last Days of the War on Drugs*. New York: Bloomsbury.

Heath, Brad. 2020. "Killed by a Cartel. Betrayed by His Own? US Re-Examines Murder of Federal Agent Featured in 'Narcos.'" *USA Today*, February 27.

Heinle, Kimberly, Cory Molzahn, and David Shirk. 2015. *Drug Violence in Mexico: Data and Analysis Through 2014*. San Diego: Justice in Mexico Project, University of San Diego; Washington, D.C.: Mexico Institute, Woodrow Wilson Center for International Scholars.

Heinle, Kimberly, Octavio Rodriguez Ferreira, and David Shirk. 2017. *Drug Violence in Mexico: Data and Analysis Through 2016*. San Diego: Justice in Mexico project, University of San Diego.

Hernández, Anabel. 2010. *Los señores del narco*. Mexico City: Grijalbo.

Hernández, Anabel. 2013. *Narcoland: The Mexican Drug Lords and Their Godfathers*. Translated by Iain Bruce. London: Verso.

Hernández, Anabel. 2016a. "El Chapo, el show y las mentiras de Peña Nieto." *Ríodoce*, January 17.

Hernández, Anabel. 2016b. "'El Güero' Palma, consentido de EU." *Proceso*, June 11, 34–37.

Hernández, Anabel. 2016c. "Emma Coronel: Su vida con Joaquín Guzmán." *Proceso*, February 28, 18–21.

Hernández, Anabel. 2016d. "Las mujeres del Chapo." *Ríodoce*, January 24, 2.

Hernández, Anabel. 2020. *El traidor: El diario secreto del hijo del Mayo*. Mexico City: Grijalbo.

Hernandez, Daniel. 2014. "Saving Mexico? Selling Mexico? Slaying Mexico?" *Vice*, February 21. https://www.vice.com/en/article/nnqz3x/saving-mexico-selling-mexico -slaying-mexico.

Hernández Norzagaray, Ernesto. 2015. "Desaparecidos y desplazamientos forzados en Sinaloa." *Sin Embargo*, October 18.

Hernández Norzargaray, Ernesto. 2020. "Nuestra turbulencia en Nueva York." *Sin Embargo*, October 10.

Hoffmann, Karl-Dieter. 2008. "Mexikos 'War on Drugs' und de Mérida Initiative." *GIGA Focus*, no. 4: 1–8.

Hogan, Andrew, and Douglas Century. 2019. *Hunting El Chapo: Taking Down the World's Most Wanted Drug Lord*. London: HarperCollins.

Honan, Edith, Mark Berman, and Katie Zezima. 2019. "El Chapo Trial Provides a Deep Look Inside the Sinaloa Cartel's Drug Empire." *Washington Post*, January 31.

Hope, Alejandro. 2013. "Violencia 2007–2011: La tormenta perfecta." *Nexos*, November 1.

Indigo. 2018. "'Este es el origen de la frase 'me canso ganso.'" *Reporte Indigo*, October 31.

Indigo. 2019. "'Me canso ganso,' la famosa frase usada por AMLO, llega a la semana de la moda en Nueva York (VIDEO)." *Reporte Indigo*, February 13.

Hsu, Spencer S. 2021. "Wife of 'El Chapo' Guzmán Pleads Guilty to Aiding Husband's Drug-Trafficking Empire." *Washington Post*, June 10.

INEGI (El Instituto Nacional de Estadística y Geografía). 2019. "Datos preliminares revelan que en 2018 se registraron 35 mil 964 homicidios." Comunicado de prensa núm. 347/19. Mexico City, July 25.

InSight Crime. 2013. "Vigilantes Fight Criminal Onslaught in Acapulco, Mexico."

InSight Crime. 2017. "Vicente Carrillo Fuentes, alias 'El Viceroy.'" March 10.

InSight Crime. 2020a. "The Invisible Drug Lord: Hunting 'the Ghost.'" March 29.

InSight Crime. 2020b. "Jalisco Cartel New Generation (CJNG)." July 8.

Institute for Economics and Peace. 2019. "Mexico Peace Index 2019: Identifying and Measuring the Factors That Drive Peace." Institute for Economics and Peace, Sydney, Australia, April 10. file:///C:/Users/16083/Downloads/MPI-ENG-2019-web.pdf.

Jiménez Jaramillo, Juliana. 2016. "'I Will Take Care of You More Than I Do My Own Eyes': El Chapo's Texts to Kate Del Castillo." *Slate*, January 13.

Jones, Nathan. 2016. *Mexico's Illicit Drug Networks and the State Reaction*. Washington, D.C.: Georgetown University Press.

Kennedy, William. 1973. "The Yellow Trolley Car in Barcelona, and Other Visions." *The Atlantic*, January 1, 25.

Kitroeff, Natalie, Alan Feuer, and Oscar Lopez. 2021. "In Blow to U.S. Alliance, Mexico Clears General Accused of Drug Trafficking." *New York Times*, January 15.

Krauze, Enrique. 1997. *Mexico: Biography of Power; A History of Modern Mexico, 1810–1996*. New York: HarperCollins.

Krauze, Enrique. 2006. "Tropical Messiah: The Troubling Roots of Mexico's Andrés Manuel López Obrador." *Letras Libres* 57 (June 30).

Krauze, Enrique. 2016. "Confidence in Mexico." *The Nation*, April 11–18.

Krauze, Léon. 2019. "Adiós al AMLO mágico." *El Universal*, April 15.

Lacey, Marc. 2009. "Mexico: Foreign Minister Disputes 'Failing State' Label." *New York Times*, January 16.

Lafuente, Hector. 2018. "López Obrador asumirá todo el control de la seguridad de México si logra la presidencia." *El País*, January 4.

La Jeunesse, William. 2013. "US Intelligence Assets in Mexico Reportedly Tied to Murdered DEA Agent." Fox News, October 13.

Lara, Luis Fernando. 1996. *Diccionario del español usual en México*. Mexico City: Colegio de México.

Lara, Ricardo. 2019. "'Me canso ganso' . . . las frases favoritas de AMLO." *Milenio*, March 7.

Le Cour Grandmaison, Romain. n.d. "The Narco Spectacle Can End." *The Battles After the Battle: Interpreting Violence and Memory in Culiacán*. Revista Espejo and Mexico Violence Resource Project. Accessed January 15, 2021. https://www.mexicoviolence.org/battles-after-battle/the-narco-spectacle-can-end.

Lencioni, Patrick. 2006. *Silos, Politics, and Turf Wars: A Leadership Fable About Destroying the Barriers That Turn Colleagues into Competitors*. San Francisco, Calif.: Jossey-Bass.

Library of Congress. 1988. *Combating International Drug Cartels: Issues for U.S. Policy: Report*. Congressional Research Service and United States Congress. Senate Caucus on International Narcotics Control. Washington, D.C.: U.S. Government Printing Office.

Linares, Adriana. 2010. "La leyenda negra." TARINGA!, December 18. http://www.taringa.net/posts/info/8416888/La-leyenda-negra-Adriana-Linares.html.

Logan, Samuel. 2009. *This Is for the Mara Salvatrucha: Inside the MS-13, America's Most Violent Gang*. New York: Hyperion.

Lomnitz, Claudio. 2016. "La religión de los Caballeros Templarios." *Nexos*, July 1.

López López, Andrés. 2008. *El cártel de los sapos*. Bogotá: Editorial Planeta Colombiana.

López Obrador, Andrés Manuel. 2007. *La mafia nos robó la presidencia*. Mexico City: Grijalbo.

López Obrador, Andrés Manuel. 2018. "Discurso íntegro de Andrés Manuel López Obrador al rendir protesta como presidente." *Animal Político*, December 1.

López Ponce, Jannet. 2019. "Gobierno no detendrá a capos; ya se acabó la guerra: AMLO." *Milenio*, January 30.

Lovell, Julia. 2014. *The Opium War: Drugs, Dreams and the Making of China*. New York: Overlook.

Luengo-Cabrera, José. 2018. "Mexico's Security Conundrum." *IP-Global Observatory*, May 18.

Lupsha, Peter. 1991. "Drug Lords and Narco-Corruption: The Players Change but the Game Continues." *Crime, Law and Social Change* 16 (1): 41–58.

Lyman, Michael D., and Gary W. Potter. 2007. *Organized Crime*. 4th ed. Upper Saddle River, N.J.: Prentice Hall.

Maas, Peter. 1986. *The Valachi Papers*. New York: Pocket Books.

Malkin, Elisabeth. 2010. "Death of a Mexican Drug Lord May Not Make People Feel Safer." *New York Times*, July 30.

Malmström, Vincent Herschel. 2010. *Cycles of the Sun, Mysteries of the Moon: The Calendar in Mesoamerican Civilization*. Austin: University of Texas Press.

Malone, Michael P. 1989. "The Enrique Camarena Case: A Forensic Nightmare." *FBI Law Enforcement Bulletin*, September.

Martínez, Fabiola, and Alma E. Muñoz. 2020. "'Fuerza moral' del gobierno, más poderosa que violencia: AMLO." *La Jornada*, July 10.

Martínez, Laura. 2016. "El Chapo Threatens Lawsuit Against Netflix for Planned Series." *CNET Techblog*, May 26. http://www.cnet.com/news/el-chapo-weighs -lawsuit-against-netflix-univision/.

Martínez Trujillo, María, and Sebastián Fajardo Turner. 2021. "Los datos de la violencia política-electoral en México 2020–21." Noria Research, June. https://noria -research.com/datos-de-la-violencia-politica-electoral-mexico-2020-2021/.

Matías, Pedro. 2014. "'Nos cazaron como perros,' dice un estudiante que logró escapar de sus captores." *Proceso*, October, 7.

McCaa, Robert. 2003. "Missing Millions: The Demographic Costs of the Mexican Revolution." *Mexican Studies / Estudios Mexicanos* 19 (2): 367–400.

McCoy, Alfred W. 2003. *The Politics of Heroin: CIA Complicity in the Global Drug Trade, Afghanistan, Southeast Asia, Central America, Columbia*. Chicago, Ill.: Lawrence Hill Books.

McCoy, Alfred W. 2018. "Searching for Significance among Drug Lords and Death Squads: The Covert Netherworld as Invisible Incubator for Illicit Commerce." *Journal of Illicit Economies and Development* 1 (1): 1–14.

McKinley, James C., Jr. 2010. "Mexican Drug Kingpin Sentenced to 25 Years in Secret Hearing." *New York Times*, February 25.

Mexico News Daily. 2020. "Prison Slated to Be Shut Down Controlled by Jalisco Cartel." October 3. https://mexiconewsdaily.com/news/prison-slated-to-be-shut -down-controlled-by-jalisco-cartel/.

Meyer, Lorenzo. 2016. "¿La 'solución Tlatlaya'?" *Reforma*, June 2.

Meyer, Lorenzo. 2017. "De encuestas y desconfianza." *Reforma*, August 31.

Meyer, Lorenzo. 2018. "Antes que la amnistía." *Reforma*, July 26.

Milenio. 2016. "¿Quién es la diputada ligada a 'El Chapo'?" *Milenio*, January 21.

Miller, Todd. 2014. *Border Patrol Nation: Dispatches from the Front Lines of Homeland Security*. San Francisco: City Lights Publishers.

Mills, James. 1988. *The Underground Empire: Where Crime and Governments Embrace*. London: Sidgwick & Jackson.

Molina, Hector. 2018. "Gabinete de López Obrador: Seguridad Pública, Defensa Y Marina." *El Economista*, November 24.

Monjardín, Alejandro. 2015. "Desplazados en riesgo." *Ríodoce*, November 29.

Montenegro, José Luis. 2016. "Californian, Businesswoman, 'Narco Junior': El Chapo's American Daughter." *The Guardian*, March 4.

Montenegro, José Luis, and Rory Carrol. 2016. "El Chapo Entered US Twice While on the Run After Prison Break, Daughter Claims." *The Guardian*, March 4.

Morris, Stephen D. 1991. *Corruption and Politics in Contemporary Mexico*. Tuscalosa: University of Alabama Press.

Muñoz, Alma E., Alonso Urrutia, and Emir Olivares Alonso. 2019. "No se violarán los DH con La Guardia Nacional, garantiza AMLO." *La Jornada*, April 9.

Murphy, Emily. 1922. *The Black Candle*. Toronto: T. Allen.

Nacár, Jonathan. 2021. "El reacomodo del partido del crimen." *Eje Central*, June 17. https://www.ejecentral.com.mx/la-portada-el-reacomodo-del-partido-del-crimen/.

Nájar, Alberto. 2016. "Las mujeres en la vida de Joaquín 'El Chapo' Guzmán." BBC News Mundo, January 12.

Nájar, Alberto. 2019. "'Ya no hay guerra' contra el narco: La declaración de AMLO que desata polémica en México." BBC News Mundo, February 1.

Neuman, Willam, Randal C. Archibald, and Azam Ahmed. 2015. "Mexico Prison Break by 'El Chapo' Is a Blow to President Peña Nieto." *New York Times*, July 13.

O'Day, Patrick. 2001. "The Mexican Army as Cartel." *Journal of Contemporary Criminal Justice* 17 (3): 278–95.

O'Day, Patrick, and Angelina López. 2001. "Organizing the Underground NAFTA: Fayuqueros and El Arreglo." *Journal of Contemporary Criminal Justice* 17 (3): 232–42.

Open Society Foundations. 2016. *Undeniable Atrocities: Confronting Crimes Against Humanity in Mexico*. New York: Open Society Foundations.

Oppenheimer, Andrés. 1996. *México: En la frontera del caos, la crisis mexicana de los noventa y la esperanza del nuevo milenio*. Buenos Aires, Argentina: Javier Vergara Editor S.A.

Osorno, Diego Enrique. 2009. *El cartel de Sinaloa: Una historia del uso político del narco*. Mexico City: Grijalbo.

Osorno, Diego Enrique. 2012. *La guerra de los Zetas: Viaje por la frontera de la necropolítica*. Mexico City: Debolsillo.

Osorno, Diego Enrique. 2015. "La (nueva) fuga de 'El Chapo.'" *Horizontal*, August 13.

Osorno, Diego Enrique. 2016. "Recaptura de 'El Chapo': Esto no es una película de narcos (ni de amor)." *Univision*, January 12. http://www.univision.com/noticias/narco trafico/recaptura-de-el-chapo-esto-no-es-una-pelicula-de-narcos-ni-de-amor.

Overa, Dulce. 2019a. "Las empresas públicas (63%) que remató Carlos Salinas Hicieron a 23 familias súper ricas hasta hoy." *Sin Embargo*, February 27.

Overa, Dulce. 2019b. "Peña dejó en PGR la foto de sus 6 años: Derroche, amiguismo, miles de carpetas a la deriva, desvíos . . ." *Sin Embargo*, May 14.

Overa, Dulce. 2020. "'Salvando México,' dijo *Time*. No se salvaron ni a ellos: Sospechosos, defenestrados. Y varios, presos . . ." *Sin Embargo*, July 9.

Pantoja, Sara. 2019. "Nombran a Luis Rodríguez Bucio comandante de la Guardia Nacional." *Proceso*, April 11.

Partida, Juan Carlos G. 2016. "En territorio huichol la siembra de amapola desplaza a la de cannabis." *La Jornada*, June 13.

Payan, Tony. 2014. "Ciudad Juárez: A Perfect Storm on the US–Mexico Border." *Journal of Borderlands Studies* 29 (4): 435–47.

Payan, Tony, Kathleen A. Staudt, and Z. Anthony Kruszewski, eds. 2013. *A War That Can't Be Won: Binational Perspectives on the War on Drugs.* Tucson: University of Arizona Press.

Paz, Octavio. 1970. *Posdata.* Mexico City: Siglo XXI Editores.

Paz, Octavio. 1978. *The Other Mexico: Critique of the Pyramid.* Translated by Lysander Kemp. New York: Grove.

Paz, Octavio. 1979. "Mexico and the United States." Translated by Rachel Phillips. *New Yorker*, September 17.

Penn, Sean. 2016. "El Chapo Speaks: A Secret Visit with the Most Wanted Man in the World." *Rolling Stone*, January 9.

Peralta González, César. 2001. "Falleció el fundador del cártel del Golfo." *El Universal*, July 12.

Pérez, Edmundo. 2012. *Que me entierren con narcocorridos: Las historias de los gruperos asesinados.* Mexico City: Grijalbo.

Pérez Magaña, Ruth. 2019. "Estaban acostumbrados a no pagar impuestos, eso se acabó: AMLO." *El Sol de México*, February 1.

Pérez-Reverte, Arturo. 2002. *La Reina del Sur.* Madrid: Alfaguara.

Pinker, Steven. 2011. *The Better Angels of Our Nature: Why Violence Has Declined.* New York: Viking.

Policzer, Pablo. 2019. *The Politics of Violence in Latin America.* Calgary: University of Calgary Press.

Poppa, Terrence E. 1990. *Drug Lord: The Life and Death of a Mexican Kingpin; A True Story.* Seattle: Demand Publications.

Poppa, Terrence E. 1998. *El zar de la droga: La vida y la muerte de un narcotraficante Mexicano; Una historia verdadera.* Seattle: Demand Publications.

Pradilla, Alberto, and Arturo Ángel. 2020. "Clasifican caso Cienfuegos por riesgo diplomático e indagatoria en curso." *Animal Político*, December 19.

President Elect Transition Team. 2018. "Plan Nacional de Paz y Seguridad 2018–2024." Mexico Office of the President Elect.

Preston, Julia, and Sam Dillon. 2004. *Opening Mexico: The Making of a Democracy.* New York: Farrar, Straus and Giroux.

Radden Keefe, Patrick. 2014a. "A Billion-Dollar 'Narco Junior' Cuts a Deal." *New Yorker*, April 10.

Radden Keefe, Patrick. 2014b. "How the World's Most Notorious Drug Lord Was Captured." *New Yorker*, May 5.

Ramirez, Carlos. 2019. "La Granja y Los Tigres del Norte; Significado político e inspiración de George Orwell." *Reporte Indigo*, August 16.

Ramos, Dulce. 2015. "¿Qué es NarcoData?" *NarcoData*, October 23. http://narcodata.animalpolitico.com/que-es-narco-data/.

Ramos, Jorge. 2014. "Las masacres y el silencio." *USA Today*, October 21.

Raphael, Ricardo. 2019. *Hijo de la guerra*. Mexico City: Seix Barral M.R.

Ravelo, Ricardo. 2006. *Los capos: Las narco-rutas de México*. Mexico City: Plaza Janés.

Ravelo, Ricardo. 2007a. *Crónicas de sangre: Cinco historias de los Zetas*. Mexico City: Random House Mondadori.

Ravelo, Ricardo. 2007b. *Herencia maldita: El reto de Calderón y el nuevo mapa del narcotráfico*. Mexico City: Grijalbo.

Ravelo, Ricardo. 2009. *Osiel: Vida y tragedia de un capo*. Mexico City: Random House Mondadori.

Ravelo, Ricardo. 2013. *Zetas: La franquicia criminal*. Mexico City: Ediciones B México.

Ravelo, Ricardo. 2018. "Capos y políticos, en la mira de Washington." *Sin Embargo*, October 19.

Ravelo, Ricardo. 2021. "El imperio de los cárteles, impune." *Sin Embargo*, January 8.

Raziel, Zedryk, and Tania L. Montalvo. 2020. "Cártel de Jalisco opera en 27 estados del país; hay otros 18 grupos criminales." *NarcoData*, September 22. https://narco data.animalpolitico.com/cartel-jalisco-27-estados/.

Redacción Animal Político. 2020. "Localizan 1,027 fosas clandestinas en 614 puntos del país." *Animal Político*, July 10.

Redacción Sin Embargo. 2019. "Durazo acepta que inseguridad no acabará de un día para otro; es un problema de décadas, dice." *Sin Embargo*, April 13.

Redacción Sin Embargo. 2020. "La Fiscalía de EU vincula a García Luna con ex policía que filtraba información a Los Beltrán Leyva." *Sin Embargo*, January 24.

Relea, Franceso. 2007. "Capturado en México uno de los cabecillas 'narcos' más buscados." *El Pais*, January 19.

Resa Nestares, Carlos. 2003. "El valor de las exportaciones mexicanas de drogas ilegales, 1961–2000." Universidad Autonoma de Madrid. https://www.research gate.net/publication/331175728_El_valor_de_las_exportaciones_mexicanas_de _drogas_ilegales_1961-2000_Carlos_Resa_Nestares.

Restall, Matthew. 2003. *Seven Myths of the Spanish Conquest*. New York: Oxford University Press.

Reveles, José. 2014. *El Chapo: Entrega y traición*. Mexico City: Debolsillo.

Reyes, Alfonso. 1952. *Cartilla Moral, 1944*. Mexico City: n.p.

Rhoda, Richard, and Tony Burton. 2010. *Geo-Mexico: The Geography and Dynamics of Modern Mexico*. Ladysmith, B.C.: Sombrero Books.

Ribando Seelke, Clare. 2009. *Mérida Initiative for Mexico and Central America: Funding and Policy Issues*. Washington, D.C.: Congressional Research Service, Library of Congress.

Ribando Seelke, Clare. 2021. "Mexico: Background and U.S. Relations." Congressional Research Service, R42917, January 7. https://fas.org/sgp/crs/row/R42917.pdf.

Ribando Seelke, Clare, and Kristin Finklea. 2014. *U.S.-Mexican Security Cooperation: The Mérida Initiative and Beyond*. Washington, D.C.: Congressional Research Service, Library of Congress.

Ríos, Viridiana. 2014. "Autodefensas: El riesgo de no aplicar la ley." *Nexos*, April 1.

Ríos, Viridiana. 2018. "Plan de seguridad: No es ideal, pero puede funcionar." *Excelsior*, November 18.

Ríos, Viridiana, and Kevin Sabet. 2008. "Evaluating the Economic Impact of Drug Traffic in Mexico." Unpublished manuscript, Department of Government, Harvard University.

Ríos, Viridiana, and Duncan Wood, eds. 2018. *The Missing Reform: Strengthening the Rule of Law in Mexico*. Washington, D.C.: Woodrow Wilson International Center for Scholars.

Rocha, Carolina, and Miguel Pulido Jiménez. 2018. *"Qué tanto es tantito": Atlas de la corrupción en México, 2000–2018*. Mexico City: Grijalbo.

Rodríguez García, Arturo. 2018. "AMLO convoca a construir la 'constitución moral.'" *Proceso*, February 4.

Rodriguéz García, Arturo. 2019. "Suman 222 fosas en cinco meses; son herencia de una política equivocada: AMLO." *Proceso*, May 14.

Rodriguez Nieto, Sandra. 2016. "Y tras 110 meses de guerra, hoy hay más sangre y tragedia." *Sin Embargo*, February 22.

Rohter, Larry. 1990. "His Widow Reveals Much of Who B. Traven Really Was." *New York Times*, June 25.

Rolling Stone. 2016. "Watch El Chapo's Exclusive Interview in Its 17-Minute Entirety." January 12. http://www.rollingstone.com/culture/videos/watch-el-chapo-s-exclusive-interview-in-its-17-minute-entirety-20160112.

Rosagel, Shaila. 2018. "Guardia Nacional en manos del Ejército. Ahora falta que el Plan de AMLO dé resultados: Analistas." *Sin Embargo*, November 14.

Rosagel, Shaila, and Sandra Rodríguez. 2016. "El GIEI desnuda 'la justicia a la mexicana': Tortura, tardanza, manipulación de la evidencia . . ." *Sin Embargo*, April 25.

Rosenberg, Mica. 2015. "U.S. Drug Case Shows European Ambitions of Mexico's Sinaloa Cartel." Reuters, December 8.

Rueda, Maria Isabel, and Gloria Congote. 2008. "Guia para entender a los sapos." *Semana*, June 6.

Sabet, Daniel M. 2012. *Police Reform in Mexico: Informal Politics and the Challenge of Institutional Change*. Stanford: Stanford University Press.

Sáinz Martínez, Luis Carlos. 2019. "En 11 meses: 53 masacres en México." *Ríodoce*, November 26.

SAJ Truthtellers. 2018. "I Felt Trapped and Scared: Al Giordano's Predatory Behavior and the Men Who Continue to Support Him." *Medium*, August 11. https://medium.com/@sajtrutht/i-felt-trapped-and-scared-al-giordanos-predatory-behavior-and-the-men-who-continue-to-support-9f43e4768bcb.

Sanchez, Cecilia, and Patrick J. McDonnell. 2018. "Herbs, Incense, a Wooden Staff—Mexico's Indigenous Cultures Take the Inaugural Stage to Purify the New President." *Los Angeles Times*, December 2.

Santamaría Gómez, Arturo, Luis Antonio Martínez Peña, and Pedro Brito Osuna. 2009. *Morir en Sinaloa: Violencia, narco y cultura*. Culiacán: Universidad Autónoma de Sinaloa.

Saviano, Roberto. 2007. *Gomorrah*. New York: Farrar, Straus and Giroux.

Saviano, Roberto. 2014. *Cerocerocero: Como la cocaína gobierna el mundo*. Barcelona: Editorial Anagrama.

Saviano, Roberto. 2015. *Zero Zero Zero*. Translated by Virginia Jewiss. New York: Penguin.

Saviano, Roberto. 2016. "El problema no es el narco, es la corrupción: Saviano." *Sin Embargo*, February 2.

Scherer García, Julio. 2008. *La Reina del Pacífico: La mujer-mito del narco mexicano; Qué significa nacer, crecer y vivir en ese mundo*. Mexico City: Grijalbo.

Scherer García, Julio. 2010. "Proceso en la guarida de 'El Mayo' Zambada." *Proceso*, April 3.

Scherer García, Julio. 2011. *Historias de muerte y corrupción: Calderón, Mouriño, Zambada, El Chapo, La Reina del Pacífico*. Mexico City: Grijalbo.

Schiavone Camacho, Julia María. 2012. *Chinese Mexicans: Transpacific Migration and the Search for a Homeland, 1910–1960*. Chapel Hill: University of North Carolina Press.

Schou, Nick. 2015. *Kill the Messenger: How the CIA's Crack-Cocaine Controversy Destroyed Journalist Gary Webb*. New York: Nation Books.

Selee, Andrew D. 2011. *Decentralization, Democratization, and Informal Power in Mexico*. University Park: Pennsylvania State University Press.

Semple, Kirk, and Paulina Villegas. 2019. "Mexico Approves 60,000-Strong National Guard. Critics Call It More of the Same." *New York Times*, February 28.

SESNSP (Secretariado Ejecutivo del Sistema Nacional de Seguridad Pública). 2019. *Víctimas de delitos del fuero común 2018: Instrumento para el registro, clasificación y reporte de delitos y las víctimas*. CNSP/38/15, Congress. http://secretariadoejecutivo .gob.mx/docs/pdfs/nueva-metodologia/CNSP-V%C3%ADctimas-2018_dic18.pdf.

SESNSP (Secretariado Ejecutivo del Sistema Nacional de Seguridad Pública). 2021. *Víctimas de delitos del fuero común 2020: Instrumento para el registro, clasificación y reporte de delitos y las víctimas*. CNSP/38/15. Mexico City: Centro Nacional de Información. Accessed June 1, 2021. https://drive.google.com/file/d/1qsSqp X7HdjwREuukdI0i9GIKuoTiPoLp/view?usp=sharing.

Shannon, Elaine. 1988. *Desperados: Latin Drug Lords, U.S. Lawmen, and the War America Can't Win*. New York: Viking.

Sheridan, Mary Beth. 2020a. "Mexico Expects Blockbuster Corruption Case with Return of Former Pemex Chief." *Washington Post*, August 16.

Sheridan, Mary Beth. 2020b. "More than 60,000 Mexicans Have Disappeared amid Drug War, Officials Say." *Washington Post*, January 6.

Sicairos, Alejandro. 2018. "Al narco, ¿amnistía o guerra?" *Noroeste*, July 12.

Sicilia, Javier. 2018. "Las contradicciones de una constitución moral." *Proceso*, September 9.

Simpson, Lesley Byrd. 1941. *Many Mexicos*. New York: Putnam.

Suárez-Enríquez, Ximena, and Maureen Meyer. 2017. "Overlooking Justice: Human Rights Violations Committed by Mexican Soldiers Against Civilians Are Met with

Impunity." WOLA Report. https://www.wola.org/wp-content/uploads/2017/11/WOLA_MILITARY-CRIMES_REP_ENGLISH.pdf.

Sullivan, Mark, Colleen W. Cook, and Alessandra Durand. 2008. "Mexico-U.S. Relations: Issues for Congress." CRS Report for Congress, November 14. https://digital.library.unt.edu/ark:/67531/metadc795618/.

Sumners, Chris. 2020. "Case Against Ex-Mexican Government Minister Accused of Taking Sinaloa Cartel Bribes Is 'Air Tight.'" *Sputniknews*, September 29.

Tercero, Magali. 2011. *Cuando llegaron los bárbaros . . . : Vida cotidiana y narcotráfico*. Mexico City: Temas de Hoy.

Tijuano [pseud.]. 2013. "'El Pozolero: A Legacy of Death by Tijuana's 'Soup Maker' (Interview Included)." *Borderland Beat*, April 10. http://www.borderlandbeat.com/2013/04/el-pozolero-legacy-of-death-by-tijuanas.html.

Tourliere, Mathieu. 2021. "Mensajes sobre Cienfuegos, gobernadores del PRI . . . y el 'amigo Osorio.'" *Proceso*, January 16.

Townsend, Camilla. 2020. *Fifth Sun: A New History of the Aztecs*. New York: Oxford University Press.

Transparency International. 2019. "Corruption Perceptions Index." Mexico. https://www.transparency.org/en/cpi/2019/index/mex.

Traven, B. 1967. *The Treasure of the Sierra Madre*. New York: Hill and Wang.

Trejo, Guillermo, and Sandra Ley. 2020. *Votes, Drugs, and Violence: The Political Logic of Criminal Wars in Mexico*. New York: Cambridge University Press.

Tuckman, Jo. 2011. "Mexico's War on Drugs Blights Resort of Acapulco." *The Guardian*, December 7.

Turner, John Kenneth. 1912. *Barbarous Mexico*. New York: Cassell.

Turner, John Kenneth. 1999. *México bárbaro: Ensayo sociopolítico*. Mexico City: Leyenda.

Unidad de Investigación Aplicada de MCCI. 2019. "El discurso de 100 días de AMLO y la corrupción: Del dicho al hecho hay un gran trecho." *Nexos*, March 14. https://anticorrupcion.nexos.com.mx/?p=833.

United Nations. 2020. "World Drug Report 2020." Vienna, Austria: United Nations Office on Drugs and Crime (UNODC). https://wdr.unodc.org/wdr2020/index.html.

Univision. 2014a. "Por primera vez habla Doña Consuelo, madre de Joaquin 'El Chapo' Guzmán." Aquí y Ahora, March 2. https://www.univision.com/shows/aqui-y-ahora/por-primera-vez-habla-dona-consuelo-madre-de-joaquin-el-chapo-guzman-video.

Univision. 2014b. "Mamá de El Chapo Guzmán, Entrevista Exclusiva HD." YouTube, March 1. https://www.youtube.com/watch?v=yVFWhmubRtY.

Ureste, Manu. 2019. "Región donde asesinaron a Los Lebarón no registra homicidios pero es disputada por cárteles." *Animal Político*, November 6.

U.S. Attorney's Office. 2010. "Osiel Cárdenas-Guillen, Former Head of the Gulf Cartel, Sentenced to 25 Years' Imprisonment: Judgment Entered Forfeiting $50 Million of Cárdenas-Guillen's Ill-Gotten Gains to the United States." Federal Bureau of Investigation. Press release, February 24.

U.S. Congress. 1988. "Senate Report No. 216: Iran-Contra Investigation Resport." Serial number 13739, 100 Congress, 1st Session, 726. https://archive.org/details/reportofcongress87unit.

U.S. Department of the Treasury. 2014. "Narcotics Sanctions Program." Office of Foreign Assets Control, July 18. https://home.treasury.gov/system/files/126/narco_overview_of_sanctions.pdf.

U.S. Department of the Treasury. 2015. "Treasury Sanctions Two Major Mexican Drug Organizations and Two of Their Leaders." Press release, April 8.

Valdés Castellanos, Guillermo. 2013. *Historia del narcotráfico en México*. Mexico City: Aguilar. Kindle edition.

Valdez Cárdenas, Javier. 2009. *Miss Narco: Belleza, poder y violencia; Historias reales de mujeres en el narcotráfico mexicano*. Mexico City: Aguilar.

Valdez Cárdenas, Javier. 2011. *Los morros del narco: Historias reales de niños y jóvenes en el narcotráfico mexicano*. Mexico City: Aguilar.

Valdez Cárdenas, Javier. 2012. *Levantones: Historias reales de desaparecidos y víctimas del narco*. Mexico City: Aguilar.

Valdez Cárdenas, Javier. 2015. *Huérfanos del narco: Los olvidados de la guerra del Narcotráfico*. Mexico: Aguilar.

Valdez Cárdenas, Javier. 2016. "Huyen 250 familias en Badiraguato." *La Jornada*, June 17.

Vega, Miguel Ángel. 2014. "Chicago: El 'Chapo' cercado por sus proprios cómplices." *Ríodoce*, May 4.

Vega, Miguel Ángel. 2019. "Estados Unidos libera a Miguel Caro Quintero, hermano de Rafael." *Ríodoce*, July 30.

Vega, Miguel Ángel. 2020. "Oficial: Los 'gringos' vienen por Caro." *Ríodoce*, February 18.

Villa, Alejandro Valencia, Ángela María Buitrago, Carlos Martin Beristaín, Claudia Paz Baile, and Francisco Cox Vial. 2015. "Informe Ayotzinapa: Investigación y primeras conclusiones de las desaparaciones y homicidios de los normalistas de Ayotzinapa." Grupo Interdisciplinario de Expertos Independientes de la Comisión Interamericana de Derechos Humanos.

Velasco, Ana. 2021. "How to Protect Electoral Candidates in Mexico?" Noria Research, June. https://noria-research.com/how-to-protect-electoral-candidates-in-mexico/.

Villareal, Andrés. 2014. "Mas poderoso que nunca el Cártel de Sinaloa: Buscalia." *Ríodoce*, November 9.

Vinson, Tessa. 2009. "The Sinaloa Cartel: A Study in the Dynamics of Power." *The Monitor: A Journal of International Studies* 14 (2): 39–53.

Volpi, Jorge. 2016. "La vida interior del 'Chapo.'" *Reforma*, January 16.

Vulliamy, Ed. 2010. *Amexica: War Along the Borderline*. New York: Farrar, Straus and Giroux.

Wald, Elijah. 2001. *Narcocorrido: A Journey into the Music of Drugs, Guns, and Guerrillas*. New York: Rayo.

Wald, Elijah. n.d. "Corrido Censorship: A Brief History." Accessed May 5, 2021. https:// elijahwald.com/corcensors.html.

Ward, Olivia. 2009. "Mexico's Human Rights Record Blasted." *Toronto Star*, February 11.

Watkins, Ali. 2018. "U.S. Puts New Pressure on Mexico in Decades-Old Murder of D.E.A. Agent." *New York Times*, April 8, 2018.

Weber, Max. 1958. *The Protestant Ethic and the Spirit of Capitalism*. New York: Scribner.

Werne, Joseph Richard. 1980. "Esteban Cantú y la soberanía mexicana en Baja California." *Historia Mexicana* 30 (1): 1–32.

Wilkinson, Tracy. 2009. "Song Banned, Band Pulls Out." *Los Angeles Times*, September 16.

Wilkinson, Tracy, and Ken Ellingwood. 2011. "Wife of Fugitive Mexican Drug Lord Gives Birth in L.A. County." *Los Angeles Times*, September 27.

Williams, Phil. 1999. "Drugs and Guns." *Bulletin of the Atomic Scientists* 55 (1): 46–48.

Winslow, Don. 2005. *The Power of the Dog*. New York: Alfred A. Knopf.

Winslow, Don. 2015. *The Cartel: A Novel*. New York: Vintage Books.

Winslow, Don. 2019a. *The Border: A Novel*. New York: William Morrow.

Winslow, Don. 2019b. "The Dirty Secret of El Chapo's Downfall." *Vanity Fair*, February 1.

Xantomila, Jessica. 2018. "La Constitución Moral fortalecerá a la cuarta transformación: Morena." *La Jornada*, November 28.

Zunzunegui, Juan Miguel. 2019. *El mito de las tres transformaciones*. Mexico City: Grijalbo. ebook.

INDEX

ABOUT THE AUTHOR

James H. Creechan is a retired sociologist from the University of Alberta in Edmonton. He has held visiting and adjunct professorships at the University of Toronto, McMaster University, Queen's University, and the University of Guelph. Between 1998 and 2012, Creechan was a member in the Faculty of International Studies and Public Policy at the Autonomous University of Sinaloa in Culiacán, Mexico, where he also served as founding professor of an MA program in U.S. and Canadian studies.